Personal recollections of the conflict over Europe, 1939-45

Theo Boiten

The Crowood Press

First published in 1999 by
The Crowood Press Ltd
Ramsbury, Marlborough
Wiltshire SN8 2HR

British Library Cataloguing-in-Publication Data

A catalogue record for this book is available from the British Library.

ISBN 1 86126 298 1

Typeface used: Garamond.

Typeset and designed by
D & N Publishing
Membury Business Park, Lambourn Woodlands
Hungerford, Berkshire.

Printed in Great Britain by T. J. International, Padstow.

Contents

Introduction and Acknowledgements

Introduction

This book is not another strategic unfolding of the great night air campaigns and battles that raged in the night skies over Western Europe for almost six years between 1939 and 1945. The strategic and technical viewpoints of the political and military leaders who masterminded these campaigns and battles have been described and analysed exhaustively in innumerable books since the end of World War II, and I have not attempted to address this subject once more in this volume.

Instead, this book offers another dimension, a human dimension. These are the personal stories of the experiences of the young men who were committed to battle by their leaders, and help us to understand, to some extent, the emotions of the bomber and night fighter crews. Tens of thousands of men, often barely out of their teens, confronted each other in the dark skies over the Third Reich, combatants in the longest and most intensive airwar campaign the world has ever witnessed. In this volume I have endeavoured to capture the personal experiences of a representative selection of veterans from both sides of the conflict, with a focus on the wide-ranging operational aspects of the night airwar. The compelling first-hand narratives are moving evocations of the defining experience of a generation of airmen. Share their hopes and fears; learn of their successes, failures and defeats in combat, of incredible feats of airmanship; feel their comradeship and loneliness, dedication to duty, patriotism, heroism and sacrifice; experience their tales of survival, injury, and witness violent, sudden or slow death. From the airmen's point of view, these stories, combat reports and poems tell the history of the parallel developments of night bombing within the RAF and night fighting in the *Luftwaffe* night fighter force in the giant and fiercely contested struggle for air supremacy over Hitler's Third Reich.

The stories are extensively illustrated with 180 rare and mainly unpublished photographs from the personal collections of the veterans. Combined, they present a vivid picture of the personal experiences and emotions of the combatants in the night airwar. I have chosen to give these narratives and photographs a historical framework, by arranging them chronologically and by detailing some of the background of the campaigns in which the events, as related by the veterans, took place.

Acknowledgements

An oral and pictorial history of the night fighter versus bomber war in World War II, drawing on the experiences and photographs of the men who were there, could never have been compiled without the aid of many people. I am therefore deeply grateful to all those veterans, next of kin, and fellow researchers who furnished such marvellous help and support throughout the research of this book: John C. Adams (Pilot 50 Sqn); Gebhard Aders; Herbert Altner (Pilot 7./NJG3, 8./NJG5 and 10./NJG11); Harry Andrews DFC (Instructor No.1 (C) OTU); Hans-Joachim Augustin (Waffenwart 5./NJG4); Frau Anneliese Autenrieth (widow of Hans Autenrieth, Pilot 6./NJG1 and St Kpt 6./NJG4); Eric Bakker; Bruce D. Bancroft DFC, GM (Pilot 158 Sqn); Paddy Barthropp DFC, AFC (Pilot 91 Sqn); Raymond V. Base (Flt Eng 115 Sqn); Nick Beale; William G. Bell (Nav. 166 Sqn); Pieter Bergman; Jack Bosomworth (WOp/AG 57 Sqn); Herman Brandt; Otto Brinkhuizen; Len Browning (B/A 550 Sqn); Don Bruce (Obs. 115 Sqn); Helmut Bunje (Pilot 4./NJG6); Caterpillar Club Association (UK); Hendrik Cazemier;

Len Collins (WOp/AG 149 Sqn); Helmut Conradi (Flt Eng Stab./NJG1); Noel 'Paddy' Corry ('A' Flt Comm 12 Sqn); Roger Coverley (Pilot 76 and 78 Sqns); Eddy A. Coward; Jim Davis (AG 90 and 7 (PFF) Sqns); *Deutscher Luftwaffenring* e.V.; Hille van Dieren; Arnold Döring (Pilot 2. and 7./JG300, 7./NJG2, 10./NJG3); Albrecht Dress; Helmut Eberspächer (St Kpt 3./SKG10); Fritz Engau (Pilot and St Kpt 5./NJG1); Wolf Falck (Founding Father of *Nachtjagd*); David Fellowes (RG 460 (RAAF) Sqn); Prof. Dr Ing. Otto H. Fries (Pilot I. and II./NJG1); Wolfhard Galinsky (Pilot 8./NJG6); Paul Gärtig (Bordfunker I./NJG3 and I./NJG4); Henry van Geffen (Special Op. 101 Sqn); Wyb-Jan Groendijk; Hans Grohmann (Daimler Benz Engine Specialist NJG1); Hans de Haan; Willi Hahn; Jack F. Hamilton (Mid-Upper Gunner 463 Sqn); Frank Harper; Heinz-Otto Hartmann (Pilot NJG1 and NJG2); Bill Harvey (Mid-Upper Gunner 415 Sqn); Leslie Hay (Pilot 49 Sqn); Graham M. Heard; *Heimkehrer* magazine (*Stimme der Kriegsgeneration*); Lothar Hemmerich (Pilot 4./NJG6); Maurice Hemming DFM (Flt Eng 97 (PFF) Sqn); Wilhelm Heuberger (Engine Fitter II./NJG5 and III./NJG6); Peter C. Hinchliffe; Ken Hodson (Obs. 107 Sqn); Hans Höhler; W.H. 'Dutchy' Holland (WOp/AG 77 Sqn); Ted Howes DFC SAAF (Pilot 106 and 97 Sqns); Gerhard Hug (Bordfunker 5./NJG2); Ron James (AG 90 Sqn); Ab A. Jansen; Graham B. Jones (Nav. 214 and 487 Sqns); Hans-Jürgen Jürgens; Luit van Kampen; Harry Kelso (Mid-Upper Gunner 101 Sqn); Charles F. Kern (Pilot 2./NJG4); Herbert Koch (Pilot IV./NJG3, St Kpt 1./NJG3); Hans Krause (Pilot I./NJG3, St Kpt 6./NJG101, Gr Kdr I./NJG4); David Leicester DFC and Bar (Pilot 158, 640 and 35 (PFF) Sqns); Chas Lockyer DFC (Pilot 608 Sqn); Denis MacKinnon (Nav./Radar Op. 85 Sqn); Norman Mackie DSO DFC (Pilot 83 Sqn and Flt Comm 571 Sqn); Len Manning (AG 57 Sqn); Marineschule Mürwik; Adrian Marks (Special Op. 101 Sqn); Ernest 'Mac' McConchie (Obs. 150 Sqn); John H. McQuiston DFC and Bar (Pilot 415 (RCAF) Sqn); Joan and Cyril Miles; Kees Mol; Alan R. Morris; Douglas Mourton (WOp/AG 102 Sqn); Jan Mulder; Frank Neale (Nav. 144 Sqn); Aad Neeven; Tony Neve MBE (Special Op. 101 Sqn); Dr Hans-Dietrich Nicolaisen; Dr Leslie P. Oliver DFC (Obs. 455 (RAAF) Sqn); Friedrich Ostheimer (Bordfunker NJG2); Maurice Paff (Nav. 100 Sqn); Roger V. Pallant (Flt Eng 158 Sqn); The Pathfinder Association; Bill Pearce (WOp/AG 100 and 156 (PFF) Sqns); C.P.C. Pechey DFC SAAF (Pilot 106 and 83 Sqns); Bryan R. Pepper; Helmut Persch (13th Vp. Flo); M.J. Peto (Flt Eng 15 Sqn); Ken Phelan (AG 214 Sqn); Bob Pierson (AG 100 Sqn); Norbert Pietrek (Pilot 2./NJG4); Tomas Poruba; John and Joan Price; Frank Pringle (Pilot 29 (F) Sqn); Frank Pritchard (AG 550 Sqn); Ron Putz; The Reverend Paddy Raine DFC (Special Op. 101 Sqn); Edgar Ray (Nav./BA 61 Sqn); Angus Robb CGM (AG 431, 432 and 405 (RCAF) Sqn); Heinz Rökker (Pilot and St Kpt 1. and 2./NJG2); Ernst Rummel (Pilot 1./JG300); David M. Russell (Pilot 109 (PFF) Sqn); Eric Sanderson (AG 578 Sqn); The Lord Sandhurst DFC (Obs. 149 and 419 (RCAF) Sqns); Dorothy Saunders; F.A. 'Sandy' Saunders (Pilot 627 (PFF) Sqn); Alan F. Scanlan (WOp/AG 50 Sqn); Kurt Schmidt (Air Gunner 7. and 12./NJG1); Hans-Jakob Schmitz; Josef Scholten (Bordfunker 3. and 9./NJG3); Wilhelm Simonsohn (Pilot 6./NJG2 and 4./NJG100); Vera Sherring; Albert Simpson (Flt Eng 419 (RCAF) and 415 (RCAF) Sqns); South African Air Force Association; 101 Squadron Association; Albert Spelthahn (Bordfunker 5./NJG2); Peter Spoden (Pilot NJG5 and 6, Gr.Kdr. I./NJG6); Wilf Sutton (FE 35 Sqn); Manfred Tangelst (Pilot 7./NJG6); Alec T. Taylor (2nd Pilot 218 Sqn); Leslie Temple (Special Op. 101 Sqn); Terschellinger Museum 't Behouden Huys; Tom Thackray DFM (Flt Eng 10 Sqn); E.J. Thomason (B/A XV and 622 Sqns); Paul Todd (Pilot 101 Sqn); Tom Toll (Flt Eng 295, 570 and 299 Sqns); John C. Turnbull DFC (Pilot and Flt Comm 419 (RCAF) and 424 (RCAF) Sqns); Dick Vimpany (Nav./WOp 254 Sqn); Rob de Visser; Todor Walkow; Bert Waller (WOp/AG and 2nd Pilot 144 and 280 Sqns); Eric Watson; Frank Westbrook; Hans Wijers; Eric Wilkin (AG 115 and 7 (PFF) Sqns); Basil Williams (AG 51, 431 (RCAF) and 432 (RCAF) Sqns); Kees Wind; Tom Wingham DFC (102 Sqn Association); Gerhard Wollnik (AG I./NJG6); Allan R. Wright ('A' Flt Comm 29 Sqn).

A special word of thanks goes out to my friends Gerhard Heilig (Special Op. 214 and 101 Sqns), who helped me splendidly with the translations of German veterans' stories, and to Jim Moore DFC (WOp/AG 18, 114, 88, 107 and 226 Sqns) for carefully proofreading the manuscript of this book.

CHAPTER 1

1940–41

When Hitler's aggression towards Poland finally resulted in the opening of hostilities on 3 September 1939, the Royal Air Force was ill-prepared for war. Its senior command, Bomber Command, was equipped with a strategic striking force of 349 twin-engined aircraft of reliable but restricted design, such as the Blenheim, Hampden, Whitley and Wellington, and its crews were only able to operate in fair weather. Daylight attacks on elements of the German fleet in late 1939 and early 1940 brought heavy losses, and therefore the decision was made to mount a future bombing offensive against Germany under cover of darkness.

War finally became a reality on 3 September 1939. Depicted are Bf 110s of II./ZG76 flying eastwards at 04.30 on the morning of the first day of World War II, on their first combat mission, against Lodz, Poland. This shot was taken by the rear gunner of M8+DK. II./ZG76 was incorporated into Nachtjagd *as III./NJG3 in late 1941.* Coll. Hans Grohmann.

In the wake of the German invasion of the Low Countries and France in May 1940, the first night raids on transportation and industrial targets in the Ruhr were attempted. The bomber crews had to learn the new trade of finding and attacking targets at night and in poor weather the hard way, suffering a high loss rate for relatively little success during 1940 and 1941.

TOUR OF OPS IN WHITLEYS

The situation that the pioneering bomber boys found themselves in is vividly illustrated by Sgt Douglas Mourton's story. On completion of his WOp/AG training and a final course at the OTU at Abingdon, Sgt Mourton reported to 102 Squadron 'B' Flight at RAF Linton at the beginning of October 1940. Within a couple of weeks the squadron moved to Topcliffe, and Sgt Mourton was crewed up with Sgt 'Ricky' Rix, a very competent and experienced pilot, having completed twenty-seven trips already. Sgt 'Stevie' Stevens, also a 'rookie', was the second pilot of the crew:

> I met up with several of the lads that I had trained with, but as yet we did not know the odds that were stacked against us. We did not realize that now it was just a question of survival. The average loss on a raid was 5–10 per cent, although it was often more. If it were known by any body of fighting men that 90 or 95 per cent would return safely, there is little doubt they would go into battle filled with optimism. If, however, they were told

83 Squadron Hampden QQ-P, taken pre-war at Scampton. This unit mounted six sorties on a raid to bomb warships in the Wilhelmshaven area on the very first day of the War. No attacks were made due to darkness descending before the aircraft had reached the target area. Having changed its wartime code to OL, 83 Squadron lost seventy-four Hampdens on 1,987 sorties during 283 raids, plus eleven in non-operational crashes before converting to the ill-fated Manchester in December 1941. Coll. Wyb-Jan Groendijk.

that those who returned would take part in a second battle, and then a third and so on to a total of thirty, each time losing 5–10 per cent, their optimism would have completely evaporated. The slim chance of survival became obvious to us after our first few raids.

102 Squadron was equipped with Whitley V bombers. They were twin-engined, sturdily built of metal, very tough and could take the roughest of landings. But they were slow, cruising at only 160mph, and did not have a high ceiling, which made them vulnerable. The Whitley was nicknamed 'The Flying Coffin'; down the length of the fuselage there was barely five inches of headroom and there were various obstructions: the flare-chute, Elsan toilet and wing spars. The rear turret was equipped with four Browning .303 machine guns with a range of 400 yards. On a winter's night it was the coldest place on earth.

Sqn Ldr Beare, commander of 'B' Flight, gave us our first assignment. Six of us were detailed to be the funeral party at two separate funerals. A couple of nights previously, the squadron had taken part in a bombing raid, and one of the planes that was landing on its return was shot down by a German intruder fighter, and as a consequence five of the crew were killed. One fellow we buried locally and it was very sad to see the terrible anguish of his wife and parents at the service. The other one we escorted to a train to be transferred to his home town for burial.

We went into one of the hangars and saw a Whitley that had also returned from this raid. The entire side had been blown out. There had obviously been a fire onboard and this aircraft had been brought back miraculously by Fg Off Cheshire. For this episode he was later awarded the DSO. The WOp had been badly burned putting out the fire and he was awarded the DFM. I know he was in hospital for a long time. Up till now our flying had been carefree, but we were now beginning to realize what we had let ourselves in for. But human nature is very optimistic. You always think it is going to happen to someone else, but never to you.

On 21 November 1940, our crew was detailed to fly our first op to Duisburg that night and bomb various factories there. In the morning we did our air test of O for Orange (P5074), to ensure that all the equipment was in perfect working order. At 2 o'clock we attended briefing in the main crew room, a new experience for me.

We were given routes to fly, wireless frequencies, met. forecasts, which incidentally were so often wrong, and areas to avoid, where Intelligence knew there were fighter squadrons based or anti-aircraft locations. In fact, we were given all the available information to help us on our journey there and back. In spite of what I had seen and heard, I had no feeling of fear or trepidation. That would probably arrive when I was over enemy territory and saw anti-aircraft fire or fighters for the first time. I didn't know what to expect, and I was a little apprehensive concerning my ability to cope with the various situations that might arise.

Bomber pioneer. Sgt Douglas Mourton survived a tour of ops flying as WOp/AG in 102 Squadron Whitleys between October 1940 and May 1941. Coll. Douglas Mourton.

Take-off time was scheduled for the unearthly hour of 2.45am. So we had a long time to hang around waiting, which was always considered to be about the worst part of the job. I went into the mess, had one or two beers and then went to the library. Here I sat down quietly on my own and composed a letter to my wife, Maisie, which would only be opened in the event of me going missing. Nearly everyone did this, and the letter was duly left in your flying clothing locker. In the event of you going missing, this locker would be emptied and the letter would be seen and sent off to the person to whom it had been addressed. Actually, the procedure was that a friend would examine all the possessions and correspondence belonging to a missing airman. Any compromising material would be destroyed. Obviously there were many illicit associations during wartime and any evidence of this received back home would cause great distress.

Although I had only been married to Maisie for less than a year, there was obviously so much you had to say when you knew that, quite likely, you were never going to meet again. This letter which follows may seem very melodramatic today, but the circumstances merited it. I was separated from Maisie, with whom I was very much in love, and from what I had observed, I was going to have to be very lucky to complete a tour of operations.

20/11/1940

My sweet darling Maisie,
You will see that I have put no address, as should you ever receive this letter I shall be by then beyond the reach of any written correspondence. But I thought it would be nice to leave a last letter for you, especially as things lately in the air are becoming more sticky. It is written, I'm afraid, in rather

a hurry, as I am visiting the Ruhr tonight and unfortunately I have not a great deal of time.

Well, my precious, I'm sorry to say that my sudden exit will cause you the sadness and heartbreaking, because I shall feel no pain and I regret to cause you suffering. But remember, my darling, a partnership like ours, which has been so full of true love, so pure and unblemished cannot possibly be ended because we leave this earthly world. I am sure that I am leaving this earth which is so obsessed with sin and greed and hate to enter a much finer place, and as certain as the sun will rise tomorrow, you will join me later on. That is why I do not wish you to grieve for me, but to wait patiently for our reunion and to have absolute faith in that reunion.

Some people will consider me unlucky to die so young, but I have had twenty-four years of happy life, and many people who die quite old cannot claim as much. The last two years have been the happiest of all for which, Maisie, I thank you deeply. Even although we have often been apart, I have been comforted by the knowledge of our love. I know you will always keep me locked deeply in your heart but should you wish later on to marry again, do not let my memory stop you. I do not expect my death to stop you loving for all the happiness and companionship you can get.

Do all the good you can, my soul-mate, and above all have faith in God. Please do not go into mourning for me, but occasionally buy some flowers in my memory. You can be sure that my last thoughts were of you, my sweet darling, who has brought me so much happiness.

Well, bye bye, my only love, wishing you happiness until we meet again, written as always with all my love,

Doug.

We set off to Duisburg as scheduled and I was in the rear turret; a rear gunner was the equivalent of having eyes in your back. But it is a very lonely position. You are a long way from the other four members of the crew, and there is a feeling that if something very serious occurs you might not be aware of it. It was a beautiful moonlit night, the weather was good and we had no difficulty in locating Duisburg and duly dropped our bombs and then turned round to come home. Although Duisburg was in the Ruhr, which was renowned for its inhospitality, we saw very little anti-aircraft fire and everything had gone very well, until we were returning home over the North Sea.

It was then that trouble developed in one of the engines, about which I knew little, and we began to gradually lose height. When one engine fails there is always the gnawing fear of coming down in the sea. In mid-winter the North Sea is very cold and probably very rough. I could hear the anxiety in the conversation between pilot and navigator; the consolation was that Ricky was probably the best pilot on the squadron. It was decided by Ricky to make for the nearest available airfield, which was Bircham Newton. We landed safely here, having been in the air for six hours. Mechanics repaired the engine and later that day we returned to Topcliffe. Our squadron sent five aircraft, of which one went missing, piloted by the Squadron Commander, Wg Cdr S.R. Groom.

About this time the Italian government announced that it had taken part in the bombing of London. This caused great indignation amongst the general population and was contributory to lowering the morale of the country. So a decision was made by the powers that be, quite illogically, to retaliate by bombing a target in Italy, the Fiat works at Turin. Large reserve tanks were fitted into the aircraft and this, of course, lowered the bomb-carrying capacity.

Previous operations to Italy had shown that they were always fraught with danger. Although the Italian defences were scorned by those more accustomed to flying to the Ruhr Valley, Berlin and so on, the sheer distance to the target, negotiating the Alps, and the uncertainty of the weather caused Bomber Command many casualties. Seven aircraft were detailed from our squadron, and once again I was crewed up with Sergeant Rix. We set off at a quarter to two in the afternoon and landed at a grass airfield at Horsham St Faith. Here we filled up again with fuel and had a meal of some sort, and set off for Italy at twenty minutes past five.

77 Squadron aircrew, under Wg Cdr Young, pose in front of a squadron Whitley V in 1941. 77 Squadron flew thirteen leaflet and three recce operations during the early months of the War, and carried out the most bombing raids (223) by a Whitley squadron in Bomber Command during World War II. For these successes it suffered the highest losses in Whitley squadrons, with fifty-six aircraft failing to return from 1,687 sorties flown. Coll. 'Dutchy' Holland.

We flew across France and then across Switzerland, where it was quite unusual to see all the lights still on amongst the snow-covered mountains. We did not fly over the Alps, we flew through them. At 15,000 feet I became acutely aware of the numbing cold that was spilling through the draughty unheated rear turret. We located the Fiat works without any difficulty and dropped our bombs. It was really poorly defended, probably by about two men and a dog.

On the way back, the met. forecast was completely wrong and instead of the skies being clear, the weather was very bad, the night very black and we had great difficulty with the navigation. We were flying in 10/10ths cloud and it was impossible to get an accurate pinpoint of our position. In those days navigation was primitive, we had no radar, and wireless communication was very erratic. When it was estimated that we were over England we tried to break cloud by coming down to 500 feet two or three times, but were not successful and now we were hopelessly lost. It is an absolute nightmare for any aircrew to be lost. We flew round just trying to see something through some break in the cloud that would identify our position.

Suddenly we were hit by anti-aircraft fire and naturally we thought we were over the French coast. We turned north and were hit again, and then we ran out of petrol. The Captain gave the order to abandon aircraft. In one way, it was a relief. I had been cooped up for twelve hours in the rear turret, at a temperature of around –30°.

My procedure should have been to leave my rear turret and open the escape hatch part way down the fuselage, climb up through it, walk along the top of the aircraft and jump off the end. However, the escape hatch would not open, so with my parachute I decided to go up to the front cockpit. The engines having stopped there was an eerie silence, broken only by the wind as we glided downwards. I wondered what height we still had. It was natural that I began to feel nervous. It was very hard to squeeze through the overload tanks that had been fitted, but I eventually got into the pilot's cockpit and there was Sgt Rix, still at the controls, holding the plane steady because he was unable to find his parachute. He asked me to find it, which eventually I did. He told me to jump and I left the aircraft as quickly as possible. It was a peculiar sensation as you jump and wait a few seconds; you wonder whether you have strapped your chute on correctly, and then you pull the handle, a canopy flies up past you and suddenly your speed is arrested and you float gently down to the ground. Of course, I was wondering where I would be landing, whether it would be in France, the Channel or England. If it was in the Channel on a cold November night there would be little hope of rescue.

When I landed, not knowing where I was, I bundled my chute up and hid it in a hedge, because if I was in France I would endeavour to return to England, probably by contacting the Resistance Movement. A parachute in an open field would have been discovered by the Germans. It was 4 o'clock on a bitter November morning and I walked along until, at last, I came to a house. I knocked on the door; there was no answer, so I threw some stones up at the window, wondering where I was and even what country I was in. Soon after a head popped out and said, 'Are you English, RAF or German?' I said, 'RAF.' 'Alright,' he said, 'I'll come down and let you in.' So he came down, let me in, and I sat in one armchair, with my legs on another one, in front of the dying embers of a fire and of course I was soon asleep. I had been very relieved to know I was in England.

Of the seven aircraft that took part in this raid from our squadron, three never even cleared the Alps and took their bombs back home. Two of the others landed in the water in the Channel and one was not heard of again. The crew of the other one, piloted by Fg Off Young, was able to launch the dinghy and board it, and were picked up later. From then on the Captain was known as 'Dinghy' Young. Unfortunately, he lost his life later, on the Dams raid. We had baled out, and the remaining one of the four that actually bombed Turin landed safely. It was a very costly operation to lose three aircraft and a crew.

I got fifteen days survivors' leave, and when I returned from leave our crew was given a lift down to a maintenance unit to pick up another aircraft to replace the one from which we had baled out. I did not operate again until 21 December, when I flew as wireless operator, still with Sergeant Rix. I have no recollection of what the target was, but one engine failed after we were thirty miles over the Dutch coast, so we turned around to return. We steadily lost height all the way back and Sergeant Rix was just able to pull the plane over the boundary hedge of our airfield.

Unfortunately, on the other side there was a Whitley parked. We went right through the middle of it, and cut it in two. Our wheels and undercarriage were ripped off and we plunged into the ground. We could not get out of the usual exit, and had to get out of the emergency one on top of the plane. Although we were expecting that the bombs might go off at any minute, there was no panic and everybody got out of the plane in an orderly fashion. But as soon as we were all out we ran like mad for a couple of hundred yards. Then

Close-up of the smashed-in nose gun turret of Whitley V N1377 DY-B of 102 Squadron. Whilst on the way back from a raid on Mannheim, the aircraft came under fire from a flak battery at Vlaardingen-Ambacht and Plt Off R.F. Beauclair was forced to put his Whitley down at Hekelingen to the south-west of Rotterdam at 01.30 on 27 July 1940. All five crew members escaped the ordeal to be taken prisoner. Coll. Kees Wind.

The Bf 110 formed the backbone of Nachtjagd *and the* Zerstörer *('Destroyer' or Heavy Fighter) arm in the* Luftwaffe *throughout the War. Here, a Bf 110 C-1* Zerstörer *of I./ZG76 has come to grief due to its undercarriage collapsing on landing at Kielce, Poland in September 1939. This unit became II./NJG1 in late August 1940.* Coll. Hans Grohmann.

we sank to the ground, tired and out of breath. But then we started laughing uncontrollably; most likely it was the reaction setting in. Sgt Rix had completed twenty-seven operations without any serious trouble until I joined him. Then the last three had all ended in near catastrophe. His last remark to me was 'Mourton, you are a bloody jinx.'

I had completed three operations, all of them ending in near disaster, and realized that a terrific amount of luck had to be available to be able to finish a tour of thirty. But I do not think any of us got into a state of despair; that's because we were young and still full of optimism.

I was now attached to the crew of Sergeant Stevens. He was a Londoner, a cockney, and he was very short indeed. I do not suppose he was more than 5ft 5in, and in fact he had to have special blocks made so that he could get his feet on the rudders. He had done three trips as a second pilot, and was now the official Captain of an aircraft. We went on our first operation as a crew on the day after Boxing Day 1940. We were to bomb the submarine base at L'Orient on the west coast of France. This was considered a good, easy target for somebody who was out on his first operation as a Captain. Stevie, as Captain, would have to make all the decisions and I was in charge of the radio. I felt we had made the grade, as I expect we all did. It was a great feeling of responsibility and we were determined to do well. There were only two crews detailed from our squadron that night, both novices. As far as we were concerned, the operation went off perfectly; unfortunately the other aircraft went missing.

There followed two further operations with Sergeant Stevens. Bremen on 2 January was a particularly difficult one; due to the intense cold four of the eight aircraft despatched returned with unserviceable engines. When we reached 10,000 feet the temperature must have been around –30°, and our clothing did little to alleviate the cold as the aircraft had no heating. We encountered intense anti-aircraft fire, but returned safely. Of the four that actually bombed, one was missing, shot down. Then Brest on 12 January, which went perfectly, no trouble at all and no enemy aircraft.

Then it snowed, and when it snows in Yorkshire it really makes a good job of it. There were mornings when I could not open the front door to get out. Due to the snow we were unable to

A member of the newly-founded NJG1 is seen here studying the victory bars on Major Wolfgang Falck's Bf 110, the 'Founding Father' of Nachtjagd. *As Staffel Kapitän of 2./ZG76, Hptm Falck destroyed three adversaries during the Polish campaign (the three kill bars on the left side of his tally). He went on to claim two Wellingtons in the Battle of the German Bight (18 December 1939, the two victory bars in the middle), and two Blenheims of 110 Squadron in the winter of 1939–40. Promoted to Kommandeur of I./ZG1, he scored his eighth and final victory over a Danish aircraft in April 1940, before he was appointed CO of NJG1 on 26 June 1940.* Coll. Hans Grohmann.

(Below) *A rare shot from* Nachtjagd*'s pioneering days. Nine Dorniers Do 17 Z-10 'Kauz II' were on the arm's strength during 1940–43, one of which is depicted here serving with II./NJG1 in June 1940. Clearly visible are the heavy nose armament of four MG17 and one MG151, and the big 1,000hp Bramo 323 P radial engines. To track down enemy aircraft, this particular aircraft was also equipped with a nose-mounted searchlight and 'Spanner', an infra-red device used, in theory, to detect the heat from bombers' engine exhausts. Spanner was a failure in practice, and* Nachtjagd *had to wait until AI radar was introduced in 1942 before the arm could really start to effectively combat Bomber Command at night.* Coll. Hans Grohmann.

operate for at least three weeks. We landed and took off purely on a grass field and when this got bogged down it was impossible to take off. When we landed at night we came in with the aid of a flare-path. There were no bright lights to illuminate the landing field, there were just some goose-necks burning paraffin that gave just a very dim light. It says a lot for the efficiency and ability of the pilots that they were able to land continuously with such poor aids.

Because of the snow, aircrews just hung about during the daytime at the airfield. I was playing cards (crib) with Sgt Elliott regularly; it passed the time away. However, all good things must come to an end and on 4 February we were detailed to bomb Bordeaux. After we had been going along for about two hours, one engine went out of action and we were forced to return. We were unable to make it to our own airfield at Topcliffe and landed at Dishforth. The fault on the engine was rectified and we returned safely to Topcliffe at 4 o'clock in the afternoon.

Our next trip, on 10 February, was to Hanover. When we were briefed, it was made clear that for the first time we were not attacking any military targets, but were bombing a town indiscriminately. A great shout of excited agreement greeted the news as most aircrews had come from towns that had suffered heavily from German air attacks. However, my conscience was deeply concerned. I had never volunteered to bomb civilians, to incinerate women and children. I seriously considered refusing to fly, but actually this would take more guts than facing the German defences. It would not be regarded as a conscientious objection but cowardice, with all the shame and degradation that would follow. I took the easy way out and carried on. The target was given as the main post office in the centre of the town. I was in the tail turret because a new wireless operator was being tried out on the set. In actual fact he could not cope and I had to take over on the return journey to get the bearings and information to enable us to land safely.

The next trip was to Sterkrade oil refinery, on 15 February, and the same arrangement took place. I was in the tail, but this time the wireless operator managed to cope with things quite satisfactorily. These trips in the tail turret were

Aircraft sound locators were used in the early war years to aid in the tracking down of Bomber Command aircraft. They were later replaced by the Freya *and* Würzburg *ground radars. Here, personnel of* Kriegsmarine *coastal battery M Fla Abt 4/816* 'Olmen' *are at work in Ijmuiden on a fine winter's day. The position of an aircraft was determined by one operator moving the vertical horns in a horizontal plane, and a second operator moving the horizontal horns vertically.* Coll. Marineschule Mürwik.

particularly boring. The turret was cramped, so you had little freedom of movement, it was very cold indeed and until you were flying back over the North Sea you dared not leave it, even to use the Elsan. On the way home crews were tired, aching and stiff. Occasionally I dozed off for a few seconds, often to wake with a start, mistaking a speck of mud on the perspex for an enemy aircraft. Several rear gunners lost fingers through frost bite when trying to clear faults in the guns, others lost the skin off their behinds when sitting on the Elsan.

On this trip, especially over the target, the anti-aircraft fire and the searchlights were extremely heavy, and it was a very unpleasant feeling to sit in the rear turret, seeing the anti-aircraft shells bursting, sometimes near, sometimes a little farther away, and wondering whether the next one would be curtains for you. However, after eight hours' flying, some of it under great stress, we landed back at Topcliffe. I had now completed nine trips and thirty seemed an awful long way away.

Our next trip on 12 March was to the 'Big City', Berlin, the most frightening target of them all. However, when we were well on our way, one engine packed up and we were forced to return. We decided to bomb Hamburg as an alternative on the way back. As we approached Hamburg, it was completely quiet. There were no searchlights, no anti-aircraft fire, nothing. I thought what a doddle it was. We carried on to the centre of Hamburg and then dropped our bombs. As soon as the bombs hit the ground, all hell was let loose. They apparently knew we were up there. They did not give the position away, because they did not know whether we had located Hamburg or not. But as soon as the bombs actually dropped, they had us in their sights, we were coned, in the middle of several searchlights, one of the most dangerous situations, one that we always tried to avoid. When you were coned you were completely lit up. It was brighter than day inside the aircraft, you could not see. You had to get down quick; if you stayed in it for long you would cease to exist.

I stood petrified in the cabin, watching Stevie weaving and seeing the ground getting far too near for comfort. Stevie threw the aircraft about in all directions; eventually we managed to evade the searchlights. We dived down to about 1,000 feet, and it took a big effort by Stevie to pull the control column back to fly straight and level. We had managed to get out of trouble and returned home. Out of eight aircraft from our squadron that took part in this raid, one went missing. Another crashed on landing and two of the crew were killed. Like most raids, aircraft were lost, but you would not take too much notice. All we wanted was to get back ourselves. You got used to it, you just carried on doing your job.

A Bf 110 C-4 of 5./NJG2 taxies out at Leeuwarden airfield for a night-fighting patrol in 1942. Coll. Heinz Huhn, via Rob de Visser.

The next night we were detailed to go to Hamburg again, this time as the official target. We had a comparatively easy trip. It was a bright moonlit night and as we were approaching Hamburg we could see another Whitley also flying along on a parallel course with us. Suddenly it exploded. What had been an aircraft a few seconds before, was now a mass of debris flying through the air. It had apparently been hit by an anti-aircraft shell, most likely in its bomb bay. We also encountered very heavy anti-aircraft barrages, and again Stevie's ability to take severe evasive action saved us. But at the climax of every trip came the long run-up to bomb, through the dazzling web of lights, the flicker of flak, the curling twisting pattern of the tracer and the glow of the fires below.

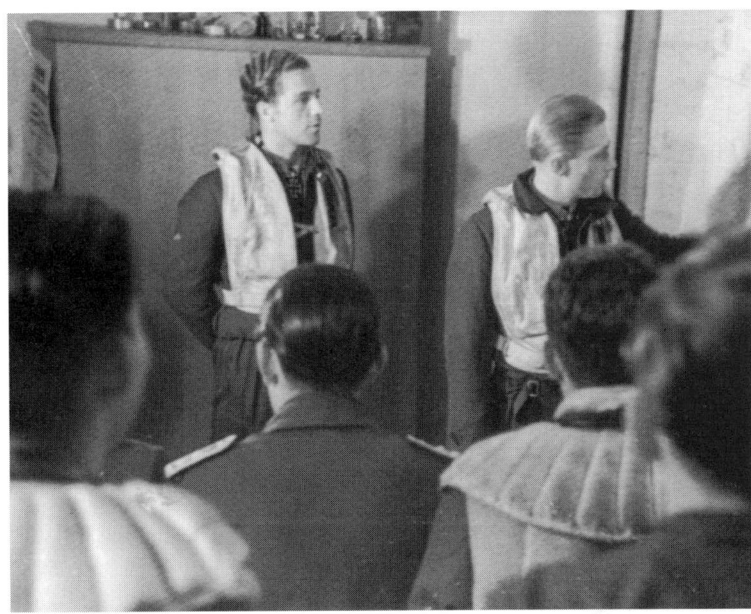

Nachtjagd *pioneers. Ofw Paul Gildner (left) and his Staffel Kapitän Oblt Helmut Lent briefing their 4./NJG1 crews in the operations room at Leeuwarden, late 1941. Aged twenty-seven, Gildner had been one of the first* Nachtjagd *pilots to receive the* Ritterkreuz *on 9 July 1941 for two day and fourteen night kills. Lent received the* Ritterkreuz *for seven day and fourteen night kills on 30 August of the same year, at the age of twenty-three.* Coll. Heinz Huhn, via Rob de Visser.

There had only been three aircraft taking part from our squadron and the one that went missing was piloted by my very best friend on the squadron, Alec Elliott. He was the man whom I had gone out with every night, and we used to play crib day after day, waiting in the crew room, and I had seen him go. He had lent me a book, *Gone with the Wind*, which, of course, I would be unable to return to him. To lose a good friend was initially very distressing. But such was the pace of our losses we soon forgot, and it served to emphasize how lucky we ourselves had been to get back.

Our next trip was to Bremen. This was comparatively easy because we did not have to fly over any German territory, and of the seven aircraft that went and took part, all returned safely. By now, having done twelve operations, I was the longest surviving wireless operator/air gunner on the squadron and the one with the most experience. The next day I was detailed to fly with our CO, Wing Commander Howes. This time the target was L'Orient in France, which as I said previously was a comparatively easy target. As far as we were concerned everything went well, but again out of the seven aircraft that took part there was one that had gone missing.

I was crewed up again with Sergeant Stevens on 23 March and the target was once again Berlin. However, once again we never made it, and again we bombed Hamburg as the alternative. Looking back now I wonder if we really did have to turn back each time Berlin was the target, or whether Stevie considered discretion was the better part of valour. Out of the three aircraft that took off that evening from our flight, only two actually located Berlin and one of these was shot down.

However, it is probably right to look at the conditions under which we were operating. The crews who operated during the autumn of 1940 and through 1941, were doing so under tremendous difficulties. The aircraft were fitted with inadequate ancillary equipment. The only navigational aid the navigator was supplied with was a sextant. The aircraft were without heating and the cold was appalling. The crews flew clothed in layers of silk, wool and leather and yet they were still bitterly cold. Vital systems jammed, wings iced up for lack of adequate de-icing gear, guns froze and the crews limbs seized with the cold.

The navigator gave his pilot a course to steer on take-off and then relied upon dead reckoning, hoping to be able to establish pinpoints on the ground below at intervals in the seven- or eight-hour flight. When visiting Germany we always flew out over Flamborough Head, then across the North Sea to the Frisian Islands off the Dutch coast. If visibility was satisfactory, both these points gave a good pinpoint. If the night was clear and the stars could be seen, then it was possible for the navigator to obtain a fix with his sextant, provided the pilot was willing to fly straight and level for long enough. That could be a dangerous operation.

War artist's impression of a Wellington Abschuss *by Ofw Gildner (4./NJG1) sometime in 1941. On this occasion, the Wimpey's fuel tanks exploded at close range, covering the German hunter in burning petrol. Gildner prepared himself to bale out, but the flames were blown away in his slipstream and he managed to return to Leeuwarden safely. Berliner Illustrierte Zeitung,* via Helmut Conradi.

It was sometimes possible for the wireless operator to obtain a loop bearing from England. But the bearing could occasionally put the aircraft on a 180-degree reciprocal course. The Germans also jammed the wavelengths. Navigators were given the weather forecast before take-off, which included predicted winds. Often the predictions were inaccurate and the winds were blowing the aircraft off track. The crews could attempt to check drift by dropping a flare; this was at best a chancy business and quite impossible in low cloud. So obviously if it was a cloudy night it was necessary to rely on dead reckoning, but there were several factors that could cause serious errors, and again and again during this period, bombs were being dropped all over Germany, in villages, farms and homes, as well as on factories and industrial regions.

Our bombing operations were not nearly as effective as the official reports and the media claimed. However, the most important point is that we were keeping up the morale of the civilian population. Our armies had been overwhelmed in France and rescued from Dunkirk, our navy was suffering severe losses, and German bombers were creating havoc and despair with their regular raids on our towns, as they only had to travel a few miles from their airfields in France. The only gleam of hope our civilian population had was to read of the exaggerated reports of the RAF bombing raids on Germany.

At the beginning of April, I found myself crewed up with another pilot, Sergeant Doherty. He was an Irishman, had not flown on operations as a Captain so far, and I presume that I was crewed up with him so as to give him the benefit of my experience. We were detailed to fly on operations on 1 and 2 April, but at the last minute both of these operations were cancelled. This was particularly stressful, as during the day you did an air test on the aircraft, flying around for probably half an hour, making sure that all the equipment was in perfect order. You attended

Illuminated night-fighting kill. Lt Hans Autenrieth of 6./NJG1 proudly poses with the roundel cut from his first night Abschuss, *Halifax I L9531 MP-R of 76 Squadron, which fell victim to his guns in a* Helle Nachtjagd *interception over Hamburg on 12–13 August 1941. The aircraft crashed at 03.16, some 500m north-east of Wittstedt, 15km SSE of Bremerhaven. Sgt C.E. Whitfield and his crew all baled out safely, but five fell into a swamp and drowned.* Coll. Anneliese Autenrieth.

the briefing in the afternoon and then hung around for several hours and then just before take-off the whole thing was scrubbed.

However, on 3 April we were detailed to Brest and actually took off. We had been flying for two or three hours when our intercom system failed, and were flying just above a bank of clouds when a German fighter was sighted. We immediately dived into cloud cover, because the task of a bomber was to carry out the raid, to evade fighters and only seek combat when unavoidable. Inside the cloud we ran into an electric storm. Sparks were flying off the propellers, there were bangs and crackles, a most eerie experience. Then one engine was struck by lightning and packed up. We had no alternative but to turn back and jettison our bombs. This then became a very tough assignment for Sergeant Doherty, being his first operation as Captain of the aircraft. Actually, without boasting, I can say it was a good thing that he had an experienced wireless operator with him that night, because I was able to consistently get courses to steer to take us back to England.

We were losing height across the Channel and I was able to get permission to land at Tangmere, which was on the south coast, and also give him courses to steer to arrive there. We landed safely. Of the aircraft that took part in this raid, none of them were actually lost over the target, but one aircraft apparently also got into difficulties in the same way as we did. They crashed on landing and all were killed. Our aircraft was eventually repaired and we landed back the next afternoon. Apparently Sergeant Doherty was now allocated a permanent wireless operator and I went back to flying with Sergeant Stevens, which suited me very well.

On 7 April we were detailed to fly to Kiel. This was a particularly long trip across the North Sea, but it had the advantage that we did not fly over much German territory. The visibility that night was extremely good. It was bright moonlight and we observed our bombs hitting the docks, which was our target. Kiel was a particularly long haul back and I was very busy on the return journey getting courses to fly and eventually we landed safely after seven hours. Seven aircraft went out that night from our squadron and one went missing.

We had arrived back at 4 o'clock in the morning. By the time we were debriefed, had our meal and I went home and got into bed, it was gone 6 o'clock. However, a despatch rider came around about 9 o'clock and told Maisie I was detailed to fly again that night. She woke me up and feeling very weary and heavy, I reported to the airfield. I had been up almost twenty-four

A fine shot of a Halifax I, taken in the Western Desert in 1942. L9531 of this type fell victim to Lt Autenrieth of 6./NJG1 over Hamburg on 12–13 August 1941. Coll. Cyril Miles.

hours the previous day, much of it under great stress, and after a couple of hours actual sleep I was due for another long stint. Once again Kiel was the target. Apparently, the raid the previous night had been so successful that they decided to make use once again of the bright moonlight and the northern lights. Ten aircraft from our squadron took part, but four never made it.

I had now completed seventeen trips out of the thirty. I was the most experienced wireless operator on the squadron, and I was beginning to see the light at the end of the tunnel, because having completed seventeen, another thirteen seemed quite possible.

Next followed a trip to Düsseldorf, which was a piece of cake. Eight aircraft took part, they all bombed successfully and returned home, which was unusual because the Ruhr was considered particularly hazardous.

The next operation on 12 April was to Bordeaux. It is quite a long haul when circumstances are good, but this particular night we had difficulty with navigation. It took us a long while to locate Bordeaux and the navigator had problems on the way back. As a consequence, our petrol reserves were becoming dangerously low. I was kept very busy on the wireless getting homings from Abingdon and we landed there, having been in the air for ten hours and our petrol almost exhausted. Once again though, it was a good night in general. Six aircraft took part and all returned safely. We landed at 6 o'clock in the morning, refuelled and took off again at 8 o'clock.

On 15 April we returned once again to Kiel. From our point of view the trip was uneventful, but of the seven aircraft from our squadron that took part, two got bogged down in the mud before take-off, two returned without having found the target, and of the three that actually got to Kiel, one was shot down. So out of the seven aircraft, only our crew and one other had a satisfactory journey.

On 17 April Berlin was the target. It was a long, arduous and nerve-wracking flight of nine hours. It must be emphasized that during that time we were really 'keyed up'. Having crossed the Dutch coast anti-aircraft fire was encountered on the way to Berlin, and when we were about fifty miles from the target it seemed impossible to penetrate the barrage that surrounded it. Searchlights had to be evaded, and seeing the occasional bomber being shot down in flames obviously heightened the tension. The pilot was weaving and turning all the time, and all of us were on a continual lookout for fighters. Of the eight aircraft from our squadron that took part that night, one aircraft was missing. Once again, this emphasized how the odds were stacked against anyone attempting to complete thirty operations.

On 25 April, Wing Commander Howes decided that he would operate once again and he had selected me as his wireless operator. The target was Kiel, it all went off uneventfully and, of the ten aircraft that took part, all returned safely.

The Flight Commander had gone missing a couple of weeks previously and at the end of

April we received a new one, Squadron Leader Burnett. He was commencing his tour of operations and I found that I was crewed up with him. Once again I had been chosen because I was the most experienced wireless operator on the squadron. So on 30 April, again the target was Kiel, but this time with Squadron Leader Burnett. As far as we were concerned the operation was a complete success. April had been an extremely good month for me. I had completed nine operations and was now well on my way to the end of my tour.

On 2 May I was crewed up once again with Squadron Leader Burnett and the target was Hamburg. It turned out to be one of the most nerve-wracking flights I had taken part in. That night I learnt that Squadron Leader Burnett was a 'press it home at all costs' type of man. The anti-aircraft fire that night over Hamburg was particularly heavy and on the run up to the target we were caught in about twelve searchlights. It was so bright it was impossible to see. If Sgt Stevens had been the pilot, he would have shouted to the bomb-aimer, 'Drop those bloody bombs and let's piss off home,' but Squadron Leader Burnett was made of different stuff.

He turned the aircraft round into an acute dive, still the searchlights held us and we knew that if we were held in the searchlights too long, we were obviously going to be shot down by a fighter or by anti-aircraft fire. However, he continued to weave and dive until eventually we lost the searchlights, but we were now almost on top of the houses in Hamburg. It took the two pilots all their strength on the control column to pull out of the dive.

To my dismay he said to the navigator, 'I'm climbing to 12,000 feet and I want you to give me a course to steer to go in again.' Laboriously, with a full bomb-load on, we climbed to 12,000 feet and the navigator gave him the course. We were on a straight and level course to bomb the docks, but the majority of aircraft had now left and once again the searchlights came on us and the anti-aircraft fire began noisily banging all round us. Somehow we got out of it, but it was purely by luck, and eventually we left the target area and returned home. Of the ten aircraft that took part that night, one was missing.

It was about this time that I began having trouble with my ears. They were discharging blood on the pillow when I slept. I think that when sometimes we dropped 10,000 feet very

Lt Hans Autenrieth (left) and his Bordfunker Gefr Rudolf Adam return to Stade airfield near Hamburg, home of II./NJG1 after a flight in their Bf 110 C in September 1941. Coll. Anneliese Autenrieth.

A Messerschmitt Bf 110 E of II./NJG1 being refuelled at Stade airfield in September 1941. Note the aperture of the gun camera fitted between the nose armament, the night-fighting crest and the Roman II, denoting that the aircraft belongs to the Second Gruppe, *and the individual letter 'C' on the nose of the aircraft.* Coll. Anneliese Autenrieth.

rapidly, the difference in pressure was causing a problem. I was also having nightmares and Maisie sometimes had to wake me up, because I was moaning and shouting.

Two days afterwards, I was crewed up once again with Squadron Leader Burnett. The target was Brest, a very easy one, but it was nice to get there and back without incident. Six aircraft took part and all returned safely.

On 9 May, my birthday, I found myself crewed up yet again with a fresh pilot, a Sergeant Dougall. It was obvious that I was being crewed up with pilots who were just beginning their tour of operations, which was a little disconcerting as the majority of losses were from pilots who were on their first five trips. So if you flew with a pilot on his very first operation, the odds were stacked against you more than usual. Our target was Mannheim, but it was an easy trip and I was kept busy on the return getting courses to fly. One aircraft failed to return.

On 11 May, again with Sergeant Dougall, we went to Bremen and got home without any problem. I had now completed twenty-seven trips, but was getting to the jittery stage which happens when you have only two or three more trips to complete. However, two days afterwards, to my surprise, the Flight Commander came into the crew room and informed me that I had completed my tour. Apparently, a new Air Ministry directive had just been issued saying that when 200 operational hours had been completed, the tour was finished, irrespective of the number of operations flown. This was to compensate those people who had flown a high percentage of long arduous trips. He wished me the best of luck and said that he was recommending me for the award of the Distinguished Flying Medal. This was not given in a lot of cases for any specific act of bravery, but just as a reward for having completed a tour of operations. It became known as the Survivors' Medal.

The feeling of relief at the completion of a tour of operations is indescribable. I had been particularly lucky. In 1940–41 only one in ten finished a tour of operations. Later on, the chances improved to one in three. By the end of my tour, almost all my friends had gone missing. The remarkable thing is that you felt no sense of loss, you did not grieve, and in a week or two you had forgotten they ever existed. I think it was because it happened so regularly and you eased your conscience by thinking they were probably prisoner of war. Of course, one had the 'I'm alright, Jack' mentality. Also, in Bomber Command you rarely saw a dead body – names were rubbed off the board in the operations room and people failed to turn up at breakfast next morning. It was inevitable that we became hardened to loss.

Looking back I am amazed at the flippant way we went about our dangerous business. In the crew room before an operation the atmosphere was such that you would have thought we were about to take a holiday trip to Spain; plenty of banter and leg-pulling, completely unforced laughter. Aircrew, by performance, lived very close together. Squadron life was an intimate experience. We were all of the same mould: young, adventurous, living life to the full, but always conscious that many who were laughing and joking with us today would probably not be around tomorrow. In operational roles, each one was directly or indirectly dependent upon the other for survival. There was mutual trust and reliance. This promoted fondness, affection and respect. Friendships thus forged had a depth and unique quality that never existed with friendships before, and for me never after. There was also a deep personal relationship between aircrew and groundcrews, who worked tirelessly at all hours and outside in all weathers, to ensure that everything worked perfectly, adding to the safety of the aircrew who would fly the aircraft. In doing so they formed a close bond with the aircrew, for whom they had a deep and lasting admiration. We were as one, winning and losing together.

Aircrews developed enormous personal loyalty to each other and had a remarkable faith in their collective ability to face the terrifying tasks that lay ahead. It is no exaggeration to say that personal safety was never considered. It was always the collective safety of the entire crew that was of prime importance. There were very few aircrew, who entered the War at the beginning, who survived to the end. A crew's efficiency, ability and competence increased their chance of survival. But I maintain that it was 20 per cent ability and 80 per cent luck.

The airwar of 1939–1945 was a period of progressive change. Conditions in 1939–1941 were completely different to those in the closing stages of 1944–1945. The earlier years were the roughest; we were pioneering and we were thrown in at the deep end. Our difficulty was navigating to a target, sometimes small, in darkness, when our only means of navigating were map-reading, dead reckoning and astro-navigation in that order, and not many aircrew were proficient in the latter. Not for us the sophisticated radar aids of later years. It was going to be a hard war; the men who survived those primitive operations of 1940 and 1941 would look back on them afterwards as almost lunatic in their crudeness compared with what came later. Aircrew, as befitted men who were statistically not long for this world, spent their last months fattened with whatever England could provide for them, unheard-of luxuries such as extra milk, sugar and real eggs and bacon.

The start of the strategic bombing campaign against Nazi Germany was marked by raids primarily on targets in the Ruhr and against ports

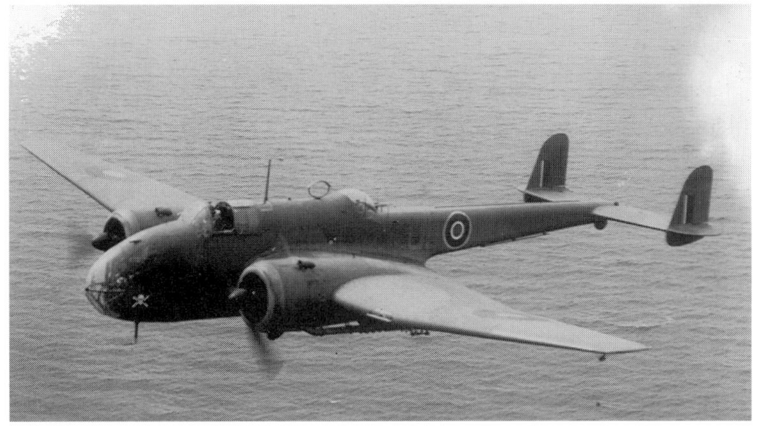

The first Australian squadron in Bomber Command, 455 (RAAF) Squadron became operational at Swinderby in August 1941. The unit flew 424 Hampden sorties in ninety-two raids, losing fourteen aircraft, before being transferred to Coastal Command in April 1942. Depicted is a squadron Hampden flying over the North Sea. Note the skull and crossbones painted on a dark flag just aft of the nose compartment's glazing. Coll. Dr Leslie Oliver DFC.

on the enemy coastline. However, it soon became painfully clear that on most raids the bomber crews failed to carry out precision attacks against the small military targets they were briefed to destroy. The main bomber types in use were simply not equipped, and their crews not trained to find and hit specific targets at night, even when operating in full-moon periods. In addition to this handicap, crews had to come to terms with operating in foul weather conditions at night, with the ever looming dangers of fog and icing.

Even though these early raids caused little damage to the Reich, Generalfeldmarschall Hermann Göring, C-in-C of the *Luftwaffe,* ordered the creation of *Nachtjagd*, a specialist night-fighting arm, on 26 June 1940, as Germany's flak defences proved largely ineffective against the British night raiders. Oberst, later General, Josef Kammhuber was tasked with setting up the first night fighter division, and creating operational units. The infant arm found itself confronted with the same difficulties as its adversary, struggling with the intricacies of night-time and bad-weather flying, for which the German crews had also not been prepared. The elements come to the fore in the following two accounts, first focusing on the British bomber crews, and then their opponents.

THE DEADLY ELEMENTS

On 24–25 October 1940, Bomber Command dispatched 113 aircraft to many targets in Germany and the Netherlands. Weather was atrocious, with crews encountering thick cloud, snow and icing. Hampered by the elements, only few aircraft made their way to their allotted targets, although Hamburg reported thirteen fires started in a particularly sharp raid. Losses amounted to a 38 Squadron Wellington IC (L7809) and Whitley V P5073 of 102 Squadron, with nine crew members perishing. Sgt Ken G. Hodson, observer in Blenheim IV T2230 D for Donald of 107 Squadron bound for Kassel, recorded:

As a member of a Blenheim crew engaged in operational flying in late 1940 and 1941 I took part in some dangerous and spectacular daylight sorties at low level, in formation with other Blenheims. Such trips were exciting and exhilarating, I loved flying at low level, however dangerous. It was, however, the night sorties, in the terrible weather during the later months of 1940, that I found lonely, terrifying, uncomfortable and nerve-wracking. They placed a great strain and responsibility on the navigator, as the navigational aids were negligible: particularly as the W/T, from which we could have got a course to steer for base (QDM) rarely, if ever, worked. The following account of a raid on Kassel is such an example.

On 24 October 1940, the weather at Wattisham, where we were based, was foul. The squadron had been detailed to carry out a raid on a factory at Kassel in Germany, beyond the Ruhr. It was one of those nights when the weather was way below the limits acceptable for night flying in those days. We thought it would be cancelled. It was not, but it should have been!

We took off and were immediately in thick cloud. We climbed to 12,000 feet to get above it, but we could not. The wings were icing up. The temperature in the cockpit was –20°C, and we didn't have any heating. We suffered touches of frost bite. En route I was able to get a pinpoint through a break in the cloud over Holland – or I thought I did – in those conditions I couldn't be sure.

At the estimated time of arrival (ETA) over Kassel, Bill Howell, my pilot, started to circle and we dropped flares to try and locate our position. We could see through small gaps in the clouds, but the glare from the flares – which gave off a bright light and reflected off the clouds, caused Bill to become disorientated. He got the aircraft on to its back. He did not realize what had happened, so put the nose down to gain flying speed. As we were upside down, this had the opposite effect. The aircraft stalled and started to fall out of the sky, spinning madly as it rapidly lost height. Bill shouted 'Bale out!' Jock Armour, the wireless operator/air gunner and I tried, but we were tied to our seats by the force of the spin. This was as well because, after

Plt Off Paul Todd peering out of the side window of Wellington R1781 SR-C of 101 Squadron, a veteran of thirty ops, at Oakington in late 1941. The 'Wimpey' remained the very reliable backbone of Bomber Command throughout 1941 and 1942. Coll. Paul Todd.

falling around 10,000 feet, Bill was able to get the aircraft under control – but one of the engines had cut. He managed to get the engine running again, but the aircraft wouldn't climb because of the weight of ice on the wings. We did not have any devices in the wings to stop ice building up. It would have greatly helped our situation had we jettisoned our bombs, to reduce the weight of the aircraft and so gain more lift. We did not jettison. We still hoped that a break in the weather would allow us to bomb the secondary target, railway marshalling yards at Hamm. There was no let-up in the weather and we did not identify that target either. We wanted to bomb a military target so we aimed at the flashes from anti-aircraft guns. It was the best we could do in the circumstances.

During the spin, some of my navigation instruments and flight plan/navigation log disappeared, lost somewhere in the cockpit. Thus, the navigation home was by guess and by God! We had little interference from the enemy – we didn't need that hassle. The weather was so terrible, it was an absolute nightmare! Fortunately, I could remember the course we had flown from the Dutch coast to the target and so we set course back on the reciprocal, adjusted to take account of the change in wind effect. At ETA Dutch coast, I altered course to strike the English coast well north of Orford Ness.

Bill was having difficulty; he was very tired – we were all very cold and tired. Until you have experienced such bitter cold, it is difficult to appreciate how cold, cold can get. We had suffered it for more than five hours. Bill had been struggling to fly the aircraft all that time – blind flying in very turbulent conditions. The aircraft was not fitted with an automatic pilot. When blind flying, the pilot relies solely on his instruments, which calls for absolute concentration the whole time, but his instruments were icing up. It is not surprising that Bill became disorientated once more and I found he was flying around in circles over the North Sea. With my encouragement he got back on course (or so we hoped) towards England. I was determined to survive! We got down on to the sea, below the clouds, to about fifty feet. We overshot our ETA by more than five minutes, and still no sign of the coast ahead, a most stressful time for us all. I was peering anxiously through the bombing panel. I can't stress too strongly the terrible feeling of isolation, of loneliness, fear and intense cold. Although we operated as a squadron, at night we rarely saw another aircraft throughout a flight – particularly in that sort of weather. I still have nightmares when I think about it!

The fuel was getting low, the radio was unserviceable. We were beginning to think we would never find England. We were, I'm afraid, on the

A Bf 110 C-4 of 5./ZG76 revving-up its engines before taking off from Leeuwarden in 1941. When crews of II./ZG76 were incorporated into II./NJG4, many retained the shark's mouth on their aircraft, but with the teeth now painted black. Coll. Kees Mol, via P. Staal.

point of giving up hope. I had never felt like that before, or indeed since. It was, in RAF slang, a 'very dicey do' [a dangerous trip]. We could have 'gone for a Burton!' [we could have been killed]. Then suddenly – there was the coast ahead of us, and we turned rapidly to port – our morale rose, hope had returned. Had this been our first operation we would, probably, not have survived to reach this point.

We were in fact some fifty miles north of Orford Ness, a coastal spit in Suffolk, which was our designated landfall when returning from operational flights. Soon we were able to identify an RAF beacon near Norwich by the letters it was flashing in code. We soon got to Orford Ness, still flying at fifty feet, but in light snow. From Orford we found our airfield beacon at the second attempt, having gone back to re-establish our position and try again. Once we identified the beacon we soon found our airstrip and landed, although it was still snowing and very dark. What a relief and joy we felt; we had survived against what seemed to be almost impossible odds. Odds against the weather, not the enemy!

An anonymous German war reporter continues to tell how the German night fighter crews coped with adverse weather conditions at night:

> When in the evening at their briefing they are given the weather data such as ceiling fifty to eighty metres, icing all the way up to 5,000 metres, upper winds 129 kilometres, diversionary airfields only here and there – then the crews look at each other in silence. It's going to be 'criminal' again, they mean.
>
> If by day an engine fails 200 metres after take-off or the radio goes dead, one takes a quick look around and makes, if necessary, a belly landing in the nearest field. At night, from autumn until spring, a technical failure can mean death. The icing alone! It means a great deal when a night fighter, who has survived many an air battle and countless heavy take-offs and even more dangerous landings at night, admits that he fears nothing so much as icing. It is a struggle against death each time.
>
> That's how it goes. Up above, high beyond the dangerous zones of icing, the enemy bombers approach from their clear bases. The night fighter

has taken off. Just now, for some seconds he had seen the red lights of the airfield perimeter – then they had dimmed and disappeared in the haze. The aircraft climbs through the grey, dark, surging cloud. What had the meteorologist said: tops at 5,000 metres? But the icing starts already at 1,000 metres. This time quite slowly. The aircraft climbs more slowly. Higher and higher. The pilot is bathed in sweat.

Aren't we hanging starboard wing down? he suddenly thinks, startled. Instinctively he leans to his left, as if he could balance it out. But his reason prevents his hands from correcting the supposed imbalance. He takes another look at the instruments. According to these the machine is on an even keel. But his senses whisper: perhaps the instruments are no longer indicating correctly! Here begins that nerve-wracking struggle which recurs with almost every flight on instruments: the conflict between one's own sense of balance, which according to experience deceives each time, and the instruments. The senses demand: believe me, don't trust the instruments. He struggles with himself, calls all proven experience to his aid, forces himself to look only at his instruments and neither to right or left. And still it remains a hard struggle.

At 4,000 metres the icing has got so heavy that he considers going down again to warmer layers. He is already far over the sea. It's obvious – up ahead there is another bad-weather front! So back and away. But he cannot risk a turn, the heavily iced-up machine has lost so much lift that it could be dangerous to do so. Behind him his radio operator and gunner. They suspect, but they do not know what he knows. So, continue with the climb. There! Aren't those stars, glimmering through the thinning haze? Another 1,000 metres, then he must be through. Then he has made it. If the icing gets even heavier in these last 1,000 metres they would be lost. Even the parachutes would not help. The sea is cold. No one would survive for more than an hour. A thousand thoughts enter his mind. He swears quietly to himself. 'What's up?' asks the radio operator on the intercom. 'Oh, nothing, we'll be through in a minute,' he replies, and tries to sound casual. But the radio operator knows him, they have been flying together for a long time. Time and again he looks anxiously at the thickening ice on the leading edges of the wings. And he cannot fail to hear the ice chunks from the propellers striking the fuselage side.

At last they are through and in clear air. Whatever might follow seems easy. What are

Plt Off Jimmy Craig and a ground-crew member prepare a Hampden of 144 Squadron for take-off at RAF North Luffenham, October 1941. Note the flame-dampers on the port Bristol Pegasus XVII engine, and the retractable D/F loop aerial aft of the aerial mast. Coll. Frank Neale.

the enemy bombers and night fighters, what the dangerous flak zones and the air battles, now that the heavenly elements have released them from their icy grip. They give no thoughts yet to the landing and its dangers. A random bullet in the radio, and the sole means of orientation in such nights without sight of the ground is gone. How often that does happen to a night fighter! Then the difficult decision: bale out or attempt the landing? For one no longer knows one's position with certainty. Still over the plain or above the mountains? Try to get down through the clouds? They hang down to within fifty metres of the earth. Perhaps he is lucky and gets through over the plain! But even then the deadly danger has not passed. Where is there an airfield? Flying at a speed of hundreds of kilometres per hour through the dark, each tiny hill, each power pylon or chimney can mean sudden disaster.

These are not selected and rare cases, but the night fighter's daily bread. From autumn until spring he must take off under weather conditions which are highly dangerous from start to finish. If the weather conditions are good the enemy no longer comes. As a result, every night sortie becomes a bad-weather sortie. They are silent tests of courage, extreme demands on the human frame, for which there are no decorations. No outsider suspects what nervous tension and what struggles are behind the simple formula of the *Wehrmacht* report: 'In spite of adverse weather conditions …'

The main problem with which *Nachtjagd*'s pioneers found themselves confronted, was how to get the night fighter aircraft to within firing range of their British adversaries in the three-dimensional vastness of the black night sky. General Kammhuber experimented with listening posts equipped with acoustic aids to track down the bombers, and with searchlight batteries co-operating with night fighters, but it was not successful. Kammhuber realized that he needed more accurate means to find the elusive bombers, and in October 1940 he got the first tools he desperately wanted, obtaining six of the new *Würzburg* precision radar sets. Quickly equipping three experimental fighter control radar stations on Bomber Command's main route to the Ruhr with the *Würzburgs*, it was only days before Kammhuber was to witness success.

FIRST RADAR-CONTROLLED *NACHTJAGD* KILL

Lt Ludwig Becker and his Funker Uffz Josef Staub of 4./NJG1 scored *Nachtjagd*'s first ground radar-controlled success on 16 October 1940, by destroying Wellington IC L7844 KX-T of 311 (Czech) Squadron. After his action, Lt Becker submitted the following combat report:

> I flew the first sortie in the night-fighting area Zuidersee, and at about 21.20 I was controlled by Lt Diehl at Nunspeet using *Freya mit Zusatz* and *Würzburg*, using morse on the tactical frequency. I was guided very well at the correct height of 3,300 metres with constant corrections towards the enemy at his starboard rear and suddenly saw, about 100 metres to my left and above, an aircraft in the moonlight, which on approaching closer I recognized as a Vickers Wellington. I closed in slowly behind him and gave a burst of about five or six seconds, aiming at the fuselage and wing roots. The starboard engine caught fire at once and I drew my machine up above him.
>
> For a while the Englishman continued, rapidly losing height; then the fire went out and I watched him spinning downward and finally crash. I observed no one baling out. I returned to my standby area.

Unseen by the victorious *Nachtjagd* crew, Sgts Emanuel Novotny and Augustin Sestak managed to bale out before their Wellington was completely destroyed in the crash near Oosterwolde, Holland at 21.45. Plt Off Bohumil Landa and three of his crew were found dead in the wreckage the next day.

ILLUMINATED NIGHT-FIGHTING

By the end of 1940, *Nachtjagd* had expanded into a force of three *Gruppen* (I., II. and III./NJG1) and three searchlight battalions, which were used in a close-range interception technique called *Helle Nachtjagd* or illuminated night-fighting, in the areas to the west of the Ruhr. When Bomber Command penetrated this area, night-fighting aircraft were scrambled to take up positions behind the searchlight batteries, in the hope of engaging bombers caught in their beams. *Würzburg* ground radars were incorporated into this system, and Kammhuber rapidly expanded his defensive line into a continuous belt stretching from the Schleswig area over Kiel, Hamburg, Bremen, the Ruhr, and Venlo to the Luik area, and further to the south into France. A second belt was constructed for the protection of Berlin, and Bomber Command crews soon learned to respect the 'Kammhuber Line', as they christened it.

Ofw Paul Gildner of 4./NJG1, who was the first NCO in Nachtjagd *to receive the* Ritterkreuz *after fourteen night kills on 9 July 1941. Gildner would add another twenty-six night victories to his tally before he was killed on 26 February 1943.* Coll. Anneliese Autenrieth.

Being entirely dependent on weather conditions though, *Helle Nachtjagd* had many limitations. Still, up to the end of 1941, forty-two bombers were destroyed, mainly by the *Helle Nachtjagd* technique, as against some thirty brought down by flak. One of these aircraft fell victim to Lt Hans Autenrieth, a pilot with 6./NJG1, over Hamburg on 12–13 August 1941. Whilst it was still fresh in his memory, two months later, Lt Autenrieth recorded his experiences.

> During the night of 12–13 August 1941, I had taken off with the first wave to area 2A on my third operational flight but, having had to abandon this sortie due to malfunction of the oxygen system, I thought myself to be dogged by bad luck. Fortunately, however, this proved not to be the case, for it gave me the opportunity to take the place of another crew of the second wave and, using their machine, to operate in area 2C which had the reputation of being the most successful one. Having orbited the radio beacon for about half an hour, I received the report 'Otto, Otto' from ground control. I flew towards the searchlight cone but was unable to recognize the target within it. As I was only a little above the target; it took a long time before I was close enough to make out the coned aircraft in the haze. I watched the enemy machine trying to escape the searchlights by diving and twisting. When at last I had approached to within about 500 metres, I was able to make out that it was a four-engined machine. As the searchlights were already at a very low angle and I was worried that the Tommy would soon have escaped from them and also from me, I opened fire. I fired short bursts at the wildly twisting Tommy who then succeeded to get out of the searchlight's cone.
>
> I was of course very disappointed at this failure. But this disappointment was not to be the only one this night. Whilst still blaming myself for this missed opportunity, I received the report of a second sighting which I was able to spot at once. I was about 2,000 metres above him and tried to reach him as quickly as I was able. Only after having dived down some 1,000 metres and having to steepen my dive even more in order to

keep him in my sights, did I realize that the Tommy was on an opposite course and that I had been in an ever steepening dive. My engines screamed, I never got a chance to fire, and I levelled gently out. The air-speed indicator showed almost 700km/h and I thought the aircraft would break up. I forgot all about the Tommy. Whilst I dived past him through the searchlights, I was blinded by one of them which shone directly in my face. When I again looked out I saw the beams hanging above me and to my left. Only then did I realize where was up and where was down. When I was at last back to level flight I found myself some 1,000 metres below the still coned enemy machine. I climbed back after him with full power. I closed steadily in, it was a Vickers Wellington. When I was about 150 metres behind him, the rear gunner of the Wellington suddenly opened fire at me. But the bullets passed to port of my cockpit. I pressed all the buttons at once and aimed the first burst at the rear turret. When this had been silenced, I went for the starboard engine and wing. The hits could be made out clearly and a long trail of smoke appeared. As my Me 110 was considerably faster than the Wellington, I was soon so close that I had to pull up above it.

Then I heard ground control shout '*Sieg Heil*' and immediately after my radio operator as well. I went into a turn to port to take a look at the burning Tommy, but to my disappointment could see nothing at all. Shortly afterwards ground control reported: 'Machine descended burning with smoke trail in direction 3.' My disappointment at this misfortune was great, in which my radio operator joined me. When I was directed at a new sighting at only 1,000 metres' height I was certain that it would be the Wellington I had just fired at. I went for him angry as hell. But when I was still at 2,000 metres the Tommy had escaped the searchlights and I climbed back to 6,000 metres and called it a day.

Towards 3 o'clock I was directed to another Tommy who was flying some 10–12km away and 1,000 metres below me. With my advantage of height I soon closed on the four-engined enemy aircraft from his rear and above. At about 100 metres I opened fire on his starboard engines and wing with machine guns and cannon and turned away to port and above for a second attack. When I had done my 180-degree turn the Tommy was no longer being held by the searchlights. But I saw a long trail of smoke which I now followed. The controller asked me whether I was still able to see the enemy aircraft. Unfortunately I had to say no. But at almost the same moment I spotted the British bomber on my starboard bow, huge and only some 100 metres below. I reduced power to adjust to the Tommy's speed and make my second attack from his port quarter and above. Unfortunately, one cannon had failed during my first attack and I no longer had full firepower. I was unable to observe the effect on the Tommy as I had to break off in order not to ram him. After this second attack I was unable to see either the Tommy or a smoke trail. Some ten minutes later my radio operator and I observed the fire of a crash. We had both guessed correctly: it was our first *Abschuss*. This was confirmed at once by the controller who reported over the radio that the Tommy had been held by the *Würzburg* radar right up to his crash. We were very pleased by this first success and returned home with two enemy contacts and one kill.

It transpired that the four-engined Halifax had continued to fly for another twelve minutes after my two attacks, until it finally went down from 1,000 metres height near Wittstedt at 03.16. The seven crew members all baled out but five drowned in a bog. The remaining two were taken prisoner.

Lt Autenrieth's first night *Abschuss* was Halifax I L9531 MP-R of 76 Squadron, which crashed at 03.16, some 500 metres north-east of Wittstedt, 15km SSE of Bremerhaven. As mentioned by the victorious German pilot, Sgt C.E. Whitfield and his crew all baled out safely, but tragically five men fell into a swamp and drowned. 76 Squadron was hit hard, with two Halifaxes failing to return to Middleton St George from the 12–13 August 1941 Berlin raid, plus L9562 crashing on return to base with its seven-men crew all perishing.

CHAPTER 2

1942

PSYCHOLOGICAL EFFECT OF OPERATIONAL FLYING ON AIRCREW

Bomber Command losses climbed steadily from 2 per cent in 1940, to 2.7 per cent in 1941 and 4 per cent in 1942. With the many dangers looming on ops, the odds were highly stacked against Bomber Command's pioneers successfully completing a tour of thirty operations. The psychological effects of this knowledge weighed heavily upon the minds of many of the young aircrew, as reflected by Sgt Don Bruce, an observer who had just turned twenty-one when he was posted to 115 Squadron at Marham on 25 May 1942. Don flew Wellingtons with the squadron until he was shot down by flak on his thirteenth trip, to Duisburg on 13–14 July 1942, in X3560 KO-K.

> Most of the aircrew I met were just mad-keen to fly. They were imbued with the spirit of flying during the late twenties and early thirties when

Wimpey on the beach. Flt Lt W.H. Thallon's Wellington II Z8370 of 12 Squadron is being inspected on the North Sea beach of Terschelling Island by the Island's garrison on 21 January 1942. It was shot down the previous night at 21.00 by Oblt Ludwig Becker, St Kpt of 6./NJG2 as his ninth Abschuss. *Becker went on to claim two more Wellingtons in the same area during a* Himmelbett *sortie in Box 'Tiger' (Z1207 of 142 Squadron at 21.07, and Z1110 of 101 Squadron, at 21.37, no survivors). Box Tiger claimed a total of 150* Abschussbeteiligungen *during the War, the large majority of its victims vanishing into the North Sea without a trace.* Coll. Terschellinger Museum 't Behouden Huys.

Oblt Ludwig Becker, St Kpt of 6./NJG2, 1942. Coll. Rob de Visser.

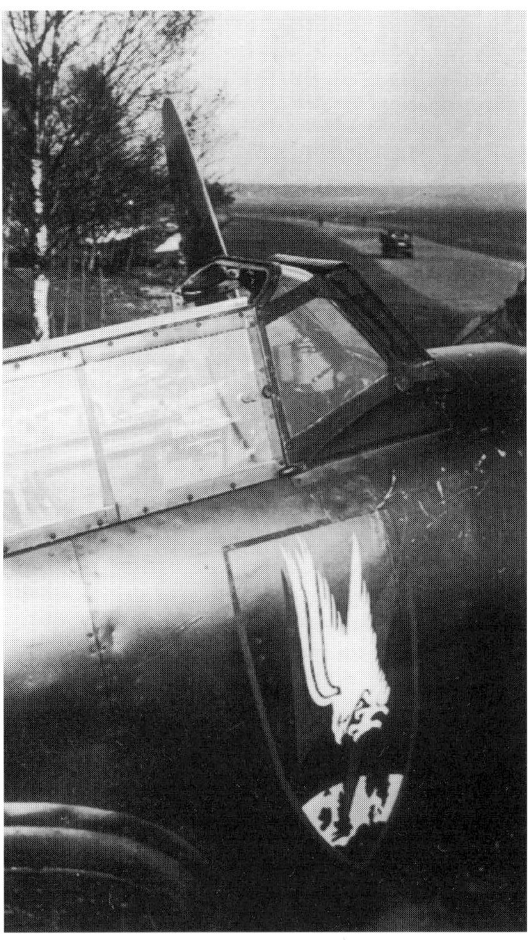

The famous Nachtjagd *crest is clearly shown on this II./NJG1 Bf 110 at St Trond in 1941.* Coll. Hans Grohmann.

momentous events were taking place in the development of flight. During our training period I don't think many of us really thought seriously about the tasks we would be asked to carry out later on operations. I know I never gave any deep thought to it, I just loved the job I was doing in the air.

When I was posted to 115 Squadron, the first five ops I flew were really exciting because it was all new and the dangers were not fully appreciated. It was wonderful to have dared and returned safely. After debriefing and breakfast it was marvellous to sink mentally and physically exhausted into cool sheets, and with the noise of the aircraft engines still singing in your ears drift into a deep sleep.

The novelty disappeared after this when I realized things could go wrong. I firmly believed that everyone was frightened on ops but you covered up and hid it from your fellow crew members. I think the dividing line between those who came off flying through Lack of Moral Fibre (LMF) and those who didn't was extremely thin. When we were being shot at by flak and the aircraft was being lifted by the blast and pieces of shrapnel were whining around inside the aircraft, I used to 'freeze'. These were short periods when I was so scared my brain refused to function properly. As soon as we were away from the flak I came back to normal, but I always had an underlying feeling of fear when on ops.

There were so many things that could go wrong. When we took off the bombers were always overloaded and difficult to get off the ground. If you crashed then it was 'curtains' for everybody. I always had on my shoulders the worry and responsibility of not getting the aircraft lost, which could easily cause us to stray across a heavily defended area. There was the risk all the time from night fighter attack and flak over the target. Then there was the difficulty of getting home, particularly if the aircraft was damaged. Landing in the darkness was also a hazard. Because of the risk of intruders aerodromes could not be lit up. As we made the landing approach the Chance Light would be turned on momentarily so the pilot could see the runway, and as soon as his wheels touched the ground it was switched off and we returned to darkness.

I'm sure no one enjoyed the open bombing of towns and cities which we were being asked to carry out. I had experienced being bombed during the Blitz in 1940 when I lived in London. That was why I felt sick when I did my first bomb-dropping on Emden (on 22 June 1942) and saw all the fires and thought of the population below. You had to put all that on one side and just do your task. We flew with Joe Richardson, who eventually came off with LMF. Also, on one trip we took a front gunner, Sgt J.B. Smith, who was suspect LMF. When we got near the target he said that his leg was playing him up. He had been wounded in the leg on an earlier occasion. Sgt Del Mooney RCAF, my pilot, told him to go back on the bed and he cowered there all the time we were in the target area and then went back into the turret later on the return journey. At debriefing he was telling the Intelligence Officer all that he had seen over the target. This was in front of us. It was pathetic and I felt desperately sorry for him. I thought this could well be me if I cracked. Del and I had to make a report to the Group Captain on him and we had to tell the truth. Del said he would refuse to fly with him if he was asked to take him again. He was posted away from the squadron LMF. The poor devils got a rough time; they were demoted and given the most menial of jobs. This happened to NCOs; I think the treatment of LMF officers was more lenient.

To sum up, I was very frightened on ops, I swore if I got through a tour I wouldn't do a second tour. When I had parachuted into Holland I heard one of our bombers overhead returning home. At first I thought how lucky they were. Then I thought tomorrow or the next day they will have to go through all that ordeal again and believe it or not I felt relieved that I was out of it.

Don Bruce briefly mentioned above the new policy of area bombing, which was issued in Directive No. 22 by the Air Ministry on 14 February 1942. Instead of attacking individual targets in a German city, the city itself now became the target. This dramatic change was prompted after an independent inquiry had revealed that, despite the best endeavours of the crews, bombs had been strewn far and wide over western Germany during 1941. Bomber Command simply did not have the tools yet to find, bomb, and destroy specific targets at night.

Another major turning point for the Command came only eight days after the adoption of the new area bombing directive, when Air Marshal Sir Arthur T. Harris was appointed as its new C-in-C. He was to pursue the area bombing campaign vigorously, believing that Bomber Command could thus shorten, or even win the War by breaking the morale of the German population and bringing about a collapse of the German war production. In his first year of command, Harris introduced several new steps in the bombing campaign. He concentrated the bombing effort into the 'one night, one main target' principle, and phased out the obsolete Whitleys and Hampdens in favour of the four-engined Stirling, Halifax and later on the Lancaster. Simultaneously, he introduced several new technological bombing aids, the first of which was 'Gee', a precision navigation aid of medium range based on beam transmissions from the UK.

THE *THOUSAND* PLAN (COLOGNE)

Within a few months of assuming command, Harris decided to stage a series of huge demonstrations of what his Command was capable of, by mounting three Thousand Bomber Raids in May and June 1942. The first raid in the *Thousand* Plan was mounted on the last night of May by 1,047 aircraft, including many from OTUs, on the city of Cologne. This night also witnessed the introduction of two major new tactics under the principle of 'concentration in space and time': the 'bomber stream', and a restricted bombing time of only ninety minutes. These tactics were intended to locally swamp the night-fighting and flak defences, and the fire-fighting services in the city under attack.

Having successfully completed a tour of ops as WOp on Whitleys with 102 Squadron, Sgt Douglas Mourton was posted to 22 OTU, a Wellington OTU for training Canadian aircrews, just before Christmas 1941. He lived with his wife Maisie quite near the aerodrome at Wellsbourne near Stratford-on-Avon, and vividly recounts his involvement in the plan.

On 25 May 1942 we were out in the garden looking down at the airfield and there was a Wellington stationary, waiting for another Wellington to come in to land, before turning in

Hptm Walter Ehle, Gruppen Kommandeur of II./NJG1, caught in a relaxed mood at St Trond in 1942. After scoring three daytime victories in 3./ZG1 and one of the first Nachtjagd *kills (either Wellington R3210 of 37, or R3165 of 75 Squadron on 20–21 July 1940) in 3./NJG1, Walter Ehle was appointed Kommandeur of II./NJG1 in October 1940. His tally mounted steadily during the difficult pioneering years, and by November 1943 he had emerged victorious in thirty-nine air combats, thirty-five by night, and was awarded the* Ritterkreuz. *Major Ehle and his crew finally met their end on the night of 17–18 November 1943 when, on finals to St Trond, the flarepath was suddenly extinguished and Ehle's Bf 110 G-4 5575 G9+AC crashed near Horpmoel.* Coll. Anneliese Autenrieth.

and taking off itself. Unfortunately, the Wellington that was coming in to land veered off course and crashed into the waiting aircraft. Both Wellingtons went up in flames and there were twelve killed including two instructors.

The next day we were all confined to camp and the rumour had it that there was something really big going to happen. No one was allowed out of camp and on 27 May, we heard that all our aircraft at the OTU were going to go on an operation, which was unusual. Almost everyone was crewed up and I considered myself very fortunate that I did not appear on the crew list. Our aircraft were old and obsolete and it was generally considered that they would be sitting targets for the German defences.

My very good friend Juggins had been crewed up with four Canadians who had not yet passed out. He decided that he was going to refuse to fly, as he thought that after surviving so long he did not want to get killed with a crew who were not very proficient. To my dismay I was substituted in his place. I went along to briefing and met my crew for the first time. They were obviously very inexperienced. The captain was Plt Off Lowe. The briefing took place in the afternoon, and we waited expectantly for the arrival of the CO. As usual we jumped to attention when he entered, then the usual 'Alright men, be seated.' The large map of Europe was on the wall and in due course the ribbon was stretched to mark Cologne as a target. When the number of aircraft taking part was announced there was a gasp of astonishment, especially as the raid was to be condensed into a relatively short space of time. The risk of collision was discussed, and the Intelligence Officer said that it was projected that only two would be lost in this way. One wag shouted out 'Yes, but which two?' A collision in the air was dreaded by all aircrew, as seldom were there any survivors. It appeared that Harris, the Commanding Officer of Bomber Command, had decided to mount a bombing operation on a town in Germany with over one thousand aircraft. It was planned not only to do severe damage to a town, but also as a good propaganda exercise. It would be a wonderful boost for the morale of people in England who were still suffering very badly from German bombing attacks.

We took off at twenty minutes to midnight, flew across the North Sea and arrived in the vicinity of Cologne which was the target. I plugged into the intercom, and although I could hear shrapnel hitting the side of the aircraft, there was no conversation going on between the crew. The rear gunner was not giving the pilot any instructions as to where the anti-aircraft was coming from and so forth, so I decided to go up into the astrodome and see what was happening for myself. We were flying along straight and level with anti-aircraft bursting on the port side. I immediately shouted to the pilot to corkscrew to starboard, which he did, and almost immediately there was a near miss on the port side where we had been a couple of seconds previously. I shouted to him and to the bomb-aimer to drop the bomb and let's get out of it as quickly as we could. We were over the town and there was no point in hanging about, especially flying straight and level, which was a sure recipe for disaster. Also, we were flying much slower and lower than the four-engined aircraft above us, and were attracting most of the ack-ack. Also, suddenly you would hear a big rumble overhead, be rocked about by an airstream and see four engines just missing you; it was very stressful. There was also the danger of being hit by bombs being released by the aircraft above.

When we had left the target area I went back to my wireless, plugged in and found that it was completely dead. I did not know for what reason. Now I realized that I would not be able to give the crew any assistance with courses to fly and I hoped that the navigator was sufficiently proficient to get us back home again. Actually things went well. We landed back just after 5 o'clock in the morning. We were debriefed and then went along to the mess to have the usual egg and bacon breakfast with two or three cups of sweet tea and always a couple of cigarettes afterwards, while we chatted away and I revelled in the fact that I had completed another trip; I had survived and everything had gone well.

No. 22 OTU had sent off thirty-five aircraft; two had returned because of faults, and of the other thirty-three there were four missing. In actual fact, out of the 1,047 aircraft despatched to Cologne, forty went missing, plus nineteen crashed in the UK, a loss figure which was considered quite acceptable. Out of 368 OTU aircraft, only seventeen were lost, so the forecast that many sprog crews would 'get the chop' was proved wrong. The following morning Douglas went out to his aircraft to see what had caused the problem with the wireless:

In fact the wireless mechanic was taking the set out. He said to me, 'Where were you last night?' I said, 'Sitting here by the radio.' He said, 'You weren't when this came in,' and he produced a piece of shrapnel measuring about three inches

A rare shot of a very rare bird: Bf 110 D-0 Dackelbauch *('dachshund belly') of NJG1, probably taken at Deelen airfield in the winter of 1940–41. In the background: Bf 110 G9+KP of NJG1. A handful of Bf 110s fitted with this type of long-range belly-tank were used in NJG1 during the summer of 1940 until mid-1941 at Deelen and Bergen aan Zee. However, due to highly explosive gases developing in the emptying tanks, which led to aircraft exploding in mid-air, the* Dackelbauchs *were removed.* Coll. Marcel van Heijkop, via Ab Jansen.

by two inches, that had gone through the aircraft where I usually sat and into the radio, but obviously it had occurred when I was supervising at the astrodome. If I had been sitting there the wireless set would have been working perfectly, but I would not have been.

Juggins, whom I had replaced, was never seen again. He had been found guilty of LMF, that is 'lack of moral fibre', and the punishment for this was that he would be stripped of his Flight Sergeant's stripes and crown and sent to another station. The marks where his Sergeant's stripes had been removed would be perfectly obvious and anybody would know what had happened to him. Besides this, he would have no trade and as a consequence would be given all the menial tasks of an air force station, such as washing up, cleaning out latrines and so on. It was quite a severe punishment for somebody who, just on one occasion, had refused to fly. And he would have been quite happy to have been posted to an operational squadron as part of an experienced crew. But LMF was never a great problem. Although most crews of Bomber Command fought an unending battle with fear, few succumbed and refused to fly.

Together with men like Werner Streib, Paul Gildner, Helmut Lent, Reinhold Knacke, and Ludwig Becker, Egmont Prinz zur Lippe-Weissenfeld was one of the driving forces in the infant Nachtjagd *arm during the early-war pioneering years. He is depicted here as Oblt and St Kpt of 5./NJG2 in early 1942, shortly before he was awarded the* Ritterkreuz *on 16 April 1942 for twenty-one confirmed night victories. Austrian Prinz zur Lippe-Weissenfeld was destined to rise to command of NJG5 in early 1944, a few weeks before he died in a flying accident on 12 March 1944. By the time of his death, he had accumulated fifty-one night* Abschüsse *and had been decorated with the Oak Leaves to the* Ritterkreuz. Coll. Anneliese Autenrieth

On the Cologne raid of 30–31 May 1942, the majority of the *Luftwaffe* night fighter effort was concentrated in the *Himmelbett* boxes on the coast and in the target area. Although the German defences were successfully 'swamped' by the new bomber stream tactic, four bombers were lost to *Nachtjagd* aircraft over Cologne. Another five were destroyed on the return journey, when the bomber stream had been more dispersed than on the way in, and it was easier for the German fighter controllers to pinpoint individual target aircraft. Four crews of II./NJG1 claimed a total of eight bombers destroyed on 30–31 May 1942, seven of which were later confirmed by the German Air Ministry. Of the remainder of the RAF losses, sixteen or seventeen fell to flak over Cologne, and twelve to anti-aircraft fire on the legs to and from the target.

The 'Thousand Force' was gathered again for two more raids in June, on Essen (1–2) and Bremen (25–26). However, the latter was only a modest success, and Essen a failure due to poor weather conditions which prevailed during the raids.

OPS IN THE AVRO MANCHESTER

During the first two years of war, a new generation of heavy bomber types was being developed by the British aircraft industry for Bomber Command, the first of which was the Avro Manchester. However, after being introduced into operational service with 207 Squadron in February 1941, it soon proved to be of limited use due to many shortcomings, the worst of which was the unreliability of its twin 1,750hp Rolls-Royce Vulture engines. Manchester crews soon found out to their cost that the aircraft could not stay in the air on one engine, as Sgt Alan F. Scanlan, WOp/AG in Plt Off Beatty's all-Australian crew with 50 Squadron experienced:

I was posted to No. 50 Squadron based at Skellingthorpe on 14 May 1942 on Manchester aircraft. With regards to the reliability of the Manchester, personally I found it underpowered, and the Vulture engines were prone to overheating. It appeared to handle quite OK when empty, however when loaded its maximum height was around 9,000 feet and when over the target you were in range for light, medium and heavy flak, plus the possibility of being hit by the bombs of higher aircraft – this was particularly the case in the Thousand Bomber Raids on Cologne and Essen. Due to the low bombing height of the Manchester, our pilot, Plt Off Don Beatty, always put the nose down and headed for the deck and flew low which allowed us hopefully to miss the night fighters and allowed us to shoot at searchlights.

In all, I completed five raids over Germany. One operation, towards the end of May 1942 before the Thousand Bomber Raid on Cologne, was aborted over the Channel through the starboard engine overheating. We had a load of incendiaries on board which we attempted to dump, however we were unable to open the bomb doors. The starboard engine was throttled back and we turned for home; on approaching the coast I radioed the signal of the day to cross the coast, and we fired the Verey pistol with the colour of the day. Plt Off Don Beatty made our approach to the 'drome nursing the offending engine as it was pretty hard to handle the aircraft with the loss of power and with a full bomb load. The flare path was lit up and Don made a perfect approach. However, on touching down the starboard motor packed up, we groundlooped with one wing down and stopped off the runway on the grass. Don yelled everybody out – unfortunately I was strapped into my radio operator's chair which was not bolted properly to the floor, and finished up on my back still in the chair and with my legs in the air. We left the aircraft to the groundcrew – we were lucky the undercarriage did not collapse.

Thirty-one-year-old Oblt Wilhelm Herget, Staffel Kapitän of 7./NJG3, depicted here on the occasion of his award of the German Cross in Gold on 16 February 1942. Wilhelm Herget was one of the more successful Zerstörer *pilots in the early war years, with nine confirmed kills over RAF fighter aircraft during the Battle of Britain, who shifted successfully to night-fighting in 1941 after the Bf 110 units were gradually withdrawn from day-fighting on the Western Front. By the end of the War, fifty-eight of his seventy-three victories had been gained at night, which earned him the award of the* Ritterkreuz *with Oak Leaves.*
Coll. Anneliese Autenrieth.

As regards the two Thousand Bomber Raids on Cologne and Essen, briefing on the first raid took place at 18.00 and we were informed that it would be the largest concentration of aircraft over a target in ninety minutes. We took off at about 23.00 through rough weather until about

A blurred but interesting shot of the inside of Oblt Eckart-Wilhelm von Bonin's Bf 110, which was probably taken by his Bordfunker Fw Johrden in early 1942. At this time, von Bonin served as Adjudant of II./NJG1 at St Trond with two or three night Abschüsse *to his credit. He was destined to survive the War in the rank of Major, with thirty-seven* Abschüsse, *and decorated with the* Ritterkreuz. *Almost all his victories, thirty-five at night plus two B-17s during the 17 August 1943 Schweinfurt raid, were gained with the help of his Bordfunker Ofw Johrden.* Coll. Anneliese Autenrieth.

sixty miles from Cologne, when clouds cleared with bright moonlight, we could see the target with fires started by the first waves. As we approached, the searchlights and flak started; I was in the front turret, some aircraft around us were hit by flak and on fire. We were coned in searchlights, but our skipper was able to corkscrew out of it. The light flak could be seen leaving the ground, it looked slow at first, then gaining speed as it reached towards us. The tracers were quite spectacular in colour, curving upwards then flashing past our aircraft, some of it quite close and looked like hitting us. I instinctively lifted my feet up at times.

The target, the old city of Cologne, was a mass of fire and smoke and still spreading, a scene hard to describe with flak bursting all around us, other aircraft coned in searchlights with flak bursting around, then some of them were hit with engines on fire and some exploding in a ball of fire.

Don Beatty put the nose down as we were briefed to do to save the chance of collision, levelling out at about 600 feet. A searchlight picked us up and I gave him a burst from my turret; it promptly went out. I must have frightened him. We arrived back at Skellingthorpe unscathed, but out of fifteen aircraft from our squadron on the raid, two failed to return.

Two nights later a repeat performance on Essen, again a Thousand Bomber Raid with much the same procedure. We were again carrying a load of incendiaries at 9,000 feet. This time, I occupied the mid-upper turret so I did not see the light flak coming up and only saw it shooting past my turret. The medium flak were exploding in groups of three, one after the other, and they were pretty accurate: you could smell the cordite when passing through the resulting smoke and hear the shrapnel hitting the aircraft like hail. Luckily we suffered no direct hits; I saw Ron Buchanan in his rear turret disappear in a cloud of smoke and thought he was hit, however I saw his turret and guns moving, watching for fighters, so thankfully he was alright. The reception from the defences appeared to be much heavier and more accurate than Cologne.

I could see 4,000 pounders or 'Cookies' falling from the aircraft way above us plus many aircraft hit by flak or fighters; we never saw any, thank goodness. After the navigator dropped the incendiaries we again put the nose down and headed for home leaving behind another enormous fire. When we landed at Skellingthorpe we examined the Manchester and found quite a number of holes in the fuselage and wings from the flak, thankfully none of the crew was injured.

My last operation ended on 6–7 June 1942. After bombing Emden, Plt Off Don Beatty put the nose down, and after pulling out low at about 200 feet over the sea near the Frisian Islands, the starboard motor packed up. The co-pilot, Sgt Ron Burton, was unable to feather the propellor, causing excessive drag on the aircraft – both pilots fought to control the aircraft which was yawing and unable to gain height. I was in the front turret and could see I was of no use there, and the North Sea was getting too close, so I climbed back up and sat behind the pilot and his armour-plated seat near the navigator, Plt Off Fred Allen, while the two pilots struggled to control the aircraft. Fred Allen was trying to plot our position and the radio operator Sgt Arthur Tebbutt sent out a 'Mayday'.

In only a short time the port engine packed up – a few seconds of silence and then the crash nose-first into the sea. I saw the second pilot hit the dashboard with his head; like me he was not strapped in, then we were under water. I must have been stunned on the floor of the cockpit, but the cold water revived me, and I made for the escape hatch above the navigator – he beat me to it and kicked me in the chest as he pushed open the hatch. The aircraft settled into the water, with the water level up to the escape hatch. I followed Fred Allen, and was about to jump into the water when I saw the navigator's curtain bobbing up and down in the escape hatch – I reached down and tore it off to find Don Beatty with a terrible wound in his forehead. I got him out, it was quiet

An unusual camouflage pattern is clearly visible on this Bf 110 of 3./NJG3, which was photographed at the snow-covered Schatalowka West airfield, near Smolensk, Russia, on 31 March 1942, prior to flying back to Germany to resume Reichsverteidigung *duties from Vechta airfield. Of interest is the absence of flame dampers on the aircraft's engines. Between 23 February and 1 April 1942, 3./NJG3 was employed in night-fighting duties on the Eastern Front, operating in the Smolensk area.* Coll. Paul Gärtig.

Death of an airman. The mortal remains of twenty-four-year-old Sgt James Adams, WOp/AG with 420 Squadron, are searched by German soldiers, before being laid into a coffin. Sgt Adams died on Schiermonnikoog Island's North Sea beach on 18 February 1942, when his Hampden AD915 PT-F was shot down by flak whilst engaged in mine-laying duties off this Frisian Island. Coll. Wyb-Jan Groendijk.

Trouble with the unreliable Vulture engines caused this RAAF crew with 50 Squadron to ditch Manchester L7471 in the North Sea, probably off Ameland on 6–7 June 1942. Six of the crew survived, the pilot later succumbing to his wounds. Coll. Alan F. Scanlan.

except for the creaking of the tail which had broken off in front of the mid-upper turret, the fuselage was at about a 45-degree angle. During the ditching there was no panic amongst the crew; it all happened fairly quickly and each did what was necessary. We knew it was going to happen and had been trained for such an emergency.

I swam Don around the aircraft in case it sank, around to the starboard side where the dinghy was, unfortunately it came out and inflated upside down – the mid-upper gunner Ron Davies cut it free from the wing without turning it over. When I reached the dinghy with Don Beatty, the rear gunner Ron Buchanan, Fred Allen and Ron Davies were there. I heard someone calling for help in the dark, so I swam out to where he was calling from, which was not far, and found the radio operator Arthur Tebbutt who said he could not see, so he hung on to me and I swam back to the dinghy. The others were already in the upturned dinghy; we heaved Arthur in and then myself. There was no sign of our aircraft, it must have sunk while I was getting Arthur Tebbutt.

There was six of us who had survived in the upturned round dinghy, as we did not want to lose anybody in the dark. We spent a most uncomfortable night, covered in oil, fluorescein, and wet. We found Don Beatty had a horrific head wound with his brain showing, Fred Allen had a broken thigh, Arthur Tebbutt a gash above his eye, the blood causing his loss of vision. I had a cut on the left side of my head and a badly bruised left shoulder, arm, side and leg.

When daylight finally arrived we all had to get out of the dinghy and back into the water while the two uninjured gunners turned the dinghy over and helped us all back in, stiff and sore. We were lucky as it was a fine sunny morning. At about 10am two Me 109s on patrol spotted our fluorescein trail in the water; they flew low line abreast over us, we waved our socks expecting them to strafe us, but they waggled their wings and disappeared.

At about 11.30am, a very old biplane with floats arrived, landed, and picked us up. The German crew put the injured on stretchers, slashed the dinghy to sink it, and flew us back to Nordeney, where a crane lifted the aircraft up on to the wharf, and ambulances took the injured to the *Luftwaffe* hospital where we stayed for five days. We were very well treated; we were all covered in oil and fluorescence. The two uninjured gunners were put in the cooler until we were fit to travel. One of the blonde 109 pilots came to see me; he gave me cigarettes, we shook hands, and although neither of us understood each other I tried to thank him for his courtesy and in saving us.

Sgt Ronald Burton, the crew's second pilot, was dragged down in Manchester I L7471 to the bottom of the sea off Ameland; his name is honoured on the Runnymede Memorial for the missing of the RAF. Fred Allen was with Plt Off Don Beatty when he finally succumbed to his severe head wounds on 10 September 1942; he was laid to rest at Sage, Germany. The crew's five survivors spent the remainder of the War in various PoW camps in Germany and Poland. Apart from L7471, among the eleven aircraft lost on the 6–7 June 1942 Emden raid were two more Manchesters, both from 49 Squadron. L7287 and L7469 disappeared in the North Sea with all fourteen crew members perishing.

Later the same month, the Manchester was withdrawn from operations. Still, despite its persistent engine troubles, the aircraft had a sound airframe. Avro therefore set about installing a redesigned centre section of the wing with four of the reliable Rolls-Royce Merlin engines. Thus, the mighty Lancaster was born, which went on to become the Command's most successful and famous bomber.

HIMMELBETT ABSCHUSS – AND A CLOSE ESCAPE

Meanwhile, General Kammhuber's experiments with radar-controlled night interception techniques (*see* page 28), had convinced him of the pressing necessity to develop fully radar-guided night-fighting systems for his arm if he were to succeed in providing the Reich with a 'waterproof roof' against the mounting Bomber Command offensive. He therefore concentrated his

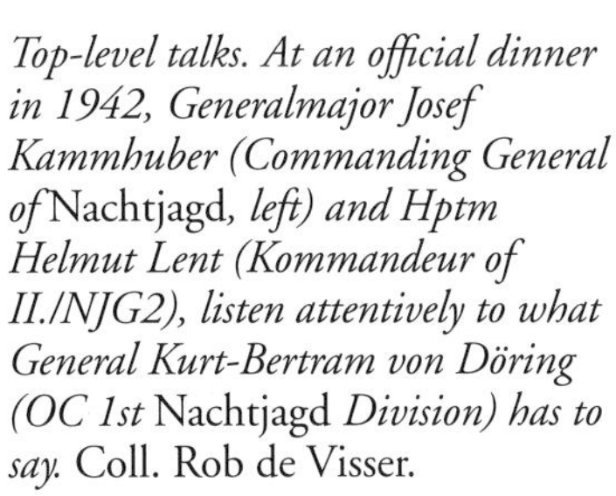

Top-level talks. At an official dinner in 1942, Generalmajor Josef Kammhuber (Commanding General of Nachtjagd, *left) and Hptm Helmut Lent (Kommandeur of II./NJG2), listen attentively to what General Kurt-Bertram von Döring (OC 1st* Nachtjagd *Division) has to say.* Coll. Rob de Visser.

energies on the development of an efficient Ground Controlled Interception (GCI) technique. The equipment necessary for this purpose was produced in the form of the *Freya* long-range radar (with an effective range of some 100km), the *Würzburg Riese* (range of 50–60km), the *Seeburg Tisch* (a plotting table within a radius of 36 km), and finally the first airborne radar, the *Lichtenstein BC*, with a forward searching angle of 70 degrees and a range of 200 to 3,500 metres.

Between 1941 and early 1943 Kammhuber used these tools to systematically build up a giant GCI belt, also called *Himmelbett*, or 'four-poster bed method', which was so named because the entire Reich, including all the occupied territories, were divided up into dozens of areas. These areas were partly overlapping circles with diameters of approximately 50km. In the centre of each was a radio beacon around which a few night fighters would orbit, waiting for orders from the area's fighter control officer. Each area had a control post from which the night fighter was guided as closely as possible to the bomber. The controller had under him a staff of specialists who kept the area under observation with their large radar sets. There was a *Freya* for the overall view and two *Würzburgs*, one of which followed a single approaching bomber, while the other was for guiding a single fighter. With the introduction of the *Lichtenstein BC* into operational use on a large scale during 1942, the Bordfunker in the fighter crew could pick up the bomber on his set during the final phase of the interception to direct his pilot to an attacking position. At a distance of some 300 metres, the pilot would have visual contact and was ready to open fire. Before that the controller would order: '*Machen Sie Pauke, Pauke*!' ['Make kettle drum!'], meaning: 'Attack!' Most of the ensuing attacks were successful, but if one failed, the next area would take over using the same procedure until the British aircraft was shot down.

After his first *Abschuss* over Hamburg on 12–13 August 1941 (*see* pages 29–30), Lt Autenrieth (6./NJG1)'s luck didn't hold. He did have an indecisive exchange of fire with a Wellington over Maastricht at 00.50 on 1 June 1942, and five other *Feindberührungen*, or 'contacts with the enemy' during the following eleven months, but none of these resulted in confirmed victories. Only on the night of 31 July/1 August 1942 did he finally get into a killing position again, and succeeded in destroying two Wellingtons at 02.03 and 02.20, which crashed near Titz and Berg, Germany, respectively. He notched up two more Wellington *Abschüsse* on the nights of 11–12 and 12–13 August (Z1404 of 460 Squadron, crashed at 01.12, 2km north-west of Eysden), before he had a very close brush with the Grim Reaper himself on 24–25th of that month. A year later, Lt Autenrieth recorded this event, which clearly illustrates the procedures in the *Himmelbett* night fighting.

> Towards 23.30 on 24 August 1942, I took off with my Bordfunker Uffz Adam from St Trond for night-fighting operations in area 6C. It was the first sortie with our new *Lichtenstein* machine for it had arrived only three days before, brand-spanking new from the factory. We hoped it would go as well as during the other sorties this month; of four Tommies which we had found, nearly all went down after our first burst, I recalled as we climbed upward.
>
> We had not reached our assigned operating height when the first Tommy was reported and we were directed on to it. I was flying at full throttle and slowly we closed on him. The Tommy is at 4,900 metres and we are at 3,500 metres and still climbing. Our bird is not climbing particularly well. The seconds drag, at any moment we can be out of the range of our equipment for we do not know where we are heading. Suddenly we get the report from the controller: 'New Tommy approaching, abandon old target.' We continue to climb to 5,000 metres heading towards him. Suddenly we hear in our earphones: 'Enemy found, he must be very close to you!' At once we both scan the dark sky but there is nothing to be seen. Suddenly there are flashes below us – three, four, five times – bomb explosions! They are in a perfectly straight line. I quickly turn on to their direction and scan the sky above. My eyes are glued to the armoured windscreen, search to the left and right, and my Bordfunker does likewise. We are

Hptm Ruppel (OC Eisbär Himmelbett *station, left) and Oblt Reinhold Knacke, Staffel Kapitän of 1./NJG1, discussing GCI night-fighting procedures in the spring of 1942. Hptm, later Major, Ruppel was acknowledged to be one of the most skilful fighter controllers in* Nachtjagd *during World War II. Reinhold Knacke became one of the most successful* Himmelbett *night fighter pilots, amassing forty-four night victories before he was killed in action on 3–4 February 1943 near Achterveld, Holland. By that time he had risen to the rank of Hauptmann and had been decorated with the* Ritterkreuz. *A posthumous award of the Oak Leaves was announced three days after his death.* Coll. Anneliese Autenrieth.

Bf 110 R4+CC (serial no. 2475) flown by Oblt Reinhold Knacke. Note that the aircraft has been equipped with Lichtenstein *A/I radar. When the A/I was first introduced, sceptical* Nachtjagd *crews dubbed the large radar direction finder antennae* 'Drahtverhau' *or 'barbed wire fence'.* Coll. Scholz, via Rob de Visser.

both calm and alert for we know that the enemy is quite close to us. Then Adam suddenly calls out, 'Herr Leutnant, he is approaching from starboard at the same height!' Sure enough, I too have spotted him; the unsuspecting Tommy is about 500 metres on our starboard bow on his homeward track to the west. I sheer off some 200 metres, then close in from behind and below towards the fellow who had still not realized his deadly danger. Slowly the Tommy assumes shape. Soon we are almost directly below him, then we recognize clearly a Vickers Wellington. Our excitement is growing all the time and neither of us speaks a single word. I quickly set the guns to 'fire', check that all their indicator lights come on, everything is in order and the reflector sight is at the right intensity. Then I carefully turn over the lever on the control column and

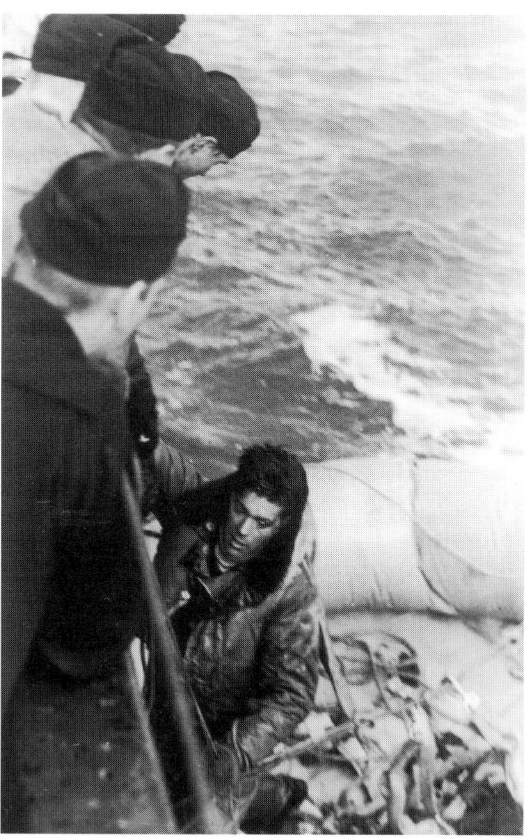

Rescued. German sailors from the 13th Vorpostenboot Flotilla help an unidentified RAF airman climb out of his dinghy and on board their flak ship, somewhere off the Dutch coast in 1941 or 1942. Coll. Helmut Persch.

take the trigger between index and middle finger, raise the nose of my aircraft, take the starboard engine of the Wellington into my sights and press the buttons. The machine guns fire but the cannon remain silent!

Jammed, went through my mind? No! Suddenly I remember, in this brand new aircraft the triggers have not yet been joined together; I like an idiot had only fired the machine guns. Too late! Temporarily blinded by the tracer I can no longer make out the silhouette of the Wellington. Fractions of seconds later I can see the rear turret of the Wellington appear before me almost close enough to touch; we had come up behind the enemy machine and are now almost exactly above him. Now away before it is too late. But the Wellington is already breaking away steeply to port without showing any damage. I also break off steeply to port and downwards but the fellow has already disappeared. Our search is of no avail. I am angry at my own stupidity and our bad luck. Then ground control reports that they have him on their screen. The fighter controller quickly gives me the enemy's height, course and distance and I react to that at once. My anger has gone, a fresh opportunity is at hand, this time he must go down. The distance to the enemy is decreasing, I check the guns, adjust the light of my sights and scan the starry sky in front.

Suddenly there is a bright white light ahead, what is that? Could this be the Tommy? I'm after it at full throttle. The thought that the Wellington might meanwhile have caught fire crosses my mind. While I am still wracking my brains about this strange light it suddenly disappears. The light can only have been in the rear turret, perhaps I had caused some confusion with my machine guns after all. Then suddenly a shadow appears in front of me and gets larger very quickly. I immediately reduce power and go lower, so low that he can no longer see me. From behind, well below, I approach the Wellington to point-blank range and open fire at some 20–30m, this time with the cannon as well. I get so close to the Tommy that I can only avoid ramming him by quickly breaking off. At the same moment there is a banging in our kite which goes down over its port wing into the darkness below. The engines scream to a crescendo, it hurts the ears; at any moment they must overspeed or break apart. I want to pull out but terror grips me, I can hardly move the stick. The controls must have become blocked through enemy fire, or has some part of the enemy aircraft struck our tail? The speed of our dive gets ever faster, the air-speed indicator already shows more than 700km/h. I pull with all my strength, for any moment we could hit the ground – but all to no avail. It is too late for baling out, escape from this devilish situation seems hopeless. I look at the altimeter – we have already dived 4,000 metres, our stricken aircraft could hardly stand that!

Then I suddenly remember the trim, the small trim wheel; very carefully I make 1–2 turns, I pull again with all my strength and the almost impossible succeeds. I pull out at less than 100 metres above the ground. I am barely conscious and do not notice that our dive has turned into a climb. As the engines turn normally again I calm down and notice on the altimeter that we are again up at 1,000 metres. I quickly check the instruments. The air-speed indicator still shows nearly 500km/h in spite of the climb; the rate of climb indicator has become unserviceable, it has turned black and is stuck against the stop, the artificial horizon is hanging in the bottom left-hand corner, the rate of turn indicator shows port, the ball starboard and to top it all the boost and rpm of the port engine rapidly drop off. I look to port and see that the port engine is trailing white smoke. I immediately snatch back the port throttle, we swing to port and I can only just manage to keep the aircraft straight. On the port engine, just ahead of the cowling illumination which is completely smothered in oil, I notice a large hole. I quickly ask myself whether there is any point in trying to get home with my damaged aircraft. As the altimeter is still showing 1,200 metres I decide to fly home and there attempt a belly-landing. I quickly order my Bordfunker to get me a course to steer to base.

Although the port engine is still giving a little power, I can no longer keep the aircraft on a straight course. The rudder cannot be moved any further. Flying wide, flat turns I wait for the bearing which never comes. Meanwhile I keep a wary eye on the port engine. Then, suddenly, it happens, bright flames spurt from the port engine. I immediately cut the engine. But when the propeller has stopped I can no longer maintain height with our 110. I realize the pointlessness of further attempts at flying and order my radio operator to get out. Without saying a word he gets out while I keep calling 'get out!' I continue trying to keep the aircraft on an even keel in order to help his escape. Once more I shout with all the power at my disposal – 'Adam, get out, I cannot hold the aircraft any longer.'

Again, all is silent. But now it is high time for myself. I hastily release my straps, jettison the cockpit roof and try to escape as quickly as possible. But I do not succeed in spite of all my efforts as our 110, having let go of the joystick, promptly turned over the dead engine and slips away. That presses me hard into the back of the pilot's seat, and as soon as I get my head and upper body out, the slipstream pushes me back and even more firmly into the seat. Only seconds are left for my escape. I sit back in the seat and am almost at the end of my tether. Then I notice that my aircraft is going down in a steep turn to port. It's now or never! In desperation and in fear of death, summoning up all my remaining strength, I have but one thought! Get out of the burning machine, which could explode at any moment, at all costs; pressing, pushing, kicking with my legs, sideways to the left over the cabin wall, thinking to fall into the port propeller and getting hacked to pieces. As I at last come clear I hear a bang and think this is it – now it's finished!

After some seconds of unconsciousness I find myself quietly floating on air. When I try to pull the rip-cord of my parachute, I find to my horror that the handle is no longer there. I think, now your life is finally finished, the parachute must have been torn off whilst getting out or been caught in the tailplane; quite calmly, in certain expectation of the death to which I am exposed without means of escape, I think of my parents and siblings. While waiting for the end I suddenly feel strong pressure against my right thigh and shoulders. I glance upwards and am startled to see all white and huge like a large tent my open parachute above me. It was like a miracle. Without having felt the jerk of its opening, without even having pulled the rip-cord, I was hanging on the open 'chute and was saved. I must have pulled the handle subconsciously as I had not been aware of its opening and I owe my escape to pure chance. I am still hanging only a few hundred metres above the earth in the dead of night and can strike the ground at any moment, so look out. But this was a mere detail against the miracle of my escape.

I strained my eyes to make out something below. And I succeeded; to my left I could make out a village and in front many small black dots (fruit trees), towards which I drift. At the very moment as I think about the landing and preparing myself for it, I feel a hard shock and lie on the ground. I get up with a violent throbbing in my head and try to stand – I manage it – try to take a few steps – which I also manage – and happy as if I had been newly born I lay down on my white parachute with but one single thought – you are still alive! When I get up again and take a close look at myself I notice a choking sensation in my throat. No wonder, the throat microphone is still around my neck while the helmet had been torn off. As I look around me I spot about 100 metres away my machine with huge flames spurting from it with its tanks and ammunition exploding. Badly shaken and fainthearted by the exertions and impressions of the past minutes I again lay down on the cool ground and wait until all the ammunition had gone off, agonized by the thought that my good radio operator had been killed in this terrible crash. In order to show him, should he be still alive, and the people in the nearest village that I am here, I pull out the signal pistol from my right overall pocket and fire three times the emergency signal. But as no one

(Left) *This snapshot of Hptm Helmut Lent was taken in the spring of 1942, shortly before he received the Oak Leaves to the* Ritterkreuz *on 6 June. At that time, the twenty-three-year-old Kommandeur of II./NJG2 was* Nachtjagd*'s top-scoring ace with thirty-four night-, and eight daytime victories.* Coll. Anneliese Autenrieth.

One wet day in the autumn of 1942, the air- and groundcrews of Hptm Lent's II./NJG2 pose on the tarmac at Leeuwarden airfield in front of Lent's Do 215 B5 R4+DC. Due to the aircraft's endurance of some five hours (1½ hours longer than the Bf 110, his regular mount), Hptm Lent flew this aircraft regularly on Himmelbett *operations at that time, especially when bad weather prevailed. He claimed four* Abschüsse *in R4+DC.* Coll. Rob de Visser.

responds, I make my way, slightly limping, to the nearest village, the direction to which I can make out by the shouting of children and people and the lowing of cattle. With one fur boot, the other had been torn off whilst baling out, and without gloves or helmet, which had gone the same way, I plod with my flashlight hanging around my neck, the signal pistol in my hand and the parachute on my back over fields and meadows and climb over fences and hedges. At last, at the edge of the village, some Belgians come towards me and approach me with greatest care and fear. Then one of them, having realized that I was just a harmless human being, offers me his bicycle and takes me to the burgomaster of the village. There I am overjoyed to hear that my radio operator had landed safely and that he was already on his way to Tongres in order to phone our comrades. But my joy increased even more when I heard that the enemy had also crashed, two minutes before us, in a suburb of Liege. The burgomaster gives me hot coffee and a bowl of plums which I polish off in my excitement. Meanwhile the entire village had been aroused by this singular occasion and has collected in the burgomaster's room in order to admire me, until after about half an hour a detachment of our group under Hptm Mayer arrives to bring me back to the operations room by car, where my comrades congratulated me joyfully both on my birthday and to my sixth night *Abschuss.*

At 00.18, Wellington III Z1594 of 101 Squadron crashed at Ougrée, a southern suburb of Liege, Belgium, some 30km south of where Lt Autenrieth and Uffz Adam came down. Flt Sgt C.S. Elkington RCAF, pilot, and his rear gunner, Sgt J.H. Garland, perished and were buried in Heverlee, the three other members of the crew escaping alive to be taken prisoner. II./NJG1 claimed five *Abschüsse* on 24–25 August 1942, but apart from Lt Autenrieth's brand-new Bf 110 G-4, the unit lost a second aircraft in the course of the night. This time, the crew of Lt Rudi Röhr and his Funker Uffz Erwin Cobi had no lucky escape when they were shot down by return fire. Both men died when their Bf 110 F-4 G9+LN crashed some 800 metres north-east of the railway station of Kottenforst.

28 AUGUST 1942 – MY FIRST ENEMY CONTACT

In January 1942, Gefreiters Otto Fries and his radio operator Alfred Staffa were posted to 5./NJG1 at St Trond, Belgium. At this stage of the War, the best and most experienced *Nachtjagd* crews were given preferential treatment in the *Himmelbett Nachtjagd,* steadily mounting their personal tally of *Abschüsse.* Green crews like Fries' had to content themselves with a place as reserves to the second or even third wave to be scrambled in the event of a British raid developing. The young and eager crews practised *Himmelbett* interceptions in daytime, and at night it was waiting, and yet more waiting, whilst the senior officer and NCO crews kept accumulating kills. Uffz Fries, writing in the third person, describes what finally happened to him after almost eight months of waiting.

It was a warm summer's night and the scent of drying hay hung over the airfield. The local farmer must have had to mow some part of it because the herd of sheep was unable to keep the grass in the huge area of the aerodrome cropped short. The machines of the crews on the battle order were parked in a row on the southern edge of the airfield, those of the first wave on the right flank nearest the take-off run, then those of the second and the third wave, and furthest on the left those of the reserve crews. His own, G9+AN was last; he was second reserve of the third wave.

In the south-eastern corner of the 'drome, behind the aircraft of the first wave, stood the crew bus; it was a sort of mobile standby room which was placed there in the evenings and moved for camouflage purposes under the cherry trees at dawn, which stood at the southern fringe of the airfield, close to the site of the fifth *Staffel,* so close together as to seem like a wood. Two months before they had picked cherries lying on their backs on the wings of their Me 110s.

Some of the crews were playing cards in the darkened bus, but most sat or lay on the grass outside enjoying the mild evening air. Permanent standby rooms were being built on a site beyond Luiker Street, immediately opposite the main gate of the airfield – but as long as the summer lasted one could make do very well with the bus. The standby rooms were not to be taken into use until mid-September. Merry tunes came over the loudspeakers; the operations room staff evidently obtained regularly the latest records from the French and German music industry.

He lay in the grass with his radio operator, together with Hanne and Mäcky, who were first reserve of the third wave. The contrast between these two frequently caused merriment, especially when they clashed over some inconsequential matter: Hanne, the quiet and sometimes somewhat obstinate one from Munich, and Mäcky, the agile and artful Berliner who could never sit still for one minute. But when it mattered they were as one. Being third reserve both crews had hardly a chance of being called for. They were nearly always 'receivers of flight rations without a flight', because the leading crews of each wave were made up of the officers of the *Gruppe*. The first wave consisted entirely of the Gruppenkommandeur with the officers of his staff and the Staffelkapitäne. The second and third waves consisted of the officer crews of the *Gruppe* and partly of the 'old' NCO crews, which left the 'young' NCO crews nearly always only in reserve – and there the chances of seeing action was at best 1:10. This fact disgusted him and he considered seriously whether he should ask for an interview with his commanding officer and request participation in an officer selection course of his Fighter Division which was due to take place during October in Gilze Rijen, in order to escape from this unsatisfactory status of reserve.

The music was interrupted: 'Attention, attention, first wave cockpit readiness!' He looked at his wrist watch: it was just after 21.00. Everyone started running about, torches flashed, shouts came from the machines of the first wave, they heard the rattle of cockpit covers as they were slammed closed. A few minutes later the music was interrupted for the second time for the announcement: 'Attention, attention! First wave take off!' They heard the rumble of the starter motors, rising to a shrill whine, engines grinding and coughing, then finally to a murmur and roar. As the first machine started to move the airfield lights were flashed on – they were not turned off until the last aircraft of each wave had taken off.

When the music came on again after the order for take-off, the lumpy voice of Rudi Schurike came over the loudspeakers with the traditional song '*Komm zurück* ...', 'Come back ...', which they called the 'QAC song'. In Morse code – now rarely used as they preferred to take their own bearings and use voice communication – there is the so-called Q-code, three-letter combinations always beginning with the letter Q. They were abbreviations with a variety of meanings; one could ask questions or give information which were mostly about flying or meteorological matters. For instance, a message from an airfield to an approaching aircraft giving QBI QGO would mean that the weather at the field was bad and therefore no take-offs or landings would be allowed. If after a take-off the radio operator sent the code QAC, then it meant that the aircraft would be returning to land. QAC fitted perfectly in place of the '*Komm zurück*' of the song. The playing of this song after having given the order for take-off expressed the sincere and well-meaning wishes of the operations staff that all the machines and night fighter crews should return safe and sound.

They sat around and waited. The odd machine returned, reserve machines had already started. Then the second wave was called for cockpit readiness. While the first wave was still hunting in their sectors, the crews of the second wave were sent to their stand-by positions over the radio beacons to ensure a neat take-over. Both waves were still in the air when he was called to the telephone. He got the order to take off immediately for sector 6A as the crew of the first wave had to be relieved in a quarter of an hour and operations were unable to make radio contact with the crews of the second wave. The aircraft had either lost their shortwave radio or the crews had selected the wrong frequency.

He was surprised that he should fly with the second wave as he had been detailed for the third – apparently some of its machines had dropped

German soldiers inspecting a crash-landed Hampden. Note the inflated dinghy, and the bomber's individual code-letter 'D'. Coll. Theo Boiten, via Eric Bakker.

out. The radio operator made a note of the required data and they went with the mechanic of their allotted aircraft with the call-sign Anton-Nordpol. On their way the mechanic grabbed one of the battery carts and they helped to drag the heavy cart to their aircraft. While they climbed into the cockpit the mechanic connected the battery cart to the aircraft, then climbed on the wing and helped them do up their harness. They put on their helmets and fastened their throat microphones. He locked the cockpit cover and switched on the electrical circuit. Each time he did that he reopened the old wound on the knuckle of his right index finger, it would no longer heal, and each time he cursed his own clumsiness. He waggled the control column about and moved the rudder pedals – the controls were free. A look around: altimeter to zero – gyro compass switched on – flaps set for take-off – propellers set to 12 o'clock – time check – oxygen indicator correct – oxygen mask tested – breathing control indicates – fuel on, throttle set slightly open, ignition on M1 + M2 – ready.

He pressed the starter for the starboard engine. The centrifugal gyro started to hum. The sound rose higher and when it had reached its typical whistle he pulled up the starting lever and put the motor into gear, which started with a cough and a spit. The port engine also caught at once. He pulled back the stick, increased the manifold pressure, and tested the ignition by switching back first to M2 and then to M1, first the starboard, then the port engine. The drop in rpm was within limits. He turned on the lighting for the engine instruments which were in a recessed panel of the engine covers: oil pressure OK, oil and cooler temperatures still on zero. The radio operator reported all set.

He briefly switched on his landing lights to indicate to the mechanic that he was ready to taxi. The mechanic disconnected the cable from the machine and pushed the battery cart to one side, then removed the chocks and cleared the machine. He taxied slowly forward, then swung to starboard on to the taxiway for the take-off point. 'Rosmarin from Adebar – taxiing out – press Christmas tree!' (switch on airfield lighting). 'Viktor-Viktor.' The airfield lights were switched on. He increased his speed and passed the machines of the third wave, which were lined up on his right. When he reached the take-off point he swung to port and stopped briefly to set the take-off time. It was 23.16. He pushed the throttles forward to their limits. Anton-Nordpol started to move with a roar, faster and faster. He pushed the stick forward to get the fuselage horizontal and the pressure on the stick slowly decreased. They were still well short of the end of the runway when the machine started to lift – and with a brief jerk it was in the air. 'Rosmarin from Adebar – are airborne – going immediately to Kleine Laterne' (the radio beacon). 'Viktor-Viktor – *Weidmannsheil*!' (good hunting).

Today he could take his time with what now had to be done, for the sky was clear, without a single cloud, and the horizon showed up so well that he did not have to go on instrument flying immediately after take-off. He reduced power, reset the propeller pitch and pressed the undercarriage button. When the altimeter indicated fifty metres and he had confirmed that he had enough speed, he retracted the flaps in stages and at each stage the machine dropped a little. During his first flights on the Me 110 that had irritated him quite a lot.

He reduced the manifold pressure and set the engines to run at 2,200 rpm. As the altimeter indicated 150 metres he turned on to course for the radio beacon 6A – 030 – and set the trim for a climb of about ten metres per second. This gave him a rate of climb of about one and a half minutes for every thousand metres. The flight time to the radio beacon was a bare eight minutes – so on arrival at the beacon he could be at a height of five thousand metres. He knew these data by heart, for during daytime they had flown countless practice interceptions for training on the equipment and to get a feeling of how accurate the guidance of the controller had to be, who issued his instructions from the plotting table in the operations room.

They were at more than 2,000 metres when the radio operator called operations: 'Gummiball from Adebar – come in – come in!' 'Adebar from Gummiball – Viktor-Viktor – I hear you.' 'Gummiball from Adebar – are approaching.' 'Viktor-Viktor – go to Kleine Laterne and make *Karussell Lisa* (orbit left) until I call you – go to *Kirchturm vier-fünf* (height 45 – 4,500 metres) – *Frage* Viktor (query understood).' 'Viktor-Viktor.'

(Left) *Uffz Alfred Staffa (left) and his pilot Otto Fries posing with their Bf 110 E-2 3738 G9+AN of 5./NJG1 at St Trond in the summer of 1942. This aircraft was shot down by a vigilant Stirling rear gunner bound for Nuremberg, during a* Himmelbett *interception over eastern Belgium.* Coll. Otto Fries.

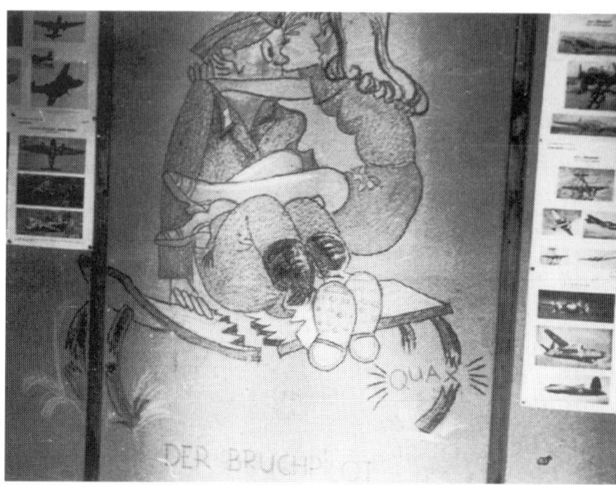

One of the mural paintings in the standby rooms at St Trond airfield, 1943. 'Quax, the hard-luck pilot' was the German equivalent of the British cartoon figure 'Plt Off Prune'. Note the Allied aircraft recognition photos pinned to the left and right of the cartoon. Coll. Otto Fries.

He had the radio operator set the loop aerial to 360 and switched to his indicator. Its pointer would show him whether his aircraft was heading for the beacon, or to its right or left. One could of course make provision for any wind effect and set the appropriate drift – but for the short distances which they had to fly in the night-fighting areas that was hardly worthwhile, especially as the wind usually veered and increased with altitude. So they preferred to approach the beacon in a 'dog-curve'.

'Put on your oxygen mask, we are at four thousand!' The wandering of the pointer showed him that they were close to the beacon. He turned starboard on to a course of 090 and had the loop aerial set to 270. The pointer moved to indicate starboard. When the beacon was on the port beam, the pointer moved to show to port. He then continued straight ahead for one minute, then turned on to 360 and the pointer again moved to starboard. In this manner they flew around the beacon in a square with rounded corners – it was called the Roland method. A year later there were frequently up to two hundred night fighters around a *Grosse Laterne* (a heavy navigational beacon) around which they would 'roland about' anticlockwise, as they called it, and wait for orders on the *Reichsjägerwelle*, the Reich fighter frequency, for *Wilde Sau* (Wild Boar) operations.

They listened in to the traffic between the fighter controller and the crews of the first wave. From the crews of the second wave, who must also have been in the area, they heard nothing. The radio operator reported later that they had had a complete radio failure. The crew of the first wave was sent on *Reise-Reise* ('travel-travel', 'return to base'), they had had some success, as they understood from what they heard.

'Adebar from Gummiball – question *Tampen* (course) – question *Kirchturm* ('Church tower', height).' 'Gummiball from Adebar – *Tampen* 180 – *Kirchturm* 45.' 'Viktor – make *Rolf* 290 - go to *Kirchturm* 41.' 'Viktor-Viktor!' He turned to starboard on to a course of 290 and let the machine sink slowly to 4,100 metres. 'Adebar from Gummiball – I have contact – Kurier approaching – *Kapelle* 42 – please wait.'

He pulled the machine fifty metres higher and prepared himself for his approach. He switched the propellers to automatic, switched the guns to ON, and turned down the illumination of the reflector sight as it seemed too bright. He raised his seat high enough to be able to see through the reflector sight without having to twist his neck. 'All clear with you back there? – Keep your fingers crossed!' 'All clear! I will turn round so I can help you searching, there will hardly be anyone behind who might want to fire

From left: Oblt Walter Barte (St Kpt 4./NJG1), Uffz Pieper (his Bordfunker), and Oberwerkmeister Adam (groundcrew) posing for the camera in front of Barte's Bf 110 G-4 at St Trond. The tally displayed on the tail unit shows nine Abschuss *symbols, dating this photograph shortly after 11–12 June 1943, when Oblt Barte shot down an unidentified Lancaster and Halifax V DK170 MP-C of 76 Squadron (crashed 4km South of Bladel, Holland), for his eighth and ninth confirmed combat victories. Barte survived the War with nineteen night- and four daytime victories in NJG 1 and 3.* Coll. Kees Mol, via Marc Deboeck.

on us!' 'Hardly!' 'Adebar from Gummiball – make *Salto Lisa* (turn port) to 120 – *Express-Express* (Hurry up)!' 'Viktor!' He pulled the aircraft around to the new course in a steep turn to port. The visibility was so good and the horizon so clear that he was able to fly the turn without losing height. He reduced the brightness of the ultra-violet light mounted on the control column by simply shoving over its cover. Even the glimmer of the markings on the instruments interfered with the finding of a bomber.

'Adebar from Gummiball – *Rolf-Rolf* (turn 20 degrees starboard) – *Marie* 90.' He turned 20 degrees to starboard – with the sensitive controls of an Me 110 it was not easy to steer an exact course, the machine was much too light and manouverable – how much easier had it been on the old Ju 52, which they had flown at the Flying Training and the Instrument Flying Schools. So: the bomber was 900 metres ahead!

'Two *Lisa* – *Kapelle* 43 – *Marie* 70.' He turned on to 120, his altimeter indicated 4,150 metres. 'One *Rolf* – *Kapelle* a little over 42 – *Marie* 60 – *Express-Express* – or you leave us!' So they were in danger of leaving the range of the ground equipment if they did not hurry. He turned 10 degrees to starboard and pushed the throttles forward to the gate. Then he pulled the machine a little higher. '*Kapelle* between 42 and 43 – *Marie* 40 – *Express-Express*!' The air-speed indicator stood at 440km/h, he pulled the aircraft a little higher still. 'It really won't go any faster,' he said to the radio operator, 'we'd need a whip!'

They were at 4,350 metres, as a quick glance at the altimeter showed. '*Kapelle* between 42 and 43 – *Marie* 30 – you should contact soon.' 'Viktor-Viktor.' Suddenly the machine was shaken about, they had got into the propeller slipstream of the bomber ahead. He went a little lower. 'Gummiball from Adebar – where is Kurier exactly?' 'High *Rolf* – High *Rolf* – you must contact!' He strained his eyes at the horizon on his starboard bow. There he was! A Short Stirling, he saw the tall fin, stuck up like a shark's fin – distance perhaps 200 metres.

'Gummiball from Adebar – I have contact!' 'Viktor-Viktor – *Horrido* (tally-ho) – Out.' They were much too fast! He snatched back the throttles. One ought to have brakes now! Instinctively he pressed his feet into the rudder pedals – only that didn't help! He was very excited – a thousand thoughts flashed through his mind. You must fire! But where is the trigger? He felt the end of the control column with his right hand – but the spoon hadn't been selected yet! He turned the

Apart from a broken back, bent props and a slightly crushed nose, little damage is apparent on Stirling I N3757 LS-G of XV Squadron, lying in a field at Hartward, Esens, Germany. Whilst on an op to bomb Bremen on 29–30 June 1942, N3757 was mortally hit by flak and skilfully belly-landed by Sqn Ldr I.G. Richmond DFC on the flat plains on the northern German coast. The whole crew of seven were subsequently taken prisoner. Coll. Ab A. Jansen.

At rest on the wet tarmac at Leeuwarden airfield, a Bf 110 F-4 of II./NJG2 waits to take off for a Himmelbett *patrol in 1942. Note that this aircraft has not been fitted with the* Lichtenstein *BC AI yet.* Coll. Rob de Visser, via Heinz Huhn.

small spoon-like lever down – you are much too fast! – slink aside and adjust your speed! No! Then he'll see you and disappear! – you can't wait any longer – you must fire! Two souls fought in his breast. The bomber hung huge ahead and above his machine – and he continued getting closer! You must fire! Now, at once!

He snatched the machine upwards. The right index finger automatically drew the spoon to the shaft of the stick, whilst the thumb pressed the cannon button. The projectiles left the barrels of the cannons rattling and thundering – it was a hellish noise and the whole machine quaked. He came up far too steep – and much too fast – and much too far! The bow of his machine almost touched the rear turret of the Stirling – and he peeled off much too late!

He saw the tracers of the rear gunner pass to the right and left of his cabin, heard the hits in fuselage and wings – it sounded as if someone were strewing peas on an old cement bag from a couple of metres height, only much louder! He felt pricks in both thighs, like hot needles. Away! Nothing but away! He peeled off to port, and when he had got the machine level again he just saw the Stirling slinking steeply downward and then disappear in the dark.

His port engine was on fire, the wing beyond it too and a long trail of smoke hung behind it. He pulled back the fire-cock of the port engine and opened its thottle to the gate – but the engine showed no reaction. The fire began to give off sparks. 'What a damned mess! Looks like we'll have to jump, for besides the engine there must be other damage!' 'A fine mess!' cursed the Bordfunker.

The flying controls were still functioning. The aircraft pulled to port as the port engine no longer had power. He increased the manifold pressure of the starboard engine and retrimmed the rudder to relieve the pressure on his right foot. The intercom was fortunately still working. He could hear the fire in the wing hissing. Thoughts flashed through his mind: What are your chances of getting the lame duck back home? Flight time about twenty minutes. If the fire goes out you'll do it, after all you are still at nearly 4,000 metres. You will of course then make a bellylanding on the emergency strip – the burst went right in underneath – the undercarriage hydraulics are surely gone – but you can extend the wheels with pneumatics – the only question is whether the tyres are still sound, if you have a flat tyre you will ground loop and the entire undercarriage will be gone.

A glance at the clock – completely unnecessary! The time didn't matter! It was 23.52. If only the flames would go out! The burning part began to give off threatening sparks. Then the starboard engine also started to stutter! He switched on the lighting for the engine instruments and saw that the oil pressure was at zero and the oil temperature well beyond the red mark. 'No chance, Fred! We have to get out, the starboard engine is also gone! Get ready to go – but wait until I have jettisoned the cockpit cover!'

He pulled both throttles fully back and trimmed out as he felt the machine slew to star-

By the spring of 1943, some 95 per cent of the Nachtjagd *aircraft were equipped with the FuG 202* Lichtenstein *BC AI radar. Depicted is a Bf 110 F-4 of II./NJG1 at St Trond in 1942, sporting the large external radar aerials which reduced the aircraft's maximum speed by some 40km/h. Note the Roman II beside the* Nachtjagd *crest denoting the aircraft belonged to the Second Gruppe in* Nachtjagd Geschwader *One. The F-4 was the first variant of the Bf 110 specifically built for the night fighter role, with more powerful engines and armament than the 'C' model.* Coll. Hans Grohmann.

board. Then he eased the stick back to reduce speed and half extended the flaps. The machine rose immediately like a lift, for his speed was still more than 300km/h. He ripped off the oxygen mask, undid the throat mike and simply flung the helmet away. 'Are you ready?' 'If it's necessary!' 'Regrettably it is!' He undid the cabin fastening. Swish! The cabin roof flew off and took the aerial mast with it. Then he heard the crackling and whistling which showed that the Bordfunker had also jettisoned his cockpit cover. The slipstream whistled – he wound back the trim to reduce the pressure on the stick. Glancing back he saw that the Bordfunker had one leg over the side but was still hesitating.

The trail of flames continued undiminished, he could see them belching out of the wing. A long stream of smoke hung on the flames. He turned his head to see whether the radio operator had jumped. He hadn't! He had pulled his leg in again and was messing about in the cabin. He had the impression that he was looking for something in his satchel – had he perhaps put his wallet into the navigation bag before the take-off and was now trying to find it? He became furious. Damn! We're sitting on a fire and the fool is calm as can be! He pulled the stick right back so that he was pressed into his seat, then pushed it violently forward. This movement must have catapulted the radio operator out of the machine, for when he looked back the cabin was empty.

Now you must jump yourself! He removed the pin of his harness and pushed himself up. He put his feet on the sides of his seat and tried to roll himself over the starboard cockpit wall. He couldn't, he was caught up somewhere. He cowered down and jerked himself upward, turning his body to the right at the same time, but he simply failed to get over the side. Damn!

Meanwhile the machine had flipped out of control and turned over to port. He pulled the stick back, then over to the right and levelled off. There he was, cowering in the seat and could not get clear. The slipstream tousled his hair and whistled about his ears. Wing and engine continued to burn. Naked fear crept over him, and a feeling of limitless solitude and abandonment came over him like the waves of a stream. One of his earliest childhood memories appeared like some traumatic vision – he must have been about two and a half years old then: he saw himself lying in his cot, looking through the bars into the room, the table with the bench behind it, the wooden chairs with their round backs, the pictures on the walls and the loudly ticking clock, the windows with the geraniums on the sill. He had woken from his midday sleep and called for his mother – but she didn't come! It was harvest time in the vineyards, she had taken him home to make the midday meal for the family and the helpers which, after she had fed him and put to bed for his sleep, she had then taken out to the vineyard. Now he had woken and called for his mother, but she did not come – either he had woken too early or, in the eager turmoil of the harvest, she was late coming back. His calls went unheard – only the clock on the wall ticked. He cried and again a feeling of limitless solitude and abandonment overcame him and dug itself traumatically into his soul. For two decades it had lain dormant within him – and now, in this apparently hopeless situation, it was suddenly there again.

Bf 110 R4+CC of Oblt Rudolf Sigmund, Gruppen Adjudant of II./NJG2 in camouflaged dispersal at Leeuwarden airfield, early autumn of 1942. By this time, Oblt Sigmund had accumulated seven night kills. He became one of the leading Himmelbett *night fighter pilots, rising to the command of III./NJG3 on 15 August 1943 shortly after receiving the award of the* Ritterkreuz *for twenty-four night* Abschüsse, *plus a B-17 and a B-24 in daylight. Only a few months later, on 3–4 October 1943, Hptm Sigmund and his crew were shot down in air combat and killed to the south-west of Göttingen.* Coll. Schmitt, via Rob de Visser.

Hptm Sigmund (with bandaged head after being injured in air combat), seen here talking to Oblt Jabs (St Kpt 11./NJG1, 2nd from left) at Leeuwarden airfield in late 1942 or early 1943. At this time, Hptm Sigmund was serving as Staffel Kapitän of 10./NJG1. Coll. Helmut Conradi.

You must get out! If not to the side, then up or down! With both his hands he pushed the stick forward with all his strength and at the same time kicked out with his legs. The centrifugal force of the aircraft's course propelled him out of his seat. The slipstream caught him and whirled him about. He saw the fuselage flash past under him and painfully felt his skull scrape along the tailplane. He somersaulted as he fell – he was feeling sick. He let himself fall and only pulled the rip-cord when he felt that he would be under the 1,000 metre level. He felt the jerk of the 'chute's opening painfully in the thighs – it felt as if a ton-weight were hanging on the soles of his fur boots. He was unable to prevent them being pulled from his feet by the jerk of the 'chute's opening. Hanging on the parachute he swung back and forth like on a pendulum and was sick several times. You got yourself a concussion on getting out, flashed through his head. His skull growled like a cello and his scalp felt as if on fire. He felt the blood running down and dripping from the ear lobes.

It wasn't particularly dark, although there was no moon. He recognized below him a wood surrounded by fields or meadows and a largish farm, towards which he slowly drifted. There was almost no wind. When he was very close to the ground he pulled the safety catch out of the harness lock and turned it to the left. As he landed he struck the lock with his fist, releasing the straps. The parachute collapsed and buried him beneath it. He extricated himself from the sheets and lines and found that he had landed in the middle of a potato field. Through the haze of the night he saw the outline of a house, not far away. He rolled up the 'chute, took it under his arm, and soft-footed it, literally, towards it. He was again sick, he felt quite ill.

Uffz Otto Fries' Bf 110 E-2 3738 G9+AN crashed at Herbesthal, Belgium, his Bordfunker having baled out unhurt. For this loss, three crews (Fw Schellwat, Lt Schnaufer and Hptm Ehle) of II./NJG1 claimed two Halifaxes and a Wellington destroyed on 28–29 August 1942, which brought the unit's total for the month to twenty-five confirmed kills. The Stirling crew that triumphed over Fries formed part of a force of 159 bombers heading for Nuremberg, which suffered a loss of twenty-three aircraft, or 14.5 per cent of the sorties despatched. An estimated fifty crews bombed the town, but little damage was reported. One-hundred-and-thirteen other aircraft raided Saarbrücken on the French-German border whilst the main attack on Nuremberg was taking place. Despite the clear moonlight conditions and Saarbrücken being relatively undefended, the bombing was scattered, and seven aircraft were lost.

Although under Kriegsmarine *rather than* Luftwaffe *control, the heavy flak batteries along the coastlines of the Third Reich accounted for many Bomber Command aircraft shot down during the War. Here we see an impressive shot of muzzle fire from battery* Neudeich *on the North Sea side of Wangerooge Island lighting up the night sky. At maximum effort, every five seconds, each of the four 10.5cm guns of* Neudeich *were able to fire a heavy-calibre shell at the bombers penetrating over the eastern Frisian Islands chain.* Coll. Hans-Jürgen Jürgens.

Coastal flak victim. Flt Sgt L.C. Shepherd RNZAF (front row, middle) and his 218 Squadron crew all perished when their Stirling BF403 HA-R was hit by Kriegsmarine *flak from a battery on the northern Dutch coast and crashed at 19.15 on 17 December 1942 into the sea between Den Helder and Texel. The crew were on their fourth op, to bomb Fallersleben.* Coll. John Price.

After convalescing in hospital, Otto Fries and his Funker were back on ops about a month later. Still, it would take almost another year before the crew finally scored their first confirmed kill, on 10–11 August 1943, over Lancaster JA716 of 97 Squadron, with Flt Lt W.I. Covington DFC and crew all baling out safely before their aircraft crashed at Hanzinelle, Belgium.

BIRTH OF AN ACE

In November 1941, twenty-one-year-old pilot Lt Hans Krause joined I./NJG3 as Technical Officer. During the ensuing few months, he flew the Bf 110 on *Himmelbett* sorties, but in June 1942 he did a conversion course at Gilze-Rijen on the Do 217, with which his *Staffel* at Rheine airfield was subsequently equipped. In his capacity as TO, he and his Funker Uffz Otto Zinn spent July 1942 at Berlin-Diepensee airfield, test-flying and calibrating the Lichtenstein-equipped Do 217 night fighter version.

Shortly after he got back to his *Staffel*, on 10 September 1942, *Nachtjagd* proudly announced its 1,000th *Abschuss* of the War. To celebrate this special event, General Kammhuber organised a 'kill-feast' on an airfield in Holland, which took place on the evening of 6 October 1942, and for which every *Nachtjagd* pilot with one or more victories was invited. Being the only pilot in his *Staffel* without any kills, Lt Krause had to remain behind at Rheine, and although adverse weather prevailed, he and his crew came on readiness late in the afternoon of 6 October.

> The meteorological briefing was to be at 17.00, at dusk. It took place as nearly always in the almost elegantly furnished common room. 'A briefing appears to be unnecessary,' remarked our always conscientiously informed weather wizard and swept his hand casually across the weather chart which covered the area of England as well. Bad weather everywhere with low rain clouds with tops of about 5–6,000 metres. A succession of depressions which could cause icing at certain levels. 'There is an exception between 22.00 and 24.00. Then there will be a break in the clouds between two fronts, enabling British bombers in Wales to take off. Possible targets could at best be in the area of Osnabrück, Rheine, Nordhorn and Münster.'
>
> But landing back at their departure points would be very problematical through the approach of the next bad-weather front, unless they were to divert to Ireland. But that had so far only happened once, and we considered it fairly unlikely that the British would do that tonight. Especially as, in our opinion, the situation would hardly be offering the British a worthwhile target.

Entrance to the operations room at Werneuchen airfield, Berlin, home of 3./NJG3 in 1942. The roundel from a Whitley V (top left) was probably taken from 78 Squadron's Z6661, which was shot down at Lorup, Germany on 18–19 June 1941 with the loss of Plt Off T.C. Richards and his crew. Coll. Hans Meyer.

Lt Autenrieth, Adjudant of II./NJG1 from St Trond, and his Bordfunker Uffz Adam claimed Wellington III BJ767 of 75 (RNZAF) Squadron at 01.33 on 12 August 1942 as their fourth Abschuss. *The Wimpey crashed 700 metres south-west of Vaals in south-eastern Holland with the loss of Flt Lt L. St G. Dobbin RNZAF, the pilot, and Sgt J.L. Jury RNZAF, WOp/AG. 75 Squadron was hit hard, with three Wellingtons failing to return to Feltwell from the 11–12 August 1942 Mainz raid.* Coll. Anneliese Autenrieth.

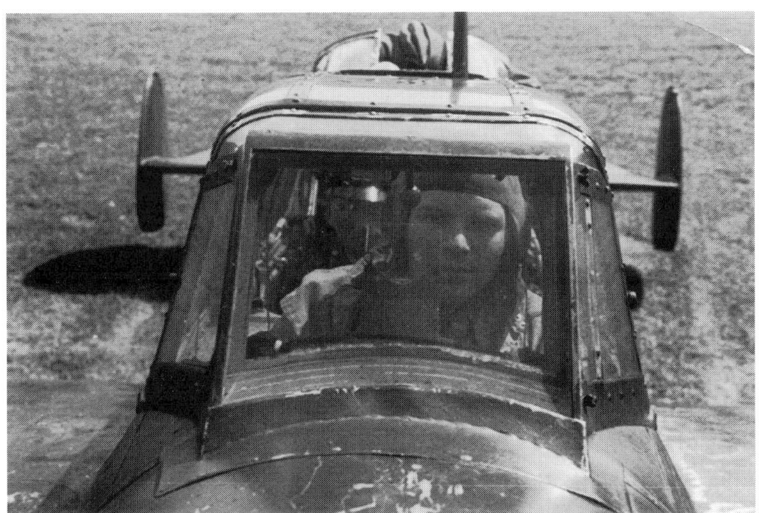

Twenty-two-year-old Uffz Heinz Vinke of 5./NJG2 at cockpit readiness in his Bf 110 at Leeuwarden airfield, 1942. Vinke scored eight confirmed night kills during 1942, twenty-nine in 1943, and seventeen during early 1944, before he and his crew were killed in action on 26 February 1944. He was decorated with the Ritterkreuz *on 19 September 1943 for twenty-seven* Abschüsse, *and posthumously awarded the Oak Leaves.* Coll. Rob de Visser.

Again and again I was surprised by the accuracy and timing of our weather forecasters who, apart from in the Reich homelands and the occupied countries, had no weather stations available to them. Although that was not quite correct, as our weather wizard explained to us. Every ship and every U-boat was duty bound to transmit weather reports. Also, we had a meteorological *Staffel*, equipped with four-engined Condor aircraft which, with auxiliary tanks and two crews, were able to remain aloft for twenty-four hours. Stacked full with meteorological instruments of every description, these aircraft took off from Bretagne and ranged far beyond the reach of enemy fighters over Greenland, west of Iceland and across the Arctic to land in Norway. As the weather came generally from the west, these reports and those of the U-boats were of great significance. Having done his job, our meteorologist then wished us with a sardonic grin a quiet night, which in fact we ourselves expected. With our chief mechanic as a fourth, we then played game after game of cards. From time to time we nibbled from the dishes of carrots standing around on the tables. Quite apart from the fact that I liked them, they were supposed to be good for night vision. It began to get boring. Now and again someone looked out at the weather, but it was still driving rain and quite cold. Suddenly, towards 19.00, the telephone rang. 'Herr Leutnant, for you,' said the operator. It was our *Staffel* commander, Hauptmann Milius, who was calling from the victory celebration in Holland in order to check up that all was as it should be. Meanwhile, it was 20.00. Then again the telephone rang. It was reported that strong radio tuning was taking place on the British island. Up to now it had always been a sure sign of enemy activity.

The wireless operators of the British bombers always checked the tuning of their sets for being on the correct frequency shortly before take-off. Was our weather wizard to be right after all about the vague possibility of an enemy attack before midnight?

The steady rain had ceased and now there were only intermittent showers. Thirty-minute readiness was ordered by operations. We strapped on our parachutes and each of us had a peculiar expectant look in our faces. Would it really work out tonight? Tonight, with no one else around, when no one could deny us being in the first wave. When all was set for a good success. Our aircraft, the radios and the *Lichtenstein* radar were in top condition, as we had ascertained during a practice flight during the previous night. There was a slight tingling feeling in the tummy region; it was not on to admit fear to the others, but a certain sense of anticipation was permissible. Then soon came the order for cockpit readiness. But already on our way to the machine, which we had been able to park right beside flying control, a red light was fired off. It had all been cancelled again. Disappointed, we turned back. But after only a few paces a green was fired. That meant the order to take off. 'Have they gone completely mad?' said Fritz, our flight engineer. But then everything went very quickly. Into the aircraft. Everyone knew the frequently done jobs. Strap in, start engines, switch on the radio, close the entry hatch, make radio contact with operations and much more. Fritz did a final check of the instruments and then I hurtled across the field for a cold take-off. The aircraft lifted off after some 500 metres. All at once fear and the tingling feeling in the tummy were gone. The aircraft and we were one, and we had our hands full. Otto, the radio operator, set the receiver on to my direction indicator and so I was able to fly towards the beacon of the ground controller. Climbing at the rate of 2–3m/sec I flew westward to my operational area. As it was a pure instrument flight, I concentrated all my attention to the dials in front of me.

The artificial horizon in particular had to receive my full attention. Before Otto had signed off on the airfield frequency we heard reports of enemy approaches with the probable target of Osnabrück. Meanwhile I had reached a height of 3,000 metres. The weather had generally cleared up, leaving the sky mainly cloudless and spangled with stars. We now made contact with the fighter controller. 'I have you on the table, climb to 4,000 metres and stay on your westerly course. Enemy bomber at the same height and on opposite course, distance 20km rapidly decreasing.' The conversations with ground control of course took place in code. Our adrenalin level rose to unprecedented heights. Thoughts tumbled through our minds. After all, it was a matter of life and death. 'You are still on parallel opposite course; Attention! Now do a steep turn to port on to 090 degrees.' I flung the machine round as steeply as I could and passed through the slipstream of the bomber, but without catching sight of him. 'You are now 6,000 metres behind the bomber and moving towards our ground station.' I applied full power. Otto had of course long since switched on his radar and Fritz stood at the coaming scanning the airspace ahead with night glasses. At last Otto was able to report: 'I have him. Distance 3,500 metres, slightly to port – now go a little lower, keep your course. Distance less than 3,000 metres.' This information came over on the intercom, but could also be monitored by ground control, which was now under absolute radio silence, by the pressing of a button. They too looked forward to the coming events with feverish anticipation. Now and then we felt the slight vibrations caused by the enemy's slipstream and therefore went a little lower. Otto now reported the enemy bomber 2,000 metres exactly ahead and a little higher. The distance reduced rapidly and Otto shouted 'Reduce speed, or we'll pass him!' At once I snatched back the throttle levers. Then Otto shouted again: 'The indication is gone, I can see nothing, the voltage is too low, we have to increase rpm!'

I adjusted the propeller pitch, thereby increasing the generator speed and power, and with it the picture on the screen was restored. With small corrections we approached the enemy to 500 metres. Our speeds were almost identical at 380km/h. Now we were able to observe the first cascades and bomb explosions at Osnabrück. I gave a little more power. The distance was decreasing slowly. At about 300 metres Fritz was able to make out the bomber with his night glasses; now he had the say and all others had to be silent. I concentrated all my attention on the instruments. I went a little lower on his directions. So far everything was going according to the book. Only at about 100 metres did I too see the enemy bomber. A huge monster, four-engined, a large fin – a Short Stirling evidently. I was now flying about 150 metres below the bomber and a little on his port quarter. We marked the enemy aircraft with all our senses, especially the dangerous rear turret with its quadruple machine guns. The barrels were pointing upwards, so we assumed that he had not spotted us. With its thirty-metre wing span and bomb load of about 6,000kg he quietly followed his course, eastward in the direction of Osnabrück. I could now use him as my artificial horizon, our instruments were dimmed, my eyes getting used to the dark. The reflector sight for the four cannon and two machine guns, set to eighty metres, was illuminated just sufficiently to avoid being dazzling. No one said a word, we hardly dared to breathe, the excitement had reached boiling point. A brief glance at the rear turret and then I decided to attack. I pressed the transmitter button and shouted: 'I make *Pauke-Pauke*!' 'Viktor-Viktor, you make *Pauke-Pauke*!' came the reply from ground control. 'You are precisely above us.' First I lowered the nose to gain a little speed, then I pulled it up. As the top of the circle in my reflector sight touched the leading edge of the enemy's wing, precisely between the fuselage and the inner engine, I pressed the firing lever. An inferno of 2cm shells from the four cannon and rifle ammunition from the two machine guns were to bore into the enemy monster, set it alight and send it down.

But not a single projectile left the barrels of my armada. I was completely baffled. How could that happen. Then, to top it all, I got into the field of sight of the British rear gunner and into the slipstream, which made my machine pretty unstable. But fortunately the rear gunner was equally surprised and made no use of his deadly defensive guns. But the Brit had spotted us, dived

Lt Heinz-Wolfgang Schnaufer (left) and his Bordfunker Uffz Fritz Rumpelhardt of 5./NJG1, dwarfed behind one of the main wheels of Halifax II W7809 of 78 Squadron, which they claimed as their sixth Abschuss *at 01.16 on 29 August 1942. The aircraft crashed between Overijse and Tombeek, 17km south-east of Brussels, after being mortally hit by Lt Schnaufer's fire at a height of 3,600 metres. Sgt J.A.B. Marshall RAAF and his crew, who were on their way back from a raid on Saarbrücken, all perished and were buried in Overijse (Tombeek) Churchyard. During August 1942, II./NJG1, based at St Trond, destroyed twenty-five RAF bombers, the crew of Lt Schnaufer and Uffz Rumpelhardt contributing five to the total tally of their* Gruppe. Coll. Anneliese Autenrieth.

Nachtjagd *aces from St Trond. Relaxing in front of the officers mess at St Trond airfield in 1942 are, from left to right: Oblt Eckart-Wilhelm von Bonin (ended the War as Major and Ritterkreuzträger with thirty-seven kills to his credit); Hptm Walter Ehle (Kommandeur II./NJG1, awarded the* Ritterkreuz *on 29 August 1943, died in a crash on 17–18 November 1943 after thirty-nine* Abschüsse*); Hptm Huchel; Oblt Walter Barte (survived the War as Major with twenty-three confirmed victories in NJG1 and 3).* Coll. Anneliese Autenrieth.

away over his port wing and disappeared into the dark. That was our last fleeting sight of him. We squatted miserably in our seats and bewailed our fate. All had gone so wonderfully well and the preconditions for our first victory on our twenty-fifth sortie could not have been better. But I was completely shattered when I noticed the reason of the failure of my guns to fire. Their breeches were empty. In our zeal, and in the hectic of the justified expectation of a victory and with it the fulfilment of an old desire, we had forgotten to do the most important thing. The state of our morale cannot be described. We hardly dared to make contact with ground control.

Against that, the fighter controller was euphoric. 'Bravo! We can hear the enemy crashing nearby!' In the background we could hear shouts of joy from the rest of the staff. We looked at each other with incredulity. Then a loud, dull bang, followed by a deathly silence. Contact with ground control had broken off and we were left literally hanging in the air. We were already fearing the worst. All our efforts to regain contact remained without success and even the radio beacon, our point of reference to the night-fighting area, had gone off the air. Any further guidance to an enemy bomber had become impossible by the total failure of ground control. The whole world had conspired against us. Meanwhile the bomber war over Osnabrück was in full spate. Helplessly we watched as, some 80–90km away, bomb after bomb exploded, and incendiaries and cascades lit up the sky over the town in a ghostly, weird and beautiful display.

It was the first time that we were to experience, more or less on our own doorstep, such an inferno. We were in the area of Hengelo and Almelo in Holland at 4,000 metres height, doing one orbit after another with our radar switched on. We hoped to be able to catch one of the returning bombers. In case that ground control might be able to hear us, we kept our transmitter button pressed so that they would be able to follow our conversations on the intercom. Suddenly Otto shouted that he had something on his radar. Orbiting, the blip appeared to the left, threatening to disappear to that side, and I had to do a steep turn to port, then to starboard and again a little to port. Slowly the course settled down. It was to the west, therefore a returning bomber which unfortunately had already deposited its deadly cargo. The distance was about 3,500 metres at the same height. No mistakes now. Slowly but steadily Otto guided us to the foe. We dropped a little lower in order to see him better against the starry sky later on. At about 500 metres we matched his speed. Now all instruments were dimmed as far as possible. Fritz was again at his post with his night glasses. Now began the phase of remoteness from worldly things, the rising of the adrenalin with the nerves exposed to the tips of our hair. One is no longer human, but a robot, ready for his final leap upon his prey. All movements are done as in a trance. Slowly we closed in

Hptm Hans Krause, depicted in February 1945, shortly after he had been appointed Kommandeur of I./NJG4 and decorated with the coveted Ritterkreuz. Coll. Hans Krause.

on the enemy. Again, at about 300 metres, Fritz noticed something, and a little later I too was able to see the enemy. It was a Vickers Wellington. The guns were armed and without further ado I began my attack. All my frustration and anger at my late mishap went into my burst. The concentrated fire was so great that the Wellington exploded in the air and fell in many burning fragments to the ground. As I sheered off to port immediately after the attack, I avoided colliding with the falling bits. Finally the burning parts struck the ground.

While the parts were still going down, we all went mad. We shouted, clapped each other on the shoulders and with a releasing bellow we shouted into the night, 'We have our first victory!' It was as if a huge load of failures, a suspicion of cowardice in the face of the enemy, but also a helpless rage at the bombing of the town where we had been reduced to passive spectators, had been lifted from us.

As our tension eased, Otto suddenly shouted 'I have another indication on my screen!' Again we stalked our prey, this time like old hands, with each move carefully calculated. As we adjusted our speed to that of the enemy I took care that the electrical power did not fail to give Otto a good picture on his screen. At last we saw the enemy about 150 metres ahead and a little higher. Again it was a Vickers Wellington. Fritz observed the enemy through his night glasses and noticed that the quadruple guns in the rear turret were pointing exactly towards us. He would certainly not have been able to recognize us as a night fighter. But, alerted by the first victory, the rear gunner would have been attentive. There was also the danger that, with the horizon behind me being lit up by the still burning town, he would be able to see me better than I him. I was now off to port and a little lower and outside his arc of fire. I decided to attack the enemy in a turn to starboard and up, hitting the port engine, which caught fire, and the fuselage. But I observed no decisive hits. In fact, the flames went slowly out and the enemy continued steadily on his course. My hopes that they might bale out were not realized. I had to make a second attack. Again I pulled my machine up to starboard and fired at the port wing with the already stricken engine and the fuselage. Now the enemy burst into flames. But I also got into the arc of fire of the rear gunner and received several hits. My armoured windscreen was struck, also the armour plating in the nose, and the cabin was holed in several places.

The rear gunner continued to fire as he was going down in flames and the enemy crashed in the vicinity of Hardenberg in Holland. No one had left the aircraft. This time there were no shouts of victory on our side; too easily it might have been ourselves.

My windscreen had become opaque through the hits and I was only able to see forward through a narrow slit. Fritz checked all the instruments but there was no drop in pressure anywhere. The engines ran smoothly, the flying instruments were in order, apparently we had been lucky once more. Then we heard, as if from far away, the voice of our fighter controller, and the indicator needle for the radio beacon came on again. Ground control had followed our on-board conversations and congratulated us on our two victories. The controller informed us briefly that the Stirling had jettisoned his entire bomb load and then made his escape. Unfortunately the bombs had fallen very close to the command post and had severed the power lines and that had put the place out of action. He had mistaken the noise from the falling bombs for the aircraft. Only after turning on the emergency power supply, which had taken some time, could a weak communication again be established.

We arranged a later and more exhaustive telephone conversation and signed off. Otto tuned in our local radio beacon and we proceeded to our home base of Rheine at 3,000 metres. Having made radio contact we were showered with congratulations but we had other things on our minds. Although everything appeared to be functioning in spite of having been hit, the tyres or the entire undercarriage might have been damaged unbeknown to us. The landing could therefore prove to be very problematic. We informed control accordingly and requested the fire tender and an ambulance to be standing by. Soon we were

Against the background of the fat belly of Oblt Hans Krause's 6./NJG101 Do 217, Ofws Otto Zinn (Bordfunker, left) and Fritz Specht (Flt Eng) are discussing night fighter tactics. Parndorf airfield near Vienna, first half of 1944. Coll. Hans Krause.

able to make out the beacon, and minutes later the brightly lit airfield and the runway. Busy activity, recognizable by the moving headlights of vehicles, gave us the feeling that all was being done to welcome us safely back on earth.

Touching down on the concrete runway was not advisable due to the possibility of sparks and we were to land parallel to it on the grass. There were now several possibilities which we discussed with the tower. Should one or both of the wheels not lock down, which would be shown by two green indicator lights, I would overshoot and make a fresh approach for a bellylanding. If both wheels lock down then there would be nothing in the way of a normal landing, unless one or both wheels had been shot through. In this case things would be critical. It could result in the aircraft breaking out to either side, or with two flat tyres tipping on its nose or somersaulting with a resulting fire. At a landing speed of around 180km/h, large centrifugal forces are created which can certainly cause bodily harm. We commenced our approach with mixed feelings. The tower informed us that all preparations had been completed. I partly extended the landing flaps, then the undercarriage, both green lights come on, this hurdle had been taken and we breathed a sigh of relief. I continued my approach parallel to the runway as agreed. Passing the touchdown point both fire tender and ambulance set off at full speed in order to be at hand if required. But they were not needed. I touched down very softly and was then able to taxi quietly in to the tower. Now we slapped each other on the shoulders, shook hands and behaved like small children. With the landing at 23.55, an eventful day had come to a successful end for us. All the others, who had had to be on duty because of us and had rather seen us go to the devil, now had to acknowledge that their presence had not only been useful, but in fact essential. I could not deny my inner satisfaction about that when I made my final report to Division. Even our doctor had to take action, for I had received a head wound from the second Wellington which I had only noticed after landing. The slight wound was cleaned and given three stitches.

With this, my report about my first two victories of my career would have been completed, had there not been a matter which had been troubling me. Something which has concerned me until this day and sometimes gives me no rest. It is not so much a guilty feeling, but it made me feel uncertain and in the end confronted me with the question of whether I had been a murderer. A discussion which, especially in the last few years, has raised a lot of dust: an assertion that soldiers are potential murderers. It had begun with a piece of paper. Three weeks after my shooting down of the two Wellingtons, I was given a piece of paper by my then Adjutant. This contained five of the ten names and ranks of the shot-down British airmen. The other five were not identifiable, so it said; what that meant I knew only too well from our own aircraft which had crashed during training – horrible is probably the most suitable expression for that. It was not usual to be informed of the names of shot-down British airmen. But, now I had them, I entered them in my log book where they remain to this day.

By the end of the War I had shot down twenty-eight enemy aircraft. We kept retreating northward and saw the end of the War on 8 May 1945 at Eggebeck. About the middle of May, the three *Gruppen* commanders of NJG4 under Major Schnaufer were interviewed by several British staff officers headed by a general. As Commander of the 1st *Gruppe* of NJG4, I gave replies to the most diverse questions for many days and hours; it is not my intention to go into these now. However, I now want to try to lead the reader to the point when I began seriously to ponder whether my feelings of guilt were justified or not. The seed of that was sown by an Englishman. Apart from the staff officers, we also talked separately with British crews who had flown over Germany, and with the British night fighter pilot who had been the most successful, with twenty German aircraft to his credit.

This was Group Captain 'Cat's Eyes' Cunningham, and his navigator, who in civilian life had a function in the Anglican Church (I hope to have given this correctly). Although the conversations with the British crews had been very much one-sided, they had been absolutely fair and almost comradely. The most interesting of these was the one with 'Cat's Eyes' and his navigator. Finally the churchman remarked that with my twenty-eight victories I must have sent at least half of the crews 'over the Jordan', and asked whether I had twinges of conscience about that. Following my remark that I had seen only very few of these escaping by parachute, he increased this arbitrary figure to about 170 airmen who had been killed as a result of my actions. A huge figure, which must weigh on my conscience like a rock and must surely be a crushing load on my soul. This did indeed strike a sensitive nerve, for I had never given it a serious thought. At first I was speechless, but then I was able to counter that he and his Group Captain had shot down almost as many German aircraft. And that for him, as a man of the Church, this must weigh even heavier. Finally I was able to reply to a further direct question, 'I have no guilty conscience.' Thereupon the Englishman explained that he had created this scenario in order to discover my attitude, for he too felt no sense of guilt. Now this was

Left to right: Ofw Fritz Specht (Flt Eng); Ofw Otto Zinn (Funker); Oblt Hans Krause (pilot and St Kpt 6./NJG101) posing in front of their Ju 88 at Parndorf, Vienna, in November 1944. Note the victory symbols on the tail unit, the crew's tally standing at twenty-four Abschüsse *at that time. Oblt Krause claimed two Liberators of 205 Group shot down within ten minutes on 5 November 1944 for his twenty-third and twenty-fourth victories. This crew was one of* Nachtjagd*'s highest scoring crews during 1944, with a total of twenty-five aircraft shot down at night over the year.* Coll. Hans Krause.

something we had in common and which was to be gone into more deeply, for it concerned the basis of human relationships. We now tried with many arguments such as the oath of allegiance, the prevention of suffering for one's own people, and finally the anonymous killing, to find some explanation for these things. One only shoots down the enemy aircraft which has entered one's own airspace in order to inflict death and suffering to its respective people with its bombs. The crew one does not see and does not know. It is merely a matter of destroying that black monster up ahead. These were the motivations which encouraged us to have no sense of guilt. And the reports did not state that five Britons or three Germans had been shot down, but one Vickers Wellington or an He 111.

Following the lost war, I had much to do to establish a new existence. Our former comrades had been scattered in all directions. Although the military zones did not make contact impossible, they did make it very difficult. It was not exactly a bed of roses upon which new families were founded. From a field of rubble without compare, the German state gradually stabilized again.

Time passed and I frequently looked at my log book in order to luxuriate in old memories. Many happenings appeared in my mind's eye, including those which would have ended fatally if my guardian angel had not taken a hand. For I am certain, and one hundred per cent convinced, that I had survived many cases of being close to death only with the aid of my guardian angel. So many lucky chances simply are not possible. But, looking through my log book, I kept coming across the names of the killed Britons and I began to have something like a personal relationship with them.

The sense of their anonimity was pushed ever further into the background and my conscience was gaining the upper hand. When later on I discovered more about their family background, that two of them had been already married, then I knew how much sorrow I must have caused their relatives. Now I did all I could to discover their graves. Using the information I had I tried to involve the British Embassy in Bonn, but without success. I inspected some of the British War graves, but also without success. Finally I got help from a British friend and his connections and I now know the graves of the killed Britons. One is in the Reichswald Forest near Kleve, and the other in the Protestant cemetery in Harderberg in Holland.

Soon I stood together with my former Flight Engineer Fritz Specht at the graves of the British airmen. What had caused us to visit them? Was it an admission of guilt and was it a guilty conscience which we had thought not to have had? We placed a wreath at the headstone of the pilot and let the events of the 6–7 October 1942 pass in our mind's eye. We asked for forgiveness. A fifty-year-old circle had closed and now I think I know why the Adjutant had given me the names of the dead. Without a word, but with a tangible easing in our souls, we turned for home.

Lt Krause's first *Abschuss* was Wellington III BK313 KO-B of 115 Squadron, which was on its way back to Mildenhall when death struck. Twenty-two-year-old Fg Off Leonard I. Smith RCAF and his crew all perished, and were laid to rest in the Reichswald Forest War Cemetery. The second Wellington that fell foul of Lt Krause was DF639 of 75 (RNZAF) Squadron, captained by Sgt G.W. Rhodes. Again, there were no survivors when the aircraft crashed in flames at 23.30 near Hardenberg in Holland.

Lancaster III ED469 of 49 Squadron, returning from a Berlin raid on 29–30 March 1943, became Lt Krause's third confirmed kill. The aircraft crashed in flames at Eilvese near Wunstorf at 03.26, with only Sgt G.A. Jones, the crew's tail gunner surviving. Lt Krause went on to become Staffelkapitän of 6./NJG101 in the summer of that year. He was one of *Nachtjagd*'s highest scoring pilots during 1944, accumulating twenty-five confirmed night victories over the year. In early February 1945 he was appointed Gruppen Kommandeur of I./NJG4, simultaneously receiving the award of the *Ritterkreuz* for his twenty-eight *Abschüsse*. He and his year-long Bordfunker, Ofw Otto Zinn, survived a total of some 150 night-fighting sorties unscathed.

CHAPTER 3

1943

DEATH OF AN ACE

When glancing through the *Nachtjagd* victory lists from the *Himmelbett* period, one always comes across the same names; the reasons for this have been explained on page 47. Oblt Paul Gildner; Hptm Ludwig Becker; Major Werner Streib; Hptm Reinhold Knacke; Major Helmut Lent; Oblt Egmont Prinz zur Lippe-Weissenfeld and Oblt Rudolf Schoenert, to name but a few, all scored in double figures against Bomber Command during 1941, 1942 and the first half of 1943. Still, despite the wealth of experience these men accumulated over the years, this did not make them invincible. A sudden and well-aimed burst of return fire from a vigilant bomber's rear gunner, engine failure during take-off or landing, icing up in bad weather: night-fighting remained a hazardous business for even the most skilled crews. This fact is clearly illustrated by the train of events on the night of 24–25 February 1943, as captured by Uffz Heinz Huhn in his wartime diary. An experienced Bordfunker, Huhn was crewed up with Ritterkreuzträger Oblt Gildner in January 1943, but was destined to survive his pilot by only a few weeks.

> On 24 February 1943, take off for Hamster. Kurier (enemy aircraft) very high, 7,200 metres. Approach, *Express-Express*. At last, contact on *Lichtenstein*, *Marie* 1.8. *Marie* 4, *Marie* 1, we're not getting closer. I think he sees us, bright flames are coming out of the exhausts of both our engines, which dazzle me. He must see that. Still *Marie* 1. Kurier lost in *Lichtenstein*, contact broken because too fast. Try again; height 6,000 metres, too far and too fast, break off. We get orders from ground to return immediately because of worsening weather. Port engine running unevenly. Half way, suddenly a brief rattling noise from somewhere under the pilot's seat. Gildner asks: 'What has just flown off?' I ask him: 'Did you fire the machine guns?' Puzzling. Fixed aerial no longer working. Aha, probably torn off. Then trailing aerial. Communication good. Suddenly vibration in port engine, heavy flames and sparks from it. Gildner stops it. Flight home on one engine. Low cloud. Unable to see airfield; I transmit that port engine is dead and request *Radieschen* (emergency flares). Takes an age until the *Radieschen* are fired off. There, a bright glow in the clouds. That must be the airfield. I switch briefly to D/F; until now we had been flying on the radio beacon. But we have already arrived. Back to voice communication. Two thousand metres high. Port engine started again. Runs normally. Good. Stopped it again to conserve it for landing. On one engine through the clouds. At about 350 metres ground contact. Airfield directly below us. We are to the left of the flare path on reciprocal course to the landing direction. Port engine started again, circuit to port. Engine loses power. Are we slipping? 'I prefer to make a right-hand circuit after all!' Gildner says. In starboard turn suddenly jerking in the port engine, then a bang and a blow, like something disintegrating. Gildner perfectly calm: 'Jump, Huhn, Jump!' '*Jawohl*, Baling out!' Pulled cabin roof release, doesn't work. I open the

The reapings of war. Thirty-five victory symbols adorn the tail unit of Ritterkreuzträger *Ofw Paul Gildner's Dornier Do 215 B-5 of II./NJG2 by the second week of June 1942. Gildner's first two kills, a Blenheim and a Morane fighter, were gained in daylight with 3./ZG1 during May–June 1940, the following victories all achieved by night in NJG1 and 2. By the time he died in action on 24–25 February 1943, Gildner had emerged as victor in forty-four air combats, and was posthumously awarded the Oak Leaves.* Coll. Hans Grohmann.

entry hatch, the slipstream blows off the cabin roof. Am sitting in the open. Climb on my seat, lie on the port cabin side. Gildner again: 'Jump!' 'I'm out!' Let myself go, my helmet is torn off and I am carried away under the tailplane. Fall backwards. Pull the rip-cord. Two seconds. Jerk. My right leg is jerked upward, my body thrown around. Hanging on the parachute. See the aircraft with its navigation lights on. Flying level, then slips down over its port wing. Earth coming up to me. Land on my left foot. Have landed on a track through fields. Foot sprained. Parachute hangs on barbed wire. The aircraft crashed about 300 metres away. Succession of explosions and smoke. Signal pistol and cannon ammunition go off. I am convinced that Gildner had baled out. I hobble along the track and finally reach a farmhouse. Leave my parachute there and have myself helped to the burning machine. On the way suddenly car headlights. I fire off signal cartridge. Then finally a red. The car turns in. Our officers. We drive to the machine. Fire crew extinguish with foam. Terrible; Gildner is inside! Failed to get out or tried crash landing. We drive home. Have to report by phone to the General and to Major Streib. Then to sick quarters: sprained ankle. Then go with aid of a stick to my barracks. Many interrogations and statements. Get to my room. Comrades sitting around, depressed. No one can understand it. The evening before we'd had NCO's bowling. On the afternoon before had played football with him and now he's dead. Vinke phones. I tell him briefly. Then phone the same night Margret [Huhn's fiancée – author] so she knows and can send a telegram to my parents. In case there is something on the radio. Am to get three weeks leave. But not yet.

On 27th, funeral in Arnhem. All the important people present, also many from Leeuwarden: Lts Jabs, Linke, Richter. General speaks. Have bought a wreath with Poppelmeyer. We take our leave. Will never again get such a pilot and comrade. He got the Oak Leaves. Hptm Becker too, who did not return from operations on the 25th. Attacked by Boeings over Wilhelmshaven by day. Attacked over the sea. Sigmund and Kraft, one *Abschuss* each. Hptm Becker shot down over the sea and never found. Spend a while after the funeral with Poppelmeyer. Then return journey.

Uffz Huhn briefly mentions the loss of Hptm Ludwig Becker on 25 February 1943. Nicknamed the 'night-fighting professor', Hptm Becker had become one of the most distinguished *Nachtjagd* pilots during 1941 to early 1943, accumulating a record forty-four night kills whilst serving with 4./NJG1, 6./NJG2 and 12./NJG1. He was also responsible for operationally testing the new *Lichtenstein BC* airborne radar in August and September 1941, scoring six kills using the revolutionary device and thus convincing the sceptics in *Nachtjagd* of AI's huge potential.

When the eighth USAAF commenced raiding targets in Germany in January 1943, the

On the wet and wind-swept tarmac of Leeuwarden aerodrome in early 1943, Lt Karlheinz Völlkopf (left) and his Funker Uffz Heinz Huhn get into full flying gear prior to setting off on an operational sortie, whilst their Do 215 B-5 is being topped up by one of the groundcrew of IV./NJG1. Note the flame dampers on the 1,075hp Daimler-Benz DB 601A liquid-cooled engine, and the Roman IV painted on the side of the Dornier's cockpit. Lt Völlkopf, a twenty-two-year-old ace with six confirmed Abschüsse *in III. and IV./NJG1, was killed when his Bf 110 G-4 G9+GT crashed whilst flying at low level near Rheine/Westfalen airfield on 21 June 1943.* Coll. Heinz Huhn, via Rob de Visser.

Oberkommando der *Luftwaffe* (OKL) decided to throw night-fighting units into battle against the Flying Fortresses and Liberators, because of their endurance and heavy armament. However, this soon proved to be a very costly business. The crews were now in action around the clock, combating Bomber Command at night and the American combat boxes in daylight. This dangerously eroded the combat readiness of the arm, with crews becoming exhausted, and many experienced crews were lost because they were not trained to engage heavily armed bombers flying in close formation in daytime. Losses included Hptm Becker, *Nachtjagd*'s top-scoring ace at that time, who went missing on his very first daylight sortie whilst engaging a formation of 44 and 93 Bomb Group Liberators over the North Sea to the north of Schiermonnikoog.

MISUSED NIGHT FIGHTERS

Fw Erich Handke had joined 12./NJG1 with his pilot, Fw Georg 'Schorsch' Kraft, in October 1942, and they were amongst those *Nachtjagd* crews ordered to fly against the American combat boxes in early 1943. In his private diary, Fw Handke recorded his thoughts on the night fighters:

> February 4 1943 was a memorable date when for the first time the Americans mounted a massed daylight attack on Emden. Four of our sections took off to intercept them on their return flight. We caught a formation of sixty Boeing Fortress II. Uffz Naumann accompanied by Uffz Bärwolf achieved his first daylight *Abschuss*. Together with Lt Völlkopf he attacked the formation head-on and shot a Fortress out of it, which dropped its undercarriage. One engine smoked, the Boeing dropped back. Naumann turned back and renewed his attack from behind. As a result both went down in flames. But Naumann was able to ditch his aircraft on the northern shore of Ameland.
>
> Hptm Jabs, commander of the 11th *Staffel*, also shot down a Boeing with his section. Uffz Scherer attacked the formation all alone. He reported: 'Contact with fifty Kuriere and making *Pauke, Pauke*.' Then he flung himself into the formation. He fired at one, but then he had to break off as his face was full of splinters; his radio operator Mehner even had the entire altimeter in his face.
>
> Then it was our section's turn, Ofw Grimm and I. We were directed by station *Eisbär* (Polar Bear) and were the last to reach the formation at 7,000 metres, 20km west of Texel. Suddenly we spotted the sixty Boeings in a heap before us. I

must admit that I had a slight twitch when I saw them! We felt so small and ugly compared to these 'flying fortresses'. We attacked from the side, with the section leader leading. But he turned in too soon so that we were not able to fire, passing behind the formation with everyone firing at us. We then attacked the last aircraft alternately from behind and above until we were both riddled. At Grimm's final attack a Boeing caught fire and crashed later on. All of Grimm's windows were shot to pieces, the radio operator, Uffz Meissner, wounded, the port engine had stopped. We also had to feather our port engine as it began to smoke. Both port tanks and the starboard rear one were shot through, the coolant and petrol pipes to the port engine and Schorsch Kraft's bullet-proof windscreen were also gone. So both of us returned on one engine. As Grimm's starboard engine also failed he had to make a belly-landing.

Three weeks later, Hptm Becker failed to return from a daylight sortie. That was a heavy loss for the *Gruppe*. We had always been of the opinion that Becker was not suited for daylight operations, and now he had not come back from his first one. We had taken off with twelve aircraft for the box Schlei with Becker leading. Quite unintentionally he was suddenly on his own. So there was no one there when it happened. We searched the sea with all aircraft until dusk, but found nothing. He had simply disappeared, together with his Bordfunker, Fw Staub. Josef Staub had been decorated with the German Cross in Gold as the first night-fighter radio operator for his part in forty victories.

On this sortie we were able to shoot down our fourth enemy. The Americans had flown into north-west Germany and were now on their way back. From Schlei our flight was sent to the north and then far to the west, until at 4,000 metres and 10km ahead we spotted six Liberators, of which the last one was some 1,000 metres behind. It was already being attacked by several Focke-Wulf fighters without success. Our flight now attacked, one after the other. We had been ordered to attack only from head-on but no one adhered to this; all attacked from the side, from the rear, above and behind, and mostly fired from too great a range, concentrating on the breaking off at the end. We almost had to laugh as each, after his attack, peeled off down, only levelling off 1,000 metres below. By the time they were back up we had completed our three attacks and the Liberator was down. We attacked precisely according to regulations, first twice from ahead. Schorsch flew on ahead to port and above until the leading Liberators had commenced firing, then I said: 'turn in', for Schorsch was unable to see behind him. After

After kill bar number eight has been freshly painted on the tail unit of their Bf 110 F-4 at St Trond, Lt Autenrieth (right) and his Bordfunker Uffz Adam of II./NJG1 are smiling for the camera in October 1942. The crew claimed a Halifax on the night of 15–16 October 1942 for their eighth kill, which was observed to crash at 21.54, 1.5km to the east of Roerdorf. The Halifax was either W1058 of 10 Squadron, or W1213 or W7850, both of 103 Squadron, which failed to return from a raid on Cologne. Coll. Anneliese Autenrieth.

> his starboard turn he closed the throttles, pushed down and fired. We flashed past the Liberator some thirty metres above it and repeated the attack from starboard ahead. Cannon strikes flashed in the wings. While I was changing magazines he now attacked from behind as the rear turret was already out of action. I did not even realize that he was attacking, I only heard the guns firing. I had just finished loading the cannon when we had approached to 100 metres. So he was able to empty these magazines as well. That was enough for the Liberator, it dived steeply into a bank of cloud. By the time we came out below the cloud, it was already in the water. It went vertically down with all engines running. No one got out.

The Liberator *Abschuss* claimed by Fw's Kraft and Handke on 26 February 1943 was one of two 44 BG aircraft that failed to return, crashing in the sea to the NNW of Terschelling. A second B-24 fell to the guns of Oblt Rudolf Sigmund, St Kpt of 10./NJG1, only minutes later. Due to the rapidly mounting losses among the *Nachtjagd* crews on the dreaded daylight sorties, the OKL adopted a new policy in April 1943, prohibiting key crews with more than twenty night *Abschüsse* flying against the Americans. This measure was intended to preserve the experienced backbone of the arm to combat Bomber Command, which had started a devastating series of attacks on the Ruhr in early March.

THE VALLEY OF DEATH

After an uneventful baptism in operational flying with a 'gardening' trip to the Frisian Islands on the night of 2 March 1943, Sgt Angus Robb, rear gunner, and his 431 (RCAF) Squadron Wellington crew were detailed to bomb Essen in the Ruhr Valley three nights later. They were part of a raid which heralded the beginning of what went into history as the Battle of the Ruhr. The ever increasing numbers of four-engined Stirlings, Halifaxes and Lancasters were led by the new target-marking Pathfinder Force (*see* page 73), and guided by the newly-introduced blind-bombing device 'Oboe'. After the long and painful struggle in its pioneering years, Bomber Command was finally capable of inflicting enormous damage to the industrial heartland of Nazi Germany. Although the Battle of the Ruhr was the first major successful wartime campaign for the Command, it was achieved at a terrible price. No less than 1,000 aircraft were lost from the 23,401 night sorties despatched between 5 March and 24 July 1943, in a grim battle of attrition with the German night defences. Sgt Angus Robb expands on his experiences:

> The Battle of the Ruhr was an attempt by 'Bomber' Harris to demolish all the cities and towns in the Ruhr Valley, and therefore cripple the production of war materials, it being the centre of the heavy industries in the Third Reich. This being the case, it was also the most heavily defended area, with the exception of Berlin, in Germany. It was considered, that to attack any city or town in the Happy Valley, as we called it, you had to fly through twenty miles of concentrated flak.
>
> Some of this was box-barrage stuff, in other words the shells were fused to go off at certain different heights which never varied but just filled the sky with shrapnel. It was no use trying to weave or dodge this type of fire. A straight and fast run was the only answer to it. The other type of fire was known as 'predicted'. This was controlled by radar and singled out one particular aircraft for attention. Very difficult to escape from if encountered over the target and mixed in with the box-barrage.
>
> Searchlights were another hazard we had to cope with. Although, by themselves, no danger, it was the feeling of being visible for miles that made the heart race. Usually used in conjunction with night fighters, but over the target they were used in collusion with the flak guns and could make life very uncomfortable.
>
> On 5 March we were detailed to participate in a raid on Essen, in the Ruhr Valley. And here I should say that very seldom did we, amongst ourselves, say we were on 'operations'. It was either 'dicing with death', 'juggling with Jesus' or

'gambling with God', reduced, in most cases, to 'dicing', 'juggling' or 'gambling'. I suppose you could say 'this was the night that changed my life'. We took off at 18.15 and for the first hour or so we flew happily over the North Sea, with, it seemed, no one but ourselves in the sky. It was strange, flying on night operations; the sky, for most of the time, seemed completely empty, although you knew for a fact that there were hundreds of your compatriots all over the place.

It was when we reached the coast of Holland things started to happen. Searchlights were much in evidence and flak, although not close, was very active. It was as we approached the Ruhr Valley for the first time that I realized I had made a mistake in volunteering for aircrew and should have accepted their offer of being a member of an air–sea rescue launch. I have never been so frightened in my life, and in fact I would better describe it as terror-stricken! There was no way, in my opinion, that any aircraft could fly into that amount of flak and come out the other side, and that was without taking into account the German night fighters that were patrolling the skies just looking for me! It really is impossible, for anyone who was not there, to fully comprehend the sheer weight of metal that was thrown into the sky over those German cities. What with that and the fiery red glow, intermixed with explosions of all colours, from the ground, it was a scene from Dante's *Inferno* brought into reality. There was also the spectacle of bombers exploding in a shower of red-hot debris when they received a direct hit from a flak shell, or had come off worst from an encounter with a German night fighter. It was a terrifying experience, and if there had been some way I could have got out of ever flying on operations again, without losing face or being graded LMF, in other words a coward, after that second trip I would have taken it.

That may seem a cowardly admission to make, but I never really believed that there were many heroes among my contemporaries, only people that had got into a situation they could not get out of without dire consequences to themselves, and just kept going on and on, with the fond hope that their God, whoever He was, would see them safely to the end. Of the 125,000 Bomber Command aircrew, 55,000 were killed and another 25,000 wounded, so if you survived, your God did look after you.

Over target. A Lancaster is clearly silhouetted against a cauldron of bursting flak shells, searchlights, exploding bombs, smoke and cloud at some 14,000 feet over Hamburg on 30–31 January 1943. Coll. Theo Boiten, via Eric Bakker.

Operational aircrew had a leave entitlement of a week every six weeks, double that of other members of the RAF. The system employed split the crews into lists of six, and when a crew reached the top of the list, off you went on leave. If, however, a crew went missing from your list, and they were above you on that list, then you automatically reduced your waiting time by one week. The losses were such during this period that we were on leave about every three or four weeks. It was the case that if you survived, your chances of survival increased. New crews were

The second four-engined heavy bomber to enter service in Bomber Command was the Halifax. Depicted is Halifax II Series 1A BB324 ZA-X of 10 Squadron, which is seen here in the spring of 1943 in the hands of Sqn Ldr Debenham, flight commander. Note the feathered port props. BB324 finally fell victim to a night fighter over the North Sea, fifteen miles west of The Hague on 22–23 June 1943. Coll. Tom Thackray DFM.

the ones at risk. You needed luck to remain alive and by keeping alive learned the skills that perhaps, but only perhaps, would keep you ahead of the game.

I should add, however, that I thoroughly enjoyed flying. There was nothing better than flying around the countryside, in fine weather, with the towns and villages set out beneath you and a view that stretched for miles in all directions. It was the operational flying that scared the hell out of me!

At no time in my RAF career can I ever recall any discussion taking place of the reason why we were dropping high explosive and incendiary devices on to German towns and cities. Neither was there any hatred for the Germans. In a strange way it was as if there was no one underneath our aircraft when we unloaded our bomb-racks, and even the defences that were trying their best to destroy you were in fact not controlled by people, but were simply machines doing these things by their own volition. So I cannot say it was with any great desire to make the world a better place to live in that I volunteered for the RAF. It was simply an ardent wish to become a pilot – and fly.

PATHFINDER DOWN

With a view to achieving further improvements in Bomber Command's effectiveness, plans were made during 1941 and the first half of 1942 to establish a specialized Target Finding Force. Gp Capt Donald Bennett was put in command of what was called the Pathfinder Force (PFF) on 15 August 1942, with five squadrons, nos 7, 35, 83, 109 and 156, forming PFF's backbone. Their main task was accurate target-marking, which was slowly but steadily brought about over the coming months, mainly with the aid of Oboe and H2S, the world's first radar ground-mapping bombing aid. W/O Angus Robb, who did a second tour of ops as air gunner with 405 RCAF Squadron PFF between August 1944 and April 1945, expands:

> The atmosphere on a PFF squadron was vastly different from what I had encountered during my time with 431 and 432 Squadrons which were both Main Force squadrons. The majority of PFF aircrew were very experienced, with at least one tour of ops behind them, and the pilots and navigators particularly were exceptionally good at their craft; they had to be as the degree of accurate flying required for the job of marking the targets for the rest of Bomber Command was very high indeed. To assist in achieving this accuracy, PFF aircraft were given their own operational height, usually 16,000 feet, in which to operate. No other planes were supposed to be within 500 feet of this altitude, so there was less turbulence to fly through.
>
> Though it was never openly stated, it soon became clear that to belong to a PFF squadron put you a 'cut above' the normal run of aircrew in Bomber Command; just the idea 'Bomber'

Harris had been against when the suggestion of a Pathfinder Force had been mooted originally. Firstly, on arrival at a PFF squadron you were given an immediate one-rank promotion; I was made a Warrant Officer on my first day at Gransden Lodge, and secondly was the award of the Pathfinder badge. This was the RAF eagle, which you were allowed to wear on the flap of your left breast pocket and highly prized they were. This was not given automatically, you had to do six 'marker trips' and then you were given a temporary award of the badge. Only when you had completed your 'tour-time' with the PFF group were you given a certificate stating that you had now been awarded the badge permanently.

Plt Off Norman Mackie started his first tour with 83 Squadron at Scampton in May 1941, doing a total of twenty-three ops on Hampdens before converting to the Manchester on the squadron, and finally completing his tour of 200 hours in March 1942. The award of a DFC was gazetted in May 1942, whilst he was 'on rest' instructing at 29 OTU. Norman rejoined 83 Squadron for a second tour in November 1942. In the meantime, his squadron had been incorporated into the new PFF, flying Lancasters from Wyton. Acting Sqn Ldr Norman Mackie tells about the Pathfinding techniques developed by early 1943, and vividly recalls his twentieth and final Lancaster sortie, as a 'backer-up' to Stuttgart on 11–12 March 1943:

My aircraft was ED312 OL-F for 'Freddie' which had been allocated to us when it arrived new on the squadron in November 1942. We had done thirteen out of our nineteen trips on this aircraft and loved it dearly. However, F for Freddie was in for inspection on this day and since John Hurry, another Sqn Ldr pilot in 'A' Flight, was on leave I was given his aircraft ED313 OL-B.

The briefing at 14.30 was conducted by Wing Commander Gillman, CO of 83 Squadron. Our target was Stuttgart with zero hour 22.45. The raid was to consist of 300+ heavy bombers (Lancasters, Halifaxes and Stirlings) led by twelve 'Y' aircraft, and backed up by sixteen other Pathfinders. The 'Y' aircraft, fitted with the blind-bombing aid H2S, were each to drop one SBC (small bomb container) of 4lb incendiaries over Baden-Baden on the outward journey, and this landmark illumination was to be maintained by the 'backers-up' in passing. On reaching the target the 'Y' aircraft were to mark the aiming point blindly with red TIs at zero –1, releasing sticks of illumination flares at four-second intervals after continuing on the same heading. The 'backers-up' were to aim their green TI's at the aiming point if able to identify it visually by the light of the illumination flares, otherwise at the centre of the concentration of red TI, or, if these had ceased to burn, at the green TI already dropped. The 'backers-up' were to attack at intervals of one or two minutes from zero +1 to zero +22. On the homeward route, aircraft of PFF were again each to drop one SBC of 4lb incendiaries at Baden-Baden as a navigational aid to aircraft of the Main Force. The route was to be as follows: 50° 00′N 01° 15′E – Chalons-sur-Marne–Bischmiller–Stuttgart–Baden-Baden–return. The route was straightforward and the met. forecast very reasonable. And so we were briefed – not being at all unhappy with the target, as generally speaking, anything in southern Germany was preferable to the Ruhr, Hamburg or the 'Big City'.

After main briefing we had our usual general crew chat before dispersing either to the sections for a further specialist briefing or back to the mess to rest up before our ops meal of egg and bacon. Our take-off was scheduled for about 20.00 and, since I always liked to have plenty of time to dress and so on, I wandered down to the flight in good time. The inevitable chat and wisecracks and then we were aboard the garry for dispersal. Our usual pre-flight external check of the aircraft and a few quick words with the ground crew and we were aboard. The rear gunner was usually first in because with his unwieldy electrically heated suit it was a fair struggle before he eventually got comfortable with his four .303 Browning guns. Of all aircrew I reckon the rear gunner required most guts. The turrets were the coldest spots, particularly the rear gunner's position, where temperatures of –40°C could be experienced and frostbite was a common occupational hazard; also he was isolated from the rest of the crew and if his intercom failed he could do nothing but wait for someone to come to his rescue and see what was the matter! Ken Chipchase, aged twenty-one and the youngest of the crew was our rear gunner. 'Jock' Lynch, our mid-upper gunner, at thirty was the oldest member of the crew. Flt Sgt Alexander Lynch had a DFM which I understood he won by downing a couple of night fighters on his first tour with 144 Squadron.

So, after settling ourselves and checking with the groundcrew that the starter battery was plugged in, we carried out the usual intercom check; but all was not well, there was something wrong with Lew Humber's (Flt Sgt L.E.J. Humber, WOp) headset in the Wireless Op's position! After a quick check it was found that his helmet was at fault and there was nothing else but for this to be changed. With a mad dash he was out of the aircraft and on his way to the Engineer Officer's van to see what could be done. As customary, each aircraft had their own start-up time, and knowing which aircraft was immediately ahead, watch was kept usually by the mid-upper gunner with his better allround vision to see when this kite started up – and then we knew it was our turn for sure. However, as engines were bursting into life all around and some started to taxi out it was clear we had missed our scheduled place in the queue. Nevertheless, to save time we started up our engines and did the cockpit checks. So when the flight van was seen tearing back and Humber scrambled aboard the aircraft, the ladder was quickly stowed, door closed and we were taxiing out, the very last as the rest of the squadron were now well on their climb away from base. Some people always wore certain items of clothing on ops and I clearly remember that Lew Humber always wore a forbidding pair of black gloves – which he said brought him luck!

A quick 'green' from the caravan and we were soon airborne. Unfortunately our route, with pretty straight legs, did not give us much opportunity to cut corners and so it was necessary to pile on 'Merlin' power (as the squadron song went – 'I like Merlin music, good old Merlin music, played by the Rolls-Royce Merlin band') and try to make up time as best we could. This was essential because being a 'backer up' we had to keep the TI's going in the target area for the Main Force, as well as the route-marking at Baden-Baden for others on their way in. The weather had been clear on take-off, but further south-east the cloud became 10/10ths with tops about 8,000 feet over France before quickly

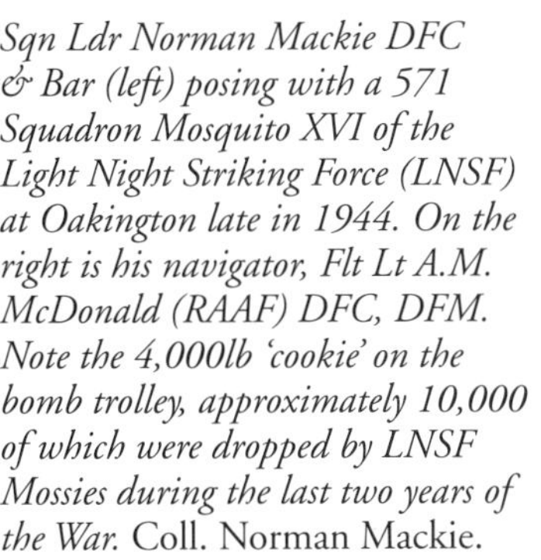
Sqn Ldr Norman Mackie DFC & Bar (left) posing with a 571 Squadron Mosquito XVI of the Light Night Striking Force (LNSF) at Oakington late in 1944. On the right is his navigator, Flt Lt A.M. McDonald (RAAF) DFC, DFM. Note the 4,000lb 'cookie' on the bomb trolley, approximately 10,000 of which were dropped by LNSF Mossies during the last two years of the War. Coll. Norman Mackie.

breaking up to nil shortly before Chalons-sur-Marne. After sporadic bursts of flak on crossing the French coast, we were flying at about 18,000 feet and in the Chalons-sur-Marne–Nancy–Metz area when we saw three aircraft shot down on our port beam. There was no flak, so clearly fighters were around and I started to weave the aircraft around with our gunners on the alert.

There was a one-third moon and visibility was excellent as the aircraft smoothly purred along at about 180 knots; it seemed so peaceful and on seeing each aircraft go down I can well remember the feeling of most aircrew when they saw the same thing: 'Poor buggers – it can't happen to us!' However, there was another feeling I had that night of being isolated – probably because of the late take-off and knowing my squadron friends were well ahead of us. Of course, we weren't all that alone as witnessed by the aircraft going down and the Main Force of 300 heavies following the same track behind. As we proceeded we could see small bursts of flak in different areas and the occasional searchlight, but nothing was so near as to cause any concern. Flight Sergeant Barrett (Flt Sgt W.E. Barrett DFM) was our bomb-aimer and the closer we got to the target the more important his job became. Lying in the nose of the aircraft his task at this time was to assist the navigator, Joe Ogilvie (Flt Lt A.M. Ogilvie DFC), by map-reading and getting an accurate ground fix if possible. Pre-war, Barrett had been to Germany where he had acquired a Nazi dagger with the inscription *Blut und Gott* which he always carried in his flying boot when going on ops.

Our main target of Stuttgart lay only forty miles from Baden-Baden and the usual searchlights and flak peppering our boys ahead could be seen. The met forecast of 2/10–5/10ths medium cloud at about 18,000 feet and ground haze was fairly accurate. The ground haze, however, was sufficient to prevent accurate pinpointing so, as instructed at briefing, we proceeded to add our green TI to others seen in the target area. The heavy flak which engaged us was inaccurate, and slight to moderate in intensity, with some light flak hosing up periodically a little way below. After bombing we set course for Baden-Baden where with other PFF aircraft we were to deposit our incendiaries to provide route-markers as a navigational aid to aircraft of the Main Force and so prevent them from straying over Karlsruhe or Strasbourg; furthermore, numerous searchlights were exposed at Karlsruhe and adjacent areas with some intermittent flak which indicated that some aircraft had already wandered off track and were possibly being harried by night fighters. I could not help thinking it was rather cruel to set fire to an ineffectual little spa town like Baden-Baden but, as Jock Lynch remarked: 'They would at least have some bloody water to put the fires out!'

Leaving Baden-Baden behind we set course for Chalons-sur-Marne about 180 miles distant. Contrails had been forecast and we had noticed them in evidence above 17,000 feet, so decided to keep below this height. There was patchy cloud and we were well settled with the occasional gentle weave for the gunners to scan around. Little was being said on the intercom and our thoughts as usual after leaving the target safely were that another op was now thankfully under our belts.

Even under ideal conditions at night the gunners could see no further than 300 yards or so, and now, with the thinnish wisps of alto-stratus, from time to time this distance could be somewhat reduced. However, it was equally to our advantage that any fighters would have similar sighting problems. We now had about eight minutes to run before reaching our turning point at Chalons-sur-Marne and Joe Ogilvie decided to ask if he could take some astro-shots. However, it wasn't far from here that we had seen an aircraft shot down when we were on our way to the target, and so I told him that as I wanted to keep a bit of a weave going in what could be a fighter belt, it would be better to delay his wish. Also, one of the engines was running a bit rough with the revs tending to fluctuate from time to time. It was about two minutes after I had refused Joe his astro-shot and I was again glancing at the rev counters when suddenly the aircraft gave a violent shudder as cannon shells thudded into the starboard wing from below, bursting the starboard engine into flames and shaving the canopy as they whipped by in a reddish stream! Almost instinctively, before Jock Lynch yelled 'Fighter – Fighter, Corkscrew Starboard – Corkscrew Starboard' as he opened fire and the tracer ripped into the metal, I was diving to starboard but not quick enough to avoid being hit. Also, on now seeing the starboard inner engine had caught fire I yelled at the Flight Engineer (Sergeant R. Henderson, a new pilot on the squadron who went on the trip instead of the crew's regular Flight Engineer, Flt Sgt Geoff Seaton, to get the feel of ops) to take extinguishing action. At the same time I realized that my dive to starboard was far too steep and on trying to lift the wing up and roll into the corkscrew climb, the ailerons didn't appear to be responding. I then noticed that the Flight Engineer had mistakenly pulled back the starboard outer throttle and not the starboard inner as he should have done, and was about to feather the good engine! There was no time for pleasantry, and knocking his hands away I powered the starboard outer engine to full boost and revs, and quickly dealt with the starboard inner myself. I then noticed that all the cowlings had disappeared from the starboard inner engine which was now enveloped in flames and belching smoke back in the slipstream across the wing. Although feathering had stopped the engine, the prop continued to slowly rotate and the controls felt very spongey; however, the wing had now started to come up and I attempted to continue a corkscrew as best I could. We had originally been flying at 16,000 feet, but with the weave and associated variation in altitude, the first attack caught us a little below this height. Having been briefed on numerous occasions that the German night fighters stuck religiously to their assigned height bands, I decided to dive to about 11,000 feet and hope the change of altitude might lose the fighter. Both gunners had started firing after the first attack commenced and Jock Lynch was trying to give me instructions as to which way to turn so that he could find the fighter. Chipchase had just said he reckoned the fighter was an Me 110 when a second attack developed and tracer was again whistling into and around our aircraft from the starboard quarter. Jock Lynch at the same time yelled 'Corkscrew – Corkscrew – I see the bastard' and the whole aircraft vibrated as he let go with his guns! I was now attempting to throw the aircraft around using my throttles and flying controls as best I could, but the aircraft continued to lose height which I was unable to stop in spite of getting as much power as possible out of the good engines. On this second attack the tracer seemed again to hit the burning starboard inner engine and I well recall thinking that the fighter must be aiming at the flames, which must be so obvious and make us a sitting target whichever way we went. Every cowling now seemed to have disappeared from the starboard inner as had also the leading edge of the inboard wing. Tongues of flame were licking around no 1 tank which still had a fair quantity of fuel and there was a horrible acrid smell wafting about in the aircraft.

Thinking there would be a big explosion at any moment and with recollections of the theory that you might put an engine fire out by diving, I stuck the nose down with some vague hope that this could do the trick, but at 6,000 feet this clearly wasn't working and I levelled out. Jock Lynch was trying to give me instructions so that he could find the fighter, but once again we were attacked from directly underneath and to port. I heard the staccato clonks as more shells whipped into the metal and then heard Jock Lynch saying in his Scottish brogue: 'I think I've got the bastard!' But now the port inner engine was obviously hit in the last attack as it started to splutter and bang with the revs gyrating all over the place. There was therefore no alternative but to quickly press the fire extinguisher and feather. Fortunately, Henderson reacted quickly to my instructions and this action was accomplished rather better than before! Realizing that we were now a sitting duck and to prevent any further blind attack developing, I dived down to about 4,000 feet. However, the whole aircraft now started to vibrate badly and although there was smoke and a strong smell of fumes in the aircraft, none of the crew reported any internal fire. My main worry, however, was that the aircraft controls didn't seem to be responding properly and made me think they were badly damaged.

Up to that point I had given no thought to abandoning the aircraft, but with the fire spreading along the starboard wing and licking around the cockpit together with the fact that the aircraft was rapidly becoming uncontrollable, I suddenly decided THIS IS IT! and I shouted: 'BALE OUT, BALE OUT!' An immediate 'Oh my God!' came over the intercom from someone whom I thought was Chipchase. I tried desperately to get the aircraft straight and level for the bale-out, but even with the aileron control hard over we continued in a slow spiral descent. The bomb-aimer, Eric Barrett, was responsible for removing the escape hatch in the floor of the nose of the aircraft, so that he could lead the bale-out followed by the other members of the crew. When he tried to eject it through the opening, it jammed, and it took him several moments to free. With Henderson breathing down his neck, he lost no further time in baling out.

Being rather occupied trying to prevent the aircraft from sliding further out of control, I hadn't given a thought to baling out myself. My parachute was stowed behind my seat and the responsibility for recovery and help in hooking it on to my chest harness lay with the Flight Engineer. However, when I looked for him I found that he had already departed and someone I thought to be Humber was quickly passing by toward the front. There was no sign of the gunners, and not unexpectedly when I called them the intercom seemed to be dead. There being no reply, therefore, I assumed they must have gone out of the main door at the back. At the same time I had the impression that Joe Ogilvie then went by and I yelled out to him to get me my parachute which he went back to do. In fact I can clearly recall him messing around behind my seat to get it. Joe certainly risked his chance of escape and, therefore, his life by spending time in both recovering the parachute and then fitting it on the hooks of my harness. The latter action was no mean feat because not only was the control column well back (trying to hold the nose up), but with my right arm and shoulder half-raised to hold the aileron control hard over to port, there was little space to get the parachute pack near, let alone on to my chest. I don't know how he managed it but remember that it was a great struggle which seemed to take some time before he had it finally clipped on, and then he was gone!

With Joe away, I was now alone and a most eerie sensation came over me as the slipstream whistled through the open hatches like a banshee and the flames enveloping the starboard side splayed back in a great big gush. I wasn't certain what the aircraft would do as soon as I released the control column and took my feet off the rudder pedals. But obviously it would spin starboard and so I extracted my legs and put them together to the right of the control column, slammed the throttles back to even any torque and simultaneously let go of the aileron control which was hard over to port. I then started to slide feet-first down into the well, but having forgotten to take my helmet off I found my head jerked back by the oxygen and intercom connections; however, lightning couldn't have been quicker as I pushed the helmet off and let my feet continue heading toward the void of the open hatch. As I suspected the aircraft had started a violent gyration to starboard and I was propelled through the opening into the night air.

Before I left I knew my altitude was about 2,500 feet and so I didn't waste time before pulling the rip-cord and then suddenly, a jerk, and I was just dangling in space. It was pitch black but I could see the canopy above and wondered if I could manoeuvre myself, but on pulling the lines all I seemed to do was lift myself up to the side as opposed to the canopy spilling out air and my sliding in the direction I wanted. Suddenly I saw a big fire-ball explosion which I assumed was the aircraft exploding some distance away. Other than this I couldn't see anything below, but all of a sudden my feet and body were carving their way through trees before coming to

Night fighter pilots of 6./NJG4 inspecting the wreckage of Lancaster ED313 of 83 Squadron (PFF), which was shot down by Fw Gerhard Rase on 11–12 March 1943 at Sogny-en-l'Angle (Marne) as his first combat victory. Left to right: Oblt Hans Autenrieth (St Kpt, survived the War with twenty-three night Abschüsse *in NJG1 and 4); Fw Gerhard Rase (survived the War as Oblt with four night* Abschüsse *in NJG4 and 6); Lt Jakob Schaus (survived the War in the rank of Oblt with twenty-one confirmed night-time and two daylight kills in II./NJG4).*
Coll. Norman Mackie.

(Left) *The wreckage of 83 Squadron's Lancaster ED313 is scattered in the woods of Sogny-en-l'Angle (Marne), after falling victim to Fw Rase of 6./NJG4 whilst returning from Stuttgart on 11–12 March 1943. In the course of this night, nine NJG4 crews claimed nine heavies destroyed, plus two probables during a raid on Stuttgart.*
Coll. Norman Mackie.

an unexpected halt, and I was hanging in mid-air. My immediate thought was to get out of my harness and so I twisted and banged the release knob. Unfortunately, I hadn't thought of judging how far I was off the ground, which I couldn't see, but soon realized it had been higher than I imagined when my legs struck the ground and a stab of pain shot through my thigh.

Acting Sqn Ldr Norman Mackie DFC went on to extract his parachute from the trees and bury it. Nearby, at Sogny-en-l'Angle (Marne), some 37km south-west of Chalons-sur-Marne, his Lancaster had crashed in flames. Both Sgt Henderson and Flt Lt Ogilvie DFC managed to escape capture, returning to the UK on 6 June 1943, but Norman Mackie, Flt Sgt Barrett DFM and Flt Sgt Humber were taken prisoner. Sadly, both the crew's gunners, Flt Sgt Lynch DFM and Sgt Chipchase were killed, and laid to rest in Sogny-en-l'Angle. Following his evasion and safe return to England, Sgt Henderson was awarded the DFM on 23 July

1943. Sadly, as captain of Lancaster JB424, he and his crew were all killed in action during a Berlin raid exactly four months later.

In fact, Norman Mackie's Lancaster had been shot down by Fw Gerhard Rase and his radar operator Uffz Rolf Langhoff, a Bf 110 crew with 6./NJG4 who claimed ED313 OL-B destroyed as their first combat victory. Uffz Langhoff had little time left to enjoy his success, as he died in air combat over Chalons-sur-Marne on 16–17 April 1943, whereas Fw Rase survived the War with four *Abschüsse* to his credit. Their unit, operating from St Dizier, had a field day on 11–12 March 1943, with nine crews claiming nine heavies destroyed, plus two probables. In all, eleven Bomber Command aircraft failed to return from the Stuttgart raid, plus two crashed on return in England. Oblt Hans Autenrieth, Staffelkapitän of 6./NJG4 recalls:

> According to a special report of our *Geschwader* we achieved our greatest success up till that time on the night of 11–12 March 1943, being credited with nine definitive and two probable kills. I personally flew two sorties, which was something we only did very infrequently, and scored my tenth kill, a Short Stirling at 00.18, which crashed 3km south-west of Chalons-sur-Marne (BF469 BU-M of 214 Squadron, six of the crew killed). Other successful NJG4 pilots who were mentioned in the special report were Hptm Materne, Oblt Kamp, Oblt Kornacker, Lt Schaus, Lt Engels, Ofw Kollak, and Fw Rase.
>
> Feldwebel Rase, together with his radar operator Unteroffizier Langhoff (who shortly afterwards was killed on another night-fighting sortie), was credited with the shooting down of Lancaster ED313. This was their first ever kill; the remains of this Lancaster were damaged but recognizable and were sought out and photographed by Fw Rase and myself a few days later. None of the Lancaster crew could be found at the site of the crash, so we assumed that they had baled out by parachute and subsequently escaped capture. Possibly, however, the dead crew members had been recovered and buried by the Recovery Team from the local *Luftwaffe* airfield sector. The operational units were never tasked with these duties. It was the policy in those days to keep our flying personnel away from the crash sites until any victims had been recovered and taken away. Understandably, one wanted to spare the crews from the sight of the often gruesome scenes at these crash sites!

As for Norman Mackie's adventures after being shot down: he was captured by a *Wehrmacht* patrol on the second night after baling out, and was imprisoned alone in a room adjoining their control post with his flying boots removed. Undaunted, he managed to force a boarded-up window and to escape without raising alarm. With the help of various French Resistance fighters, Norman reached Switzerland in early April. At first, he was imprisoned in the Prison de St Antoine, Geneva, but was later released and classed as an Internee. During the second half of 1943 he worked for the British Air Attaché, before making a clandestine departure from Switzerland on 6 December 1943. In the company of Capt Jeff Morphew SAAF (a fighter pilot who had flown Tomahawks in the Western Desert before becoming a PoW in Italy and escaping to Switzerland in March 1943), the two men escaped through France to reach Spain on 20 December. A short spell of imprisonment followed in Figueras, but eventually Norman was released, safely reaching England via Gibraltar on 17 January 1944.

On return to the UK, he briefly served as Lancaster Flying Instructor at PFF NTU before he was appointed as Sqn Ldr Flight Commander to form a new LNSF Mosquito Squadron, No. 571, in 8 Group on 23 April 1944. He went on to complete another forty ops, being awarded a DSO before he was finally rested from operational flying in December 1944.

NACHTJÄGER BEGINNERS' TROUBLES

With virtually all the raids on the Ruhr and northwest Germany being routed in and out over the Netherlands, the *Himmelbett* night-fighting units operating over Holland scored heavily against

On the occasion of Christmas 1942 and wearing their flying overalls and silk scarves, this green 11./NJG3 crew had their picture taken. Left to right: Fw Herbert Koch (pilot); Uffz Werner Gärtner (Bordfunker); Uffz Otto 'Peter' Prinz (flight mechanic). The crew claimed their first kill on the night of 20 April 1943; Herbert Koch went on to become an ace with twenty-three confirmed night victories by the end of the War. Coll. Herbert Koch.

Bomber Command. Raum 101, consisting of nine *Himmelbett* boxes in the northern half of the Netherlands, was particularly successful, accounting for 782 bombers destroyed from August 1941 to February 1944 under the guidance of *Nachtjagd*'s leading fighter controller, 'Raumführer' Hptm Ruppel.

On completion of their night-fighting training, Fw Herbert Koch and a dozen other young pilots were posted to Stade airfield in November 1942, and subsequently were distributed over the four *Gruppen* of NJG3. Koch's future *Staffel* was to be 11./NJG3 at Grove, which he firmly believed to be in Holland, the night-fighting eldorado.

> This went as follows. The Adjudant asked us 'Who wants to go to Schleswig, who wants to join the unit at Westerland, and so on.' Whilst he posed these questions to us, the thought crossed my mind 'what should I do here up in the north? I want to go to Holland, to the eldorado of the night fighters!' When he asked, who wanted to go to Grove, I thought, 'Grove? Never heard of the place, but surely it must be in Holland!' I volunteered with another comrade to be sent there. After we had all been split up, we took a close look at the map of Holland, but searched in vain for the location of Grove aerodrome. Eventually, the Adjudant pointed out its whereabouts to us. It was the most northerly operational 'drome of any *Nachtjagd* Gruppe, the IV./NJG3! We immediately asked for a transfer to another area of operations, but this was turned down.
>
> My first operational sortie, on the night of 13 December 1942, ended in disaster. I had taken off from Grove at 01.40 in Do 217 D5+BW for a patrol in the local *Himmelbett* station *Schakal* ('Jackal'), situated to the east of Jütland or at Fünen. Actually, my crew and I were already in bed when the order came to scramble, so under my flying overalls I only wore my pyjamas. There was no 'trade' for us, but when we were about to return to base, suddenly a thick layer of ground mist spread over Denmark and northern Germany, and there was no possibility of landing anywhere! So, after having been in the air for 315 minutes, my crew and I had no option but to bale out, which we did at 06.55. We all came down safely in Schleswig, and after being picked up by the police, I could only identify myself as a German airman by showing them the name of the parachute manufacturer, which had been printed on my 'chute!
>
> Only on my nineteenth operational sortie, on the night of 20 April 1943, did I get into combat with an enemy aircraft for the first time. Take-off from Grove was at 23.16 in Ju 88 C-6 D5+BW, and I seem to recall that the weather

Frontal view of Wellington X HE690 of 420 (RCAF) Squadron at Oostvoorne, 13 March 1943. On the previous night, whilst crossing the Dutch coast on its way to bomb Essen, this Wimpey was hit by flak and crashed at 22.26. One of the occupants, Sgt A.R. Dawson, was killed by an exploding flak shell, the other four crew members having a lucky escape to be taken prisoner. Coll. Kees Wind.

conditions were good, perhaps there was even a moon shining. After circling the radio beacon of *Schakal* for about an hour, the Fighter Controller guided me on to an enemy bomber which had entered the box. It was a thrilling and most exciting moment when I heard his voice announcing: 'I have a Kurier (heavy bomber) for you! Steer 270 (degrees), distance 10 (km).' Several changes of course followed, then I heard him again: 'Distance 8, 8, 5, 7, 6, 5, 4, 3, 2, 1, you are in visual distance now!' I cannot put the tension I felt in those few minutes into words. Then, after another 'You must be able to see him now!', I caught my first glimpse of the enemy machine. Whether it was a Lancaster or a Halifax, I could not discern, but what mattered most, I could clearly identify the exhaust flames from its four engines! During my subsequent night combats, those four engines were always the first sight of the enemy.

I throttled back in order to position myself behind the aircraft, and slowly descended to some fifty metres beneath and behind it. After adjusting my speed to that of my adversary, I went into the attack in the way I had learned at the Night-Fighting School: pull up, let the enemy wander through the reflector sights and then ease the stick forward. Of course, all this whilst bringing the guns to bear. Still nothing happened! I had made the classic mistake of the beginner, and had forgotten to arm the guns! Instead, I was now on the receiving end of the enemy's defensive fire; I saw lines of tracer shooting in my direction. Quickly diving away, I immediately armed the guns and pulled up for a second attack. Our lines of tracer now crossed, I felt and heard many bullets smashing into the fuselage and cockpit of my machine. At the same time, I saw many hits striking into the fuselage and left wing of my adversary, but despite all this, he did not go down.

My machine was hit so badly in the combat, which took place over the Baltic Sea, that I had no choice but to break off the fight and turn for home. The return flight on one engine and with my crew (Uffzs Werner Gärtner, Bordfunker, and Otto 'Peter' Prinz, Flight Mechanic) wounded was as exciting as the whole combat, and I was very relieved when I put her down safely in an emergency landing back at base, at 00.47, after a flight of ninety-three minutes. At debriefing, I could not submit a claim for a destroyed enemy bomber, but weeks later I received news that it was confirmed as a definite

> kill. It appeared that as a result of a combat which matched up with my area and exactly the same time as my encounter, a British aircraft had crash-landed in Sweden.

Fw Herbert Koch's victim was probably Lancaster I ED312 OL-F of 83 Squadron (PFF), which had lifted off from Wyton at 21.23 in the hands of Plt Off C.P. MacDonald DFM RCAF. Whilst just about on the return flight having dropped its load of target indicators on Stettin, it was badly shot up by a night fighter which attacked the Lancaster at 16,000 feet, wounding Flt Sgt C.J. Ford, the rear gunner. Plt Off MacDonald decided to set course for Sweden with the port inner tank badly holed, but a subsequent landing attempt at Malmo was unsuccessful. He then turned back towards the sea and ditched, which went well, and all the seven crew members escaped alive. They were returned to the UK within a few weeks, resuming their operational tour with 83 Squadron.

Fw Herbert Koch went on to serve with 11./NJG3 at Grove and Schleswig until D-Day, when he was detached to Cologne and Düsseldorf airfields to fly forward defence missions over France. Meanwhile commissioned and promoted to Oberleutnant, he was sent back to Denmark to take over command of 1./NJG3 at Schleswig in August of 1944, with his tally steadily mounting to twenty-two confirmed victories by April 1945.

FLYING STRESS

Throughout the War, each Bomber Command aircrew member had to come to terms with stress on operational flying. The impact of the manyfold dangers of flying on ops on the average aircrew is reflected upon by Flt Sgt Maurice 'Frank' Hemming DFM, who served as a flight engineer with 97 Squadron on Lancasters during 1943:

> We were scared, yes. When briefing was over and time for departure arrived, some six or so crews would clamber into the back of a truck with their kit and be transported and dropped off at their aircraft dispersal points. One could look at the crews and tell who wasn't coming back; now, that to me took guts.
>
> For me, the most anxious time was at take-off – hurtling down the runway, in the dark, willing the aircraft into the air and hoping against hope that a tyre didn't burst. Once airborne, our trust was in each other. I was very lucky with my choice of crew, led by Sgt D.I. Jones, a nineteen-year-old pilot who looked as though he wouldn't say boo to a goose, but who proved to be very calm and collected and totally in command of his aircraft at all times and was an inspiration to the crew.
>
> On what to us were short trips – to the Ruhr – on take-off, each aircraft had to circle the 'drome, gaining height to 10,000 feet before setting

16–17 April 1943 was a black night for Bomber Command, when fifty-four aircraft (or 8.9 per cent) of two raids on Pilsen and Mannheim failed to return. These represented the highest losses suffered so far by the Command during the War, night fighters accounting for at least fifteen bombers destroyed. One of these was Halifax II DT670 MH-M of 51 Squadron, which had lifted off from Snaith at 20.23 for the Pilsen raid. Whilst on its way back home, it was surprised in an attack by a Bf 110 D-3 flown by Oblt Autenrieth, Staffel Kapitän of 6./NJG4, and suffered damage to its engines. At 03.50, the Halifax crashed 15km SW of Chalons-sur-Marne, France, with the loss of Sgt D.F. Inch and four of his crew. The buckled tail unit of DT670 was photographed by Oblt Autenrieth next day. Coll. Anneliese Autenrieth.

course. This was alright when there was no cloud, but very often it would be cloudy. Having to perform this, knowing that several other airfields' 'outer circuits' overlapped your own and the same was being done by them, involving what could be up to 200 aircraft, made my eyeballs stand out like organ-stops, especially when the aircraft rocked in another's slipstream. This was to me the most frightening of times.

Our pilot had worked out a wonderful weaving pattern to confuse ground radar control. We were always thankful to see searchlights pop up in a spot of sky we had just left. Often one would see other not so lucky aircraft 'coned' and shot down.

Once over the target things were a lot more hectic, as it was necessary to fly straight and level, under the bomb-aimer's guidance. It was then that ground gunners were able to get a good 'fix' and flak would be thick and heavy, with shrapnel bouncing off the aircraft. This was the most likely time to get coned in searchlights. Another fear at this time was of hitting other aircraft, or being beneath another aircraft's falling bombs. We as a crew often thought that 50 per cent of our losses were due to these two causes.

DEATH AT HOME

One of the statistical facts of the Bomber Command offensive which is easily overlooked is that an estimated one in every six bomber losses occurred over the United Kingdom and not over enemy territory, due to crashes on take-off or landing, or aircraft limping back from the Continent with heavy battle damage and crash-landing on British soil. Sgt Angus Robb, rear gunner with 431 (RCAF) Squadron recounts such episodes:

> There was the occasion when a 51 Squadron Halifax, stationed at close-by Snaith, landed at Burn for some reason, and on take-off back to base developed a fire in one of the engines, which spread rapidly. The rear gunner must have seen the flames passing his turret and decided to get out. At the height he jumped his parachute did not open before he hit the ground, killing him instantly. The irony was, the pilot made an emergency landing with the wheels up, the Halifax split into two pieces and the rest of the crew scrambled out, unhurt.

One of the 1,000 Bomber Command aircraft that failed to return from the Battle of the Ruhr, 5 March to 24 July 1943. Sgt J.W. Newport's Stirling I EF348 LS-N of 15 Squadron was on the outward leg to Mülheim on 22–23 June 1943 when it was badly damaged in a night-fighter attack. It turned back and was attacked for a second time over the southern Dutch border by the ace crew of Oblt Hans Autenrieth, Staffel Kapitän of 6./NJG4 and his Bordfunker Uffz Rudolf Adam. Five of the Stirling crew baled out before their bomber crashed 600 metres west of Kessenich, Holland at 01.30. Sgt Newport and his rear gunner, Sgt W.C. Macaulay, died in the crash and were buried in Heverlee. EF348 was Oblt Autenrieth's twelfth confirmed night victory. Coll. Anneliese Autenrieth.

Another Halifax from the same squadron, coming back from 'ops' badly damaged, attempted a landing at Burn but did not make a landing on his first approach so tried to go round again. Unfortunately, he did not have the power to gain enough height, and in doing a banking turn hit a small brick-built hut at the end of the runway with his wing tip. This caused the Halifax to start cart-wheeling from wing tip to wing tip, coming to rest a good two miles across the fields. When the medics got to the wreck, the crew were smashed to pulp with being thrown about so violently during the last few moments of their existence.

It was a strange time, with injury and death ever present, and yet a few hours after the incident I have just described, we would be drinking with gusto and making plans as if the War did not intrude into our lives at all. Do not get the impression that it was all doom and gloom, rather the reverse. Losses were accepted as part of the game and in many ways it was a game to us; it would happen to that crew over there but not you.

GARDENING

Every one in ten sorties undertaken by Bomber Command during the War was devoted to minelaying, or 'gardening'. At the end of the War, gardening had turned out to be one of the most effective campaigns in which Bomber Command had participated. Apart from impeding U-boat training in the Baltic and putting an enormous strain on the vitally important coastal convoy lanes and causing hundreds of German and German-controlled ships to be damaged and sunk through mine explosions, by 1944 it also forced the German *Kriegsmarine* to engage 40 per cent of its forces in mine-sweeping.

Bomber Command crews usually regarded the gardening trips as something of a 'rest trip' from the more demanding bombing raids over the mainland of the Third Reich. Casualties on mining operations, however, could be heavy on a percentage basis for the following reasons: a few isolated aircraft in a particular dropping zone were more easily detected; the mines had to be dropped after an accurate fix had been obtained, requiring an area search; a low-level timed run of three to five minutes from this fix to the dropping point had to be straight and level; at the dropping height of 600ft, the gardening aircraft were highly vulnerable to enemy flak defences, both from shore batteries and

Flt Lt Jones and crew, with their groundcrew, posing on top of Lancaster OF-Q for Queenie of 97 (PFF) Squadron, at Bourn in May 1943. Conspicuous is the streamlined ventral plastic radome housing the H2S scanner, and the open, 33-feet long bomb doors. H2S, the world's first radar ground-mapping bombing aid, was first used operationally against Hamburg on 30–31 January 1943 by PFF aircraft. Coll. Maurice Hemming DFM.

from flak ships guarding the convoy lanes. Sgt Angus Robb, rear gunner on Wellingtons with 431 (RCAF) Squadron, expands on this topic.

On 3 June 1943, we made, for a Wellington, the long trip to St Nazaire to drop our two sea-mines in the harbour. Mining was not an easy option for bombers. The Royal Navy was most explicit as to the exact spot they wanted the 'vegetables', as they were code-named, dropped. To achieve the accuracy required, on most occasions 'time and distance' were made. This meant flying from an identifiable point on the coast to the dropping point using a stop-watch and a careful monitoring of the air-speed. It seems a simple enough task, but bomber crews did not like the restriction of having to fly straight and level at low altitudes into heavily defended harbours. There were many anxious airmen, I can tell you, until the navigator, with the stop-watch, said 'NOW!', and the bomb-aimer said 'mines gone'.

The dropping of sea-mines was done from a fairly low altitude, and to ascertain the exact height, someone had come up with the idea of fixing a Very cartridge into the base of a cocoa tin, with a lead weight in the bottom and a nail sticking into the base of the cartridge. The rear gunner dropped the contraption out of the turret and told the navigator, who started his stopwatch. When the gunner saw the light from the can appear, he passed the message on, whereupon the navigator stopped the watch. From the time taken for the can to reach the surface of the water, he could work out the height of the aircraft above the sea. And they say today is the age of the technocrat.

On 5 July we did another 'gardening' trip to St Nazaire, our only operational sortie of the month. At the end of the month we were on our way to another Canadian Squadron, No. 432, which was still flying Wellingtons, stationed at Skipton-on-Swale. We did six mining trips and one bombing trip in August. Four of the 'gardening' exploits were to the Dutch coast, the other two to Brest. The trips to Brest became very hazardous indeed. The channel to the mouth of the harbour was marked by normal light buoys, which we followed to the inner harbour where we dropped our mines. One night the Germans replaced the buoys with flak ships, displaying the same light pattern. We lost a number of aircraft that evening from that ploy and it made it, from then on, a very dangerous place indeed.

TARGET FOR TONIGHT: HAMBURG

After the successful, though costly, execution of the Battle of the Ruhr, Harris turned his bombers on to Hamburg. Between 24–25 July and 2–3 August 1943, Germany's second largest city, housing the Reich's most important ship-building yards, was subjected to four major raids. During the first three attacks, 2,164 bombers rained down 6,928 tons of high explosives and incendiaries on Hamburg. The raids were very concentrated, both in time and space, which was a result of the accurate Pathfinder marking on H2S and the prevailing

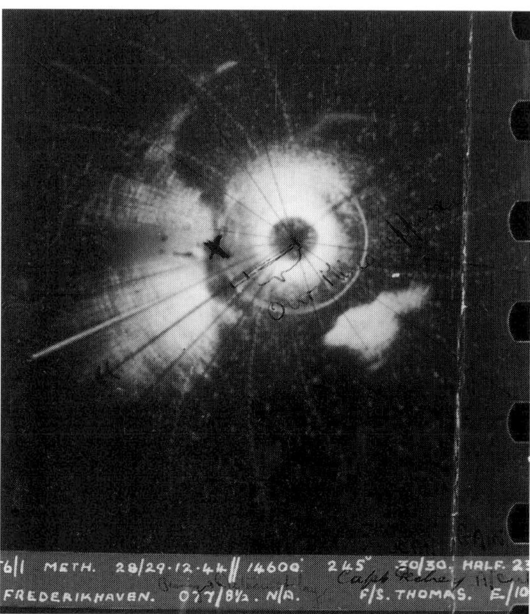

Typical H2S picture, showing Frederikhaven and taken from Lancaster 'E' of 106 Squadron by the set operator Flt Sgt Thomas at the time of dropping a load of parachute mines off Oslo on the night of 28–29 December 1944. Coll. C.P.C. Pechey DFC.

Victor. Oblt Autenrieth, Staffel Kapitän of 6./NJG4 posing with the remains of his fourteenth Abschuss. *Stirling III BF501 HA-N of 218 Squadron, captained by Sgt J.W.D. Hoey RCAF was outbound for a raid on Wuppertal when it was intercepted and shot down by Oblt Autenrieth and his Bordfunker Uffz Adam. BF501 crashed at 01.59 on 25 June 1943 some 2km WSW of Diest, Belgium with the loss of all on board.* Coll. Anneliese Autenrieth.

clear weather conditions. Only the fourth raid (of 2–3 August) can be classed as a failure due to the bombers meeting a massive thunderstorm. Losses during the battle were kept low at only eighty-seven aircraft (or 2.8 per cent) due to the introduction of 'window'. These were bundles of metallized strips of paper thrown out by every aircraft in the bomber stream, which effectively swamped the radars of *Nachtjagd* and the flak arm with false echoes. On the second raid (of 27–28 July), a firestorm was born in the district of Hammerbrook in which an estimated 40,000 people died, and a million others fled the stricken city.

Sgt Ron James, mid-upper turret gunner in Fg Off Bill Day's 90 Squadron crew, did his first trip to Essen on 25–26 July 1943, after which the Stirling crew became involved in the Battle of Hamburg, as Sgt James recalls.

> Hamburg was the next target we visited on 27 July, followed by a return visit on the 29th. The route was similar to the first one, into Hamburg from north of the Elbe, and apart from some problem with the engines (luckily they all kept going) we arrived over the target and dropped our bombs. Night fighters were about in strength, and on four occasions we had to shake them off by violent evasive action without a shot being fired.
>
> After crossing the German coast on the return journey, Don reported: 'Have some hangs-up skipper, am going to jettison.' There was a short silence from Bill, then, 'We came here to bomb Germany, and that is what we are going to do.' With that 'Roger' was turned around and we were back over 'Hunland'. Don managed to find a small port along the coast and let go the rest of our cargo. Needless to say Bill's action did not receive the approval of the rest of us, and later we had a lot to say about it. We still had plenty to learn about the hazards of operational flying, but I think Bill realized later that he had put us in peril by returning to Germany, and we never had a repeat performance.
>
> It was shortly after this particular incident that both Mitch in the rear turret and I spotted two aircraft coming up behind us. The one nearest to us was twin-engined, single-tailed, and possibly a Ju 88. An unusual feature was that it had what appeared to be two forward lights showing. It occurred to us that it might be enemy aircraft working in tandem, one to attract our attention, the other to attack. Positive identification was difficult even though the moon was fairly bright. I told Bill to change course to see if they would follow. 'No, hold it,' from the rear turret. Mitch fired on the aircraft nearest to us, the one with the lights, now about 200 yards away. The plane seemed to stop in its tracks, then disintegrated into three flaming parts as the fuel tanks blew up. We circled and watched the wreckage plunge into the sea.
>
> Of the second aircraft no more was to be seen, but a combat starting up not too far away brought us quickly back to our senses, and it was

Ju 88 C-6 D5+GX of IV./NJG3 showing its graceful yet warlike features in this fine air-to-air shot taken over Denmark sometime in 1943. Coll. Theo Boiten, via Eric Bakker.

full speed for home. At the debriefing Mitch stated that we had been attacked by a Ju 88, and although I knew this to be incorrect I kept silent. I had my doubts whether it was even German. The deed was done, and anything that I said would have helped no one, least of all Mitch.

Long after the War I decided to research this episode, and according to German sources they recorded no losses in this area. From British records it appeared that a Mosquito night intruder had disappeared in roughly that vicinity; one that was returning to base with engine trouble!

The following night we travelled to Remscheid, a town near Cologne. It housed many chemical establishments, and the raid was so successful that it never received a second visit from Bomber Command. Then, after a welcome day's stand-down, we were back on the old target again – Hamburg! At briefing we had been told that the weather over northern Germany would be clear, but in the event we encountered a storm of unbelievable severity. Of the seventeen Stirlings sent out from 90 Squadron, ten failed to get through and returned to base, and only two of the remaining seven actually bombed the target – ourselves, and Plt Off Appleby's crew.

The ferocity of that electrical storm still remains fresh in my memory: the plane going up

Whilst chasing Flt Lt C.C. Stovel DFC RCAF's Halifax II DT749 of 408 Squadron at low level over the North Sea on the night of 27–28 July 1943, Lt Hermann Stock's Ju 88 C-6 of IV./NJG3 almost came to grief when its propellor tips touched the water and, as a result, they were chopped off. Groundcrew are seen here discussing the damage in a maintenance hangar at Grove, after the crippled aircraft had been safely nursed back home. Flt Lt Stovel's Halifax was later brought down by Lt Gotthard Sachsenberg of II./NJG3 to the west of Neumünster, with the loss of five of the crew. Coll. Theo Boiten, via Eric Bakker.

The bombing tally of an unidentified Halifax, which was on its twenty-fourth op to Cologne, has been removed after being shot down by Lt Hager and his Bordfunker Uffz von Bergen of 4./NJG1 on 29 June 1943, and is seen here on display at St Trond airfield. Note the final bomb symbol which has been adorned with a skull, probably by personnel of II./NJG1. On 28–29 June 1943, II./NJG1 claimed nine Cologne raiders destroyed in air combat. Coll. Hans Grohmann.

and down like a lift, ice forming on the wings, with pieces breaking off and rattling on the fuselage. Even though in thick cloud, 'Roger' was bathed in light: the propellers were giant Catherine wheels, a continuous spark encircled the turret, and another charge joined the ends of my guns together. Inside the turret too it was far from pleasant, for I was wearing electrical gloves, and every time my hands neared a metalled surface, sparks would shoot across – it was scary!

Only by a stroke of luck did we find the aiming point. Momentarily, the cloud cleared over the Elbe and we were almost over the dock area. Thirty bombers were lost on this operation, most of which I feel sure succumbed to the weather conditions, not enemy action.

Indeed, at least four aircraft, and probably more, went down through icing, turbulence or after being struck by lightning on 2–3 August 1943. The large thunderstorm encountered over Germany effectively prevented the 740 Bomber Command aircraft carrying out another devastating raid on Hamburg, and many crews were forced to turn back early or to bomb alternative targets.

MY SECOND DOUBLE

The first use of 'window' during the Battle of Hamburg threw the rigid *Himmelbett* fighter control system into chaos. Both the ground and airborne radars in use in *Nachtjagd* were rendered virtually useless in one stroke, being swamped with echoes, only one in twenty to thirty of which represented a real bomber. What this meant for the German crews trying to get at the British bombers is vividly illustrated by Lt Norbert Pietrek, a pilot who had become operational in 2./NJG4 in January 1943, flying Bf 110s from Florennes airfield in southern Belgium. He had scored his first 'double' on 16–17 April 1943, his victims being an unidentified Lancaster which flew into a hill surrounding the River Meuse whilst being chased by Pietrek at low level, and Stirling BK653 of 214 Squadron, which came down at Bonneuil-les-Eaux in the Oise district at 23.45 (four evaders and three PoWs) after a prolonged battle. Lt Pietrek now tells of this incident:

The date is 9 August 1943 and we are once again lounging about in our operations hut, wearing our full flying kit. My radio operator Otto had gone down with hepatitis and was in hospital. Uffz Paul Gärtig, who at the time had no 'driver', had been assigned to take his place. We had already got to know each other in the course of other operations and I had found him to be a very good radar and radio operator. I called him Paulchen (little Paul), although he was older than me, but he had not taken this badly.

It is just past midnight. The 'little Kadi' (Hptm Wilhelm Herget, *Gruppen* Kommandeur) had assigned me a few days before to the first wave of his operational area 7B, which had made me feel quite proud (in the first wave, the best and most experienced crews were usually scrambled). In charge of this fighter box's *Seeburgtisch* is Ernschtle, the best JLO, (Jäger Leit Offizier, or Fighter Controller), which is practically a guarantee for an *Abschuss* if the Tommies should come. None of us of course want them to come, for we could never shoot down all the bombers but only a small fraction of them, leaving more than enough others to destroy a German city with their bombs.

Will they be coming tonight, and if so, through our sector? The chances are not bad. The Tommies have good weather for taking off and landing, the night is dark with no moon. These are good conditions for we night fighters as well.

While we are still quietly dozing away we suddenly get the order: 'First wave cockpit readiness!' and we rush out to the bus which brings us to our machines. So they are coming, the Tommies. In no time at all we, Paulchen, Moritz (flight engineer) and I, are on board and are waiting for the order to take off. After only a few minutes it comes.

The engines fire at once, thanks to the efforts of Moritz and my ground mechanic Alwin Athen, and I take off. I climb, orbiting, with full power, while Paulchen is seeking radio contact with Ernschtle, which isn't easy, for the Tommy's jamming is considerably worse tonight than usual, which almost certainly means that they will be coming through our sector. Then it sounded to me as though the starboard engine wasn't running quite right; in any case its rpm had dropped somewhat and I had to adjust it. I ask Moritz what might be wrong, and whether he thought that we should turn back. He asked me for the oil pressure and the oil and cooler temperatures, then thought that we should continue. Without Moritz I would probably have turned back.

Now, as I am almost at a height of 6,000 metres, Paulchen got contact with the JLO through the dreadful cacophony of the jammers, and he 'serves me up' with a Tommy. He is on a course of around east-south-east and still quite some distance away. I must therefore give

With twilight setting-in one evening in August 1943 over Florennes airfield, Lt Norbert Pietrek of 2./NJG4 is sitting in his Bf 110 3C+HK for a spell of cockpit readiness, and ready to be scrambled. Coll. Norbert Pietrek.

chase with full power. We get some minor course corrections and I gradually close with my opponent. He is pretty fast, it must be a new model, perhaps one of the new Lancasters? We should soon find out.

We have been chasing the Tommy for some minutes and are closing in. He is dead ahead, only 500 metres away, and I am straining my eyes to see him. There, or am I mistaken? No, he really is there! The black outline with the four faintly glimming exhausts. I ease a little lower and a little to the right in order to identify him and to get out of the rear gunner's arc of fire with his four machine guns. It is, in fact, a Halifax. Then I slide under the Tommy, adjust to his speed and ease up until I am about twenty metres below him. Now my friend, now you're for it!

I had decided on his starboard wing as my aiming point, pulled up, rising barely five metres behind the Halifax whilst firing a full burst between the starboard engines where his fuel tanks are, and the kite bursts into flames in the starboard wing and plunges burning over his port wing. We follow him down until we see the flash of his crash and report our success to base. After the crash we can hardly believe our eyes: it looks like a regular fireworks with variously coloured rockets. We had apparently caught one of the illuminators. He will not be able to set his markers over the city to be attacked. Perhaps we had saved a lot of peoples' lives there. But now back to radio beacon 7B!

Only now do I realize that my two 2cm cannon had not been fired, only my four machine guns, and of these one had failed and cannot be cocked. What's up? Has the armourer, Ofw Habermann, made some mistake? Well, I'll give him what for when I get back. Now I'll have to carry on with only three guns!

Flying westward to the radio beacon we hear from the JLO that he has lost us and cannot find us again because 'the sky is full of Tommies, but none of them are continuing on their way', as good old Ernschtle puts it. He is unable to find me and guide me to another enemy. I make that out through the chatter and noise in my earphones as I notice to our starboard, at about the same height, a small shadow, no larger than a wasp, flit past in the opposite direction at about 500 metres distance. Could that have been a Tommy? Without thinking long about it I swing off to the right and was not a little surprised to find myself exactly fifty metres beneath a Lancaster. Paulchen and Otto behind me were startled by my sudden manoeuvre but I had had no time to warn them.

Now I have my second opponent of the night before me. So I am to shoot him down with only three machine guns, but how does one do that? Will I manage it and set him on fire like the Halifax before? Let's try it. Now, as before with the Halifax and at least a hundred times before at practice, I position myself twenty metres beneath him, then I pull up and fire a full burst into the two starboard engines. No success! I must have hit him, but the Lancaster continues steadily on his east-south-east course to bring its bombs to their destination. Now I notice that another gun had failed to fire and that I have only two left. That makes it practically impossible to shoot down a *Viermot*, but it's worth a try and I want my second victory.

After my first attack I had placed myself to the right and below, to observe my opponent and consider how I might 'with only two thin squirters' as the Little Kadi expressed it afterwards, sweep him from the sky. To set the engines or tanks on fire is, as the first attack had proved, pointless. That leaves only the fuselage as aiming point and if possible the 4 × 1,000 rounds of ammunition in the rear turret. Normally we don't aim at the fuselage, but only at the tanks and the engines in the wings. The enemy crew should have the chance of escaping with their parachutes. They were only doing their duty, just as we were doing ours, and they could not be blamed that 'Bomber Harris' had ordered them to destroy German cities instead of the German industry. But now I have no choice than to try to set fire to the ammunition in the rear turret in order to stop the enemy from reaching his target. That would make it unavoidable that some of the crew would be killed, at least the rear gunner. I feel sorry for him, but how many Germans might be killed by his bombs?

Now the enemy knows that he is being stalked by a night fighter and he will be very much on the alert. I sneak under him, into the blind spot of his defences, for the second attack. The rear gunner had evidently spotted me, had realized that he no longer had a chance, and abandons his turret to save himself by parachute. But as I am already very close beneath him, which the poor fellow could not have seen, his head hits my port wing, where afterwards we found a scrap of skin with a bunch of red hair. Pity, I would rather have had him land unhurt.

Now I must try to eliminate the mid-upper gunner; I would have to pursue the Lancaster for some while yet until I should manage, if at all, to set the rear turret ammunition afire, and the propeller wash of the four Lancaster engines would fling me several times upwards into the field of fire of the two machine guns of the top turret. I therefore fired, already pulling up, into the area of the mid-upper turret and I must have got him, for he doesn't fire a single shot, although I am thrown about a lot and several times into his field of fire. I am now literally poking around with my two guns at no more than ten metres' range in the bottom right of the rear turret where two of the four ammunition boxes are located and, indeed, after about ten seconds there is a flame. Now the same again in the bottom left with the same result. Then I move off to starboard to observe what happens next.

At first nothing happens, the Lancaster continues on course to his target. Either those in front have not noticed the fire in the rear turret, or they think that it will burn itself out. I almost thought so myself, for the flame disappeared for a few seconds, only to reappear even larger. It looks as if the Lancaster is alight at the back like a cigar. After five minutes, however, the Lancaster turns back and tries to get away homewards. But after a few minutes the crew must have realized that it was useless, for suddenly the Lancaster dives steeply down and in the bright glare of the crash we see four open parachutes descending. The rest of the crew must have bought it, pity. I have done it, shot down a *Viermot* 'with only two thin squirters', something not to be emulated easily. But, now that the ammunition

'The rear gunner evidently spotted me, realized that he no longer had a chance, and abandons his turret to save himself by parachute. But as I am already very close beneath him, which the poor fellow could not have seen, his head hits my port wing, where afterwards we found a scrap of skin with a bunch of red hair. Pity, I would rather have had him land unhurt.' (Lt Norbert Pietrek, 2./NJG4.) This artist's impression of a similar incident which befell Oblt Egmont Prinz zur Lippe-Weissenfeld of 4./NJG1 during 1941 was published in the Berliner Illustrierte Zeitung. Coll. Helmut Conradi.

(Right) *Uffz Paul Gärtig, Lt Pietrek's Bordfunker during August 1943, relaxes on the side of his position in the Bf 110 before setting off on an NFT in the summer of 1943.* Coll. Paul Gärtig.

for my two guns must be almost exhausted, and my fuel too, I report my return and fly home.

During the chase of the Lancaster we had heard over the radio a succession of fighters leaving Florennes and reporting in 7B, the Little Kadi, my Staffelkapitän Rudi Altendorf, Luk Meister and also Fritz Gräff. Would some of those also down one or more Tommies?

After fifteen minutes I am over the airfield and land. I taxi over to refuel; I wanted to take off again, should the Tommies return through our area – perhaps I could get a third one! I stop the engines and call for the armourer to give him a ticking off about the cannon which had failed to work. Habermann comes, looks at the guns, then says that both are in order, but that all four machine guns would have to be changed. I then realize that I had not been flying my own 'H', which had all the guns on the trigger of the control column, but Rudi Altendorf's reserve machine 'B', and that one had only the machine guns on the trigger and the cannon separately on a button, and I had, as I had been accustomed to do on my 'H', used only the trigger. I feel a fool and apologize to Habermann. So there is no question of another flight. The three of us make our way to the operations room.

There we get a great welcome and are congratulated on our success. All the others who had taken off for 7B after my first success had now also reported their return. None of them had found an enemy because, as it now became clear, the Tommies had dropped masses of *Düppel* (window) which had so interfered with our radar that neither our ground nor our airborne instruments had been able to make them out, and with only the naked eye no enemy aircraft had been spotted. This night, mine had been the only success of the Western defensive chain.

At 01.00, Lt Norbert Pietrek's first victim of the night, Halifax II HR872 LQ-K of 405 Squadron, crashed at Awenne, Luxembourg, near the Belgian border. Skippered by Flt Lt K. MacG Gray RCAF, it had left Gransden Lodge just over two hours earlier for a raid on Mannheim. All seven crew members, of which six were Canadians, perished, and were buried in Florennes. Lancaster I W4236 QR-K of 61 Squadron fell foul of Lt Pietrek twenty minutes later, and crashed at Marbehan, Luxembourg. Three of the crew were killed, with Sgts J.T. Kendall RCAF, G.W.S. Spriggs and N.T. Holmes finding their last resting place in Florennes. As Lt Pietrek witnessed, the remaining four men in this all-NCO crew baled out safely, managing to escape capture. Their aircraft was a veteran; it had been on 61 Squadron's strength for almost a year, flying a total of 639 hours 55 minutes.

NACHTJÄGER VERSUS FORTRESS – THE SCHWEINFURT AND REGENSBURG RAIDS

As previously described by Fw Erich Handke, *Nachtjagd* crews were doubly burdened after being ordered to fly both day and night-time operations from early 1943 onwards. With the exclusion of the indispensable ace crews, the bulk of *Nachtjagd* continued to be sent up on the suicidal daylight missions against the American combat boxes throughout 1943, this 'misuse', as Fw Handke described it, reaching a crescendo during the famous 17 August 1943 raids against Schweinfurt and Regensburg. Uffz Otto Fries, a Bf 110 pilot with 5./NJG1 at St Trond, vividly recorded in the third person what happened to him and his Bordfunker on 17 August 1943.

On the night of 17–18 August 1943 he was Duty Officer and was sitting in the operations room instead of in his G9+EM – but he could not have flown on this night anyway as the guns of his machine were being changed and adjusted. During daylight operations on 17 August two machine guns and one 2cm cannon had jammed due to burst cartridge cases – and all of the reserve aircraft of the *Gruppe* had already been allocated.

Shortly before he had passed on the take-off order from division for the first *Wilde-Sau* operation of the *Gruppe* and thirteen Me 110s had signed off by radio and were on their way to Grosse Laterne Berta, a heavy bomber stream was apparently heading for Berlin. In fact, at least thirty machines should have taken off, but these thirteen were all that were left after the heavy losses against American bombers that day. All the others had been put out of action through battle damage, diversions and other unserviceabilities.

When he had gone to briefing he had been hoping for a quiet night and a good night's sleep in his bunk in the operations room; in the last six nights he had had barely more than four hours sleep and his eyes were pretty well down to zero. But now thirteen crews were airborne and he had to await their reports by telephone after landing. He probably would have had no sleep anyway after the turbulent happenings of the day.

He had only got to bed after sunrise and had intended to sleep through lunch in the mess, he was not due to take off before late afternoon for target practice in area Kolibri. But towards 10.30 his radio operator Fred hammered against his door and chased him out of bed with the words 'cockpit readiness'. He shot up and tore off his pyjamas. In no time he was dressed and had put on his fur-lined boots. No wash, no shave, no cleaning of teeth! He strapped on his pistol and ran off. As he passed the wash-room he stopped briefly to clear the sleep from his eyes with a handful of water.

Downstairs, in front of the cadet school the crew bus was waiting with the engine running. It filled up in no time at all. The door was barely closed when it turned into Luiker Street to speed along to the crew room opposite the airbase gates.

They rushed out of the bus and dashed into the barrack hut and to the cupboards holding their equipment. Flying trousers and jackets were hurriedly donned, signal pistol ammunition belts were strapped on and flying boots fastened, gauntlets and radio operators' satchels torn from the shelves. Then off at a jog-trot across Luiker Street to the operations room behind the guard room to the left. The Commander and the Staffel Kapitän were already there. The Adjudant checked and reported the complete assembly of the crews of the Second *Gruppe*.

The 'Old Man' (Major Walter Ehle) reported that several American bomber formations had taken off in England and that they were already over the Channel in their approach – target unknown. Following briefing all crews were to go to cockpit readiness, just in case. Should division order take-off, it would be signalled by the firing off of a *Radieschen*, a 'radish flare'. After take-off, assembly in a wide turn to port over the airfield, staggered in height: Staff Flight and 4th *Staffel* at 500m, 5th and 6th *Staffel* each 50m higher. Radio communication over the operations room frequency. After the take-off of the first aircraft, a continuous note of thirty seconds at one-minute intervals would be transmitted for ten minutes by operations for tuning-in purposes. General radio silence except for orders and instructions from the Commander, who would also give out departure, course and height. Other exceptions: important reports from crews.

They ran to the bus which turned at once on to the perimeter track to the dispersals – the one of the 5th *Staffel* was the last one. Konrad, the mechanic of their G9+EM, was already standing on the wing in order to assist them in putting on their parachute harness and seat belts. He closed the cabin cover and struck it with his fist to indicate that he should not forget to lock it. He unlocked his shoulder straps to give him greater freedom of movement and switched on the electrics, Konrad had already connected the battery cart. He checked the instruments and the controls for freedom of movement and Fred, behind him in the machine, checked his radio gear. Having found everything in order, he turned off the electrics again.

They did not have to wait long before the 'radish flares' went off into the air with a bang. He turned on the electrics again and pressed the starter button of the starboard engine. The rising tone of the centrifugal starter fascinated him each time. He pulled the clutch, the engine turned and gave a couple of puffs, but it did not start. He repeated the process – again nothing. Engines were roaring everywhere. Angry, he tried again three more times – the damned engine simply would not start. The other aircraft were already taxiing out. He swore to himself and decided to try the port engine. At last, at the third attempt, coughing and spitting the propeller began to turn. The mechanic signalled: battery cart empty! So he had to try to start the starboard engine using the generator of the port engine; the fetching of a fresh battery cart would take far too long. He tried it time and again, the damned engine simply would not start.

The engines roared above the airfield, all the aircraft must have taken off. He decided to make one last attempt; if it did not work this time he would have to change over with a heavy heart to the reserve machine, one by no means popular with the crews and generally known as the '*Staffel* whore' – and that name said it all. He increased the revs of the port engine and pressed the starter button of the starboard one – croaking and putting forth a blue-grey cloud the engine came to life.

'Halleluia!' Fred called out behind him. Konrad pushed the battery cart to one side, removed the chocks and gave the clear sign. Slowly he taxied out of the hangar to the perimeter track, turned to the right and hurried to the take-off point. 'Lampion from Adler 98 – taxiing for take-off – question *Tampen* (course) – question *Kirchturm* (altitude).' 'Adler 98 from Lampion – *Tampen* one-zero-zero – *Kirchturm* four-zero – *Horrido* (tally-ho) – out.'

He paused briefly at the take-off point, locked his shoulder straps and set the take-off time on the clock – it showed 11.30. He opened the throttles and took off. Having retracted the undercarriage and flaps he set a course of 110 degrees. He flew at excess boost and a rate of climb of only five metres per second to keep up speed – he wanted to catch up with the *Gruppe* as quickly as possible. Fred had tuned his receiver to the operations room frequency to keep a listening watch – but apart from background noises there was nothing to hear.

The cathedral of Tongres had long been left behind and they were approaching the River Meuse. He had reached a height of 5,000 metres and trimmed the machine for level flight. They had already donned their oxygen masks at 4,000 metres. It was a glorious summer's day, not a cloud in the sky, only a slight haze which covered the countryside beneath them in a thin smoky-grey veil. Aachen appeared on the port bow and some kilometres straight ahead in the haze he saw widely scattered aircraft of his *Gruppe* engaged with single Boeings. Why only single

A fine shot of a formation of Bf 110s of I./NJG4 during a daylight training flight sometime in mid-1943, taken from the Bordfunker's position in the camera aircraft. Note the long-range auxiliary tanks fitted to 3C+KK, flying closest to the camera. Coll. Paul Gärtig.

machines? Where were the formations? Later on he heard that individual aircraft had been cut out from a formation, whether by single-engined fighters or by the Aachen flak no one really knew.

He opened the throttles to take-off power and turned on the propeller automatic in order to utilize the power available to the maximum. The breeches of the guns clattered to the firing position as he turned over the lever. On switching on the reflector sight he noted with pleasure that Konrad had removed the night filter – and he remembered that he had forgotten to ask him about it before take-off, for it was important to be able to use the reflector sight as no tracer ammunition had been loaded. At night he preferred to use 'dark' ammunition – well, Konrad was a perfect mechanic who thought about everything!

He dived off his excess height and quickly approached the scene of the action; he decided to go for the group to starboard as it was the closest. There, two Me 110s were engaged with a Boeing which had evidently already been hit, for its starboard outer engine was trailing whitish-grey smoke. By Jove – that was a big one! When he had got within range, still some fifty metres above the bomber, the two Me 110s had just made an attack in night fighter fashion, from behind and below, and had dived away to starboard. He was behind and to one side of the Boeing, broke off to port and let his sights run between the engines and along the starboard wing. A brief burst of fire, he saw the strikes in the wing, then he had dived away to port below the bomber. Whether he had been fired at he did

Flt Lt Harry Watkins and his 61 Squadron crew pose with a 4,000lb 'cookie' in front of Lancaster III ED860 QR-N for Nan at Skellingthorpe, autumn of 1944. Lt Pietrek of 2./NJG4 destroyed 61 Squadron's W4236 QR-K on 9–10 August 1943. ED860 served with 156 and 61 Squadrons, successfully completing 130 trips before it swung out of control and crashed on take-off from Skellingthorpe on 28 October 1944. Coll. Edgar Ray.

not know, it had all happened so quickly – and it had been so exciting to have flown an attack on such a large ship in broad daylight. In any case, his machine had received no hits, for he knew that impertinent knocking sound only too well – he would certainly not have overheard it, in spite of his excitement.

He drew his aircraft up again in a turn to port and saw the other two again attacking the bomber. Its starboard wing suddenly burst into flames – it was like an explosion. Bits detached themselves and before very long the first 'packages' dropped from the Boeing, plunging downwards and suddenly hanging on their parachutes.

There was nothing left for them to do here. He looked around to see where the others had gone to – but apart from a fire on the ground there was nothing to see. The other two machines circled the burning bomber. He did not want to wait for them and went back on to his old course. There was not an aircraft to be seen anywhere. 'Listen out on your radio to find out where they've got to.' The radio operator gave no reply, he had obviously switched off his intercom. He always did this when he was working his gear, seeking a transmitter or getting a bearing. Once, when he had complained about this, his radio operator had countered: 'You only interfere with your chatter, and generally at the most inconvenient moment.' He briefly waggled his wings. 'What's up?' 'Try to get the fighter broadcast, they always give a situation report.' 'Am doing it already – just a moment, the frequency is jammed.'

He continued on his course of 110 degrees. He turned off the propeller automatic and went on to economic cruise to save fuel. 'They have turned off to the south, they are probably heading for the Rhein–Main area or Karlsruhe–Stuttgart.' He went on to the south and increased power to gain more speed. They must be somewhere over the south Eifel – down below another bomber was burning; it looked as though it would start a forest fire. The Mosel appeared up ahead. Far off to port, in the haze and just discernible, he saw the Deutsche Eck. 'Anything new on the fighter broadcast?' he asked the radio operator after he had waggled his wings. 'No, they are still up ahead – can't you get your horses to run a bit faster?' 'Certainly, where are they now?' 'The map reference given should be north-west of Mainz. On the operations room frequency there is nothing except a constant rustling and odd words which make no sense. I'm staying on the fighter frequency, if there is any news I will let you know. I'm switching you off again.' 'Very well, thanks!'

He gave a little more power and went into a slow climb in order, later on if required, to exchange height for speed. He looked around him; there were no aircraft to be seen, neither own nor enemy ones. Nahe appeared down below, he recognized Mainz to port. Its inhabitants would all be in their air-raid shelters. He was approaching his home grounds. The propellers turned, the engine noise was soothing, all instruments indicated what they should. The air-speed indicator showed just below the 420km/h mark.

Something appeared to be happening ahead on the port bow. He opened up the throttles to the gate, turned 20 degrees to port and turned on the propeller automatic again. He crossed the Rhine. Up ahead he saw a formation which appeared to be surrounded by fighters swarming around like a bunch of hornets. He would have liked to have whipped up his horses some more, but did not want to open his throttles beyond the gate. He gave a brief waggle. 'What's up?' asked Fred. 'There's a heavy formation up ahead – let's see what we can do, our ammunition can't be exhausted by a long chalk yet.' 'Well, let's go then!'

Ahead and a little lower a single Boeing appeared, its port undercarriage leg hanging down. Three Me 109s circled around it. He had the impression that they were unable to attack further due to lack of ammunition. He approached very fast, much too fast, and snatched the throttles closed. Seconds later he peeled off to port and sent a long burst into the starboard wing. He passed the bomber close above him, opened the throttles again and took the Me 110 around in a steep turn to port. When the Boeing came back into view he saw that the starboard wing was afire and that parachutes were hanging in the air. The bomber continued briefly onward, then went down over the starboard wing and exploded shortly before reaching the ground. The parts fell widely dispersed into a wood to the north-east of Mannheim.

Weeks later he heard by chance that the crews of the Boeings would lower their undercarriage if they wanted to surrender. The fighters would then cease their attacks in order to give the crew a chance to bale out. He felt very ashamed afterwards – and cursed the fact that night fighters were ordered up by day without making them acquainted with the usages of day-fighting. It might be that the old sweats of his night fighter unit, who had come from the *Zerstörer* units and had partaken in the early campaigns and the Battle of Britain, were familiar with these customs. He, who had come straight from night fighter training, had only the faintest idea of the tactics and conduct of the day fighters. His misdemeanour made him feel sad.

The three fighters were still circling the crash site, then they formed a vic and flew off eastwards. He had lost contact, apart from a few crash fires there was no sign of friend or foe. He turned his equipment to normal flight and set a course of 150 degrees. He saw the Königstuhl on his port beam. *O alma mater heidelbergensis* – would he ever return to the university?

Fred, who had been silent during this time, spoke up: 'That one won't drop any more bombs, anyway!' 'You're right, but I have lost contact – listen in to the fighter broadcast, they must still be around nearby.' 'I'll call you right back!' The machine was approaching the Kraichgau and the silhouette of the Black Forest appeared in the distance. 'They have turned off to the east. We were both so occupied with the bomber that we had not noticed it. The formations are supposed to be in map references Toni/Toni and Toni/Ulrich, that must be the area south of Würzburg. They are on an easterly course. We have got much too far to the south.'

He looked at the map in his mind's eye: 'I assume that north-east would be about the right course.' Fred took the navigation chart from his satchel. 'We are about north of Karlsruhe, I think 045 degrees would about do.'

He turned on to north-east and increased the speed. He pulled out the plugs of the pneumatic fuel gauges to check the contents. He had more than an hour's fuel left. He never trusted the fuel gauges, it had happened more than once that they showed zero although he had only been flying for one hour. According to the elapsed time the gauges could be correct, in spite of the increased consumption caused by the propeller automatic and the increased speed, for they had only been flying for just over an hour.

They crossed the Neckar. His thoughts went back to the past: how often had he paddled here at weekends and spent the night in a tent with his friends. It seemed as if decades had passed since that time. O *Gaudeamus igitur* ...! When had he last sung it in the circle of his friends?

It would certainly not do to dream during a sortie against the enemy – gross reality recalled him at once: a formation of Boeings appeared over to port, they were approaching each other at an acute angle. 'What a bunch of bombers!' came Fred's voice. 'There must be more than thirty of them – and not a single Me 109 to be seen. What are you going to do?' 'I don't know yet!'

He had heard somewhere that day fighters would attack from ahead and above, take one of the leading Boeings into their sights, fire, then dive down and away through the formation. Then, if they had not been damaged themselves, they would pull up and around and repeat the process. The Me 109 was a small and manoeuverable aircraft, against which his night fighter Me 110 seemed like a fat and lame duck. Would he be able to carry out an attack in a like manner? The chances of being hit oneself appeared considerable – but they still had their parachutes as a final consolation! An attack from behind and above or in the night fighter manner from behind and below were out of the question considering the fire power of thirty Boeings. That only left an attack from abeam, perhaps at an angle from ahead and above.

He did not know which would be the right method for himself and his aircraft, but it was clear to him that he must do something, and wanted to. 'Well now, Lofty, I've had a few things going through my head. I believe it would be best that we pull up and make an attack at an angle from ahead and above – or have you a better idea?' 'Hardly – and what are the chances of not being hit?' 'Very small – is your parachute harness secure?'

Silence ... 'Your ideas have become superfluous – look there!' A Boeing left the formation and turned off to the south. He had to admit that he felt a great relief. 'Why is it turning away – does it have some special orders or is it damaged?' 'Perhaps they want to escape to Switzerland because they don't like this dangerous game!'

He put his aircraft into a steep turn to port and followed the bomber which was about fifty metres below him. It appeared to have been damaged after all. As he got closer he thought he could recognize holes in the rear turret and the fuselage – and the propeller of the starboard outer engine appeared to be turning only by the slipstream. 'I hope I have enough juice in the cannon. You can forget the machine guns where such a heavy is concerned.' 'But you haven't fired that much so far, there must be enough left!' 'I hope so – hold tight!'

He was no longer excited, he was quite calm and turned on the propeller automatic again. He held his height and placed himself on the starboard quarter of the bomber. It certainly was a very heavy one – why did they not fire, he was well within their range! He peeled off to port, aimed at the starboard inner engine and pressed both firing button and lever. Only one of the cannons fired a short burst and not all of the four machine guns fired. He dived down below the Boeing and pulled up his machine in a steep turn to port. 'Damn it! The cannon are empty and it looks as though only two of the machine guns are working. What rubbish!' Angry, he flew two further attacks at the starboard inner engine with the remaining machine guns. At the second attack only a couple of bullets stuttered out, then it was finished. 'That can't be true!' He turned the switch for the guns off and on again and tried both triggers. Nothing happened, machine guns and cannon remained silent. 'The devil! Such rot! Now it's your turn, Fred!'

Lt Johannes Hager (right) discussing the performance of his Bf 110 G-4 on return from an NFT at St Trond, 1943, with Uffz Hans Grohmann (Daimler Benz engine specialist, middle), and his leading mechanic. Lt Hager joined Nachtjagd *in the autumn of 1942, and soon became a leading ace with twenty-two confirmed victories during 1943, including a B-17 during the Schweinfurt raid. He survived the War with forty-eight kills to his credit, and was awarded the* Ritterkreuz *on 12 March 1945.* Coll. Hans Grohmann.

As he pushed the aircraft downwards, two 'packages' dropped out of the Boeing and two parachutes opened. 'They seem to have given up after all!' He sheered off to one side and waited, flying at the same height as the Boeing – three minutes – five minutes – nothing happened. 'Well, what's up with you, my friends!' said the radio operator. The bomber flew onwards as though nothing had happened, the starboard outer engine was obviously dead. 'I am now going to place myself below him and draw slowly ahead. You must direct me into the right position and then aim for the starboard inner engine. Then fire until nothing more comes out of your barrels!'

Before joining 419 Squadron on 29 May 1943, Fg Off Stan Heard served as a flying instructor in Canada during 1941–42; he is seen here on the left with his first pupil to go solo at No. 32 EFTS. Coll. Graham H. Heard.

He went down a little, pulled over to port and increased his speed. 'Stop, that's good, you can go a little higher.' He gently pulled on his stick. 'Stop! No higher!' He held the machine rigidly on course and height – it was no simple matter as he was unable to see the Boeing. Four or five bursts clattered, then he heard the resigned voice of his radio operator: 'Any number of holes in the tin – and the engine is still running. My ammunition's all gone.'

He sheered off to one side and they continued alongside the bomber for a short while to see whether the crew would not give up after all – but the Boeing continued steadily onwards. 'There's not much point in hanging on any longer, he'll surely go off to the Swiss.' (Weeks later it became known that the Boeing did indeed fly at low level across Lake Constance in the direction of the Swiss bank.) 'Let's find a place to land. Our fuel might last as far as St Trond, but I do not want to fly without ammunition. Perhaps Echterdingen with its Night-Fighter School might suit, the people there are familiar with the Me 110.' 'I'll see if I can find the frequency in my lists, then I'll give you a bearing. I'm switching off.'

He set course westwards and before the radio operator had reported he saw a motorway up ahead. It could only be the road from Munich to Karlsruhe – but was he now north or south of Stuttgart? He was not familiar with the area. It had been an age since he had flown here during his blind-flying training – and then the windscreen of

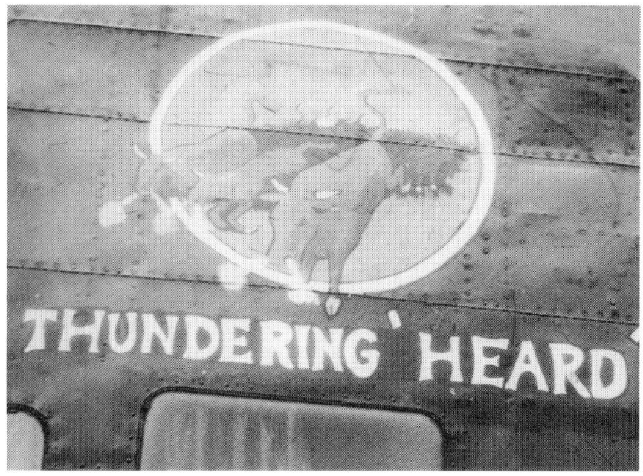

Halifax II JD258 VR-K, Fg Off Stan M. Heard RCAF's personal aircraft with 419 Squadron, was adorned with this painting of a thundering herd in the first half of 1943. On his fourteenth op, the Peenemünde raid of 17–18 August 1943, twenty-three-year-old Fg Off Heard, a farmer's son from Piapot, Saskatchewan, and his crew were all killed when their aircraft JD158 VR-D was shot down and crashed in the Baltic in the general area of Stralsund-Gross Zicker. Only in June 1992 were the relatives of Stan Heard informed that he was laid to rest at Greifswald, but his name is also still commemorated on the Runnymede War Memorial for the missing. Coll. Graham H. Heard.

his Ju 52 had been obscured as he, sitting beside his instructor, had been practising flight on instruments. Instinctively he turned off to the north and minutes later he recognized the airfield of Echterdingen. 'You needn't trouble yourself any more, there's Stuttgart up ahead.'

He landed at precisely 13.00 and taxied immediately to the hangars. The armourers found that one cannon and two machine guns had been jammed by burst cartridge cases. As a change of guns would have taken far too long, he had the magazines of the remaining guns filled up and taxied over to refuel. They took off about two hours after landing and arrived at 15.30 in St Trond, where he handed over the machine to the armourers. On his way he allowed himself a small detour to the north, however. When the Vogese came in sight, he swung along the edge of the hills to the north until the Weintor on the borders between Alsace and the Pfalz came into view. This was the beginning of the wine road of the Pfalz which went through Winzerdorf where he had been born. He circled three times at low level over the hill where, nearly 1,200 years before, his home village had been built. Everywhere in the vineyards people were waving, his mother stood on the stoop and waved too. Such digressions were officially called 'infringements against the aviator's proper behaviour', but without an accuser there could be no judge. And where operational crews were concerned, they usually turned a blind eye.

The rattling of the field telephone standing on the table before him tore him out of his reminiscences of the turbulent happenings of the day: the first crew of the *Gruppe* reported their landing at an airfield in Mecklenburg of which he had never heard, although he had flown a lot in that area during his C-training days. Berlin had not been the target for the bombers but an area further to the north. The pilot at the other end of the line was unable to give more detailed information. It must have been a major attack for he had observed a great many fires and bomb explosions and many aircraft being shot down during his approach. He himself had arrived too late because due to wrong information he had made a detour via Berlin where bombs had also fallen; evidently a diversionary attack had prevented him from flying directly to the north.

The telephone kept on ringing. Within a bare half hour all crews except three had reported back, with claims for eight aircraft shot down. He was not worried about the remaining three, he knew from experience that the lines were frequently hopelessly overburdened after an operation. Later on it transpired that the other three crews had baled out and that a further five enemy aircraft had been shot down. The target for this night had been Peenemünde.

After division had issued the code-word 'Finally Crow', he lay down on his bunk to spend what was left of the night asleep. In dozing off he took stock of the events of the day: the daylight sortie had been a completely new experience for him, with exhilaration on the one hand, and disappointment on the other because he had not succeeded to shoot down that last Boeing. And, considering the imbalance between the day's successes and losses of his night fighter unit, daylight operations against American formations appeared to make no sense at all. According to the law of averages, his *Gruppe* would hardly have any aircraft left for night operations if it went on like this for another week. With this dreadful thought in his mind he fell asleep.

In all, fifteen II./NJG1 crews were scrambled from St Trond on 17 August 1943 to combat the American formations heading for Schweinfurt and Regensburg. Uffz Fries' first victim was Capt Ash Tyson's B-17 of the 390th BG, the exploded remains of which came down at Bringen, on the western banks of the river Rhine. The second Fortress which came under his and his Bordfunker's fire was a 100 BG kite, which Lt Don Oakes managed to nurse to a safe landing at Dübendorf airfield, Switzerland. Although a total of seven B-17s fell foul to II./NJG1 during the day, four of the unit's Bf 110s and one pilot were lost through return fire and in combat with Thunderbolts of the 56th FG, and almost all the other Messerschmitts returned with such severe battle damage that they could not be sent off to hunt for Bomber Command aircraft raiding Peenemünde the next night.

Twenty-one *Nachtjagd* aircraft were lost during the daylight operations of 17 August 1943, plus an estimated thirty damaged, and fourteen crew members being killed or severely injured. Instead of the *Nachtjagd* knife cutting at both edges as originally intended by the OKL, it was thus transformed into a blunt weapon at an alarmingly rapid rate. After the American combat boxes were accompanied by escorting fighter aircraft from the late summer of 1943 onwards, these were taking an unacceptably high toll on the lumbering twin-engined machines and crews. The *Luftwaffe* leaders therefore finally relieved *Nachtjagd* of its day-fighting duties in early 1944, much to the relief of the surviving crews.

PATHFINDER TO BERLIN

Having delivered the Germans two consecutive heavy blows in the Battles of the Ruhr and Hamburg, in the autumn of 1943 Sir Arthur Harris felt that his force was ready to undergo its greatest test of the War, by unleashing a series of night raids against the Reich's capital itself. He believed that the destruction of Berlin, or the 'Big City' as it was respectfully called by his crews, would force the Nazi regime to surrender, perhaps even without first having to commit the assembling Allied land forces to a costly invasion of the European continent. In what has gone down in history as the Battle of Berlin, Harris's bomber crews flew a total of nineteen raids between 23–24 August 1943 and 24–25 March 1944 to Germany's most heavily defended city, entailing many long and fatiguing hours of flying in the worst weather of the year.

On 23–24 August 1943, the first major raid in the Battle of Berlin took place. Sgt Wilf Sutton was a veteran flight engineer in Plt Off Laurie E.N. Hahey's RAAF crew, who had flown on ops with 77 and 35 (PFF) Squadrons from February 1943. On the historic 23–24 August raid, 35 Squadron was leading a force of 710 Lancasters, Halifaxes and Stirlings, plus seventeen track-marking Mosquitoes. Plt Off Hahey and crew flew Halifax II HR865 A-Able on their twenty-eighth sortie, as Wilf recalls:

> We were a senior Pathfinder squadron. The experience of flying in Pathfinders was first class. We were a group of very experienced flyers; also we had special navigating equipment and we were in constant training to improve our target finding. We, as Pathfinder crews, were proud of the job we were doing and in spite of the fact that we were more exposed to flak and night fighters, if we were the early main markers our morale was high.
>
> On 23 August 1943, we took off from our airfield at Graveley in Huntingdonshire at 20.15. Having reached our operational height of 22,000 feet we flew towards the target. In those days we had several gadgets which helped us, to some degree, to know when other aircraft were astern or to the quarter, one of which was called 'Monica'. As soon as another aircraft flew to within 1,000 yards behind you Monica would begin to pip. It sounded rather like the BBC pip and as the aircraft flew closer the bleep and the frequency increased. Now, as I said, 35 Squadron was leading some 700 Bomber Command aircraft, not to mention the *Luftwaffe*, and Monica could not distinguish friend or foe. We crossed into Holland in heavy cloud and after an hour or so of pipping Monica we decided, as a crew, to switch it off. We broke cloud east of Hanover and within minutes we were straddled with 20mm cannon shells from a Junkers Ju 88.
>
> I had gone to the flare chute to distribute 'window'. As soon as the first shells hit us the skipper went into violent evasive action, in other words he flew like a corkscrew and succeeded in getting away from the fighter. When he righted the plane I could see what a mess we were in. Cannon shells had ripped through the fuselage within an inch of my flare-chute position, torn the starboard wing apart, set the two starboard engines on fire and the 1,000 gallons of petrol. None of the seven crew members were touched.

We do some daft things under the most trying circumstances, and in this instance I uncoupled my oxygen and intercom, went to the centre of the plane, got a tiny fire extinguisher and tried to put out 1,000 gallons of fuel against a slipstream of 250mph. It didn't work. Then the mid-upper gunner motioned me back to the flare-chute where I reconnected my oxygen and intercom to hear the skipper calling to the crew to abandon the aircraft. When a plane is flown like a corkscrew, everything not strapped down whirls around the fuselage, in this case me and my parachute, on which I was sitting to lob out the window. For my good fortune it had landed where I was sitting so I put it on, opened the rear hatch and disappeared into the moonlight. I landed without injury in a potato field, buried my parachute and having found the North Star headed towards Stettin in the hope that I could get a boat to Sweden.

After being chased through some fields by a horse in the darkness, I fell fast asleep sitting beside a tree. Next morning, having removed the Air Force markings from my battle dress and the top of my flying boots to make shoes out of them, I set off to find better shelter. I was walking along a path in countryside that seemed just the same as at home and for some time I could not accept the fact that I was in Germany. I even passed farmers who said '*Morgen*' which sounded to me like 'Morning', and I felt on top of the world thinking I could make my escape without too much difficulty. However, it took only about ten minutes before I was challenged by three farmers with a shotgun. They shouted '*Flieger*' and although I spoke no German it was obvious what they meant so I replied '*Ja*' and from that moment on they were quite convinced that I spoke their lingo.

They took me to the nearest village called Gintine where I was handed over to the police and kept in the Mayor's house until late afternoon when the *Luftwaffe* came for us. Us, by the way, meant Dave Cleary my wireless operator and Scotty Hogg the rear gunner. We were taken to Berlin, which at that time was a beautiful city and bomb damage was hardly noticeable. We were taken to a *Luftwaffe* barracks and joined up with about ninety prisoners picked up from the last night's raid.

In fact, all seven members of Wilf Sutton's crew baled out safely from their doomed Halifax to be taken prisoner. The 23–24 August 1943 Berlin raid had turned out to be a black affair for 35 Squadron, with four aircraft failing to return, all falling victim to night fighters. On board Flt Lt H. Webster DFC's HR928 TL-R was Gp Capt B.V. Robinson DSO DFC & Bar AFC, who had recently been appointed Station Commander at Graveley. Neither he, nor twelve other 35 Squadron aircrew survived this first raid in the Battle of Berlin. In all, fifty-eight out of 710 heavy bombers were shot down by the fierce flak and fighter defences, plus five more crashing in England. A loss percentage of some 9 per cent represented Bomber Command's greatest loss in one night so far in the War. In and around Berlin, 854 people were killed, and 2,661 buildings were seriously damaged or destroyed, although much of the bombing attack fell outside the 'Big City'.

Nachtjagd recovered remarkably fast from the devastating blow rendered by 'window'. 'Delousing' solutions to the jamming of the *Freya* and *Würzburg* ground radars were feverishly sought, and found, and a new AI set, the SN-2, working on a jam-free wavelength and a range of between 300 and 4,000 metres was introduced into the arm in October 1943. Most of the night-fighting aircraft were fitted with the obliquely upward-firing *Schräge Musik* guns, making them almost invulnerable to rear gunners' return fire. Furthermore, *Naxos* and *Flensburg* were installed into the aircraft to home on to the emissions of the British H2S navigation radar, and the Monica tail-warning device respectively.

Simultaneously, the rigid system of ground-controlled *Himmelbett* night-fighting was largely abolished. Twin-engined crews were sent off into the night sky on freelance patrols, operating on information about the position, course and height of a developing raid supplied in a running commentary, which was broadcast on the Reich Fighter Frequency by various ground stations. Also, three new *Geschwader* of single engined Bf

FRONTPOST

NR. 4. WOCHENBLATT FUER DEUTSCHE SOLDATEN 25. NOVEMBER 1943.

DRITTE NOVEMBERWOCHE

Bisher grösste Luftangriffe

DREI GEWALTIGE ANGRIFFE AUF BERLIN IN SECHS NAECHTEN

Die R A F richtete in den Naechten vom 18. zum 19., vom 22. zum 23. und vom 23. zum 24. November drei äusserst schwere Luftangriffe auf Berlin.

[illegible]

Das Verkehrsnetz des Ostheeres zerrissen

[illegible]

BERICHTE VON DER SUEDFRONT

[illegible]

VERKEHR MIT DER HEIMAT

This leaflet was dropped over Germany by Bomber Command in late November 1943, and under the heading of 'Biggest Air-Raids So Far' informs the German people about the successful Berlin raids of 18–19, 22–23 and 23–24 November 1943. On the latter two raids, an estimated 175,000 Berliners were bombed out, a further 3,500 were killed, and a vast area of destruction was created throughout the Reich's capital. Coll. Frank Westbrook.

109s and Fw 190s, christened 'Wild Boars', were rapidly formed to give Bomber Command a hard time over the cities under attack (*see* page 132).

FIRST TRIP TO MANNHEIM/ LUDWIGSHAFEN

These factors combined made Bomber Command's losses rise steeply by the early autumn of 1943. Once more, the skies over Germany were a lethal place for the hard-pressed bomber boys, as is demonstrated by the following story of Plt Off Lawton who describes what happened to him on his maiden trip to the Reich, on 5–6 September 1943. On this night, a force of 605 aircraft (299 Lancasters, 195 Halifaxes, and 111 Stirlings) was despatched to bomb Mannheim and Ludwigshafen. It turned out to be a successful attack, but thirty-four aircraft (thirteen Halifaxes, thirteen Lancasters and eight Stirlings, or 5.6 per cent) were lost. On the German side, three twin-engined aircraft were recorded as lost in action on 5–6 September 1943, with three crew members perishing. Plt Off Reg Lawton, the navigator in Stirling III EE973 of 196 Squadron, outlines events as follows:

> This was our first trip to Germany. It was the night of 5–6 September 1943 in Stirling 'U', piloted by Sqn Ldr D.M. Edmondson. This was his second trip, as he had done one as observer and he came back and thoroughly alarmed us.
>
> Anyway, this trip went well until we reached the target – Mannheim/Ludwigshafen. As we approached, the pilot told me to leave the navigating and come up and sit in the right-hand seat and open the bomb doors. This was a big mistake. It was completely unexpected as it was not my job – I didn't even know how to do it and I lost my night vision. I worked in a curtained cabin and when I left it I was horrified at the sight of what was going on outside, so many of our own planes in almost daylight with enemy flares lighting up the sky.
>
> I remember thinking we were risking our lives for nothing because the target seemed to be one vast fire, without our load. We were hit repeatedly by flak and I hurriedly got back to my navigation as the bombs were going. The bomb-aimer and rear gunner both called out 'enemy fighters attacking' and we went into violent evasive action for some minutes.
>
> I should never have left my work as I was now called on for a course for home, with all my timing lost as well as courses flown during the evasive action. The pilot was exhausted. He had operated the fire extinguishers in both inboard engines which was successful, and he then restarted both these engines – and they worked!

(Bristol radials – marvellous.) The starboard outer engine was almost all missing – just tangled struts in a huge hole in the wing. This engine gave all the power to our instruments. I gave a course for our next turning point (which was half way between Paris and the coast).

We started back at 12,000 feet having bombed at 17,500, which was the maximum a Stirling could get to. We were very slow and steadily losing height. After a bit I took an astro-fix but the plane was vibrating so much I took no notice of it. It put us well south of track and actually was dead right; for a long time later I was just going to give the pilot the change of course north for the coast when we were plastered with flak again. We had flown straight and alone into the defences of Paris.

We survived this and after some minutes the pilot called me up and told me to go forward and see if I could pinpoint our position as we crossed the coast. I gingerly went down the steps into the nose, because some of the extreme front had been shot away and the bomb-aimer (Sgt C.H.A. Redding) who was injured in the eyes was resting in the fuselage. So there was quite a wind blowing, and it was cold too. I saw the coast pass under us but could not locate the area and I didn't know, in the dark, where to plug in my intercom. So when I climbed back the pilot was very relieved as he thought I had fallen out of the aircraft. We were now down to 1,000 feet and the engines were on fire again; the flight engineer had been telling us long ago we were out of petrol and at this height we flew right through the London Balloon Barrage.

I don't know why we didn't make for one of the 'crash' aerodromes, but in fact I got us back to our own station. As we were now burning, we came in to crash-land without any preliminaries, such as doing a circuit. As we had no flaps we came in much too fast and as we touched down the fuselage broke in two at the trailing edge of the wings. The front bit we were in skidded a long way off the runway, heading straight for the control tower, which gave them a fright. We all scrambled out and were all OK except for the bomb-aimer who soon recovered.

No one commiserated with us, no one praised us. No medals were offered. We were shaken and worried that all trips were like this. I can't remember being even frightened at any stage (six hours, fifty minutes' flying time), nor did the rest of the crew seem to be.

Our next trip was uneventful, being the bombing of the entrance to the Mont Cenis tunnel in France. That made us a lot happier, and then Stirlings were taken off bombing as they were outclassed by Lancasters and were deathtraps – 5,000 feet below the Lancasters, just right for all the flak – and bombs from the Lancasters above.

Stirling EE973 was written off after the crash-landing at Witchford.

DOWN IN THE DRINK

Hundreds of Bomber Command aircraft were lost to enemy action and mechanical failure over the North Sea during the War, with most of the crew members declared missing. This dreaded fate was known to aircrew as going 'down in the drink'. On 22–23 September 1943, Bomber Command mounted a heavy raid on Hanover, with 711 aircraft despatched for the first major raid of a series of four on this city; twenty-six aircraft failed to return. Sgt Len Tierney had lifted Wellington X LN547 QO-G of 432 (RCAF) Squadron off Skipton-on-Swale's runway at 19.07, and his twenty-one-year-old rear gunner, Flt Sgt Basil Williams RNZAF, recalls what happened:

The trip to Hanover was reasonably quiet until we were about to make our bombing run, when all hell broke loose. We were coned in the searchlights with all the flak coming up. The pilot put the plane in a steep dive, losing a few thousand feet, then pulled it up abruptly. I thought that the turret was going to come away, my head seemed as if it was parting company with the eardrums ready to burst. I was held in suspension even with the safety belt on. According to the pilot the speedometer hit the maximum.

When we pulled out and regained some height, the pilot circled again and we dropped our bombs, then he called for the petrol to be checked. The reply from the navigator: 'sixty gallons'. A pause, then he checked again, answer: 'NOTHING!'. That left us the nacelle tanks plus something if there was any not registering on the gauges. How far can we get? And where to from here? The questions for the shortest way home. On to Sweden or do we bale out over enemy occupied territory, or last, head for the North Sea, hopefully to be picked up by air–sea rescue? No panic by anyone; we were all young and invincible and supreme optimists, aged twenty to twenty-three. As I had experienced another crash, when I was dragged out of the rear turret, my thoughts before ditching were that I had to get out. I turned the turret at right angles to prepare for the landing.

The force of the ditching turned the turret a few degrees making it a tight squeeze getting out. Also, from the turret to the tailplane was quite a step. Whilst standing on the tailplane in the pitch darkness I saw the white face of the WOp getting past fast; I shouted 'grab the tailplane', then he went under. That call, as he later said, saved his life, as it helped break the shock cycle.

My next job was getting up to the fuselage. Being in the turret the bombing jacket was too bulky; my clothing was two pairs of aircrew underwear, electric waistcoat, roller neck sweater, battledress, and Mae West. The bomb-aimer and myself had bought small sheath knives while on leave in Kilmarnock, his home town. My next move was from the tailplane up on to the fuselage, then sliding along towards the front using the knife to make a grip in the canvas. I could not see very far at this stage.

The waves were now coming over the plane; my thought was 'where am I going?', so I paused with my knife in the fuselage. I was laying flat down, the swell lifted me up, I swallowed sea water, and made another move. About this time I saw the bomb-aimer and the navigator standing on the wing, and I joined them on the right wing on the outside as I appeared to be the last. At this time the plane was going down fast, I thought 'what a way to go', no one would know what had happened, a known grave seemed lovely.

From out of the darkness we heard a whistle, then the pilot with the dinghy came up, a welcome sight! As I was closest to him I got in first, not the easiest when you are saturated. I turned to get the navigator and told Len that Johnny had gone. Len said 'No, he is slipping away'. Len moved over to balance the dinghy while I pulled Johnny in; he had a badly gashed forehead and was almost out. Next in came Dickie the navigator. My thoughts at this time went to the railway

431 Squadron RCAF, 4 Group Bomber Command, Burn, Yorkshire, summer of 1943. Left to right: Sgt Len Tierney (pilot); Sgt (later Plt Off) Dick Sewell (nav.); Sgt Johnny Mercer (WOp); Sgt (later Plt Off) Les Whetton (B/A); Flt Sgt Basil Williams (R/G). Whilst serving in 432 Squadron RCAF this crew survived more than eighty hours in their dinghy, after being shot down on the 22–23 September 1943 Hanover raid. Coll. Basil Williams.

station at Great Yarmouth where Dick's widowed mother asked me to look after him, so he was the fourth one in the dinghy. It was heavy work, with one more to go. Les, who was six foot was just holding on, even asking him to exert himself did not make much difference: he was too shocked. We got him almost half in, then with some help he was home for the night.

The next thing to happen was that I brought up the sea water swallowed on the way down the fuselage, a delayed reaction probably. We surveyed our plight. A sheath knife was found on the rubber floor so we threw everything sharp overboard as our well-equipped dinghy had no leak stoppers or storm sheet. When the pilot had got out, he had stepped straight into the dinghy, and with the high sea that was running, he did not like getting wet with the water coming over the side. Even while soaked and very cold, the extra spray was not very comfortable. We had not felt the cold from the sudden immersion as that, at the time, seemed inconsequential. We all passed out from exhaustion the first night, the wireless operator being semi-conscious. Next morning we rode the waves, they seemed ten foot high. One minute we were on top, the next instant we were at the bottom of the trough. While at the bottom, we sighted a Beaufighter pass overhead. It would have been impossible for the crew to have seen us.

The nights were the worst, as one had dreams. One of the nights I dreamt that we had landed in South Africa, and that they had offered us some wine which I refused, as I only wanted water. The large sea eventually settled down. The known record published at this time for RAF aircrew being in the sea was seven days, so the five supreme optimists of us thought that we would start to worry after that seventh day; then, on being rescued, join the Goldfish Club, and have ten days' survivor leave, which would have been the second such leave for me.

We rationed out the water at one mouthful per day, along with a few horlick tablets plus one square of glucose or barley sugar, only one of them in the four days. The third day we saw some small birds which moved the navigator to suggest that we were in the Wash (England), and should be close to home. By this time, with the cold, it was hard to move one's legs as they got tangled up with the others'. Owing to cramp one had to use one's hands to lift them. The beaker or whatever for measuring water was used for urinating in, which owing to the cold was a continuing project.

Early on the fourth day a Ju 88 flew over us, then later a German flying boat circled and dropped a flare to mark the spot colouring the sea red. Our chemical was green, the German chemical was far better. Ditched RAF aircrew could be recognized by the greenish dyed uniforms. This sighting by the Germans inspired us to start paddling again; naturally we got nowhere. Much later on the fourth day a German air–sea rescue boat arrived, we threw our escape packs away with the foreign currency. They laughed; we had to be helped aboard and 'For you the War is over.' How wrong they were.

When we were all in the cabin we got undressed, quite a task as our arms had swollen, and everything had shrunk, including our stomachs. The German crew were very kind and offered us some cognac, and told us that they had been looking for us for days.

The Wellington crew were taken to Borkum Island, where they were rudely interrogated, the Germans threatening to shoot Plt Off Les Whetton, the bomb-aimer, if he continued to refuse to give them anything but his name, rank and service number. Three days later, the five men were taken by train through Holland and the Ruhr, and the journey finally ended in Sagan prisoner of war camp for the two officers, and a camp in Lithuania for the three NCOs.

BOMBING HAPPENINGS, 1943–44

The largest group in Bomber Command was the Canadian No6 (RCAF) Group, which was founded in January 1943. Built up to full strength in the autumn of 1944, it comprised fifteen heavy bomber squadrons, and was able to put 280 Halifaxes and Lancasters into the air. For a total of

39,584 sorties flown from its bases in the vale of York, the group lost 784 aircraft (or 2 per cent) on ops during the War. Nineteen-year-old Plt Off John Turnbull, a pilot from the prairie village of Govan, Saskatchewan, and his crew first joined 419 'Moose' Squadron at Middleton St George on 29 August 1943, a relatively comfortable peace-time permanent station. Having successfully completed seventeen ops and promoted to Flt Lt on 21 January 1944, John and his crew were posted to 424 'Tiger' Squadron, where he became Deputy Flight Commander. Flying from Skipton-on-Swale which, like so many airfields throughout Britain, was hastily built during the War, they safely completed their tour of ops at daybreak on 11 September 1944, with a trip bombing German troop concentrations on the outskirts of Le Havre. By then, John's crew had all been commissioned, with John having been awarded a DFC on 27 June 1944. His crew were all decorated with the DFC after completion of their tour. John, together with his brothers Bob and Walter (who flew as a navigator), formed 'The Flying Turnbulls' in Bomber Command. Between the three of them, they completed 108 operational sorties flying in Whitleys, Halifaxes and Lancasters between May 1941 and December 1944, Bob Turnbull finishing the War as Gp Capt DFC and Bar, DFM, AFC, MiD, C de G, and CO of 427 'Lion' Squadron. John Turnbull gives an impression of his tour.

I had a well-disciplined and competent crew and, I guess, we were 'lucky' in our operational tour. As a pilot and captain, I completed thirty-four sorties; each of them flew a few less due to illness or for some other reason.

Taking off from the northern country meant longer hours, as we flew down England to join with squadrons rising from airfields in mid- and southern England ready to swing eastward toward targets in Nazi-occupied Europe. The skies were thick with droning aircraft climbing to their set-course heights. Our friends, the British on the ground, often remarked how they took to heart watching and listening as the flocks of bombers crowded the sky overhead. We, too, in our 'kites', experienced some of that awe as, in the fading light of a sunset we viewed the expected increasing number joining the stream. That stream became more and more concentrated, in depth and width, as we crossed the water and then the 'enemy' coastline (it was hard to think of the Dutch, the Belgian or the French coasts and those of other conquered nations as 'enemy').

Seldom, if ever, did the route go directly to the target; we always flew a few diversionary legs before the final run-in to the target. Often, too, the main stream would divide at some point(s), with some attacking, in major numbers or otherwise, other targets while the main force struck the main target. Such was the night of

A fine shot of Halifax II Series 1A LW282 'S' for Sugar of 419 ('Moose') RCAF Squadron at Middleton St George, October 1943, with, from left to right: Sgt Ron Gillett (WOp, RAF); Sgt 'Dusty' Hutt (mid-upper gunner, RCAF); Fg Off Earl Albert (nav., RCAF); Fg Off John Turnbull (Pilot, RCAF); Plt Off Harold McBain (B/A, RCAF); Sgt Joe Malec (R/G, RCAF); Sgt D. Board (substitute Flt Eng; the crew's regular Flt Eng was Sgt Frank Michael, RCAF). Coll. John C. Turnbull.

The Turnbull Flyers. Left to right: Bob, Walt and John. Taken on the event of Christmas 1943, whilst staying in Surbiton, Surrey at the home of their Australian hostess and 'Aunt' Peggy Brown. Between 1941 and 1944, the Turnbull brothers completed 108 operational sorties in Bomber Command. Coll. John Turnbull.

November 26–27, 1943, for example, when 178 of us swung toward Stuttgart while Berlin targets received major attention. Stuttgart defences were strong that night! I can recall that fighter flares lit the sky and attacks began about Frankfurt, which the German controllers had incorrectly guessed to be the target, and flak was heavy over Stuttgart. And, of all things, our bomb-aimer found it necessary to call a 'dummy run', forcing us to circle back into an individualized bomb-run which received much individualized attention from the defenders ... not a pleasant manoeuvre, but we made it! Then we had to push to catch up with homebound friends (was that the night the upper gunner suddenly called attention to an Me 110 so close above us that we could have touched it? Well, almost! We wondered after who was getting his attention!). 'Mac', our bomb-aimer, called a dummy run one further time, causing his crewmates to subsequently observe that 'one more time and we'll drop you and keep the bombs!'

Additional to attaining the turning points on a route, the height and time-on, and maybe airspeed, which were stated at the pre-flight briefings, the final run-up to the target and release of bombs were closely stated. Without exception, the bombing height was according to plan and the aircraft of each squadron had a specific gap of three minutes to be on and off the target. It was a bit crowded up there! The gunners (419's mid-upper became a mid-under gunless lookout when we removed the upper turret) in particular were alert to potentially dangerous situations, friend or foe; a friendly aircraft in the stream was suddenly very close to colliding, or was directly above with its bomb-bays open ready to release its load (or vice versa, if we were the aircraft above), or a night fighter was closing for a kill, or ... !

From the ground, searchlights probed the black sky and, as we approached, light flak stabbed the lower levels to discourage our Pathfinders, those expert and exceedingly courageous crews searching to visually confirm the aiming point at a close range and identify it to the bomb-laden aircraft above at heights usually of 18,000 to 20,000 feet (the Wellingtons and Stirlings couldn't make those heights; the first Halifaxes with their lower-powered Merlin engines struggled to attain them). The lack of a designated bombing height, which wasn't often, prompted pilots to see what their favourite kite could do, and I have memories of coaxing our Hally III to 25,000 feet over Berlin on February 15–16, 1944 (but my fellow pilots pooh-pooh my claim; and I don't see it written in my pilot's log book!).

The *Luftwaffe* control sent its night fighters to attack our bombers in the stream as identified by its ground radar (and just as we were beginning to savour the more easily attained accurate navigation resulting from our airborne radar boxes (H2S; Monica; Fishpond) it was determined that the *Luftwaffe* night fighters were able to home-in on those radar emissions!). As soon as Command Intelligence determined that our airborne radar could be followed by the *Luftwaffe*

Flt Lt John C. Turnbull, Deputy Flight Commander with 424 ('Tiger') Squadron warming up the engines of his Halifax III at Skipton-on-Swale, early 1944. Note the flame dampers on the large 1675hp Bristol Hercules XVI air-cooled radial engines.
Coll. John C. Turnbull.

fighters we were told, and intermittent usage rather than full-time was established. As the summer of 1943 progressed, it was time to jam the Germans' detection equipment … strips of thin paper with aluminium foil stuck to one side (so silver-shiny one side, dull black on the other), about 2cm wide and 27cm long, scattered from each bomber's 'window chute' by the tens-of-thousands made a few aircraft appear as a major attack on ground radar screens, making assignment of defensive fighters extremely difficult.

As the bombing waves passed over the target, the results of their work were exhibited to following waves first as a glow in the sky and then as fires and explosions on the ground. Target-markers, in colours made known at the pre-op briefing particularly to navigators and bomb-aimers and placed by the Pathfinder squadrons, were the guides, and a sophistication was a Master of Ceremonies' voice broadcasting supplementary instructions on poorly placed colours due to surface winds or those faked by the defenders. To one side or another at a distance from the perceived target, faked targets might appear to tempt the wasting of bombs on their simulated burning streets and local explosions and lights.

And among all the confusion of flares, bomb bursts, explosions, fires, and smoke would be the photo flashes timed to facilitate determination of where the bomber's load had struck ground (an interesting activity not having much credence, in my mind, because there was little chance of the camera being on a steady plane with flak bumping the wings, slipstreams from aircraft ahead wobbling the controls, evasive action being called or one movement or another. Straight and level was not a possibility, nevertheless, it was a proud day when a crew's photo showed an aiming point!).

One had to steel oneself to fly into a wall of powerful searchlights and exploding flak. There would be intense bluish master beams surrounded by several lesser beams slowly moving and waving in circles, probing into the incoming bomber stream. By the light of that master beam, a newspaper could be read at 20,000 feet … or, as one pilot put it, he could read his Prayer Book! … and one could be blinded if one looked down into it. I resisted the temptation to dive and corkscrew as the beam encompassed us; rather, if possible, we turned carefully toward its approach to move through it expeditiously and flew as smoothly as conditions allowed to minimize glints and reflections from any oil leaked on to the engine nacelles … it worked! Fortunately for us, after a brief pause which seemed hours, that master beam didn't gather its juniors to set us into a cone but moved on to catch a less fortunate approaching crew. Sadly, we witnessed others, possibly friends, involved in frantic evasive tactics trying to shed a cone into which circling fighters were emptying their guns; often blinded and spinning out as they lost flying control in a stall. We knew that if the beams suddenly dropped and all went dark they did so on orders of an attacking *Luftwaffe* fighter protecting his eyes for the kill. At the same time, flak bursting around the coned bomber would suddenly drop from its apex. Then, that was the moment to swing into vigorous evasive action!

The above tells of situations often encountered. My pilot's log-book record of our ninth op (4 October 1943) states 'Frankfurt: Wall of search lights and plenty of barrage flak; good fires and huge explosion'. The tenth op (8 October 1943): 'Track heavily concentrated with both bombers and fighters; many searchlights but little flak over target'. A Stuttgart target, our thirteenth op (26 November 1943), had us airborne for eight hours 40 minutes – 'long stooge; hundreds of fighter flares, but only two sightings; our guns u/s'. Memory recalls one night (over Kassel, I think, 3 or 22 October 1943) when, after a rather zigzag dog-legged route into the target area, we approached what seemed to be an extraordinary wall of searchlights with no recourse other than to fly steadily into them while praying that that bluish master light with its lesser beams waving around it would keep moving (I believe that was the night we counted twelve bombers being killed as we flew our target run-up with bombs ready to fall from our open bay doors; that was something one didn't record in a log book!).

Memory tells me one thing about my thirty-four trips, the records often indicate something a bit different! For example, on our seventh op, on the night of 16–17 September 1943, when 419 Squadron was among those targeted for the marshalling yards at the Modane Pass. The route was surrounded by the Alps which, our Briefing Officer told us, would appear to be much higher than our flying height. He was correct! I recall it was a beautiful night as we flew through what we considered as wispy cloud over the mountains. But, only twenty minutes from our target, we experienced the formation of ice on our wings and propellors and in spite of opening our throttles we began to sink and lose precious height. A dark, dark valley seemed to be below us. I began a slow 180-degree turn, descending into it, hoping it to be open enough and that we would not accumulate more ice which, as a consequence, would cause a complete loss of flying stability. It was a frightening experience. Gradually, the ice began to melt and loosen and fly off our aircraft's surfaces and we were able to level-out at about 9,000 feet … too low to try another journey up and over those mountain peaks and, in any event, now too late to rejoin the bombing stream. So, in spite of the dangers of being a lone, easily discovered aircraft over

With Sgt Clayton towering some twenty-two feet above the ground, 15 Squadron's Stirling LS-W for Winston is depicted at Bourn in the autumn of 1943. In the course of 353 raids, 15 Squadron suffered the loss of ninety-one Stirlings, plus thirty-eight being destroyed in crashes, before converting to Lancasters in December 1943. The unit carried out more bombing raids (263) than any other Stirling squadron, and suffered, with 218 Squadron, the highest casualties in Stirling squadrons during the War. Coll. M.J. Peto.

enemy territory, we had no alternative but to set a course for home. On the way, we lightened our bomb load (mostly incendiaries) over some ships not far off the continental coastline and proceeded safely. Due to bad weather, our squadron's aircraft were diverted to land at airfields in southern England and remain there for two days. 419 (Moose) Squadron's Operational Record for that night agrees with my memory and my log-book entry!

Our sixteenth op, on the night of 29–30 December 1943, saw us over a Berlin target which, although obscured by 10/10ths cloud, was marked to the bomber force by pre-arranged identifiable coloured flares of the Pathfinders. The clouds, aglow from the fires and searchlights, silhouetted aircraft around and below us. There was a lot of flak and, suddenly, as we closed our bomb doors, a loud explosion just aft of our tailplane blew the control column out of my hands. Our trusty Halifax (JP151 'S') went into a vertical dive, gaining excessive speed and resisting my efforts to level-out. When I finally succeeded, I recall being fearful that we were then so low that we might be at the height of Berlin's barrage balloons. There was little we could do about that except try to gain back some altitude as we tried to follow the track back to base. The navigator, Fg Off Earl Albert, scooped what seemed to be pounds of nuts and bolts and dust from his table and the other crew members similarly reorganized themselves in their respective positions. We wondered if there was any vital damage, but we landed at base safely and ground inspection and definitive servicing proved otherwise. My Pilot's log book (and my memory) recounts this Berlin event, but the official record doesn't make note of it!

On 21 April 1944, our twenty-third op was mine-laying. In Brest harbour we were hit by predicted flak (it was said later that two of our aircraft ran in on track a few minutes early). We 'planted our vegetables' and climbed away. Then, whilst I quietly inspected a severe pain which all but immobilized my left arm, I asked Flight Engineer Frank Michael to hold the 'stick' for a moment or so. Finding nothing wet, such as blood!, on my elbow, I came to the conclusion that the flak explosion had knocked the 'funny bone' of my elbow on to the fuselage clip of my oxygen tube. Having caused some anxiety, I was almost too embarrassed to announce my discovery to the crew! We returned to base safely on three engines. My log book doesn't record other than being hit and the loss of the starboard outer engine. 424's Ops Record merely says 'Some opposition at the target but a good trip …'

Many battle-damaged bombers were glad to see an airfield on returning from a night raid on 'Fortress Europe'. This Stirling crash-landed at Ford airfield, probably in early 1944. Coll. Frank Pringle.

Proudly smiling over the award of his Wings, eighteen-year-old Sgt pilot David Leicester RAAF poses for the camera in May 1942. Two years later, at twenty, he was the youngest Squadron Leader in the Royal Australian Air Force serving with Bomber Command in the UK. Coll. David Leicester.

(Below) *Second to none. Plt Off Dave Leicester RAAF's Halifax II HR738 NP-Z 'Zombie's Zephyr' of 158 Squadron being topped up with 100 Octane at Lissett in July 1943. This aircraft completed thirty-two sorties before it was shot down by a night fighter and crashed at Dumberg, Germany on 31 August–1 September 1943 in the hands of Sgt W. Kidd. It was one of four squadron aircraft failing to return from this Berlin raid.* Coll. David Leicester.

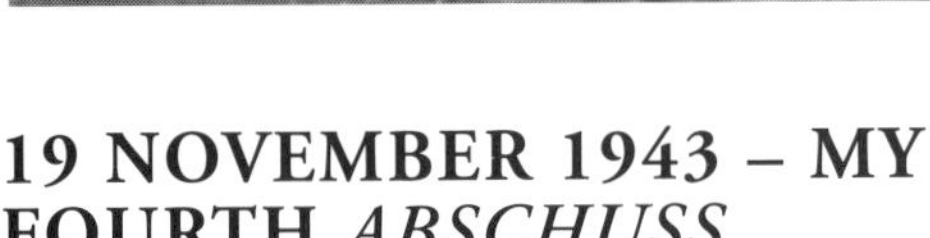

19 NOVEMBER 1943 – MY FOURTH *ABSCHUSS*

Although the introduction of 'window' during the Battle of Hamburg effectively rendered the elaborate *Himmelbett* GCI night-fighting system obsolete in the course of just one night, Kammhuber's brainchild was not abolished altogether. Freelance Wild and Tame Boar night-fighting had been hurriedly introduced as the standard night-fighting tactics, in an effort to overcome the devastating 'window' blow, but the traditional GCI method remained in full use along the coastlines of the Low Countries, north-west Germany and Denmark. *Himmelbett*-guided night fighters remained effectively employed against Bomber Command stragglers, RAF mine-laying aircraft and anti-shipping strike aircraft roaming the coastal convoy lanes. The following story by Lt Otto Fries, written in the third person, serves to illustrate the situation for *Nachtjagd* by the late autumn of 1943. Lt Fries had scored his first three victories during the chaotic months following the Hamburg disaster, and had recently been appointed Technical Officer of II./NJG1 at St Trond.

At briefing, the type of tactic to be used had been left open; should there be an attack, the fighter division wanted to leave the decision whether to use *Himmelbett* or *Zahme Sau* (Tame Boar) to the last moment – the development of the weather conditions would also partly influence this decision. At briefing, the weather conditions did not look particularly good: heavy haze, complete darkness, the cloud ceiling was at 200 metres, the tops of cloud unknown. The weather wizard assumed, however, that the clouds would extend up to at least 4,000 metres, probably with zones of icing. But during the night a considerable improvement in the weather could be expected, at the Channel coast the cloud was already broken with the ceiling at about 1,000 metres.

The approach of the bomber stream was reported shortly after briefing, but in the north, far outside of their operational sector, probably through that of the fourth *Gruppe* of their *Geschwader* which was stationed at Leeuwarden.

Towards 18.00 they went to cockpit readiness. At first they thought it was for the approach of another bomber stream, but then they were told by fighter division that it was for the return of the bombers which had flown in in the north.

They were always amazed that the British did not return the way they had come. The night fighter units who had borne the brunt of the approach were generally unable to combat the returning bombers in full strength. Some of the machines dropped out during the first attack and the returning aircraft had to be refuelled and possibly rearmed before they could be used again.

They had taken off at 18.16 in G9+EM, a machine borrowed from the 4th *Staffel*, with orders for a *Himmelbett* hunt in area 6C. Meanwhile the weather had improved, the cloud ceiling was a little over 500 metres, and their altimeter showed 1,000 metres as they emerged from the murk. They had noticed no icing. Above them a starry sky, completely free of cloud or haze.

Some ten minutes after take-off the radio operator had established contact with the operations room of 6A. They had been ordered to a height of 7,000 metres and they had been wandering around on varying headings, guided by *Würzburg Riese* blue. He was on a course of 090 when the controller came on the air: 'Adler 98 from Feuerwerk – Adler 98 from Feuerwerk – Kurier approaching – continue 80 – go to *Kirchturm* 50 – question Viktor.' 'Viktor-Viktor.' He pulled the throttles right back, turned propeller pitch to automatic and pushed the stick forward. The rate of descent indicator went to the bottom stop. He looked at the clock – it was 19.41. He raised his seat until his eyes and the reflector sight were on one level. He switched on the sight's light and adjusted its intensity. Then he turned over the gun switch; he was always surprised at the noise the repeating mechanisms of the guns made. The red indicators glowed: all guns cocked!

'Adler 98 from Feuerwerk – make *Salto Lisa* to 270 – go *Express* to *Kirchturm* 40 – question Viktor.' 'Viktor-Viktor – 270 and 40.' The altimeter showed 5,500 metres and as he turned off the autopilot, all he had to do was to slide his left hand down the control column. He flung the machine in a steep turn to port until the compass approached a course of 270. As he levelled out, the altimeter showed the required height – the machine had slid down over its left wing. He was very fast and could feel the vibration of the wings, so he opened the throttles only very slowly. He switched the autopilot back on, for now it was important to follow the instructions of the controller very precisely until either the radio operator had the enemy aircraft on his radar or he could see it himself.

'Adler 98 from Feuerwerk – make twice *Rolf*.' 'Viktor – twice *Rolf*.' He applied aileron and turned the course indicator on the stick until the pointer on the compass indicated 290. 'What does your magic lamp say, Fred, no blips yet?' 'None.' 'Adler 98 from Feuerwerk – make three times *Lisa*!' 'Viktor – three times *Lisa*.' He turned 30 degrees to port.

'I have a blip on the screen, distance 2,000 metres, slightly left, higher.' 'Feuerwerk from Adler 98 – contact with Emil-Emil!' 'Viktor – contact – good hunting – out.' He eased the aircraft up and turned off the autopilot. He did not require it any more for now his radio operator would guide him with the *Lichtenstein* radar set – it was really amazing that it was not getting any interference. 'A little higher, distance 1,200, closing fast.' He took off a little power. 'Higher, port a little, distance 500 – you are much too fast!' He pulled the throttles back to idling. He searched the horizon. 'Where is he exactly – what distance?' 'Slightly left, slightly higher – 300 metres.'

'There he is! A Short Stirling – on the port bow and just above the horizon!' He saw the tall rudder, the squat fuselage, the wings narrow like the back of a knife and on each side two engines with faintly glowing exhausts. He was much too fast for a sensible attempt. Although he had spontaneously attacked when much too fast the last time – and it had worked. But one could not be so lucky every time! And especially with the Short Stirling he had to be particularly careful. He remembered only too well his first meeting with this type of bomber. He had, without matching his speed, spontaneously attacked when much too fast - and it had all gone wrong! On no account should it be so tonight! He slunk off to the right and kicked alternately the rudder pedals without using aileron. Although it was unpleasant being pushed sideward right and left, it was an old proven method to 'tail away' speed.

There, suddenly the bomber dived away to starboard! He must have realized that a night fighter was clinging to his tail. There had been rumours that the British bombers had an accoustic warning device installed which sounded an alarm on being approached from the rear – but there was no real knowledge about it. As the Stirling dived away it went right through his sights. He could not resist and spontaneously pressed the trigger – it was like some reflex action. Only a short burst though. He had a feeling of having hit the bomber, but it showed no effect.

'Fred, note the time! It's 19.53.' He dived in order to keep the bomber above him, so he could keep the Stirling in sight against the lighter sky. 'Feuerwerk from Adler 98 – have made *Pauke-Pauke* – Kurier shows no effect – keeping contact.' 'Viktor-Viktor – *Weidmannsheil*!' The Stirling twisted like mad, down and up, did what they called a 'corkscrew'. He followed the corkscrew, but less violently. 'He'll soon have a bellyful of his twisting and turning! What, do you think, will the pilot now hear from his crew – especially from the rear gunner!' They called him 'sniper', or 'tail-end Charly', that man in the rear turret with his quadruple machine guns, and they treated him with respect.

Some minutes had passed since the first attack; the Stirling gradually ceased its twisting about and resumed its steady flight. They surely thought to have shaken him off. He was under the bomber to starboard, about 200 metres below and slightly behind. Slowly he rose, very slowly. When he was to starboard of the bomber, at almost the same height and about seventy

Safely back. A 432 Squadron Halifax III coming in for a three-point landing at Eastmoor in September 1944. Coll. John McQuiston DFC and bar.

metres behind, he kicked into the rudder and slunk to port. He gave a burst of fire as the starboard wing passed through his sights, then a second into the port one. Then he peeled off to port to get out of the rear gunner's arc of fire. The tracers flashed past his stern like maddened glow worms – like a fiery fan!

He saw a faint glow in the Stirling's port wing, which suddenly spread like an explosion and then encompassed the fuselage. Single parts detached themselves and flew off - were they crew members who had jumped? He could not be sure. Within seconds the whole bomber was aflame – it reared up, fell over on its port wing, then plunged down like a stone streaming flames like the tail of a comet. The flames disappeared in the clouds, which moments later were lit by a red flash, to be followed by a steady red glow. The clock showed 19.59. 'Feuerwerk from Adler 98 – report *Sieg-Heil* – note position – over!' 'Adler 98 from Feuerwerk – Viktor-Viktor – position noted – congratulations!' 'Thank you!'

A teleprinter message received by II./NJG1 at St Trond the following day revealed that Lt Fries' fourth victim had crashed near Horrues, 35km south-west of Brussels. The markings on the fuselage were still clear, reading JN F, and it was identified as Stirling LJ442 of 75 (RNZAF) Squadron. Four crew members were found dead at the crash site: Sgt M.I.R. Day (rear gunner), whose name was found on an envelope, Sgt S. Watkins, Flight Engineer, who was identified by his clothing card, and two others (later identified as Plt Off W.R. (Bill) Kell RNZAF, WOp, and Sgt W. 'Jack' Gilfillan, mid-upper gunner). The crew's bomb-aimer, Sgt Jack Hyde RNZAF, had baled out only moments before the aircraft exploded in mid-air, being injured on landing, and was taken to the *Luftwaffe* hospital in Brussels-St. Gilles. Flt Sgt N.N. Parker RAAF, the experienced captain, and his navigator, Sgt Robert E. Griffith, evaded capture after baling out of their crashing aircraft, and reached England early in the following year. Parker subsequently volunteered for the Pathfinder Force and survived another fifty operations, acting on some of them as Master Bomber.

TOUR IN STIRLINGS

Berlin proved a costly target for the Short Stirling. On 23–24 August 1943, the opening raid of the Battle of Berlin, sixteen out of 124 participating Stirlings were lost; a week later seventeen out of 106 failed to return from the 'Big City'. At losses averaging 10 per cent on deep penetration raids, it would be a matter of only weeks before the whole of the existing Stirling force would be wiped out.

Whilst the Pathfinders were re-equipped with a better type of H2S for more accurate target marking during September and October 1943, the Big City was not sought after by Harris's heavies. Even so, over the period August to mid-November 1943, Stirling losses averaged 6.4 per cent, forcing Harris to withdraw the oldest of his four-engined bombers from the main offensive at the end of November. Fg Off Harry Barker, bomb-aimer in 218 and 623 Squadrons, was one of those few fortunate Stirling aircrew to complete a tour of operations between May 1943 and July 1944.

We all knew that in 1943 the average 'life' of a crew was ten operations, so you can imagine that everyone was a bit jumpy at their thirteenth! If you really began to analyse it the options open to us were limited. We had to consider the following: (1) We had all volunteered to do the job. (2) We all wanted to hit back at the enemy, who were attacking London, Coventry, Liverpool and so on. (3) The camaraderie was so strong on the squadron that no one would seriously consider letting his friends down. (4) There was a keen determination to achieve thirty ops and complete the tour. (5) The alternative was refusal – followed by a court martial and the awful consequences. (6) The reward on returning from an op was a breakfast of bacon and eggs, a luxury only available to aircrews.

When you take this lot into account, together with the youthful confidence that believed that 'only other crews get shot down', you may understand how we felt about the incredible risks we were taking. It is similar to the attitude of cigarette smokers who are all convinced that it is only other people who get lung cancer!

In general the morale of aircrews was good. It was easier for the young, unmarried and unattached men to cope than it was for those with wives, children or steady girlfriends. One could cope with the prospect of death if this did not result in misery and hardship for others. This inevitably caused some differences in attitude to the War and the way we behaved under fighting conditions. I am not saying that the men with family commitments were any less dedicated to the job, but I believe they were under much greater strain than many of the rest of us.

We did tend to 'let ourselves go' when off duty. We drank a great deal of beer and used any excuse for a party (commonly described as a 'piss up') either in the mess or at a local pub. We got to know the locals who were always friendly and understanding. Some shared their Sunday dinners with us, and of course there were the girls …

Life on the squadron was a mixture of fun, laughter, friendship, excitement and hell just around the corner. In the officers' mess we had a very high standard of living; the food was very good. Sleeping quarters were comfortable and we had either a batwoman or batman to look after us, cleaning shoes, brass buttons, pressing uniforms and making beds. I usually had a cup of tea brought to me in bed every morning!

I am one of the few who survived and it seems dreadful to admit that I enjoyed the life on the squadron. The only way I can admit this is in the belief that my friends who were lost also shared the good side of this battle for survival. That is how we saw it. The tragedy was in fact that so many did not survive.

OPERATIONAL DIFFERENCES BETWEEN THE HALIFAX AND THE LANCASTER

The withdrawal of the Short Stirling from the Battle of Berlin left Bomber Command with two types of four-engined aircraft to carry on the night-bombing offensive. The famous Lancaster has gone down in history as the symbol of the Command's might, whereas the Halifax is usually cast in the role of the ugly sister. The truth is that the Lancaster could fly farther and carry a greater bomb-load, but the Halifax was more rugged and a faster aircraft with a better rate of climb, to mention but a few of the differences between the two aircraft. Australian L. David Leicester flew twenty-seven ops in Halifax Is and IIs with 158 Squadron, plus four more in Halifax IIIs with 640 to round up his first tour in late March 1944. He then volunteered for the Pathfinders, joining 35 PFF Squadron and completing another tour of thirty-seven ops in Lancasters over the following eight months, nine as a Master Bomber. He rose from Sgt Plt to Sqn Ldr in just seventeen months, being awarded a DFC and Bar, and at twenty years of age was the youngest Squadron Leader in Bomber Command. David is therefore well qualified to comment on the following.

Over the years since the end of the War, I have had many discussions and arguments (sometimes heated) on this very subject with ex-pilots, but I always have great difficulty convincing them of my preference for the Halifax. I readily concede that, from an economic point of view, the Lancaster was superior as it took a bigger bomb-load a further distance and used less fuel, and it was only natural, therefore, that it should be preferred by Bomber Command and the Air Ministry, but for flying capabilities when fully loaded (bombs on) at height (approximately 18–20,000ft) over enemy territory and when attacked, I would prefer the Halifax. Of the two aircraft, the Lancaster was possibly the easiest to fly in terms of pilot handling, as it was slower to the pilot's control actions but, for an evasive action or corkscrew manoeuvre, I preferred the Halifax as it responded to control more quickly and more viciously when required to get me out of trouble and to escape flak, fighters and searchlights, and that was extremely important when being attacked.

It would be hard to say which of the two aircraft took more punishment from German defences, possibly the Lanc because it was used in greater numbers, but, with the great amount of German flak and fighters, it was almost impossible for an aircraft to avoid damage of some description, especially with shrapnel holes and so on. Perhaps the greatest danger was the risk of having control cables hit and severed by flying pieces of flak, and, of course, the risk of having the glycol tank of the Merlins holed, thus causing the engine to overheat. It was often referred to, jokingly or facetiously, that if an aircraft returned undamaged and on four engines there was doubt as to whether the crew had been to a specific target.

When the two aircraft were designed I do not think the designers had crew comfort in mind but, being wartime, the need was for additional bomb-loads but I do not recall being troubled by discomfort. The famous, or infamous, main spar of the Lanc was always troublesome to negotiate with equipment (parachutes for example) but did not present a real problem. As far as I can recall there were never any complaints from other crew members, even though their compartments, especially the navigator and wireless op, were very cramped.

It has been recorded that because of the bad siting of the escape hatches on the Lancaster, chances of survival in the Halifax were much better. Per seven-man crew, 1.3 survived escaping from the Lanc and 2.45 from the Halifax. That, of course, was very important, and no doubt many lives were saved on that factor alone. In both aircraft armour plating was removed, except for that behind the pilot's head, to allow for a greater bomb-load. I know that I was satisfied with the armament protection available.

Whenever Air Force pilots were sent to an HCU to be trained on four-engined aircraft, they would invariably convert on a Halifax I or II which had already completed dozens of ops and was therefore, more or less, almost ready to be put out of service. The pilot would then be posted to a Lancaster squadron and hence fly a near-as-new-Lancaster. To compare the two aircraft under those circumstances was grossly unfair to the flying capabilities of the Halifax.

The 'Hally' III, with its Taurus radial engines, was superb, although I had great admiration for the Rolls-Royce Merlins as well. To compare the performance on ops between the Merlin and the Taurus is difficult. The Merlin was fantastic but had its faults. It was dangerous for aircrews because the exhaust pipes of each engine became red hot and were therefore like beacons in the sky, thus allowing the keen sharp eyes of the German night fighter pilots to clearly see each aircraft (which were otherwise blacked out). Being liquid-cooled, the Merlin engines were subject to overheating and eventual feathering of the props if the glycol tank was holed. Many aircraft returned with engine failure simply because of that fact alone. The Taurus radial engine, being air-cooled, was not subject to similar damage. Perhaps the radials were most satisfactory, but why were more radials not used – the RAF's preference seemed to be for the Merlins. I cannot recall consciously knowing any difference in speed between the Lancaster and the Halifax, especially with the Merlins, but suspect speeds with the radials would be slightly faster.

To sum it up: my vote is for the Halifax. I understand the Halifax I with its triangular fins and rudders was not satisfactory for many reasons, but once the square fins and rudders were designed, it was terrific and flew beautifully. It was my privilege and pleasure to fly the Halifax Is, IIs and IIIs and found all of them to be just great – the best in fact – and I will never change my mind and will never be convinced there was a better four-engined bomber.

NIGHTMARE: COLLISION

Statistics have never been compiled to establish how many Bomber Command aircraft were destroyed in operational collisions during the War, although it is generally accepted that relatively few bombers were lost that way. Still, many aircrew in Bomber Command were nervous about collisions with other aircraft in the enormous bomber streams. This nightmare came true for Plt Off John C. Adams RAAF, pilot, and his 50 Squadron crew on 26–27 November 1943. To the crew's dismay, their regular Lancaster III DV368 S-Sugar

(Right) *Lancaster III DV178 VN-N of 50 Squadron came to grief in the shallow waters of Wilhelmshaven Bay after colliding with another Lancaster on the 26–27 November 1943 Berlin raid. German soldiers are inspecting the wreckage the next day.* Coll. Hille van Dieren.

Plt Off John C. Adams RAAF was left sitting looking into a 200mph –40°C gale after colliding with another Lancaster on 26–27 November 1943. This close-up clearly shows the extent of the damage inflicted by the offending bomber's right tail fin to the cockpit area of DV178. Coll. Hille van Dieren.

was unserviceable, and they had to take the squadron 'jinx' DV178 N-Nuts to Berlin instead. For this raid, Plt Off Adams took on board Flt Sgt Thomas, a Gunnery School instructor who needed to experience an operation.

> The night of 26 November was a particularly cold one. A cold front had come down from the North Atlantic. It was just after the shortest day of the year and Skellingthorpe was fairly dark by about 4.30 in the evening. However, at briefing we were told that we could expect reasonably clear conditions over the target but to conserve our fuel as we might find ourselves being diverted to another airfield on our return. Our route was to take us into Germany, south of the heavily defended Ruhr Valley. This route was chosen in the hope that the defences would expect an attack on one of the cities near to our track and that they would assemble their night fighters south of the route followed by our main force. The route home was to be directly west, taking us out over northern Germany and across Holland.
>
> All the 50 Squadron Lancasters were loaded to an all-up weight of 66,000lb. This consisted of around 2,100 gallons of fuel and 10,000lb of bombs – a 4,000lb 'cookie' and the balance incendiaries. We were off the ground after using the full length of the runway at 17.15. By this time it was quite dark and overcast. We were not too familiar with the aircraft and so I had Tom Midgely our Flight Engineer pay particular attention to the engine temperatures. Sure enough, by the time we were well clear of the ground, they were on their limits. I eased off the throttles while Tom reduced the engine revolutions to normal climb/cruise settings and settled down to see if the temperatures would come down. They remained fairly high but just within their operating limits and we resigned ourselves to a long period of slow climbing.

By the time we reached 10,000 feet my windshield was iced up and it took a constant effort on Tom Midgely's part to keep it clear enough for me to see to fly the aircraft. This meant that I was flying on instruments for most of the journey. This was no real problem but it was always nice to be able to look out and see some stars on the horizon. Tom began by trying to wipe the ice off the screen with a rag but he seemed to be making very little progress. He then came up with the idea that he could clear the icing and stop it by using Glycol anti-freeze. This worked to some extent but he left the glass badly smeared. I just had to carry on with a semi-opaque windscreen. It was back to flying on instruments and I flew the whole way from then on as though the aircraft was in cloud. This was a particularly cold spell of weather and when we had reached 18,000 feet the outside temperature gauge was showing –40°C.

Our route took us in over northern France and when we headed east our course took us in the general direction of Frankfurt. This city had been attacked the night before and I think it was intended that the enemy should anticipate a follow-up raid. We only saw one aircraft shot down in that area.

We finally arrived at our turning point south of the Big City and made our bombing run on the flares which the Pathfinders had dropped. Our run-in to the target was without incident and we completed it without any trouble. We bombed at about 21.20. It was clear over the city, the searchlights were very active and there was a very heavy barrage of flak at about our level. Our luck held and we escaped being coned in the lights and suffered no damage from the flak. This was consistent with our luck so far; we had never had a bullet hole or a flak hole on any of our operations.

I could only get a general idea of the success of the raid because of my restricted vision. I thought that it had not been a particularly successful attack as, to me, it appeared scattered and lacking the tight concentration we wanted. After we had unloaded our bombs we continued north for a few minutes to clear the defences of the city and then turned for home. I asked Flt Sgt Thomas, our passenger, if he had had a good view of the raid and he said that he had and that he thought that it was a spectacular sight. I had been talking to Bill (Sgt W.J. Ward, bomb-aimer) as he took me in on the bombing run. Jimmy (Sgt J. Rawcliffe, navigator) had given me the course to fly on our return to base. I checked with the gunners and they both reported that they were all right. Cyril (Sgt C.W. Billet) had been quiet down in the rear turret and George (Sgt G.M. Hastie) in his mid-upper turret, as usual, had very little to say. I cautioned them both to keep a good look out for other Lancs, not just night fighters, because we were still in the most concentrated part of the bomber stream. George said that he could see a Lancaster on the right side and behind us.

One hazy day in late 1943, Bf 110 G-4s G9+DK (left) and G9+BB of II./NJG1 are depicted whilst on a formation flight. The aircraft are equipped with both the Lichtenstein *BC and the SN-2 radars, and with auxiliary underwing tanks for* Zahme Sau *(Tame Boar) operations.*
Coll. Otto Fries.

Just then, it happened. There was a crash and the perspex above my head and the windscreen disappeared. I was left sitting into a 200-mile-an-hour, –40°C wind. The aircraft lurched down to the left, the left inboard engine was screaming with the rev counter going off the dial. The outer rev counter was fluctuating wildly. I automatically applied full right rudder and brought it back to straight and level and somewhere near the course we had been flying. (I have since concluded that we were hit by the rear of the other Lancaster. Its right tailfin took out the perspex above my head and demolished the windscreen. Its tail-wheel hit our inboard propellor very hard, breaking up the reduction gears and housing, while its left tailfin came in contact with our outboard propellor.)

As I was getting the Lancaster back under control I was aware that someone had brushed past me and dived down into Bill's bomb-aimer compartment which was also the forward escape hatch. Tom showed a lot of presence of mind and immediately shut down the inboard engine and tried to feather its propellor. It continued to windmill. The reduction gears and their housing had been broken. It was throwing off sparks but luckily there was no fire. We had to feather the outboard engine. When it stopped we could see that the propellor tips had been badly bent. The tips of all three blades were bent almost at right angles. This left us with two engines. I applied full right trim and continued to fly on the power from the two starboard engines. I then had time to realize that my face felt frozen and that I had some difficulty seeing. My goggles were hanging down the back of my helmet. With Tom's help, I put them on and found I was better able to cope with the icy blast of wind. At least I could see. At that height it was impossible to maintain height on two engines, especially with one propellor windmilling, so I decided to lose a few thousand feet in the hope that the cold at lower levels would be less severe. The wind was ripping straight into the flight deck and down the fuselage. It had blown all the charts off Jimmy's navigation table and they were scattered about somewhere in the rear section.

It was now time to take stock of our situation. I checked with the gunners and they told me they were all right. George said 'That was close!' The tail of the other Lancaster had only just missed him. Doc Crawford (Flt Sgt D.R. Crawford RAAF), the wireless operator, was shaken by the experience. However, by this time he was checking that he still had his radio aerials. Flt Sgt Thomas was still with us, just wondering what would happen next. Then the conversation on the intercom went like this: 'Where's Jimmy?' Bill: 'He's down here. I think he's passed out!' 'He probably needs oxygen. Connect him to your spare outlet and plug him in to the intercom.' 'OK Skipper, he's plugged in.' Then a little later: 'I think he's coming around.' 'Jimmy, can you hear me?' A very groggy voice said 'I'm here Skipper.' 'Jimmy, we're still flying and we aren't bailing out yet. You'd better get back up here, I'll need a new course to fly soon.' Then to Doc I said 'Doc, send a message to base telling them that we bombed the target, we have had a collision with another Lancaster and lost two engines and we are losing height.'

When Jimmy returned to his navigation table he found that all of his charts had disappeared. They had been blown down into the back of the fuselage. I continued to fly the original course allowing for the aircraft 'crabbing' a few degrees sideways because all the power was coming from one side. I was using full power on the two starboard engines and I began to worry about whether we would use up all our fuel before we got back to England. In addition to worrying about the fuel, I was concerned that those old suspect Merlins might overheat and fail us. Tom began to transfer fuel from the tanks in the port wing to replace what we were using from the other side.

We were down to about ten thousand feet when, a long way ahead, we saw that the Pathfinders had dropped some track markers. They seemed to me to be far too far north of where they should have been. I discussed this with Jimmy and he agreed with me – they were a few miles north of where we thought they should have been. This was a great concern to me and I had to make up my mind whether to acccept that they had been dropped in the correct location or to continue on the heading we had been flying. We were virtually without navigation ourselves, so it seemed the best thing to assume that PFF were right and we had drifted well to the south. We accordingly headed in the direction where we had seen the markers.

We were still losing height and we had descended to five thousand feet. I felt it was decision time. We would either bale out or try to get old 'N' to carry us home to England. At about this time the windmilling port inner propellor did the right thing – it fell off! This had the effect of reducing the drag on the left side. It was just a little easier to hold our course without it and we seemed to lose height more slowly. It was obvious to me that we wouldn't make it on two engines so I suggested to Tom that we should start up the outboard engine and see what happened. To our surprise, it started and ran almost normally. There was some vibration from the unevenly bent propellor tips, but it was contributing some power – probably a bit better than half of normal.

We had a conference over the intercom – I asked the crew if they wanted to bale out. I explained that we were a long way behind the rest of the bomber force and that we would be on our own for much of the trip home. They all said they would rather stay with the aircraft. I've always admired them for the way they came to that decision. I told Doc to send to base that we had restarted the outboard engine, that we were maintaining height and that we were trying to make it back to base.

Unfortunately, from there on things went badly wrong. We should have backed our own judgement and continued on our original course instead of heading north. Jim was unable to find his charts and as he had no other means of determining our position, we were virtually without a navigator. I talked our situation over with him and we concluded that the best course was to get out of enemy territory as soon as possible. We decided to head in a north-westerly direction which would take us out over the coast to the North Sea. Once over the sea, the plan was to head due west and when we were near to England, Doc would get us a course to steer for base.

We knew that the coast of Germany was defended by a lot of light anti-aircraft guns so it would be too dangerous to cross it at five thousand feet. We couldn't climb to a safer height so the only alternative was to cross it as low as we dared. This would give the gunners on the ground the minimum time to fire at us. Of course the wind was still roaring into the cockpit and even with glasses I couldn't see very much. Bill was keeping a good look-out down in the nose, so to some extent he was the eyes of the aircraft. I just kept flying on instruments. When we judged that we should have been near to the coast, I came down to about 400 feet which I thought was about as low as it was safe to fly. Actually the barometric pressure over Germany varied from that over England so that the altimeter was at least 200 feet out. We were flying a lot lower than I thought.

Suddenly Bill said that he had seen a building pass only just below us. The next moment he said that we were over water. I presumed that we had crossed the coast and started to make a turn to the right which would take us straight out to sea. Just then we were caught in a searchlight from off to our right. I instinctively started to turn away from it. This was against the side where we had very little power and we lost some more height – I must have overbanked. Bill shouted 'Look out Johnny!'

Before I could react to his warning, we hit the water. Old 'N' bounced once, spun half round and hit the water again, breaking off the rear section of the fuselage. In one way we were lucky – we'd landed in relatively shallow water and the body of the Lancaster sat on the bottom with about a third of the fuselage out of the water. This meant that six of us were able to escape through the flight deck escape hatch out on to the right wing where the rubber dinghy had emerged automatically and was waiting for us. Bill must have been knocked out when we hit the water and he did not appear. Cyril was in the broken-off rear section, and to get out of his turret he had rotated it and baled out backwards into the water.

Unfortunately, there was a strong current running which swept Cyril away from the aircraft. The six survivors tried to paddle after him in their dinghy, but it was in vain. In an effort to mobilize German help searching for his rear gunner, John Adams fired two flares from a Verey pistol which he had found in the dinghy. An enemy launch soon arrived from Wilhelmshaven Bay, where the Lancaster had come to grief, but by then it was too late for Cyril, who had drowned. Both he and Sgt Billett were initially buried in Wilhelmshaven, and after the War were laid to rest in Sage and Becklingen respectively.

From a total force of 443 Lancasters and seven Mosquitoes, twenty-nine Lancasters were lost on 26–27 November 1943 Berlin raid, five of which have been identified as victims of night fighters, and seventeen more crashed in England. It had been a costly night for Bomber Command, with nine Halifaxes failing to return from a diversionary 178-aircraft-strong raid on Frankfurt, plus Stirling III EF511 of 90 Squadron crashing on return from a gardening trip to the Frisian Islands. Plt Off John Adams concludes: 'We had come to the end of our career as members of 50 Squadron. I had made a total of sixteen sorties while, as a crew, we had attacked the enemy fifteen times. We were just half way through our first tour – a time when I felt that we had at last become competent at our job. We were sad at losing two good friends and bitterly disappointed to finish as prisoners of war because of a collision with one of our own aircraft.'

THE BATTLE OF BERLIN – A SENIOR FIGHTER CONTROLLER'S VIEW

The first period in the history of German nightfighting, under the aegis of General Kammhuber, was characterized by systematic development of the *Himmelbett Nachtjagd* along preconceived lines. It was a period of mounting success against a still relatively limited bomber offensive. This ended abruptly when the clouds of 'window' rained down for the first time during the Battle of Hamburg, swamping the German radars with false echoes. *Nachtjagd* now entered a new era, in which General Schmid held the reins. The period of September 1943 until the end of the War was typified by every kind of makeshift and expedient being utilized to overcome the deficiencies of a machine which had been thrown out of gear by British countermeasures.

From the autumn of 1943, *Nachtjagd* fought an uphill struggle – and not only the aircrew, but also the men on the ground. It was of paramount importance for the German ground controllers to identify Bomber Command's main route and target in the earliest stages of a raid, in order to infiltrate the Tame Boars into the inbound bomber stream, and to be able to assemble the Wild Boar units over the intended targets before the bombers arrived there. During interrogation of some of the leading German fighter controllers immediately after the end of the War, it was clearly established that Bomber Command's effective use of ('window') spoof raiding broke the morale of the German ground controllers. Obtaining a true picture of the air situation in the chaotic conditions after the Battle of Hamburg was one of the most exciting and difficult functions within *Nachtjagd*, and the ground controllers were usually reduced to wrecks, both mentally and physically, after one night's duty in the operations room.

One of the men serving in the centre of *Nachtjagd*'s giant ground controlling 'spider's web' during the Battle of Berlin was Oberst Wolfgang Falck. The 'Founding Father' of *Nachtjagd*, Wolf Falck had commanded NJG1 until 30 June 1943, when he was called to duty in various organizational tasks in the arm. When Bomber Command started pounding the Reich's capital in the autumn of 1943, Oberst Falck was appointed 'Ia Flieg' (senior fighter controller) in *Luftflotte* Reich, Germany's main air defence organization, a position he held throughout the battle.

The *Luftflotte* (Air Fleet) Reich was responsible for the day and night air defence of the entire Reich, amongst others for the flak and the day and night fighters. Headquarters were at first at the Reichssportfeld, the former site of the Olympic Games of

1936, with the operations room in a bunker, then it was transferred to Berlin-Wannsee, to the former Air-Raid Defence School, and the operations room was in a specially constructed new bunker.

The next in rank below the Commander of the Air Fleet was the Chief of Staff, a Lieutenant General; below him the Ia Flak and the Ia Flieg, both Staff Colonels. Normally there is only one Ia in a staff. But owing to the size of the *Luftflotte* Reich there had to be a division between the flak and the fighter units. From the autumn of 1943 I was Ia Flieg at the *Luftflotte* Reich and responsible for the day and night operations of the fighter units.

The operations room was the heart of operational control. Here all the decisions were made, the operations ordered and their progress monitored. Also, an essential task of this centre was to maintain liaison with the flak divisions, the fighter divisions, industry, the railways, hospitals, the *Gauleiter* (provincial governors), the Organization Todt (labour corps), the *Luftwaffe* construction battalions, the Red Cross, the fire brigades, and all organizations responsible for the repair of damage and assistance to the civilian population.

The daily routine began with a situation briefing during the late morning, usually attended by

Spiders in their web. With the change from close-controlled Himmelbett *to broadcast-controlled Wild and Tame Boar night-fighting in the summer of 1943, the night air battles over the Third Reich were directed from five huge* Divisionsgefechtsstände *or Divisional Battle Command posts positioned in Holland, France and Germany. The central HQ during the Battle of Berlin, depicted here, was the Battle Room of* Luftflotte *Reich in Berlin-Wannsee. Generalmajor Andreas Nielsen, Chief of Staff of* Luftflotte *Reich and the officer in overall control (right) and Oberst Wolf Falck, Senior Operations Officer, responsible for the deployment of all operational* Nachtjagd *units (left), keep a close eye on the development of a Bomber Command raid during the Battle of Berlin. Note the brightly painted telephone in front of Falck, which was his 'Hot Line' with Göring.* Coll. Wolf Falck.

(Left) *Together with Oblt Wever, one of his aides and the son of General Walter Wever, the first* Luftwaffe *chief of the General Staff who was killed in a flying accident in 1936, Oberst Falck is tracking the progress of the bomber stream and the positions of his own* Nachtjagd *units in the Battle Room of* Luftflotte *Reich in Berlin-Wannsee, 1943–44. Generalleutnant Nielsen, right, is concentrating on the giant map of the Third Reich on which the movements of all attacking RAF forces (in red dots) and the* Nachtjagd *units (in blue dots) are projected, whilst liaison officers are seen in their 'Reporting Boxes' in the background. These latter men kept in constant touch with all official bodies affected by a Bomber Command raid.* Coll. Wolf Falck.

(Left) *Fw Friedrich Ostheimer, Bordfunker, taken in 1943. Until the death of his pilot and Kommodore of NJG2, Major Prinz Zu Sayn-Wittgenstein on 21–22 January 1944, Friedrich survived some three months of operational flying in Wittgenstein's crew. During this period he participated in the destruction of sixteen RAF heavies.* Coll. Friedrich Ostheimer.

Eichenlaubträger Major Prinz zu Sayn-Wittgenstein enjoys a coffee at the open fireplace in his bungalow at Deelen, Holland. This photo was taken shortly before he was killed in action east of Magdeburg on 21–22 January 1944. In the hours before he died, Wittgenstein claimed five Viermots *to become the top-scoring night fighter pilot ever with eighty-three confirmed kills in just over 1½ years of action, including sixty RAF bombers.* Coll. Friedrich Ostheimer.

the Commander, the Chief of Staff and all departmental chiefs. So also on the morning of 23 November 1943. During the previous night the RAF had made its heaviest attack so far on a target in Germany and the target had been Berlin. Berlin was the heart of the Reich: seat of the government, concentration of industry, traffic and culture, and control point of the Party. For the Allies, the crippling of this centre was a matter of prestige. From our point of view the weather had been bad, allowing only radar-controlled firing by the flak and severely limiting the use of night fighters. Berlin had become an inferno. Entire sections of the city were destroyed, with huge fires everywhere, especially in the residential areas. For the RAF it was a success, for us a bitter night. In the morning I myself had gone into town in order to get an impression of the extent of damage, fires and casualties amongst the civilian population. It was a dreadful sight to see.

The briefing began with the Ic reporting the events of the past night: the damage, losses, own operations and successes. There was then usually a discussion to determine what could be learned from these experiences, what improvements could be made and what additional preventive means might be employed. Next, the meteorologist gave a report of the current weather situation over England, so far as it was known to us, and for the coming night over Germany. This would give us operations officers the initial considerations of which targets the RAF might choose for the coming night.

The *Luftflotte* had of course a large establishment for monitoring enemy radio traffic. We also knew where the individual units were stationed and their call-signs. All bomber units which were to operate during the coming night tuned their radio sets in the course of the afternoon. From that, the monitoring station was able to inform us which units were to operate at night. From this, and linked with the weather situation, it was possible to predict already in the afternoon which areas would be attacked.

Having considered all aspects we decided that the attack would again be on northern Germany and probably again on Berlin, in order to cause further damage and to interfere with clearance and fire-fighting.

These considerations led to night fighter units being transferred from southern Germany to the north, to airfields north and west of Berlin, in order to set up some sort of barrier to approaching formations. At the same time all command centres, authorities and organizations were alerted, construction units moved, the railways warned, industry informed and so on. Liaison officers were detailed for all these communications who, later on during operations, sat behind me maintaining contact with their particular departments whilst having an excellent view of the huge map showing the movements of the attacking forces as well as those of our own units.

The main operations room was manned fully in the late afternoon with tense expectations. The *Luftwaffe* auxiliaries sat behind the map with their pencil-light projectors. Each girl received data of friendly and enemy movements from a ground radar station which was then shown on a huge map of the Reich by means of a pencil-light projector, showing red dots for enemy aircraft and blue ones for our own. That provided a clear picture of the situation for all present. In front of me, as operations officer, were the liaison officers for the individual fighter divisions, to the left the meteorologists and behind me the row of liaison officers as already described, and the boxes of the contact men to the various agencies and organizations, similar to today's reporters at sporting events. Beside me were the places for the Commander and the Chief of Staff. Both their telephones were connected so that they were able to listen in to any conversations conducted by me. At a prominent place on my desk there was another, special telephone: it was the 'hot line' direct to Göring, irrespective of where he might be at the time. This telephone was in the same light colour as Göring's uniform, with some thin gold lines, and over it all a glass cover with a light which glowed whenever Göring called me or I him. Its purpose: to indicate to all present that there must be absolute quiet in order not to disturb the conversation.

Beside my desk with all the maps and references stood an assisting officer of my staff, as well as a navigator, whose task was to continuously calculate the courses and speeds of both the approaching enemy and our own formations. Fully staffed we were able to observe, soon after they had taken off, the bomber formations assembling and then setting course. Most of the approaches were across the North Sea and Jutland to the Kattegat, then on a southerly course to Berlin.

And so too it was this time and the facts confirmed our assumptions. But it was important that we should not allow ourselves to be deflected from the main objective through diversionary attacks on secondary targets. Tensely the entire complement of the operations room now watched the development of things. Göring, who had already had himself informed about the situation and the measures taken during the late afternoon, now, as the bomber stream approached, called ever more frequently about the issued orders and measures taken.

Once it had become fairly clear that Berlin was the probable target, our warnings went out to all concerned, including the hospitals to enable them to get their patients into the air-raid shelters in time, the railways to halt their trains, for industry to take appropriate measures and so on.

Meanwhile, the night fighter units had been assigned their radio beacons where they were to assemble to make their attacks in good time. Orders for take-off were accordingly given, not

Berlin Raider. At 16.40 on 26 November 1943, 166 Squadron's W/O J.E. Thomas DFC lifted his heavily loaded Lancaster III DV247 AS-F off Kirmington's runway for a Berlin raid. It was the crew's twentieth trip. The outward trip was uneventful, but over the Big City they were caught in search-lights, a very nerve-wracking experience. By using all his skill, the pilot was able to climb to about 28,000 feet and got away from the beams unscathed. However, on their way back and approaching the German-Dutch border, an unseen Bf 110 suddenly riddled DV247 with cannon fire. The bomb-aimer, Sgt Jimmy Edwards, was badly wounded with part of his left hand shot away and with a gaping wound in his left thigh. Sgt W. O'Malley's voice announced over the intercom that he was trapped in his rear turret, whereupon Sgt A.V. Collins DFM immediately replied that he was going to help his mate. W/O Thomas shouted that he was unable to hold the aircraft much longer, as it was well and truly disabled, and gave the order to bale out. Five men successfully jumped, but the two gunners didn't get out and were killed in the aircraft when it crashed; both rest in the Reichswald War Cemetery. The crew's navigator, Sgt Bill Bell, made three attempts to escape from various PoW camps during 1944, but was caught each time after being on the loose for a few days. Here is the crew depicted in happier days at Kirmington. Coll. Bill Bell, via Eric Watson.

too early in order not to waste flying time which would later be badly needed, but in no case too late for meeting the attackers before the target to prevent them from dropping their bombs. Once the order had been given, fate took its course and everyone stared tensely at the huge situation map. And then hell broke loose. The first bombs were dropped, the first damage and losses, but also the first shootings down were reported. All assisting forces were brought closer to Berlin to be ready to go into action the moment the attack was over. In between were calls from Göring, possibly Goebbels, Berlin authorities, army, Party and various organizations and the police. There was no hectic activity in the operations room, but full concentration. Each one there knew his responsibilities and gave his best.

After a while, but much too long a time!, there were only sporadic bombs, the fire of the flak decreased, the night fighters reported that there was barely any activity left over Berlin, that they would take up the pursuit of the bombers and land at one of the western airfields, which were immediately informed by us.

Now came the agonizing calm after the storm. All rescue services were sent into Berlin to save what there was left to save. Then reports from the flak about successes and losses came in. And finally the landing reports from the night fighter units and their reports of successes and losses. But then there was the great anxiety about the night fighter crews who had not yet reported in. Was the crew lost, had they made an emergency landing somewhere, or had they baled out and not been able to report in yet? Some anxious hours, and at the operations room of the First Fighter Division, to which I had previously belonged, the gramophone played the song *Komm Zurück* ('Come Back') until certainty had been reached about the fate of the crews or no hope remained.

We of the operations room remained together for a long time and discussed the happenings in detail, until we too retired to our quarters in the early hours of the morning, tired out and fatigued.

CHAPTER 4

1944

Obgefr Gerhard Wollnik, who served as air gunner in the crew of Hptm Heinz Reschke, Kommandeur of I./NJG6 between 19 February and 24 April 1944, and contributed to the destruction of four Lancasters during February and March 1944. Coll. Gerhard Wollnik.

THE *ABSCHUSS* WHICH WAS IDENTIFIED IN THE AIR

With a view to establishing a better defence of the Reich's capital city, which was suffering from Bomber Command's onslaught during the winter of 1943–44, detachments of the 1st and 2nd *Gruppen* of NJG6 were shifted from Mainz-Finthen and Schleissheim airfields to Stendal on 16 and 17 February 1944, where they reinforced NJG5. Earlier that month, Obgefr Gerhard Wollnik (AG) had joined the crew of Hptm Heinz Reschke, Kommandeur of I./NJG6, and his Bordfunker, Uffz Josef Fischer. During the ensuing months they scored four Lancaster *Abschüsse*, plus one damaged: 19–20 February (a 460 (RAAF) Squadron aircraft at 03.55, crashed north of Torgau near Jessen); 25–26 February (possibly JB742 of 460 (RAAF) Squadron, Flt Sgt R.C. Martin RAAF and crew all killed, crashed near Stetten to the west of Rottweil, at 00.27); 1–2 March (probably 44 Squadron's ND566 of Plt Off Oakley and crew, one man killed and six PoW, crashed 30km south of Reutlingen at 03.30); 15–16 March (at Jussy near Belfort, at 22.32), and finally a Lancaster claimed damaged on the night of 30 March 1944. Gerhard vividly recalls his first *Abschuss* in Hptm Reschke's crew, on 19–20 February 1944:

> At midnight on 20 February 1944, strong RAF bomber formations (an estimated 300 aircraft) were reported approaching the German Bight and Jütland, and heading on an attacking course towards Berlin and Leipzig. After a long

spell of cockpit readiness, we were scrambled at 01.55 in our Me 110 G-4, coded 2Z+KK, for a Wild Boar mission over the western approaches of Berlin. Visibility at our combat height of 4,500 metres was good, and we experienced no weather problems.

We approached several British bombers, but never succeeded in getting into a good attacking position. At last, our Bordfunker Unteroffizier Fischer identified a clear blip from an enemy bomber on his SN-2 radar set. It flew at our height and some 300 metres in front of us; we could already feel the turbulence from its propellers. Slowly, we approached the enemy aircraft. We thought it was a Lancaster, judging from its green exhaust flames which were clearly visible. If it were a Halifax, the flames would have been more reddish. Hauptmann Reschke pushed our Me 110 down to about 100 metres under the Lancaster. It was a giant bird, with gun barrels protruding from its defensive turrets. The Lancaster crew had not yet spotted us. Complete silence reigned in our machine. Our pilot had decided upon carrying out an attack with his obliquely mounted guns, from a position underneath the bomber. These guns, code-named *Schräge Musik* consisted of two 2cm cannons, which had been installed very close to my gunner's position. The barrels of the guns pointed upwards and forwards at an angle of 80 degrees. At this time, the *Schräge Musik* was still top secret, and in the case of being diverted to a strange airfield, we had orders to hide them from view.

The moment of the attack was now drawing near: Hauptmann Reschke slowly approached the enemy bomber from underneath. Our Me 110 now hung some fifty metres underneath the Lancaster, and still we had not been spotted. Then a short burst from the oblique guns; in all, Hauptmann Reschke only fired nine 2cm rounds. The shells struck home between the two engines in the right wing, and immediately the bomber started burning fiercely. It trailed a long sheet of flames, which covered almost the complete fuselage. The aircraft lost height at once, and plunged towards us in a right-hand turn. Hauptmann Reschke swerved to starboard to avoid a collision. The flames burned bright in a yellow-red and trailed back towards the blue-white-red roundel. They clearly illuminated the squadron code on the fuselage too; I could make out the capital letters AR, and made a note of this. A few minutes later, we watched how the Lancaster hit the ground in a sheet of flames. The time was 03.55.

After one of our longest night-fighting sorties so far, of 190 minutes, we landed at Jüterborg at 05.05. Having touched down safely, I reported my observation of the squadron code AR on the enemy bomber to Hauptmann Reschke. Only

II./NJG5 aces at Parchim, spring 1944. From right: Oblt Josef Kraft (survived the War with fifty-six night Abschüsse *as Staffel Kapitän of 12./NJG1, decorated with the* Ritterkreuz *with Oak Leaves); unknown; Oblt Helmuth Schulte (Staffel Kapitän 7./NJG5, decorated with the* Ritterkreuz *on 17 April 1945 for twenty-five night victories when Kommandeur II./NJG6); Hptm Leopold 'Poldi' Fellerer (Kommandeur II./NJG5, received the* Ritterkreuz *on 8 April 1944, survived the War credited with forty-one combat victories); Lt Peter Spoden (survived the War with twenty-four confirmed night victories as Kommandeur I./NJG6); unknown.* Coll. Peter Spoden.

after I had showed him my notes did he stop looking at me in bewilderment and believe me. My whole crew was filled with great joy, because now the written report on our *Abschuss* was also confirmed visually! A few hours later, we received a phone call from the Burgomaster of the village of Jessen, to the north of Torgau, during which he confirmed the crash of our Lancaster. The squadron code AR was still visible on its fuselage. The wreck of the machine lay just a few kilometres from Torgau, the place where, in April 1945, the Soviet armies met up with the Americans on the bridge over the River Elbe. No one of the seven-man crew had been able to bale out of their doomed Lancaster. We had no explanation as to why the crew had not been able to save their lives, as Hauptmann Reschke had deliberately not aimed at the cockpit area.

On this night, our *Gruppe* destroyed eight enemy bombers, for the loss of two Me 110s and six crew members killed.

Hptm Reschke's victim was either Lancaster III JB610 AR-H or ND569 AR-E of 460 (RAAF) Squadron. Both aircraft had left Binbrook at 23.34 and 23.48 respectively for an attack on Leipzig. Two men from each crew survived their ordeal to be taken prisoner, three members of JB610 were buried in Hanover, and the seven remaining men were never found. On this raid, seventy-eight

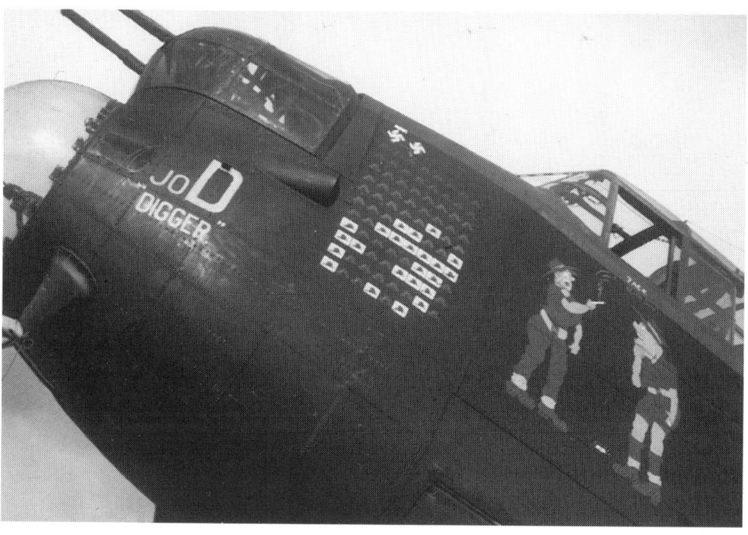

Nose art decorations applied to Lancasters in 1944. (Top) *PO-D 'Der Tag' of 467 Squadron, showing an impressive bomb log of fifty-seven trips.* (Below) *LL847 JO-D or 'Jo the Digger' (Australian slang for an Australian) of 463 Squadron. The two Aussies 'Bluey and Curley', a pair of characters from an Australian World War II cartoon, are playing a game with coins called '2-up'. Although illegal, this game was widely played during the War. This particular aircraft was lost on its ninety-third sortie on 17–18 December 1944 during a raid on München, with the loss of Fg Off K.E.H. Bennett RAAF and his entire crew. LL847 crashed at le Gros-Theil, the eight-men crew finding their last resting place in the local cemetery. Their average age was twenty-one. After a long-term restoration to static display configuration of the Aviation Heritage Museum of Western Australia's Lancaster VII NX622, it has been completed with the application of the authentic nose art of LL847.* Coll. Jack Hamilton.

(Right) *Area bombing load. A 4,000lb 'blockbuster' or 'cookie' (right) and smaller type bombs are being loaded on to a 463 Squadron Lancaster in 1943 or 1944. As a usual bomb load for Main Force pattern bombing attacks during the second half of the War, the bomb-bay of an RAF heavy bomber was typically filled with one 4,000lb high explosive 'cookie', and surrounded by some 6,000lb of small bombs and incendiaries. The 'cookie' was a thin-cased can with over 80 per cent of its weight being explosive. It was intended as a blast bomb for use among compact building complexes, being complemented in the bomber armoury by a variety of incendiary bombs. The most commonly used was the hexagonal-shaped 4lb incendiary, a simple stick of highly inflammable magnesium which burned fiercely on contact.* Coll. Jack Hamilton.

(Below) *The coffins containing the mortal remains of Hptm Reschke and his crew photographed during the funeral ceremonies at Illesheim airfield in late April 1944. Note the Bf 110 of I./NJG6 in the background.* Coll. Gerhard Wollnik.

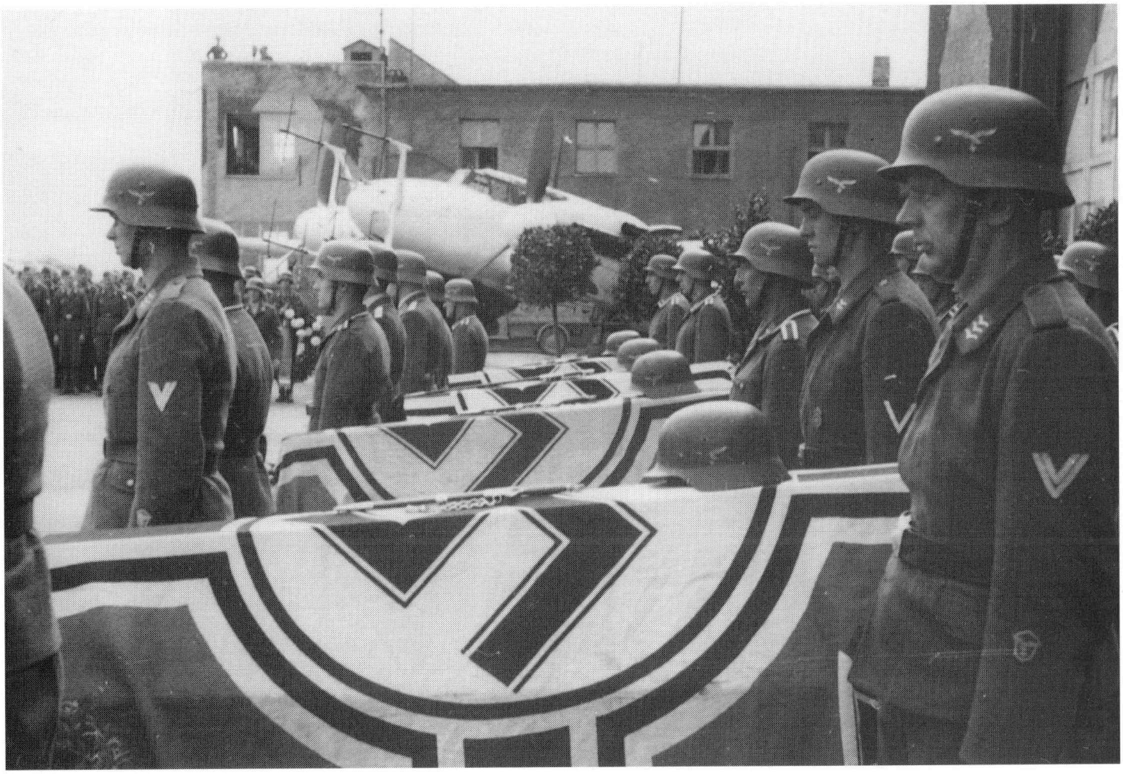

aircraft (forty-four Lancasters and thirty-four Halifaxes) were lost out of the 823 strong Main Force. Gerhard Wollnik was posted to Pilot Training School A 116 at Göppingen on 1 April 1944, and instructed there until February 1945.

Together with hundreds of other grounded *Luftwaffe* aircrew, he was engaged in the ground-fighting during the desperate final months of the War, first against the Americans and then, during April, in the defence of Berlin. On 1 May 1945, he was injured by Russian gunfire, and spent the remaining days of the War in hospital. His old pilot, Hptm Heinz Reschke and Uffz Fischer were killed when their Bf 110 G-4 2Z+KB collided with Bf 110 G-4 2Z+CK (piloted by Fw Georg Walser) whilst returning to Illesheim from an operational sortie on 24–25 April 1944. A few weeks previously, Gerhard Wollnik had been replaced by Gefr Werner Hohn when he left I./NJG6 for instructional duties. Gefr Hohn was injured in the crash on 24–25 April. By the time of his death, Hptm Reschke's tally had risen to six confirmed night kills in I./NJG6.

WILD BOAR

In an effort to meet the radar crisis following the catastrophe of Hamburg in the summer of 1943, three single-engined *Jagdgeschwader* (JG300, 301 and 302) were quickly established in the so-called Wild Boar night-fighting, with a view to combating Bomber Command visually over the burning cities under attack. One of the pilots employed in Wild Boar night-fighting was Ofw Ernst Rummel, who had served as a flying instructor at the Blind-Flying School at Brandenburg Briest for three years. Ofw Rummel received further training at the Night-Fighting School in Altenburg/Thüringen, and was posted to 1./JG300 at Bonn-Hangelar in the early Spring of 1944. He gives a vivid impression of events:

> At this time the RAF came to Germany in all weathers. Now only the *Dunkle Nachtjagd* could be used, and *Helle Nachtjagd* (target area night-fighting) was hardly able to offer any defence. Radio communication was useless as our frequencies were being interfered with by the enemy.
>
> It was very difficult to fly the Me 109 by night. It had no de-icing equipment and its narrow undercarriage made take-offs and landings very difficult. Only very experienced pilots with blind-flying training could do it. Fifty per cent of the losses were not in action but due to the problems at take-off and landing. The same applied to daytime operations as well. We experienced old pilots could not understand why Hitler did not use the much better Me 262. For only this fighter could have been successful against the enemy's vast superiority.
>
> I was shot down for the first time on the night of 24–25 April 1944. I took off from Bonn-Hangelar in very cloudy weather, and flew alone in the direction of Frankfurt at about 8,000 metres. I tried to get through two cloud layers in order to find the enemy bomber stream. Radio communication was interfered with. No information came through. Now and again enemy propaganda could be heard over the radio. I lost some height in order to get a glimpse of the enemy bombers. Suddenly my aircraft was struck with a hard bang. But I could not make out either tracers or flak. I turned to the east, but no longer had full control over my aircraft. The smell of burning was increasing. I decided to bale out. I found that my cockpit cover had jammed and I was unable to jettison it. I suspected that the fuselage had been twisted. At last I managed to jettison the cover and get out. I had managed to loosen the cover with a large screwdriver which was mounted on the fuselage side. These situations were known. As I had lost all orientation I pulled the rip-cord right away. But I was still very high. All was dark around me. I only heard loud engine noise from a large bomber stream. Then the noise was overhead and moved on. I noticed a bright mirror surface below me and assumed that it was a lake. I wanted to inflate my life jacket but discovered that the CO_2 bottle was empty. Then the bright patch disappeared and I was in total darkness.
>
> Then I felt fir branches against my face. I hoped that my parachute would be caught by a

Bf 109 G-6/R6 'Yellow 7' of 3./JG300, taken at the end of February 1944. By this time, losses among the Wild Boar Bf 109 and FW 190 units due to the bad winter weather had risen to such a high level that, early in the next month, it was decided to dissolve the 30th Jagddivision *and transfer JG300, 301 and 302, and their surviving pilots to the day fighter arm.* Coll. Kees Mol, via Roba/Lorant.

tall tree to stop me from crashing to the ground. Now everything happened very quickly; I struck the ground with full force and broke my ankle. It was precisely 01.30, pitch-dark and pouring with rain. I fired several times with my signal pistol, but to no effect. I wrapped myself in my parachute and waited for the dawn. As soon as it got lighter I fired off some more cartridges. Then I cut myself a stick and stumbled through the forest. Fortunately there was a kind of track through the wood. Then I heard the sound of bells coming from a small chapel. So there was a village nearby. I fired off my last signal cartridges. Now I could go no further. I noticed some people approaching stealthily through the trees. Only when they were within calling distance and heard my shouts in German did they come closer. Their caution had been due to an Allied crew which had recently landed here. On approaching them, they had been fired at. Now I discovered that I had come down in the Forest of Spessart. After a very friendly welcome I was taken to the hospital in Lohr am Main, where I spent some weeks recovering from my injuries.

After time in hospital I returned to my old unit at Bad Wörishofen via the frontline pilots' assembly unit at Quedlinburg. Sadly I found that of my seven comrades at the Night-Fighter School only two were left at the unit. They had all been shot down and killed. As JG300 was no longer used for night-fighting, I was converted by my Staffel Kapitän to day-fighting. Until the end of the War we were stationed at various airfields for the so-called *Reichsverteidigung* (Reich Air Defence).

JG300, 301 and 302 were credited with a total of 330 RAF bombers destroyed between July 1943 and March 1944. However, losses amongst the Bf 109 and Fw 190 Wild Boar pilots, mainly due to the bad autumn and winter weather, rose to such a high level that in mid-March 1944 the three *Geschwader* and their surviving pilots were withdrawn from *Nachtjagd* and retrained for day-fighting. They put up a good fight against the American day raids during the summer of 1944, but were almost completely annihilated in the process.

FIRST DEEP-PENETRATION RAID

From the fifty-five raids mounted by Bomber Command between the end of August 1943 and the end of March 1944 (or roughly the period spanning the Battle of Berlin), a staggering 1,578 aircraft failed to return. This represented an average loss rate of 5 per cent per raid, or the equivalent of twice the front-line strength of the Command. This meant that only some 20 per cent of the bomber crews successfully managed to complete a tour of thirty operations in this period of the airwar.

After having flown as 'second dickie' to Stuttgart in a 10 Squadron crew on 21–22 January 1944, Flt Sgt Bruce 'Doug' Bancroft RAAF and his crew joined 158 Squadron at Lissett in late February 1944. The crew was 'blooded' in three raids against French railway marshalling targets before they were detailed to attack their first German target, Stuttgart, on the night of 15–16 March 1944. Flt Sgt Bancroft recounts what happened to him and his crew on the raid:

> Naturally, I wondered about the reaction of my young crew members to this long journey over enemy territory and to the heavy defences that would threaten us to and from and especially over the actual target.
>
> 158 Squadron detailed nineteen aircraft of the 863 laid on by Bomber Command and I was to use Halifax III LV792 NP-E in which we were airborne at 18.50. All of the attacking aircraft were to assemble over Selsey Bill headland on the south coast of England and to set course from there at the same time (theoretically, that is) and in order to do so, aircraft arriving early, as we did, would alter course in a dog-leg manner to lose time before coming to the rendezvous point. We were back on course and heading for Selsey Bill when I suddenly saw a Halifax aircraft aiming to cross our track at right angles from the starboard side and level with us, with the absolute certainty of colliding with us. To pull up the nose of our aircraft would have meant 'squashing' into the offending aircraft and in the split second that I had to react, I pushed the nose of our aircraft hard down as the idiot passed over the top of us, catching us in his slipstream and clearing us by just a couple of feet. Being a clear night, the pilot of the other aircraft should have clearly seen us as we were on his port bow, and in any case should never have tried to join or cross the main stream of aircraft at 90 degrees. It was bad enough in the general mêlée over the target area and I would say this particular character must have had his head hidden between his knees and possibly flying on automatic pilot with the attitude of 'it can't happen to me'. It certainly appeared to me that he had a very limited future and his crew would also suffer. My crew realized then that there could be other dangers as well as the enemy endeavouring to bring us down.
>
> From Selsey Bill the route was to a point on the French coast south-west of Le Havre at 48° 18′N 00° 05′W, then to a point near Chartres at 48° 10′N 01° 30′E, then on to a more easterly course to close to the Swiss border at 47° 55′N 09° 00′E before turning on the final leg almost due north to the target. It was a fine clear night, and on approaching the target area the

The German Mosquito. The all-wooden Ta154 V1 Moskito was built to a 1942 RLM specification as the antidote to the British Mosquito and test-flown in mid-1943. The second prototype reached 435mph, but the design was plagued by engine problems and structural failures. Three aircraft were produced as Ta154 A-2/U4 all-weather fighters, and four more as Ta154 A-4 night fighters during 1944, equipping Stab I./NJG3, III./NJG3, and III. (Ergänzungs)/JG2, but the Moskito was most probably never committed to battle. Coll. Theo Boiten.

Unfulfilled potential. In July 1943, General Kammhuber requested 2,000 of the high-performance He 219 A-2 to be built, but the intented standard night fighter type for Nachtjagd *never reached full maturity, mainly due to stiff opposition from the RLM.* Coll. Pieter Bergman.

bomb-aimer, Fg Off Eric Tansley, advised me that the PFF markers were quite some way off the prescribed aiming point and I instructed him, if he were sure such to be the case, to ignore the markers and aim for the correct aiming point. The result on the bombing photograph showed a direct hit in our case, although most of the bombing from the force fell in open country. The enemy night fighters were delayed by our approach route towards Switzerland but arrived just before the bomber force reached Stuttgart and combats ensued. The return route was more northerly, across France to the north of Paris and to cross the French coast between Le Havre and Boulogne then to Selsey Bill and north to base where we arrived without further incidents after being airborne for eight hours and twenty minutes. It was well after 5am before we went to bed following debriefing and a talk amongst ourselves about the night's events.

From these discussions I realized more than ever what an excellent crew I had gathered around me. No one spoke of being frightened during the course of the operation although, quite naturally, there was a certain amount of tension in the expectation of our being hit by anti-aircraft gunfire or of being attacked by a night fighter. At no time was there any idle chatter over the inter-communication system as everyone was concentrated on doing his own particular duty to assist in the safety of us all as far as possible and press home a successful attack. I had always insisted that only necessary information be passed over the intercom system in relation to the job in hand. I did impress on each man the absolute necessity of remaining fully alert throughout the whole of the time from take-off until return to base and the aircraft was in its dispersal area. So much could happen at any unspecified moment as it did on a few occasions later on.

Although this operation was virtually incident-free for us, and being our first action against a large, well-defended city, my crew were deeply impressed at the result of mass bombing even although this attack was something of a failure. I know that on seeing the great opposition to the attacking force by way of searchlights, anti-aircraft gunfire and the visible attacks by the night fighter force, it was fully realized what it was going to be like in the future.

THE NIGHT OF THE STRONG WINDS

The final raid in the Battle of Berlin was mounted on 24–25 March 1944, when Harris dispatched 811 aircraft to attack the Reich's capital city. The

HX356 'Goofy's Gift', a Halifax III was taken on 158 Squadron strength on 9 January 1944. It was destined to complete eighty-two sorties before being completely destroyed in a crash on 8 November 1944 at Gembling, Yorkshire in the hands of Flt Sgt W.M. Freeman RCAF, and with the loss of the whole crew. Seen posing with 'Goofy's Gift' in the summer of 1944 are Plt Off Bruce 'Doug' Bancroft RAAF DFC and his crew, plus groundcrew. Coll. Bruce Bancroft.

raid went wrong from the start, as an unforecasted strong wind from the north blew the bomber stream off track, and made accurate target-marking impossible. On the homeward leg in particular the bomber stream became very scattered, with flak and night fighters taking a grim toll on the attackers. Seventy-two aircraft, or 8.9 per cent of the force, went missing. One of the crews involved in this raid was Flt Sgt Bancroft RAAF's of 158 Squadron, who lifted off from Lissett's runway at 18.59 in Halifax III HX334 NP-C. 'Doug' Bancroft shares his experiences of that night:

> We were one of the sixteen aircraft despatched by 158 Squadron which were divided between waves two and three of the five waves of the complete force. Zero hour on the target was timed at 22.30 with each wave being allocated three minutes over the target area. We were detailed as a Windfinder crew for the operation, and were briefed to attack in wave three between 22.36 and 22.39.
>
> The met report at briefing advised good weather conditions all of the way with little cloud, and winds only light and variable. We were detailed to fly below 1,000 feet across the North Sea to keep below the enemy radar screen until Anrum Island – about 100 miles from the enemy coast – at which point we were to begin our climb to our bombing height of 20,000 feet. From previous experience we knew that our aircraft, NP-C, would be struggling to reach 18,500 feet but that was the least of our worries as it so happened.
>
> We were on track as verified by fixes taken by the navigator (Flt Sgt Alwyn Fripp) until over half-way across the North Sea, where we had commenced our climb to bombing altitude and intended to cross the Danish coast at 55° 12′N 08° 40′E. On reaching the coastline the navigator advised me that we had drifted over fifty miles south of our flight-plan track and that he had calculated a wind velocity of 100mph from the north and that our ETA target would be 22.52 – some fifteen minutes late. The wireless operator, Sgt Leonard Dwan, was instructed to immediately advise Group Control of the wind velocity and direction and the navigator to give me a new course directly to the northern side of the target area in an endeavour to make up some of the time. We would then be able to attack the target on the

Special Duties crew. 101 Squadron's Plt Off Ken Fillingham (back row, 2nd from right) and crew depicted just before boarding Lancaster G-George for a raid sometime in 1944. Note the golliwog pinned to George, which was the crew's lucky mascot. It was removed before boarding the aircraft and taken on every raid. 101 Squadron was the only unit in Bomber Command to perform the ABC role, even after 100 Group was formed. It operated as a normal bomber squadron in 1 Group, but its ABC-equipped aircraft were spaced throughout the bomber stream to provide ECM cover from start to finish. This meant that elements of 101 Squadron were expected to fly on most of the major raids until the end of the War. Even when 1 Group was not operating, six or eight 101 Squadron Lancasters would be operational and consequently their casualties were high. From 4,895 sorties in 308 raids, 113 Lancasters failed to return, plus another thirty-three were destroyed in crashes. Externally ABC aircraft were easy to spot. They carried three large aerials, two on the upper fuselage and one under the bomb-aimer's position. There was no H2S dome. Internally three 'jostle' transmitters were installed just forward of the mid-upper turret and aft of the main spar. There was also equipment for transmitting slow morse and false radio beacons. Plt Off Adrian Marks, RAAF special duty operator (front right) has vivid memories of the Neuremberg raid of 30–31 March 1944:

> *At briefing, we were advised by the met. officer we would have some cloud cover to and from the target. This was not so – it was a bright full moon and little cloud cover.*
>
> *Our usual aircraft G for George was not serviceable at that time, so we were allocated another Lancaster, J 2, whose crew were on leave. Once airborne we had a very real problem. The aircraft could not gain altitude at the speed of the bomber stream, so we had a choice. To keep up with the others and be well below their height, or climb to the height of the others but fall well behind, with the possibility of arriving over the target alone. The crew discussed the options over the intercom and all agreed to gain the operational altitude of the stream rather than have bombs of our own aircraft falling around us and possibly on us, whilst accepting the risk of being a lone aircraft to and from the target.*
>
> *Some twenty-five or so minutes prior to the time the raid was scheduled to begin, I picked up on my ABC receiver the message 'Achtung Nuremberg', the target having been identified. I warned my crew of that fact and that we could expect more night fighters than usual. As usual it was a zig-zag course to and from the target and I often wondered if someone back home had been careless in their conversation and it had been picked up by an 'unfriendly' person and made known to the Germans.*
>
> *We arrived over Nuremberg some 20–25 minutes late, all by ourselves, but at the correct altitude. The city appeared to be on fire in several areas as I could see the target once the bomb doors were open. We dropped our bombs and got the hell out of the area and headed for home. At no stage did we encounter any enemy aircraft despite the fact that ninety-five aircraft did not return that night. It was the heaviest loss recorded by RAF Bomber Command on any one night.*

101 Squadron despatched twenty-six ABC Lancasters on 30–31 March 1944. The Neuremberg raid turned out to be a pitch-black affair, with six aircraft failing to return to Ludford Magna, plus one more crash-landing on return near RAF Welford, Berkshire. Forty-seven men were killed, eight taken prisoner, and one (Sgt D. Brinkhurst) escaped capture. Coll. Adrian M. Marks.

planned heading of 206 degrees T. We arrived in the target area some ten minutes late and I could see that the bomber stream was very widely scattered, no doubt by reason of the fact, as was revealed later, that quite a large number of the crews were adhering to the met forecast winds.

When we arrived in the target area there was about 9/10ths cloud cover and we were able to get glimpses of the ground area from time to time and were actually able to bomb visually on to the aiming point. The PFF marking was very scattered and so was the bombing generally. Some markers and bombs were as much as ten miles off-target and a number of crews bombed as much as fifteen miles short of the area in their haste to set course for their home bases. I witnessed several mid-air collisions, no doubt caused by aircraft which had gone wide of or to the south of the target area turning back directly into the main stream which was entering the area from the NNE.

Anti-aircraft gunfire was very concentrated (I am advised that there were some 1,500 guns protecting the city) and masses of searchlights

Flt Lt H.D. 'Roger' Coverley peering through the side cockpit window of his 76 Squadron Halifax. Whilst at the controls of LK795 MP-P, Coverley was shot down by a 'Schräge Musik'*-equipped Bf 110 on the disastrous Nuremberg raid on 30–31 March 1944, as the twenty-second bomber to go down. He was captured four days later.* Coll. Roger Coverley.

'Watching take-offs of fully tanked Lancasters presented an artistic spectacle. Fuel bleeding from the tanks formed pretty cones of vapour behind the airscrews. Pretty but disconcerting. I have never seen this effect shown on any films of Lancaster take-offs. Joke – we were so heavily laden the rear gunner had to fire a burst before we could get off the runway.' (Flt Sgt Edgar 'Ted' Ray, nav./bomb-aimer 61 Squadron 1944.) Depicted are two 49 Squadron Lancasters, with 'U' on the left, being waved on to an operational take-off at Fiskerton in 1944. Coll. Leslie Hay.

ringed the city. In addition, groups of night fighter aircraft began their attacks well before the target area was reached and these were also very active even amongst the flak. We were able to make a good bombing run up to the target and drop our load of incendiaries and high explosives right in the target area from our height of 18,000 feet without being attacked by a night fighter at that crucial stage or being hit by the mass of anti-aircraft shells exploding around us, although we were bounced about considerably by the force of these explosions.

Once the bombing photograph was taken it became a matter of getting out of the heavily defended area as quickly as possible and trying to avoid being caught in the beam of the searchlights, especially a blue-coloured radar-controlled master light. I put the nose of the aircraft down and increased power on the motors to gain more speed and, when several lights converged to form two cones in the sky, we were able to dive through the space between the cones, and then to head for our turning point for the route back to base.

Still using the wind velocity and direction as calculated by the navigator, Flt Sgt Fripp, we were able to maintain the original flight-plan tracks for the whole of the homeward flight. When passing well north of the Ruhr area I could see that many of our aircraft had drifted well to the south beyond Osnabrück and were caught in the heavily defended area down there and were being shot down by those defences.

SCHNAUFER KILL

Eddy A. Coward was just fifteen when he lost his brother Plt Off Cliff Coward, navigator with 49 Squadron. Cliff was shot down by Oblt Heinz-Wolfgang Schnaufer, Kommandeur of IV./NJG1, whilst returning from a bombing op to Aachen on 11–12 April 1944, and perished with his comrades when Lancaster LL899 EA-P crashed in flames in a field at St Lenaerts/Belgium. This sad personal loss inspired Eddy to compose the following two poems:

SPIRITS IN FLIGHT

I saw them return, seven spirits in flight.
Engines fired by the sparks of night.
Lumbering, throbbing like a battered ghost.
So thankful for a friendly coast.

Glowing and gliding, it roars without sound.
The rubber screams, as it kisses the ground.
Perfect touch down, on a deserted plain.
Now a corn field, a field with no name.

Night after night, mission after mission.
Helmets, visors, masks and ammunition.
The Seven Sky Warriors from long past.
All knowing tonight, could be their last.

I hear the fields, alive with noise.
Filled with brave men, some are just boys.
I see them walk, in their suits of leather.
Slowly and proudly, they walked together.

Where their plane rose, to meet the foe.
Now the larks rise, from their nests below.
Down the runway, only peace is heard.
Save for the wind, and the song of a bird.

Time passes – January to December.
From spring to winter, the years drift on.
Every April, every Easter – I will remember.
Cliff, Al, Pete and John – Nick, Stan
and Skipper Don.

A FLEMISH FIELD

A field far away, but brought so near
By loving memories we hold so dear,
They were too young, and fresh from the womb,
To end their youth in this grassy tomb.

They flew twenty-two, without any fuss,
They flew and fought for the like of us,
The celestial hanger called out that night,
We are receiving seven spirits in flight.

Like a wooden cross, stood a single tree,
Looking down on their destiny,
Giving comfort to one of the crew,
His moments left were just a few.

The soldiers came and circled their craft,
Standing sentinel, silent, fore and aft,
Grim faced lads from a foreign land,
Doing a duty, I'll never understand.

The grass grew greener over the years,
Warmed by our love, watered by our tears,
The scar in the soil has long been healed,
Now its a meadow, and a Flemish Field.

I walked alone through that grass to find,
A mark, a sign, for peace of mind,
I looked through time, a void to fill,
Visions came, but I am searching still.

I know it is written, I know it's decreed,
But why destroy this happy breed,
Manhood severed, and their fate was sealed,
To greet their Maker in a Flemish Field.

Schnaufer kill. In his 'Leistungsbuch' *('Book of Achievements'), twenty-two-year-old* Ritterkreuzträger *and Gruppen Kommandeur of IV./NJG1 Oblt Heinz-Wolfgang Schnaufer noted on his fifty-third* Abschuss*: 'Lancaster or Halifax. Date 11.4.44. Time 23.25. Place 2km north St Leonhard. Height 5,300 metres. Eye witness Fw Topp, 12./NJG1. Comments: Crashed in flames after one attack, received defensive fire. Confirmed kill Nr. 435/44.' Flt Lt Don Bacon DFC (sitting in the middle) and his 49 Squadron crew, returning from their twenty-third op to bomb Aachen, all perished when Lancaster LL899 EA-P crashed at St Lenaerts, Belgium. Lt Fritz Rumpelhardt was Schnaufer's Bordfunker, destined to finish the War as the* Luftwaffe*'s most successful Funker with 100* 'Nachtabschussbeteiligungen'*, and decorated with the* Ritterkreuz*: 'Heinz Schnaufer always tried to shoot at the wings, between the engines, since this would have the greatest effect because of the fuel tanks, yet allow the crew the chance to save themselves with their parachutes. However, if the aircraft spiralled and made evasive movements, it was very difficult for the pilot to shoot precisely and to make a hit in the way he had intended. I suspect that this was the case on 11 April 1944, as the bomber crew shot at us, very intensively, without hitting our plane. This was one of the few air combats in which we experienced strong retaliatory fire. Generally this was not the case because we would fly horizontally and shoot upwards, with guns directed vertically. Thus we made use of the little corner which the machine guns of the bomber could not reach. This, however, was not possible in the case of Lancaster LL899. The crew was a very strong opponent for us.'* Coll. Eddy A. Coward.

(Right) *The Night Ghost of St Trond. This photograph of Hptm Heinz-Wolfgang Schnaufer, Kommandeur of IV./NJG1, was most probably taken on the occasion of the award of the Swords to the* Ritterkreuz *with Oak Leaves on 30 July 1944. Schnaufer received this high decoration after scoring his eighty-seventh to eighty-ninth night victories on the night of 28–29 July 1944.* Coll. Anneliese Autenrieth.

THE TABLES ARE TURNING

Although *Nachtjagd* had grown into the *Luftwaffe*'s most powerful and effective branch by the end of the Battle of Berlin, the writing of its decline shortly after was already on the wall. Pressure mounted steadily on *Nachtjagd*; its bases in the Low Countries and France came under increasing air attack, both by day and by night. II./NJG1, for example, had been moved into St Dizier, France in early 1944, where it was subjected to a devastating bombing raid by 148 B-24s of the 2nd Bomb Division on 24 March. In a hail of 463.7 tons of bombs raining down on the airfield, the operations room and nearly all the other buildings, including flying control, were destroyed. The bombs fell right into the middle of the aircraft park of the *Gruppe*, two hangars and the aircraft parked there being completely destroyed by fire, and fragmentation bombs causing heavy damage to the aircraft in the other hangars. Sixteen *Luftwaffe* personnel were killed, among them some female signals staff. Other bombs had fallen on the part of the town nearest the airfield causing fires and heavy casualties amongst the French civilian population.

Other factors contributed to a steadily mounting pressure on *Nachtjagd*: 100 Group's jamming of radio and radar traffic were giving both the ground controllers and *Nachtjagd* crews a severe headache. This, combined with Bomber Command's skilful use of diversionary and faint raiding made it increasingly difficult for the Germans to identify the Command's main target(s), and direct the available night fighters on an accurate intercepting course. To make life even more difficult for the German night fighter crews, a few dozen Mosquito night intruders accompanied each Bomber Command raid, taking a rising toll of the *Luftwaffe* night hunters. Furthermore, spare parts to keep the *Nachtjagd* aircraft in the air frequently did not reach the operational units, and last but not least, the rapidly diminishing fuel reserves gave reason for grave concern.

By the third week of April 1944, Lt Otto Fries of II./NJG1 had become an ace, with nine confirmed victories. In his capacity as Technical Officer, he was responsible for the state of aircraft serviceability in his *Gruppe*, which was lacking at that time. Probably in an effort to improve this situation, Fries received strict orders to devote his full efforts to this problem, which excluded him from any further operational flying. He explains, in the third person, the situation at that time:

> He had asked the Adjutant for an appointment with the Old Man, but the Commander had flown immediately after the night's stand-by for a Commanders' Conference at the *Geschwader* in Arnhem, most likely concerning this very business. His Highness Hermann the Fat was probably in a bad mood and dissatisfied with his night fighters because these lame ducks did not shoot down enough of the enemy.
>
> He was hopping mad. The Old Man should get himself a non-flyer as TO. He had become a pilot in order to fly, and not to sit at a desk and push paper around or keep statistics about serviceable, part serviceable, unserviceable or written-off operational aircraft – and to make life hell for his technicians who he knew were doing all that was humanly possible. It wasn't the mechanics' fault that their *Gruppe* did not have sufficient reserve aircraft, and that due to excessive operational demands the aircraft were in constant need of servicing because equipment became unserviceable, suffered hits, or fighter-bombers damaged hangars. What fault was it of theirs that the delivery of spare parts failed because fighter-bombers were continually attacking the supply lines and deliveries were frequently delayed for weeks. Together with the engineers of the *Staffeln* and the workshop section he had at times set up servicing in three shifts, had established priorities for the damaged aircraft. But what was the use of all that without the necessary spare parts. In the end he had decided on the cannibalization of the last two aircraft on the list. At some point, when the missing parts turned up, they could be rebuilt. More he could not do, whether at readiness or flying, or whether he sat around at the flights or in the workshops.
>
> The following afternoon he went to see the Commanding Officer and asked for his relief as TO. Although his reasons were accepted, his

Lancaster ND787 'F' of 49 Squadron in a lovely spring setting at Fiskerton, spring of 1944. This aircraft became operational with 49 Squadron on 5 April 1944 and flew some forty-nine ops before it was replaced by a 'Village Inn'-equipped aircraft. Coll. Leslie Hay.

relief was refused. After all, where was the Old Man to find an officer in a hurry, who was both willing and suitable to fill his function. The remaining officers of the *Gruppe* either had a function already or were themselves pilots such as he. He went through the list in his head – of those who could be considered, not a single one would have been prepared to give up flying in favour of a staff job as TO.

The Commander promised him however to turn a blind eye – and so they agreed that he would be grounded until further notice during the moon phase and permitted to fly on operations during the moonless period – this agreement remaining, of course, strictly between themselves. Besides, the Old Man was of the opinion that this ban on flying could not be kept up indefinitely, they were aware of that even at division level, and one fine day it would simply be forgotten. This consoled him a little, although the solution reached left him less than fully satisfied.

During his 'rest time' he got the *Schräge Musik* installed in his G9+CC: two 20mm cannon, the barrels of which protruded from the fuselage behind the gunner. They fired upward, slanted slightly forward at about 80 degrees to the fuselage axis. The gun selector on the control column was adjusted accordingly: The forward firing guns, two MG 171/20 and four MG 17 to be operated as 'fighting trigger' by the 'spoon', and the upward firing ones by the button on the top end of the stick. During normal flight the spoon was in the upward position over the button, blocking both triggers. A second sight for the slanting guns was mounted in the roof. For aiming upwards he would have to move his head far back; this was very unpleasant as it meant losing all feeling of the aircraft's attitude. He had difficulty getting used to this, but the advantages of the slanting armament were obvious: during an attack his own aircraft would be in the blind spot of the bomber's guns, out of reach of the 'tail-end Charly', as the rear gunner of the British bombers was sometimes called – how often had they been spotted by him!

He was very pleased when, on the evening of 18 April, he was again able to drive out for readiness with the operational crews. They soon took off as a railway station in the vicinity of Paris was being attacked. But the order for take-off came much too late and the Y-control was extremely poor because interference made communication with ground control almost impossible. They hung around and could see the fires and explosions, but by the time they had arrived it was all over – the attack had only lasted a few minutes.

On 20 April 'increased readiness' was ordered because of the 'historic occasion' (Hitler's birthday). Towards 22.30 they went to cockpit readiness and at 22.46 he opened the throttles, without being troubled by long-range night fighters. This night too their communications were interfered with, they were sent around Paris, Rheims and Metz, saw 'Christmas trees' and bombing far away, and landed again at 01.42 at St Dizier – having achieved nothing.

On 21 April they remained in their quarters as the weather was very bad, but on the following evening they again went out to readiness. It was to be *Zahme Sau* again, although this had not

End of Tour party, East Kirkby, late April 1944. All smiles for this 57 Squadron crew, who were one of the lucky few to complete a tour of ops during the period of the Battle of Berlin, when average Bomber Command losses rose to an alarming 7 to 10 per cent on deep penetration raids. Flt Lt Johnnie Ludford was awarded an immediate DFC for his skilful flying and for safely bringing back heavily damaged Lancaster JB526 D-Dog after being attacked by a Ju 88 whilst on their way to bomb Leipzig on 19–20 February 1944. With the intercom dead, an engine loose, and the hydraulics u/s as a result of the sudden night fighter attack, the crew 'pressed on regardless', dropping their bombs on target before struggling back to East Kirkby. Coll. Jack Bosomworth.

worked properly on the past few nights. The order for take-off came almost at the same time as two nights before. This time he managed to be the first to take off; at 22.53 he set the time on his clock and started out. This time too it was the same stupid game as on the previous nights: they got no clear instructions from ground control as the communications were being interfered with and finally broke off altogether. 'What a mess!' cursed the radio operator. 'But something must be going on tonight, otherwise the Tommies would not be causing such complete interference. Let us fly to some particular place, somewhere in the north, perhaps we'll be lucky and see something.'

The radio operator tuned in the radio beacon *Wilhelmine* and set the loop aerial athwartships. Then he switched on the autopilot to steer towards it. He reduced power in order to save fuel and reset his propellers accordingly. The altimeter showed a bare 4,000m. He and the gunner looked around to see if they could spot anything on either side and the radio operator sat at his radar set. He suddenly saw some 'Christmas trees' light up on the starboard bow, took out the autopilot and turned towards them. 'There are markers on the starboard bow – do you have anything on the screen?' 'Not yet.'

He increased the manifold pressure and turned on the automatic propeller pitch control. A glance at the instruments showed that all was in order. He had 340 on the compass. He raised his seat, set the illumination of the reflector sight and set the guns to fire. The clock showed 23.20. Five minutes later the radio operator had an indication which approached very fast. 'Someone is approaching from ahead – a little higher – watch out!' He stared ahead, then the Viermot rushed past, perhaps fifty metres above them. He disengaged the autopilot with the switch on the stick and flung the machine in a steep turn on to the opposite course – the horizon was so clear that he could allow himself this manoeuvre. As the machine levelled out his radio operator reported a contact: 'I've got him – distance 30!'

Could it be the same bomber he had just seen? That one must have been much further away than three kilometres by now. 'No matter – whip up the horses!' he told himself and opened the throttles. The radio operator gave him some course corrections and kept up a running commentary on the distance. When they were within 300 metres he saw him: four-engined with twin fins – Lancaster or Halifax? – at this distance it was not possible to be sure –

but certainly a *bahnhof bomber* ['railway station bomber'; aircraft involved in the Allied *Transportation* Plan].

He remembered that he still had the auxiliary tanks hanging from his wings. They couldn't be quite empty yet, but as he now had the Tommy in front of him it would be safer to get rid of them – there was no trusting the tail-end Charly! He pulled the jettison levers and the machine reacted with a little hop. He pushed the machine a little lower to make himself smaller and edged a little to starboard. He was approaching too fast and reduced power a little. When he was almost abeam he moved to port and positioned himself exactly under the bomber – judging by the engines, which projected far out in front of the wings, it looked like a Lancaster, but he was not quite certain. It hung hugely above him, he estimated the distance about 200 metres, and went a little higher.

It was really very unpleasant, with the head tipped far back all sensation of flying was lost. He looked down again and checked the attitude of his machine – all was in order. 'Let's go then!' he ordered himself. He tipped his head back again and took aim at the bomber. Slight pressure on the left rudder, and the vertical line of his sight moved to a point precisely between the two port engines. He pushed the stick slightly forward, and as the sight reached the trailing edge of the wing he pressed the trigger and let the sight wander over the wing – he fired for only seconds. The machine shook and in the cabin it stank like after some fireworks.

The bomber showed no effects – that could not be true! Somewhere ahead there were flashes as from light flak – but that could not get up as far as 4,000 metres…! Then it dawned on him: they were the explosions of his own two-centimetre shells – in the excitement of the moment he had pressed the wrong trigger!

'You're crazy!' barked the radio operator. 'He's up there!' 'I know I'm stupid! But he hasn't noticed anything – he too thinks it's light flak!' How lucky that he did not use tracer, only 'dark' ammunition. He repeated the aiming sequence and this time pressed the right button. A short burst – they saw the strikes, right between the engines. The wing immediately burst into flames, he had hit the tanks. 'Note the time! It's 23.35.'

With all its details splendidly revealed in the early spring sunshine, this fine shot of He 219 A-5 DV+DL was taken at München-Riem airfield in April 1944. It was used as a flying test-bed for different types of A/I radar and is seen here equipped with both the FuG 212 Lichtenstein *and the FuG 220 SN-2 radars.* Coll. Albert Spelthahn.

The bomber went downwards, flames streamed from its port wing, pieces detached themselves and flew off. He drew off to one side and also went into a descent. As he went down he saw, over to his left and almost on the opposite course, another four-engined one coming up over the horizon. He pulled back the stick and went into a turn, losing sight of the burning bomber in the process. 'I have another one – keep an eye on the burning machine – I must not lose sight of the other one!' His position in relation to the second bomber was most unfavourable, he could not turn tight enough to keep him in sight. He dragged the machine round with all his strength, but he lost him. When he thought to be on the right course, he levelled off. 'Look at your screen – I've lost sight of him!'

The first bomber crashed down below, the gunner reported: '23.38.' He wandered to right and left to give his radio operator a wide area to scan – but no blip appeared on his screen. After a few minutes they flew back to fix the place of the crash, for after so many changes of course they only had an approximate idea of where they were. The *Abschuss* was on a bearing of 090 to the radio beacon *Chameleon*.

They continued to fly in the area, saw far off to the north-west markers and bombing, but nothing seemed to be happening in their own vicinity. It was shortly after a quarter past one when he decided to turn for home. The radio operator tuned in the beacon of St Dizier and switched the autopilot to it. When they thought themselves to be close enough, the radio operator called their own operations room and advised them of their imminent landing. 'Adler 98 from Pfauenauge – do not go to Gartenzaun (home base) – just laid eggs – go to Haus 73 – question Viktor.' 'Viktor-Viktor – to seven-three – out.' 'Where is that?' he asked. 'Just a minute, I'll look it up – it's Jouvincourt.' The radio operator tuned in the beacon of Jouvincourt and gave him the course. They landed at 01.48 and he taxied the machine to the control tower. They climbed stiffly out of the aircraft and while he and the radio operator went to operations the gunner saw to the refuelling.

They phoned operations at St Dizier and asked why they had sent them away. They were told that some minutes before they had reported their return the place had been attacked by Mosquitos. From operations it had looked as if the bombs had hit the runway. But an inspection had since shown that the bomb craters were close beside the concrete strip and the runway itself had not been damaged. He decided to fly back that night as soon as the enemy activity had ceased. So they waited, drank some coffee, and when the air was clear they set out. They took off at 02.45, flew at low level to the radio beacon, and landed at St Dizier at 03.11.

When he drove out to the field the next day, the armourer reported that only seventeen rounds had been fired from the two MG FF of the *Schräge Musik*. He thought it had been a very economical *Abschuss*.

Lt Fries' tenth *Abschuss*, on 22–23 April 1944, was most probably one of a force of 181 bombers attacking the railway yards at Laon, near Rheims with devastating effect. In all, nine Lancasters, Halifaxes and Stirlings were shot down on this raid, at least seven of which were claimed destroyed by night fighters of II. and III./NJG1 and I./NJG2.

IV./NJG6's mascot dog 'Trolly', having enjoyed a ride on board a Bf 110 G-4 in 1944, is lifted to his usual habitat, Mother Earth, again. Coll. Hans Meyer.

(Right) *In the evening of 22 May 1944, Plt Off F.N. Henley (on extreme left) lifted Lancaster NE127 DX-J of 57 Squadron off East Kirkby's runway for a raid on Braunschweig. The crew never reached their target; to the west of Groningen, NE127 was intercepted by a Bf 110 G-4 of 8./NJG1, in the hands of twenty-one-year-old Uffz Herbert Beyer and his Bordfunker Uffz Hans Petermann. The burning Lancaster was seen to thunder over Hoogkerk village, before being ripped apart in a violent explosion near Dorkwerd at 23.45. Five of the crew, all British, perished in the crash. Only the mid-upper gunner, Paul Dalseg RCAF (2nd from left), was able to bale out before the bomber exploded. Miraculously, Norman G. Wharf, the Canadian rear gunner (4th from left), came down in his turret and landed in a deep ditch. This saved his life, although he was badly wounded. Both survivors were soon captured by the Germans. It was a bad night for East Kirkby, with 57 and 630 Squadrons losing three and two Lancasters respectively. Almost one month later, on 21 June, the victorious 8./NJG1 crew, flying Bf 110 G-4 740076 G9+NS, were killed over Eelde airfield at 15.19 in a surprise attack by a Mosquito of 515 Squadron flown by Sqn Ldr Paul Rabone DFC and his nav. Flt Lt Frederick Johns DFC.* Coll. Alan R. Morris.

No longer missing. Whilst returning from a bombing raid on synthetic oil plants at Sterkrade (Ruhr) on 16–17 June 1944, this 77 Squadron crew was shot down at 02.05 by a Bf 110 flown by Ritterkreuzträger *and Kommandeur of III./NJG1 Hptm Martin Drewes. A veteran of sixteen sorties, Halifax III NA508 KN-A 'Apple' crashed in a ball of fire on farmlands in the Bovenkerker polder at Amstelveen (near Amsterdam), the forward section of the fuselage penetrating deep into the soft soil. One crew member was found at the crash site and buried as an unknown airman, but recovery attempts during 1944 and 1953 only unearthed the remains of two others. In 1990, after forty-six years, a third attempt was undertaken, this time successful, and the mortal remains of the missing four young men were finally laid to rest at Bergen op Zoom. Depicted here are the Australian members of the crew, (left to right): W/O Johnny O'Meara (WOp); Plt Off Lance Pratt (nav.); Plt Off Bob Blair (pilot); Flt Sgt Gordon Armstrong (BA); Fg Off John Date (RG). Not included in this picture are Sgts Lou Moore (Flt Eng) and Denis Tustin (mid-upper gunner), both RAF. 77 Squadron paid a heavy price on the 16–17 June 1944 raid against Sterkrade, with seven out of twenty-three Halifaxes despatched failing to return.* Coll. Dorothy Saunders.

'OWL' DOWN

The He 219 *Uhu* ('Owl') was *Nachtjagd's* most advanced night fighter aircraft during World War II. Fast, manoeuvrable, heavily armed and fitted with SN-2 radar and ejection seats for the crew of two, General Kammhuber planned to make it the standard front-line aircraft for his arm by the spring of 1944. This, however, was not to be. Due to various political machinations and other reasons, between mid-1943 and late 1944 only 195 'Owls' were delivered to operational units, mainly to I./NJG1 at Venlo, Holland. Another seventy-three aircraft were used as test-beds, or never reached the front due to being damaged or destroyed in Allied bombing attacks. The *Uhu* proved to be very successful in combat: statistics compiled for the period 12 June 1943 – 2 July 1944 confirm that twenty *Uhu* pilots destroyed 111 Bomber Command aircraft, including seven Mosquitoes. The top-scoring He 219 pilot over this period was Hptm Ernst-Wilhelm Modrow (Staffel Kapitän 1./NJG1) with twenty-five kills, followed by Hptm Heinz Strüning (Staffel Kapitän 3./NJG1) with fourteen, and Oblt Josef Nabrich (3./NJG1) with eleven *Abschüsse*. Despite all these favourable figures, by January 1945, He 219 production was stopped in favour of the Ju 88 G ('Gustav') series.

Even the formidable He 219, however, was no real match for the Mosquito night intruder, and losses built up when Mosquitoes were sent in numbers to mingle with the bomber streams bound for the Reich. Between 12–13 August 1944 and 13–14 April 1945, a total of eleven *Uhu*'s were claimed destroyed by Mosquitoes of 100 Group (with eight He 219s shot down), the 2nd TAF and the ADGB (with claims for three 'Owls'). One of the earliest He 219s destroyed by an unidentified prowling Mosquito, He 219 A-0 G9+DC (srl no. 190116) was flown by Lt Otto Fries, TO of II./NJG1. He describes, in the third person, what happened to him and his Funker on 19–20 May 1944:

> The British were a cunning lot: It obviously amused them greatly to lead the German night fighters astray from time to time. They began in the early afternoons: A great number of radio transmitters were tuned and masses of coded messages were sent – in short, they acted as if a major raid was to take place during the night. As a result of these activities, which had been carefully monitored by the German wireless service, at the evening briefings the words 'increased readiness' would be added to the codeword '*Fasan*' (Pheasant). But during the night mostly only single Mosquitoes would turn up which, by dropping 'window', would give the appearance of a major raid, resulting in the night fighter force in the affected area being ordered into the air, only to be recalled when the true situation had been identified. However, sometimes it happened that a real raid did take place, but an hour later, after the fighters had landed and whilst still in the process of being refuelled.
>
> On that mild night of 19–20 May such a major raid had been assumed by the night fighter control with the words 'increased readiness'. The crews therefore left their stand-by quarters immediately after their briefing and went to their Staffel dispersals in order to be ready to board their machines the moment the order for take-off came. The weather over England was supposed to be good – at least the weather wizard had said so at briefing. Our own field was covered by a thin layer of cloud at between eleven and twelve-hundred metres, which was of no significance.
>
> When at midnight the first hint of an RAF aircraft appeared on radar, the entire Second *Gruppe* of NJG1 was ordered into the air. His *Gruppe* was in the process of converting from the Me 110 to the He 219. The First *Gruppe* in Venlo, which had already been converted, had lent them four of their lamest ducks. Now he had a host of engineers engaged in inducting the mechanics of the *Staffeln* and workshops into the secrets of these new kites. He himself had already carried out some flights on the new type and it was obvious that he would be the first of the *Gruppe* to try it out on operations in his capacity of TO.
>
> The He 219 had been conceived as only a night fighter; it had not been tested at Rechlin, but by the First *Gruppe*. It was different in many respects than the other types used for night-fighting. The pilot sat in a perspex cabin in the bows of the aircraft with a fantastic all-round view. The radio operator sat behind him, back to back, separated by the high backs of their ejector seats with their headrests. The propeller arcs lay about two metres behind the radio operator and almost touched the fuselage. It was impossible to bale out normally in an emergency as one would certainly be caught by the propellers. For that reason, ejector seats operated by compressed air had been installed for the crew. The radio operator was ejected with an atmospheric pressure of sixty and the pilot with ninety. This means of baling out was most reassuring.
>
> They took off at 01.25 and were guided by the Y-method. They had been on a southerly course

for some twenty minutes when they received the following instruction: 'Rübezahl to all Adler – make *Reise-Reise* – I repeat: make *Reise-Reise* – Out.' His Bordfunker said, 'Now we are up here we could try out this new kite to our heart's content. Up to now we have only flown it at low level.' 'Good idea,' he said, 'let's do it!'

They called it *Erfliegen*, flying in, when they wanted to familiarize themselves with a new machine or a new type. This involved a whole series of different manoeuvres: extreme steep turns, single-engined flight port and starboard with and without trimming out including turns into and away from the stopped engine, and stalls, where it was important to find out whether the aircraft simply sagged or went into a spin. He also checked the automatic pilot and the, as yet unknown, three-axis trimming, and did a number of other manoeuvres to familiarize himself with the characteristics of this hitherto unknown type of aircraft – after all, he was to fly it on operations in due course. The Bordfunker also checked the panoply of his equipment and occupied himself with the 'piano' – as the long row of switches for the electrics were called – for in an emergency he had to find the right one at a touch.

After about ten minutes he turned on to course for home, throttled back the engines and put the aircraft into a slow descent in order to maintain speed. But the aircraft had hardly been on course for half a minute when there was a bang and vibration, the port engine bursting into flames. 'Long-range night fighter!' shouted the Bordfunker.

He threw the aircraft into a steep turn to starboard and opened the throttles to their limit. At the same time, in one movement, he closed the fire cock of the port engine to shut off the fuel flow. Once the petrol remaining in the lines had been used up, the fire should go out. He continued in the steep turn to starboard in order to make it more difficult for the Mosquito to renew its attack and hamper its aim.

The thrust of the port engine got less and the pressure on his right rudder pedal increased; he trimmed it out to ease his right leg. The difference in rpm caused the aircraft to shake. The port engine, still afire and with its propeller driven by the slipstream, continued to turn with reduced revolutions, and these different revolutions caused the aircraft to swing about. In order to stop the port engine from continuing to turn he feathered its propeller.

The port engine stopped and the shaking ceased; although the fuel supply had been shut off, it continued to burn. Then it began to give off sparks like a Christmas candle. He was irritated and felt unsure of himself. Had it been his familiar old Me 110 he would not have cared – but he hardly knew the He 219 and he had no idea why the engine continued to burn. And he knew of no way by which he might douse the fire.

The sparking increased. Desperately he continued to turn and slowly descended. The distance to the layer of cloud, where he might have found cover from further attacks, was too great to reach it in a dive. A glance at the altimeter showed that they were still at more than 5,000 metres altitude. The stopped and still burning engine and the resulting reduced manoeuverability of his machine put a close limit to his options.

The engine began to spark like a rocket. 'It stinks!' he said to his radio operator. 'If only I knew why the engine continues to burn when it no longer gets any fuel. Perhaps it is the oil, and I have no idea what I can do about that. As we cannot continue to turn for ever, I will try to reach the clouds in a steep spiral and then set course for Deelen. To be on the safe side I will jettison the cabin cover so we can bale out quickly if necessary. If anything goes wrong, press the button and jump – is that clear?' 'Nice prospects!' said the radio operator, 'only the Tommy worries me – I wonder why he hasn't made a second attack! – Well, go to it then!'

The cabin roof of the He 219 was in two parts and they were connected with a hinge. On operating the jettison handle – according to the type handbook – springs should raise the front part, enabling the slipstream to get a grip and tear away both parts. When he operated the jettison mechanism however, the roof merely moved backwards. He had raised his seat into the attacking position so that his eyes were in line with the reflector sight. The rearward moving cabin cover struck heavily against his head, just above the hair line. He collapsed, unconscious. As he had loosened his backstraps in order to have more freedom of movement whilst flying, his body fell forward against the control column and put the aircraft into a steep dive.

'What's going on?' called the radio operator. He could not reply – he was out for the count. Squinting past the back of his seat the radio operator saw his pilot hanging like an empty sack over the stick. He shouted at him again but the pilot did not move. The diving aircraft accelerated – and the engine sparked. Then the radio operator tore open the safety lid of his ejector seat and pressed the operating lever. With a loud bang he was catapulted out of the diving aircraft.

What happened to him then he was never able to remember. They both tried to reconstruct the events but never achieved any convincing solution. Although the radio operator questioned it time and again, it could have happened as follows: In the excitement of the assumed loss of his pilot – the long years of flying and experiences together had made them friends – he pulled the rip-cord of his parachute without first having released the straps which held him in his seat. The parachute opened because the tumbling motions of his fall had torn it out of the bucket of his seat, but the seat straps held the lines of the 'chute in such a way that he was hanging in them upside down. He landed at a dropping rate of at least five metres per second in a field. His last memory of his fall – he was unconscious for three whole days – were his desperate efforts to do someting about his predicament, but he remembered more about what he had been wanting to do.

He, the pilot, regained consciousness as his aircraft dived into the clouds. He was hardly able to make anything out as blood had got into his eyes. Instinctively he put both his arms around the control wheel and, with his feet braced against the rudder pedals, pulled it with all his strength against his chest. The centrifugal force drained the blood from his head and he blacked out, but he did not loosen his grip until the aircraft shot out of the clouds again. During the dive it must have achieved a great speed and it was a miracle that the wings had not been torn off.

He called the radio operator, and when he did not reply he turned around and saw that the cabin behind him was empty. The wound on his forehead burned. Blood ran over his face and he felt it dripping from his nose and his chin. A dark veil seemed to descend on his brain – he had the feeling that his capacity to think was fading. He felt that he would not be able to fly his aircraft much longer. The engine was still burning and emitting sparks. He realized it quite clearly: he must bale out as soon as possible before his brain gave way. He vaguely remembered the fact that he would have to use his ejector seat for getting out.

He had the faint memory that some emergency switches were mounted on the bottom left of the instrument panel – certainly on the Me 110; but when he felt for them with his left hand he could find nothing there. He was barely able to see anything as, in spite of constant wiping, the blood kept running into his eyes. He continued fingering around the instrument panel, there must be something there! He pulled a button, but only the armour plating of the windscreen popped up. Continuing his fingering he unintentionally extended the undercarriage, he could hear the rumbling, and finally the flaps as well – the aircraft rose like a lift. He desperately tried to remember the operation of the ejector seat, but he was not able – his capacity for thought had been totally confused by the blow on his head.

The port engine was still burning and sparking. Naked fear overcame him, combined with immeasurable anger. He was unable to comprehend that the much-vaunted hero's death could be such a banal affair! He forced himself to be calm and concentrated his mind; then he remembered the torch he had hung about his neck. He wiped the blood from his eyes, switched on the lamp and let its beam wander systematically over the instrument panel. Then he discovered, on the right-hand strip along a row of electrical switches, the red safety lever. With a sigh of relief he lifted it up and struck the pin with his fist with all his might. A loud bang, his chin was forced on to his chest and he felt as though his neck had been broken – but he was free and was tumbling about in the air. He released his straps and got clear of his seat. As he entered the clouds he felt the damp on his hands and his face, pulled the rip-cord and opened the parachute. Hanging in the lines he swung back and forth and was violently sick: the cabin roof had given him concussion.

Blackness yawned below him, he was unable to recognize anything. He remembered his signal pistol which must be in the right-hand side pocket of his trousers, secured by a strong line. He drew it out and fired, one after the other, three parachute flares from his ammunition belt which was fastened around his left lower leg. Continually wiping the blood from his eyes, he was able to make out below him fields, meadows and a village with houses on either side of a winding road. A mild breeze drifted him towards it. He landed with a bump in a meadow and at once released the parachute harness with the quick-release clasp on his breast. The parachute collapsed over him and he extricated himself from the tangle of lines and panels. There was a large cowpat right beside his place of landing and his first thought was: some luck that you did not sit yourself right into it!

Both Lt Fries and his Bordfunker Fw Staffa were admitted to the hospital at 's Hertogenbosch in southern Holland, their aircraft having crashed three kilometres south of this town. Apart from his head wound, Fries suffered from concussion; Staffa, having landed head first into a field at high speed, sustained extensive contusions and a heavy concussion. Only in July 1944 were the crew declared fit to fly on ops again, and they were posted to I./NJG1 at Venlo. They were to add eight more night *Abschüsse* to their tally whilst flying the He 219, ending the War with eighteen confirmed victories.

D-DAY

Following the Battle of Berlin, Bomber Command was temporarily directed to carry out precision raids on tactical targets, mainly in France, during April, May and early June 1944, in preparation for

Victim of the 'Transportation *Plan'. Whilst on its way to bomb the railway junctions at Revigny in northern France in the early hours of 19 July 1944, Lancaster III JB318 DX-L of 57 Squadron was hit in its port wing by* Schräge Musik *cannon fire from Bf 110 C9+AS of 8./NJG5, flown by Ofw Herbert Altner. The blazing bomber crashed and exploded with its full bomb-load only minutes later at 01.21, at La Boue, Bassevelle, killing four of the crew. These burnt-out remains of its tail unit were photographed the next day. The 5 Group Lancaster force bound for Revigny suffered heavily from night fighter attacks, with twenty-four aircraft (or almost 22 per cent) failing to return, Ofw Altner claiming five heavies destroyed in just over half an hour for his 17th–21st victories. Herbert Altner recalls: 'After getting my first adversary of the night into the* Schräge Musik *sights fitted to the roof of my cabin, I close my eyes to avoid losing my night vision temporarily by a possible explosion of the Lancaster, and press the gun tit of the 20mm cannon at a range of some 50m. I hear my crew exclaiming "He's burning!", whereupon I swerve off to the left and level off my good old 110 outside of the danger zone. It is 01.01 and I've conquered my first adversary of the night. At 01.34, after downing my fifth adversary without return fire, I feel that I have stretched my airman's luck far enough and decide to head for base. We touch down in one piece at 01.59 at Laon-Athies. The main task for Karl Braun, my Flight Engineer is now, as it is after each mission, to light one cigarette after the other and put them into my mouth, to steady my nerves again.* Coll. Len Manning.

the invasion of Normandy. Under the codename of the *Transportation* Plan, the British heavies successfully demolished or severely disrupted the German transport and supply lines in the hinterland of the invasion coastline, thereby denying the Germans the opportunity to reinforce their forward areas in the first crucial days following D-Day. These short penetration raids gave *Nachtjagd*'s Tame Boars little time to find their prey, and losses amounted to only 525 aircraft or 2.2 per cent during this period.

By early June 1944, twenty-eight-year-old Hptm Helmut Eberspächer was serving as Staffel Kapitän of 3./SKG10, at Tours, some 200km south-west of Paris. Helmut had flown on ops since July 1940 as a reconnaissance pilot in 7.(F)/LG2, both on the Western and on the Eastern Front. In January 1943, he received further training as a ground attack pilot and became engaged in the highly risky business of hit-and-run attacks against targets in south and south-east England whilst flying the FW 190 in 3./SKG10. Apart from these 'Jabo'-sorties, his Staffel was used as 'Jack-of-all-trades', also being employed in reconnaissance, day-fighting, and long-range night intruding over England. Hptm Eberspächer vividly recounts a very special recce sortie he carried out on D-Day:

The Transportation *Plan in operation: bombs (extreme right) raining down from a 550 Squadron Lancaster during a daylight raid on marshalling yards, probably in the late summer of 1944.* Coll. Len Browning.

> It is not incorrect to call 6 June 1944 the beginning of the military end of the War. In the early dawn of this June day, when the Americans and the British crossed the Channel with their huge armies and landed on the coast of Normandy, 'Zero Hour' really struck; even if it took more than another 330 days of agony before the capitulation was signed at Rheims.
>
> On that beautiful June day I was at Tours on the Loire as Staffel Kapitän of a *Kampfgeschwader*. Since the beginning of the year we had been expecting the Allies to land on the coast of France on a night with a full moon; it was the subject of our daily conversations. Naturally, the enemy would make use of a moon phase favourable to his purpose. Only, precisely when and on which sector of the Atlantic coast remained unknown. Whether our reconnaissance and espionage had failed, or whether their reports had been disbelieved, I do not know. There were, as always, many conflicting rumours. In Paris, my wife was told by her neighbour, who had close contacts with the *Abwehr*, the secret intelligence service, late in the evening of 5 June, 'tonight they will land'.
>
> The *Luftwaffe* was part of the German Armed Forces, but it was no longer much of a 'force', for nearly all airfields in northern France and Belgium had been ploughed up by bombs. What aircraft and crews were still available were no longer able to take to the air. At that time soldiers used to say: if you see a blue aircraft in the sky it is American, a red one is British, if you see none it is German. The *Luftwaffe* in the West was virtually no longer in existence. My own unit was one of the few exceptions for, after the US Air Force had made our airfield at Tours unusable, we had been able to make use of a meadow on the banks of the Loire with our few remaining aircraft where, like by some miracle, we remained undiscovered by the Americans who totally dominated the air. We carried out our operations against southern England only at night and after returning before dawn were

After shooting down an 801st BG B-24 Carpetbagger on a supply-dropping mission south of Brussels (crew all safe) at 01.30 on 30 May 1944, from left to right: Ogefr Werner Klix (Flt Eng), Lt Karl Kern (pilot), and Ogefr Johannes Langowski (Bordfunker) of 2./NJG4 were decorated with the EK II at Cerfontaine, Belgium later the same day. This crew was bounced by a Mosquito in the vicinity of Laon-Athies airfield in Ju 88 G-1 Wrk.Nr. 751167 on 15–16 June 1944, Lt Kern managing to bale out with severe facial burns, but his crew perished in the crash some 17.5km east of Laon, France. Coll. Charles F. Kern.

able to camouflage our machines so well in a wood that they escaped notice by American reconnaissance aircraft who kept a daily eye on the whole of north-western France. They were able to fly around almost unhindered and without serious opposition. Had the French 'Resistance' really functioned as well as had been boasted for decades after the War, then our landing ground, which was known by the entire population in the vicinity, should have been reported to the other side. Our operations would then have been quickly at an end. As it was, we were able to take off and land without disturbance until the American tanks thrust to the south and occupied Tours. We never noticed any signs of 'Resistance' activity.

During the day we sat around in a chateau-like house on the banks of the Loire, at constant readiness for an American attack on our landing ground – not knowing whether reconnaissance had spotted us or not. Then came the night of the 5–6 June, when towards 3am we were startled by the report that the enemy had landed with parachute troops and gliders at various places in Normandy. At this stage we knew nothing of attacks from the sea. We received orders from *Luftflotte* 3 in Paris to reconnoitre the French Atlantic coast from Caen to the west. As we had only half a dozen servicable FW 190 aircraft, a handful of pilots were given orders to watch a section of the Normandy coast. Following a number of decoy attacks by British paratroops, during which sandbags but no soldiers had been dropped, we were sceptical whether this time it would be the real thing. Against that was the report of gliders, with which the British could hardly make a dummy attack.

It was still pitch dark and our excitement – fear would be a better expression – was great. There was a full moon, but partly obscured by clouds. The take-off from the country meadow on the Loire proceeded as on every night. The strip was only sparsely marked with a few lamps – one was practically tapping in the dark. At that time 'radar' was a virtually unknown German concept; we flew by compass, clock, and the certainty that the sun would rise and light up the familiar landscape of Normandy. The aircraft had been brought out of the forest clearings on to the field and the engines warmed up, then stopped – it was really like on any other night. Everyone climbed aboard, the mechanic helped with the straps, one received reports on the serviceability or otherwise of engines, guns and other matters, pressed the starter button, the BMW 801 engine sprang to life, the mechanic jumped down, waved 'clear' with his torch – and one sat alone in the tight cockpit. There is not much time for thoughts at such a moment – but Schiller's cavalry song flashed through my mind: 'no one else will take his place, he alone must make his race'.

Take-off from a meadow in the dark with a single-engine fighter which had been constructed for daylight operations was a tricky thing. To begin with, the pilot was unable to see ahead and was therefore unable to judge whether he was running straight or in a curve. It was as if the windscreen had been obscured in a car. But all went well that June night; I set course for the Cotentin peninsula, the distance to the sea near Bayeux was about 200km – about thirty minutes' flight with an FW 190. The ground below me was still dark, but the closer I came to the coast, the more frequently the horizon was lit up by flashes from guns or bombs, which were indistinguishable from the distance. There was no doubt – down there hell had broken loose, only I was unable to get a clear picture yet as I could make out no details. I was flying at about 1,000 metres, between me and the moon there was a thin, translucent layer of cloud like a veil. There was something ghostly and threatening about it all.

I had been given no specific objective for my reconnaissance; I was to observe the line Caen–Bayeux–Carentan along the Normandy coast. Gradually it got lighter along the horizon and with each minute I was able to distinguish more clearly what was going on down below me. It was indeed gigantic. Out at sea the contours of hundreds of ships of all sizes became more clear. Directly before the coast and parallel to it lay the heavy battleships which were firing broadsides with all their guns at the German bunkers of the Atlantic Wall. In between, like strings of pearls, the landing craft heading for the coast. For me, flying at some 450km/h, the scene below hardly seemed to matter. But my imagination was sufficient to enable me to guess what was going on – with myself right in the turmoil of muzzle flashes, bombings and signal flares. There was no longer any thought of the supposed dummy attack, this was the real thing, and with no doubt about it. At such a moment one no longer thinks of safety, fear has been swept away, one is in the midst of events, for it was clear that it was the beginning of what we had been anticipating for months. Now they were here, not the hoped for, but the long-expected landing.

In order to see as much as possible, in fact everything, I forgot all caution and went down to a few hundred metres and overflew a heavy battleship which, however, did not fire a single shot at me, although it could have cut me to pieces with its dozens of anti-aircraft guns. Years later I read that the American General Bradley had ordered the fleet not to fire at aircraft as the risk of confusion with Allied aircraft at night – at that stage – was too great. Amongst hundreds of aircraft there could only be a single German one and an attack on a battleship would be most unlikely. So they let me go unscathed.

In my excitement I no longer knew exactly where I was. But in the face of the immense events that did not really matter very much as I would be able to report having observed a never-yet-seen giant armada with hundreds of vessels, which I was unable to count, landing on a wide front on the south-eastern coast of the peninsula. A few dozen more or less would not matter.

My aircraft had fuel for a maximum of two hours and time was pressing for my return. I knew that I had to fly due south, 180 degrees on my compass, in order to reach the Loire to the right or left of Tours. I had just gone on this course when, flying below a thin layer of cloud with the full moon shining above, suddenly there appeared above me and below the cloud layer the silhouettes of several Lancaster bombers looking like shapes projected on to a magic lantern screen. We were at war, the enemy had to be fought and I was in a good position for an attack. The Lancaster crews would hardly be able to see me as the ground was still in the dark. I was in a favourable situation as I was able to see but could not be seen myself and I was able to fire from the dark into the light. And that I did, three times. Within minutes, three Lancasters caught fire, they fired back and hit my aircraft – but I did not notice that and only discovered it after my landing. Whether the Lancaster crews were able to save themselves with their parachutes or not I was unable to observe, but it is probable.

Now time was getting short if I was not to become a victim on the morning of the invasion by having to force-land somewhere due to lack of fuel. The hinterland, the Department with the sympathetic name Calvados, was bathed in the light of the rising sun, and gradually the historical significance of what I had, more or less, accidentally seen and experienced became clear in my mind. It was nothing less than the turning point of the War and I had gradually come to realize this during my two hours over Normandy and the sight of the fire-spitting fleet. I was unable to get an idea of the events on the ground, but if the Allies were able to form a secure base in Normandy, the German *Wehrmacht* would no longer have a chance.

I was now flying at low level towards Tours and felt, nearly 100km from that witches' cauldron, utterly safe and undisturbed. I had not considered that now, after sunrise, the news of the landings would have spread throughout France down to the last flak battery in the hinterland and that the last gunner would be sitting behind his gun with his finger on the trigger. And so it happened that such a dutiful gunner sitting on a church steeple took a bead on me and sent his tracer up towards me. If only one out of a hundred projectiles hits the right place the flight would quickly be at an end. This hundredth one must have found its mark, for suddenly my engine started to run rough; it vibrated, indicating a hit. It could not last long, but then Tours and our secret landing ground came in sight and the engine held out just long enough for a landing. After touching down on the grass strip it turned out that it had not been only a single hit, the undercarriage had only extended on one side which meant that the machine did not keep straight but did a groundloop in an uncontrollable wide arc at some 200km/h. Any obstruction in the way, perhaps a petrol bowser, and it could have been my last flight. The German gunner or a British rear gunner had hit the hydraulic system which operated the undercarriage. Another bullet had bitten a piece out of the propeller; this had upset the smooth running of the engine and I had sat in my cockpit as if in a vibration test bed. But these were only minor matters, though they made me forget temporarily the great world events by bringing me back to mere routine daily happenings.

Shaking, happy to be alive, but unhappy about what I had seen and what would follow, I stood beside my damaged aircraft; thankfully no bowser had stood in the way. Never before had my reports been received so eagerly. It turned out that I had been the first to have overflown the decisive sector of the coast and as such had been the first German to have observed the Anglo-British invasion fleet in its entirety. Everyone congratulated me, there was much speculation about further events and getting a telephone connection to the *Luftflotte* in Paris took, as usual at that time, nearly an hour. When at last the Chief of Staff finally came on the line and received my report, I heard him say to the commander of the *Luftflotte*, Field Marshal Sperrle, who evidently stood beside him: Eberspächer has seen them. Evidently they had not received an authentic report in Paris before mine.

My memory abandons me in recalling the further events of 6 June. But after all the comrades of my *Gruppe*, even if damaged, had landed safely, I am certain that the red Burgundy and the friendly Calvados managed to distract us a little from the historical events of the day. That was the way of an airman's life during the War – one either lived quite well, or one was not alive any more.

On the night of the D-Day landings, Bomber Command despatched a record total of 1,211 aircraft, the majority bombing the coastal defence batteries on the Normandy coast. One-hundred-and-ten aircraft of 1 and 100 Groups carried out extensive bomber support operations, and fifty-eight aircraft of 3 and 5 Groups were employed on a variety of vitally important operations to conceal the true location of the Allied landings for as long as possible. Only thirteen aircraft were lost, eight of which fell to either flak or night fighters. Hptm Eberspächer's victims were probably all Lancaster IIIs engaged on bombing sorties on the French coast, four of which failed to return. NE166 of 582 Squadron (Sqn Ldr A.W. Raybould DSO DFM and crew) went missing without a trace, and 50 Squadron's ND874 (piloted by Plt Off R.G. Ward RAAF) crashed with the loss of six men. 97 Squadron lost two aircraft with all fifteen men perishing (ND739 in the hands of Wg Cdr E.J. Carter DFC, lost without a trace; and ND815 of Lt F.V. Jespersen RNAF and crew, which crashed at Osmanville).

After D-Day, Hptm Eberspächer's 3./SKG10 was mainly employed in the ground-attack role on the invasion front, both by day and by night, being renamed 3./NSG20 in October of the year. Eberspächer led his men in the thick of the action during the Ardennes Offensive, receiving the award of the *Ritterkreuz* on 24 January 1945. He survived the War with 170 operational sorties under his belt, and with seven aircraft shot down on the Western Front.

FIFTY-EIGHTH AND FIFTY-NINTH *ABSCHUSS* – AND A PARACHUTE JUMP

In the immediate aftermath of D-Day, Bomber Command's main thrust of operations continued to be directed towards transportation targets in France, in tactical support of the advancing Allied ground forces. Only a few deep-penetration raids were mounted on German cities in the period prior to mid-September 1944, as becomes clear in Fw Handke's story. Fw Erich Handke, born on 2 November 1920 in Darmstadt, was trained as Bordfunker during 1941–42, crewing up with Fw Georg Kraft and joining 12./NJG1 in October 1942. The team rapidly made a name for themselves, accumulating fourteen kills during the following months. Their partnership came to a violent end when Fw Kraft, whilst flying with another Bordfunker, was shot down by Wg Cdr John 'Bob' Braham DSO, DFC and bar of 141 Squadron on 17–18 August 1943. Kraft was killed, his body being washed ashore in Denmark four weeks later. Fw Handke now joined the crew of Oblt Heinz-Wolfgang Schnaufer, with whom he claimed five *Abschüsse*, before briefly flying on ops with Ofw Karl-Heinz Scherfling and contributing in the destruction of two more bombers. Shortly before the turn of 1943, Handke teamed up with Hptm Martin Drewes, who at that time was Staffel Kapitän of 11./NJG1 and an ace with seven confirmed victories, and Ofw Georg 'Schorsch' Petz, air gunner. On 1 March 1944, Drewes assumed command of III./NJG1, and the team went on to score an amazing thirty-seven kills in the space of less than five months.

> After a long lull, the first major action came on the night of 20–21 July 1944: Duisburg and the Ruhr were again attacked. We were the last to take off, as the situation was not clear. In the box Eisbär we were merely told: Situation uncertain, so we continued to box Hase on the southern edge of the Zuiderzee. There we were informed that a formation was entering the Schelde estuary; we at once flew towards this on a south-westerly course, but I remained on the frequency of GCI station Hase, which suddenly reported a new formation of 100 aircraft by Amsterdam. We turned immediately back to Hase, where six machines of our *Gruppe* had meanwhile collected. The fighter controller of Hase gave an excellent commentary, according to which the enemy aircraft should fly right through the area. When we were back at the beacon I initiated a turn to port, we must be very close; Schorsch (at 5,500 metres height) spotted three of them flashing past on an opposite course. As we turned I saw one more. Immediately afterwards I had the first two in the SN-2, two kilometres ahead, when I discovered a weak blip at 300 metres, probably behind us, but before I had said anything Schorsch had seen him behind and above. We adjusted our speed to his and slowly placed ourselves beneath him. Meanwhile we had discovered another half dozen machines all around us; we had excellent visibility, up to 800 metres. It was a Halifax, under which we were, then Drewes fired from fifty metres into the port wing, it caught fire at once, but also in the fuselage and in the starboard outer engine, which we did not particularly take note of. Probably one of the cannon mountings had come loose, causing this scattering of our fire. The Halifax went into a left turn downwards, the fire went partly out, increased again, it dived ever steeper, finally a long flame shot out of the fuselage and at about 2,000 metres the plane exploded into three parts.

Hptm Martin Drewes (middle), and his III./NJG1 crew of Fw Erich Handke (Bordfunker, left) and Ofw Georg 'Schorsch' Petz (air gunner) have every reason to put on a broad smile after having brought down five Lancasters within forty-five minutes on the Mailly-le-Camp raid of 3–4 May 1944. Coll. Martin Drewes, via Rob de Visser.

We went straight back on to the approach course (100 degrees) and were immediately again right in the bomber stream and tucked ourselves under a Halifax which weaved back and forth. I had been giving a running commentary not only to ground control, but also to our other machines. All of them had seen our first *Abschuss*, but in spite of all that none had found the stream and failed to make an attack! Our Halifax now cut under a Lancaster coming from starboard which was flying a steadier course. As I saw the Halifax disappearing to the right, Drewes had already placed himself under the Lancaster which I had not even seen. At fifty metres range Drewes aimed at the port inner engine, but close to the fuselage (as I could see by the aerial mast on top of the cabin roof in front of me), but before I could say anything he fired. Schorsch had already said we were too close, but then it happened, we must have hit the entire bomb-load, because after the first shots the Lancaster above us disintegrated into a thousand pieces! Our machine was struck several times and all at once we went steeply down out of control, all around us white flames, a thousand green stars, the Lancaster must have been a Pathfinder with flares; we had no intercom, we were thrown about, most of the time I was stuck against the cabin roof. We had gone down perhaps some 1,000 metres (the attack had been at 5,800 metres), when I said to myself it is no use, Drewes can never regain control, I must get out. I gave two tugs of the roof jettison lever (Schorsch had done the same at the rear), the rear cabin roof flew off, I pushed off a little to the rear and was caught at once by the slipstream and pulled upwards; my heel just touched the tail, I was clear of the machine and went down, somersaulting, suddenly no more engine noise, and I briefly saw our machine and the burning wreckage of the Lancaster going down.

Then I found myself turning horizontally in the air, drew in my legs and kicked out again, which made me tumble over forwards. I took my time to pull the rip-cord because I wanted first to break my fall (the straps are only designed for speeds up to 400km/h, and the jerk of the parachute's opening could break one's thigh), and we'd had at least 550km/h on the clock. The air whistled past my ears, in the end I wanted to pull, but I only found the handle after some difficulty, I had to steady my right arm with my hand to keep it steady, then I pulled, then an enormous jerk and I hung on the 'chute. At first I got no air, I must have stopped breathing throughout my fall. Suddenly all was quiet, only a soft rustle from the parachute, I hung jammed in the straps because the CO_2 bottle of my lifejacket must have gone off and inflated it, it was pushing my head forward and

I couldn't see the 'chute above me. On top of that there was blood running from my forehead and nose. I looked at my watch, it was 01.20, then discovered that my fur boots had been dragged off at the opening jerk of the parachute, even though my overalls had covered them. Then I started to swing back and forth which made me feel quite sick. On the forward swing I saw the fire on the ground and, about 200 metres below me, in the faint light, a second parachute swinging (it was Drewes). When I went down I was at first angry that we had been torn out of that beautiful stream where we could have shot down so many more, then I had been afraid that I had jumped too soon leaving the others to continue on their own until I saw the parachute below me, then the swinging about made me feel ever more sick. I was drifting away from the fires, at first all was dark below me, then suddenly I could distinguish fields and meadows, a tree came towards me, I held an arm in front of my face, swished through the leaves, the 'chute was caught in the tops of a poplar arresting the fall, and I gently fell into a meadow. I looked at my watch, it was 01.27.

Then I was sick, but as I felt the firm ground under my feet I felt well again. I tried to drag my parachute off the tree but it was firmly caught. Just before I landed I had seen lights from a signal pistol below me, now I saw more and in their light I saw Drewes no more than fifty metres from me in the meadow. We called to each other and rejoiced at having found each other again. He had only recognized me by my voice as he could hardly see, his eyes having suffered some light burns; they were blood red, but after two weeks they were sound again. On top of that he had strained his left arm and could not fly for eight weeks. We now both shouted for Schorsch who replied after our third call from behind a hedge some 200 metres away. Leading Drewes by the hand, in my stockinged feet and firing Very lights, we finally found Schorsch after having stumbled across several ditches, barbed wire fences and hedges. Leaving our parachutes behind, the three of us set off and by the light of signal lights quickly found a farmhouse. The farmers were already about, they were Dutch. A kilometre away we still heard explosions from the crashed wreckage. We were twenty kilometres north of Enschede, close to the German border. The Dutch were still somewhat confused, they gave us warm water for washing our injuries and a labourer went to fetch a doctor who arrived after half an hour. Having first bandaged Schorsch (I only had a slight cut on the forehead), I put on his fur boots (which were much too large for me) and walked under the guidance of the labourer twenty minutes to the next village to telephone. I got a connection right away to the airfield of Twente some thirty kilometres away where our 8th *Staffel* was stationed. Olt Schmidt was very surprised at my call as our flight time was not up and we were not yet overdue. He also had had two *Abschüsse.* Forty-five minutes later he arrived to fetch us with his car. Four weeks before it had been the other way round, he had baled out with his crew and Drewes had gone to fetch him. Then we drove to the nearest hospital on the other side of the border to get ourselves properly attended to. It turned out that Schorsch had a bomb splinter in the left forearm and a flesh wound in the right. He got plaster casts on both. (He was left with a stiff finger.)

Drewes said that as soon as he had released his harness straps, he was simply catapulted out through the cockpit roof which was torn off and left hanging around his neck, and which he only managed to get rid of with some difficulty. In doing so he had dislocated his arm, but at the farm it snapped in again when he leaned on a table. He had jumped after us but had pulled the rip-cord later, thus landing before us. His singed boots showed that the fire had started up front, which we had not even noticed at the back.

Two days later we went back to Leeuwarden by train. At the site of the crash, my radio operator's leather satchel had been found, undamaged but empty, by the labourer one kilometre away. (Back home I checked on a graph and found that seven minutes' parachute descent corresponded to about 4,000 metres altitude.) On the same night Ofw Scherfling was shot down by an intruder, the third time in six weeks, and this time he was killed; he had survived his award of the *Ritterkreuz* by only three months, he was forever unlucky; had he not been such a good pilot he would have bought it much sooner. He had thirty-one *Abschüsse*. His gunner, Fw Winkler, was also killed. Fw Scholz, his radio operator, was severely injured.

As there was no home leave, we were sent to a convalescent home of the First *Jagdkorps* in Hellbeck on Seeland in Denmark for three weeks, Drewes with his wife and Putzer, Schorsch and his wife, our first mechanic with his wife, our armourer and myself. First we were allowed eight days at home. The night we left, 23 July, three more crews of our *Gruppe* were shot down by Mosquitoes: Hptm Jandrey and crew dead, Uffz Huxolt, the radio operator of Fw Lahmann, dead, and the crew of Lt Hettlich baled out! We all recuperated splendidly in Denmark; during the whole time, which lasted 4½ weeks, I did not even have a cold. I, the only one unmarried, was rewarded by meeting my future wife. On the journey back to Heidelberg via Berlin I caught a bad cold, it did not get better until I had returned to Leeuwarden. Drewes still could not fly because of his arm. We expected daily that Leeuwarden would again be bombed.

His eyes still bloodshot as a result of having to bale out over the German-Dutch border on 20–21 July 1944, Hptm Martin Drewes, Kommandeur of III./NJG1, was photographed at Leeuwarden after being awarded the Ritterkreuz *on 27 July 1944.* Coll. Martin Drewes, via Rob de Visser.

Hptm Drewes' Bf 110 G-4 720410 G9+MD crashed to the north-east of Tubbergen, near the Dutch-German border. The ace crew's first victim of the night was Halifax MZ511 LK-M of 578 Squadron, a veteran aircraft of thirty-two sorties which had left Burn at 23.05 for a raid on Bottrop. Although the crew were warned of a possible night fighter attack when a blip appeared on the Monica set, Drewes' attack came as a complete surprise. The skipper Flt Lt Alastair T. Hope-Robertson must have realized that the aircraft was mortally hit when he gave the bale-out signal 'J' over the visual intercom. Only two men escaped alive: Fg Off Kenneth Parsons (bomb-aimer) and Plt Off Jack Smith (navigator) were probably both thrown clear when the Halifax exploded, and landed unconscious beneath their opened parachutes. At 01.30, MZ511 crashed near Heerde, where Flt Lt Hope-Robertson and four of his crew were laid to rest. The Bottrop raid turned out to be a very black affair for 578 Squadron, with four aircraft failing to return, plus two more colliding in thick cloud on return to base.

The *Nachtjäger*'s second victim of the night was a Pathfinder Lancaster, PB174 LQ-P of 405 (RCAF) Squadron. The twenty-eight-year-old skipper from Toronto, Ontario, Flt Lt J.D. Virtue RCAF, and six of his crew perished when their aircraft exploded, and were laid to rest in the Roman Catholic Cemetery of Tubbergen on 24 July. The crew's sole survivor, Flt Sgt M.S. Stoyko RCAF (rear gunner), came down safely and was hidden by Dutch Resistance fighters.

As Erich Handke briefly mentioned, twenty-five-year-old Ofw Karl-Heinz Scherfling, a thirty-three-victory ace in IV./NJG1, fell victim to a surprise Mosquito attack on this night, leaving

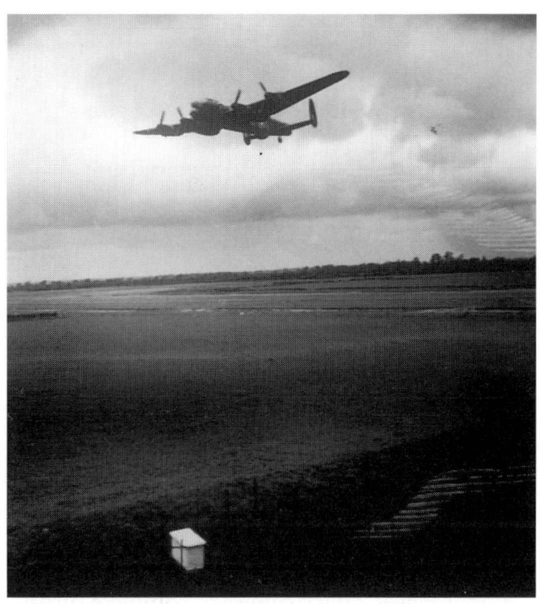

Lancaster JB399 'A' of 49 Squadron, in the hands of Fg Off George Lee, setting out from Fiskerton for the squadron's first daylight operation on 18 July 1944, when 16 squadron aircraft bombed troop concentrations near Caen. On this day, and for the loss of only six aircraft, Bomber Command disgorged over 5,000 tons of bombs on five fortified villages to the east of Caen, making a most useful effort in direct support of the Allied Armies which were about to make an armoured attack in 'Operation Goodwood*'. The bombing badly crippled elements of two German divisions, the 16th* Luftwaffe *Field Division and the 21st* Panzer *Division.* Coll. Leslie Hay.

behind his three-months pregnant widow. Whilst still recovering from his wounds, on 27 July Hptm Martin Drewes received the *Ritterkreuz* for his forty-eight victories. He would add one more kill to his tally before the end of the War, on 3–4 March 1945, and was decorated with the Oak Leaves to his Knight's Cross three weeks before the capitulation of Nazi Germany. Fw Erich Handke's fifty-eighth and fifty-ninth *Abschussbeteiligungen* earned him the rare award, for a Bordfunker, of the *Ritterkreuz* which he received from the hands of General Schmid together with his pilot on 27 July. Both men survived the War unscathed.

BLITZING *NACHTJAGD*

Fw Erich Handke's fears of *Nachtjagd* airfields becoming subject to Allied bombing raids came devastatingly true on 15 August 1944. Sqn Ldr Charles Sherring DFC flew as 97 Squadron's Gunnery Controller on board a Lancaster captained by Wg Cdr Woodroffe on this day. He tells about his forty-fifth trip with Bomber Command as follows:

> The programme was a combined blitz by the Americans and all Bomber Command on German night fighter aerodromes, about twenty of them all told, with about 100 bombers to each. Our target was Deelen aerodrome, just west of the Rhine near Arnhem. It was the loveliest day for flying I could have ever imagined. There wasn't a cloud in the sky and you could see as far as the horizon.
>
> We formed our own lot up between Grantham and Coningsby and then went across the Wash past Wells to Cromer, where the rest of our show joined us. We headed straight out towards Holland at 18,000 feet. Halfway across you could clearly see England and Holland at the same time. We went in close to Ijmuiden, north of Rotterdam, and then south of the Zuyder Zee, and passed an aerodrome that had just been bombed by six Group – smoke was up to 12,000 or 14,000 feet and it looked an awful shambles below. We were eleven minutes late, as Woodroffe was quite inexperienced at leading. There were about thirty or forty heavy guns firing from the aerodrome, which you could see quite clearly from some way away, runways, buildings and all. Then we started our bombing run. The aircraft next to us to port got a direct hit and blew up in the air. It just disintegrated completely before it even began to fall. I'm afraid there was no chance of survivors.
>
> The flak was being pretty accurate and then our bombs started to go off. We were carrying maximum load – fourteen 1,000lb and one 500lb and the result below from 100 aircraft was staggering. All the bombs were on the aerodrome, which just disappeared in a cloud of smoke and dust, and a great column of smoke

came up to nearly our height. As we turned for home you could see far into Germany, no haze and no cloud, and here and there a great pillar of black smoke where another aerodrome had just been bombed. There had been a fighter patrol over all the aerodromes for the morning to prevent any of the night fighters taking off. The damage must have been appalling.

Lindsay, who was flying the other side of the aircraft which had blown up, closed in next to us. Before we were clear of the target area he got a direct hit on his two starboard engines. He got the fire under control but lost half his height and a lot of speed. He kept calling up for fighter support, which went to him and kept with him. He kept going down on two engines till finally he was at 2,000 feet trying to clear the coast, where he was hit again by light flak and another engine went. He lost more height and came down in the sea ten miles off Holland off Ijmuiden. We left the formation to go on on its own and went back to Lindsay. The fighters were circling round them. We gave out wireless fixes and so on, and finally beat them up at really low level. The aircraft tail was still afloat and he and all his crew were near it in their dinghy, all looking really miserable. We left them, as the fighters turned for home as well, and turned back over the sea.

Lindsay got an immediate DFC. The ASR people got going and picked him up from within ten miles off Ijmuiden, and that same evening he was back in England. We passed one speed launch going out as we came back. They kept a fighter patrol over him till all was OK.

Fg Off B.B. Lindsay RAAF and all of his crew managed to evacuate their Lancaster III PB358 OF-J before it disappeared below the cold water of the North Sea off Ijmuiden. Within two hours the seven men were picked up by an RAF HSL. The Lancaster that exploded over Deelen was LM263 EM-N of 207 Squadron, which was captained by 1e Lt Vlieger G.A.C. Overgaauw, who originated from Amsterdam. Overgaauw had escaped from occupied Holland to England in 1941, and was on his thirty-seventh trip in Bomber Command when he and his whole crew met a sudden death over Deelen. Only one other British aircraft, Lancaster X KB749 of 428 Squadron was shot down on the large-scale operation of 15 August. After receiving a direct flak hit whilst bombing Soesterberg, it exploded in midair, throwing clear W/O1 A.P.A. Jakeman RCAF (pilot) and his Flight Engineer Sgt S.W. Wright. Both survived the ordeal to be taken prisoner. The other five crew members all perished and were laid to rest in Amersfoort General Cemetery.

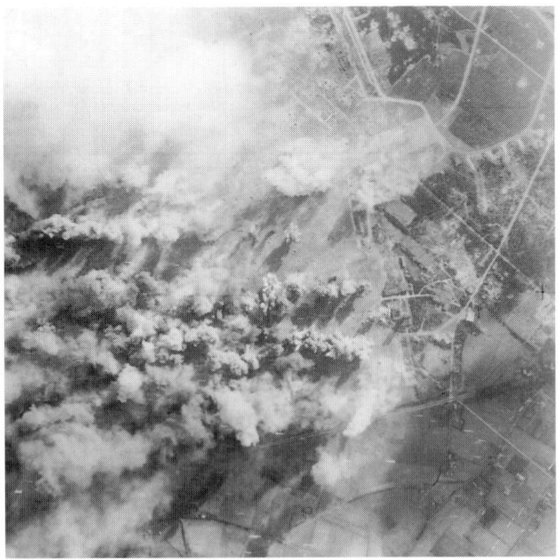

Blitzing Nachtjagd. *A 550 Squadron Lancaster took this target photo of Deelen or Gilze-Rijen airfield under attack, probably during the daylight raid of 15 August 1944.* Coll. Len Browning.

In all, Bomber Command dispatched 599 Lancasters, 385 Halifaxes, nineteen Mosquitoes and one Lightning (flown by Master Bomber Wg Cdr Guy Gibson VC) on 15 August 1944. The American 8th USAAF contributed 517 B-17 and 415 B-24 sorties. This combined force carpet-bombed seven night fighter airfields in the Netherlands, five in Belgium and nine in north and west Germany. Three-hundred-and-ninety-three Mustangs and Lightnings supported the American air armada, with a further 168 Thunderbolts and forty-seven Mustangs escorting Bomber Command on the Dutch airfield raids. Total American losses amounted to twenty-two aircraft.

DOWNED BY A MOSQUITO

The final decline of *Nachtjagd* as an effective fighting force commenced in August 1944. The arm had been rendered 'blind' again by the British jamming of the SN-2 AI radar; its early warning radar chain and VHF Y-navigation stations were run over by advancing Allied ground troops in France, and the British long-range Mosquito night intruder offensive was stepped up with dire consequences for the German night-fighting crews. After a long and distinguished career, during which he had accumulated twenty-three night *Abschüsse* and had risen to command of 6./NJG4, Hptm Hans Autenrieth finally fell victim to one of the dreaded Mosquitoes on 3–4 August 1944. Almost half a century later, he vividly recalls events:

> My *Staffel* (6./NJG4) was stationed at Coulommiers (previously at Tavaux, near Dole, and St Dizier). At briefing we were informed that the invasion forces in the area of Avranches had succeeded in a breakthrough at Rennes and that we were to participate in the ground battles with our armament (four 2cm MG 151s). During the previous night (2–3 August 1944) whilst on a low-level sortie in the area of Avranches, my Ju 88 G-1 had received a number of hits from US flak and, having lost one engine, had had to make an emergency landing at Coulommiers. As night fighters we had had only limited success in such operations and the low-level attacks resulted in unnecessary losses of qualified crews. This situation of course dampened our spirits.
>
> This only improved when we got fresh orders for night-fighting patrols in the area of Brest. Our night fighter control there was expecting the landing of American or British paratroops or other airborne forces in the area. I still remember well this, my last operational flight. After take-off from Coulommiers towards 22.30 in the company of six other aircraft from my *Staffel*, we experienced a dreamlike beautiful night during our climb to 3,000–4,000m height: clear skies, bright moonlight and gleaming white cumulus clouds continuously approaching and then slipping by below us. We had the impression of flying over huge snow-covered mountains and were fascinated by this display of nature under a star-spangled sky. Not one of us thought about the War at this moment.
>
> We were soon brought back to the hard facts of life when we heard over the radio that the operations in the area of Brest had been cancelled and we received orders to fly low-level attacks on enemy positions in the area of Avranches–Rennes as during the night before. We found these operations pointless as we were neither bombers nor fighter-bombers, but night fighters who were only trained and equipped for air combat. We had expressed these opinions during the past briefings and to our superior officers, but our high command had insisted on these operations because it had recognized the great danger of a decisive breakthrough of the Americans in the direction of Rennes–Laval and Flers. It was prepared to sacrifice us.
>
> As, following orders, we abandoned our course to Brest and headed for Avranches, we were suddenly fired at and hit by flak from the American occupied area. A loud bang indicated that we had received a hit in the fuselage of our Ju 88. I tried to avoid further firing by twisting about and checked the instruments in the cockpit. Suddenly my radio operator Rudi Adam shouted 'Aircraft behind!' – but at the same moment we were taken under fire by a British Mosquito long-range night fighter. He hit the port engine and wing of our machine which caught fire at once. I gave my crew orders to bale out and had my hands full keeping the aircraft level long enough for Rudi Adam and then Schorsch Helbig to get out.
>
> I released my straps and could tell by the strong whistle of the slipstream that the floor hatch was open and that both had left the aircraft. When I let go of the controls in order to get out as well, the aircraft immediately flipped over to port as the engine on that side had stopped. But with a final effort I managed to get out of the aircraft which was going down over the port wing. After a few seconds of free fall I tumbled several times over backward and then pulled the rip-cord handle. As the parachute opened with a

mighty jerk and I was hanging in its lines I saw the crash of my downed Ju 88. I was only at a height of a few hundred metres and could see some houses beneath me, I swung violently and drifted towards a house at the edge of the village. I feared to land on its roof, but then fell backward into a tree standing beside a small stream in a meadow. I sprained my left ankle on landing as I had lost one of my fur boots whilst baling out. As I lay on the ground I suddenly heard a loud noise approaching me, which at first I thought were Americans or local residents, but they were only some curious cows which were in that meadow. I released my parachute and hid it in a nearby bush. When I had recovered from my fright I approached the village (whose name I have forgotten). I limped towards a farmhouse in which a light was still showing – it must have been near midnight. My calls were followed by a man opening the door. With my small knowledge of French I explained my situation. He took me into his house where his wife met me. I discovered that the place and its surroundings had been occupied two days before by the Americans and they advised me to give myself up the next day. This I declined, under no circumstances did I want to be taken prisoner but to try, hiding by day and sneaking through the enemy lines by night, to get back to my *Staffel* and my comrades.

Nachtjagd *ace down. Hptm Hans Autenrieth served as Staffel Kapitän of 6./NJG4 in France (operating from St Dizier, Tavaux, Dyon, and Coulommiers) between March 1943 and August 1944, amassing twenty-three confirmed victories during 139 night sorties. Whilst operating over the Invasion front on 3–4 August 1944 in Ju 88 G-1 712343, he and his crew of Fw Rudolf Adam (Bordfunker) and Uffz Georg Helbig were surprised by a Mosquito attack. Hptm Autenrieth and Uffz Helbig baled out safely to be taken prisoner soon after, but Fw Adam has not been traced.* Coll. Anneliese Autenrieth.

Hampered by a badly sprained ankle, Hptm Autenrieth limped eastward, managing to hide himself at daytime, and trekking at night-time for the next two days and nights. After being overcome with sleep on the third day, his hiding place was found by French partisans, who took him with them for interrogation. A few days later, the Frenchmen brought him to a nearby forest with the clear intention of shooting him, when an American armoured truck appeared on the spot. He was handed over to the Allied troops, and, after further interrogation in Cherbourg and the UK, he spent the next one-and-a-half years in a prisoner-of-war camp in the United States.

Hptm Autenrieth's air gunner, Uffz Georg Helbig, had also managed to bale out before the stricken Ju 88 G-1 712343 3C+KP crashed at Fougeres, north-east of Rennes at 01.30. He was soon taken prisoner by Allied troops, but no trace has ever been found of the Bordfunker, Fw Rudi Adam, who possibly died at the hands of French partisans. An interesting résumé of the interrogation of the two surviving members of the crew has been kept in ADI(K) Report No. 463/1944, stating: 'The pilot, who holds the *Deutsches Kreuz* and EKI, is known to have been the Staffel Kapitän of 6./NJG4 for some time. He is a born line-shooter and his morale is high. In interrogation he showed a nice discrimination in the value of intelligence; he had been in the habit of lecturing his crews on

Bomber Ace Crew (I). This 115 Squadron Lancaster crew completed a tour of twenty-nine trips from Witchford between February and August 1944, before moving, as a crew, to PFF Navigational Training Unit. They went on to complete a second tour in 7 (PFF) Squadron during the remaining months of 1944. Fg Off Eric Wilkin, mid-upper gunner (third from left next to his Skipper Flt Lt D.S. McKechnie RCAF) then volunteered for a third tour in a new sky marker crew with 7 Squadron before finally being taken off ops in March 1945. By that time, Eric had completed seventy-two operational sorties, plus a leaflet-dropping trip at OTU. Coll. Eric Wilkin.

behaviour when captured. The gunner's morale was not high and he was willing to talk, but he is a rather dim ex-dance band trumpeter, more interested in jazz than in the German Air Force.'

ENCOUNTERS WITH *NACHTJAGD*

Especially after the introduction of the obliquely upward-firing *Schräge Musik* guns in *Nachtjagd* from August 1943 onwards, using non-tracer ammunition, Bomber Command crews who got shot down hardly ever knew what had hit them. It took a very experienced bomber airman to 'smell' *Nachtjagd* aircraft equipped with this deadly armament before it had closed in for the kill under one of the wings or belly of its bomber target. One such man is Sqn Ldr Noel Corry, who joined No. 12 Squadron (known in Bomber Command as 'The Shiney Dozen') as 'A' Flight Commander on 31 May 1944, with well over 1,000 flying hours under his belt. These included some 300 hours on a tour of night-fighting operations with 25 Squadron during the Battle of Britain. He reflects on his crew's encounters as follows:

Because of my 1940–41 experience as a night fighter pilot, I could 'smell' the German night fighters and read the signs when we were out on bombing raids. Much depended on the weather conditions, lighting in the sky and so on, but there were ops on which, for quite long spells, I rarely flew straight and level for more than a minute or two. I took the view that our job was to get to the target, deliver our bombs on target and get back safely to base so that we could do the same thing the next time. That meant avoiding combat, where possible, by keeping alert so that we saw the German night fighter before he saw us. That did happen on a number of occasions and we were able to slip away and melt into the darkness before he saw us, or perhaps he preferred to leave us alone and turn his attention to another bomber where the crew would be 'easier meat'! I took the view that, in order to survive, it was essential for us to see the night fighter before he saw us.

Early on our tour of ops, I started the practice of calling up each member of the crew on the intercom from time to time, softly, so that, if they were alert and heard me, they were required to respond. On one occasion Sgt 'Ozzy'

Osborne, our mid-upper gunner failed to respond. I then called the wireless operator, Sgt 'Wally' Waldron softly and asked him to check if 'Ozzy' was asleep and, if so, not to waken him but to report back to me. 'Wally' reported that the mid-upper gunner was asleep. I told him to climb on to the deck on top of the bomb-bay (where he would be on much the same level as Ozzy's backside) and to kick him as hard as he could on the backside. This he did – there was a yell, partly of pain and partly of terror; it was harsh treatment, but 'Ozzy' had learnt his lesson. On our return to base I took him aside and explained that, if it happened again, he would 'get the sack'. Fact was, a sleeping gunner could have got us all killed.

We had a determined attack from a Ju 88 nightfighter on our eleventh raid whilst flying Lancaster LM230. The date was 23 July, 1944, and the target was Kiel naval base; we took off at 22.30 from Wickenby and we were airborne for a total of five hours. I have no record of the actual time of the combat, but we were attacked shortly before reaching the 'enemy' coast. There was a new moon and Sgt Frank 'Piwi' Faulkner, the rear gunner saw the Ju 88 coming in from about 800 yards on the port quarter at our level. 'Piwi' opened fire and alerted the crew and 'Ozzy' also opened fire. 'Piwi' called immediately for 'Corkscrew Port'. I threw the Lanc into a corkscrew to port – it was my practice to yell, 'Brace, Brace, Corkscrew!' as I rolled the aircraft into the vertical to start the corkscrew – but the Ju 88 persisted with his attack, despite the ferocity of our evasive action, through two complete corkscrews, and had closed up with us

Sqn Ldr Noel 'Paddy' Corry, 12 Squadron 'A' Flight Commander giving the 'thumbs up' from the cockpit window of his personal Lancaster LM230 'Shillelah'. Wickenby, July/August 1944. Coll. Noel Corry.

Painting of Lancaster LM230 PH-A of 'A' Flight, 12 Squadron, which was collected brand-new from Ludford Magna by Sqn Ldr Corry and his crew on 4 July 1944. It was christened 'Shillelah', emblazoned on the nose of the aircraft beneath a large shamrock. A 'Shillelah' was a club or cudgel, originally made in Shillelagh, a town in County Wicklow, Ireland, and used as a weapon. Whilst Sqn Ldr Corry was on leave, his Deputy Flight Commander, Flt Lt Charles Taylor RNZAF and his crew took 'Shillelah' on a raid to Kiel on the night of 26–27 August 1944 from which they failed to return. Flt Lt Taylor and his crew are listed on the Runnymede Memorial panels as having no known graves. Coll. Noel Corry.

considerably when suddenly all our rear turret guns went u/s and ceased firing. Fortunately, just then the Ju 88 broke away to starboard down into dark sky, the enemy pilot probably deciding that it would be prudent to seek another target with less alert gunners. There was no indication to our gunners that they had hit the Ju 88 severely; during the combat 'Piwi' fired 400 rounds and 'Ozzy' 200 rounds.

We only had one other actual combat with a night fighter; it was on the night of 23 September 1944, while we were on a five-hour-fifteen-minute trip to bomb Neuss, near Düsseldorf. My gunners saw the twin-engined night fighter as he swung in to attack us and gave him a long burst as he scampered away after we had taken violent evasive action. Again, I think the night fighter pilot broke away into the darkness to seek easier prey.

I see from my records that earlier, on our eighth raid on 4 July 1944 (a night of the full moon!), while on a six-hour-ten-minute trip to bomb marshalling yards at Orleans, I and 'Wally' (having a break from his W/Op duties and on the look-out while stretching his legs), spotted an Fw 190 a little below us in the moonlight, but we immediately altered course to slip away from him and there was no combat. Others were not so fortunate that night for we saw three aircraft shot down over the target.

WAHRSCHEINLICHE/NICHT ANERKANNTE ABSCHÜSSE, AND *FEINDBERÜHRUNGEN*

During World War II, the *Luftwaffe* operated a system of three different categories to differentiate between the various encounters with Allied aircraft. In the first place, there was the category of air combat leading to a claim for an *Abschuss*, or confirmed victory. Then there was the *wahrscheinliche* or *nicht anerkannte Abschuss*, equivalent with the Allied possible/probable kill, which was not credited to the claimant as a confirmed victory due to lack of sufficient hard evidence. Third, there was the *Feindberührung* (*mit Luftkampf*), or contact with the enemy (with air combat). Airwar historians usually concentrate on researching the confirmed kills, or *Abschüsse*, category. However, for every one of the 5,833 confirmed Bomber Command aircraft shot down by *Nachtjagd* during World War II, at least one *nicht anerkannte Abschuss* or *Feindberührung* was claimed by night fighter crews. To illustrate this fact, Hptm Hans Autenrieth, an ace with twenty-three confirmed kills in NJG1 and 4, sums up all his claims in these latter two categories:

FEINDBERÜHRUNGEN (MIT LUFTKAMPF)

(1) 30.9.1941 – Towards 00.15 enemy contact with Vickers Wellington north of Hamburg in searchlights.

(2) 30.9.1941 – Towards 01.00 enemy contact with assumedly Hampden/Hereford north-west of Hamburg in searchlights.

(3) 12.2.1942 – Towards 19.15 enemy contact by day with Halifax over the Channel during Operation *Donnerkeil* ('Channel Dash') in section led by Ofw Schönherr. Halifax immediately went into cloud and jettisoned bombs without hitting the ships' formation.

(4) 26.7.1942 – Towards 01.40 near Louvain/Belgium enemy contact with Bristol Blenheim (long-range night fighter) at 300m height.

(5) 29.7.1942 – Towards 03.30 near Hasselt/Belgium enemy contact with long-range night fighter Blenheim at 500–1,000m height.

(6) 17.4.1943 – 02.00 south of Turnhout/Belgium enemy contact with Short Stirling. Due to excessive speed only short burst at short range at rear turret. Hits observed without effect. No defence. Enemy aircraft lost turning in the dark.

(7) 29.6.1943 – Towards 02.15 enemy contact with four-engined enemy aircraft near Liege/Belgium.

(8) 22.4.1944 – Towards 01.30 enemy contact with Short Stirling (agents' aircraft) near Macon/France. Fired at dropping zone. (Do 217.)

(9) 2.5.1944 – Towards 00.35 enemy contact with about four aircraft (probably Lancaster). No attacks possible due failure of guns.

(10) 6.6.1944 – Towards 01.00 enemy contact with single-engined aircraft (probably Hurricane

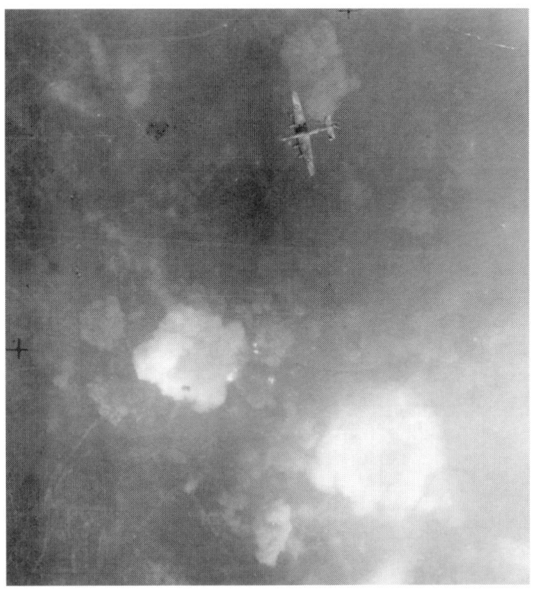

A low-flying Lancaster is clearly silhouetted in this target photograph of a night raid on München, which was brought back by a 550 Squadron Lancaster during late 1944 or early 1945. Coll. Len Browning.

Supporting the Army. Target photograph taken by Flt Lt Watkins' Lancaster LL911 'X' of 61 Squadron looking down at Le Havre from 11,500 feet, 10 September 1944. LL911 added 13,875lb of bombs to the similar loads of almost 1,000 bombers carrying out a concentrated daylight attack on eight German troop positions at Le Havre, without loss. After another (smaller) bombing raid next day, two British divisions launched an attack on this French key coastal port and the German garrison surrendered just a few hours later. Coll. Edgar Ray.

or Defiant) on Channel coast near Fecamp. Attack broken off as not clearly recognized as enemy aircraft.

(11) 3.6.1944 – Towards 00.50 enemy contact with three Lancasters west of Paris, lost due to flying on opposite course.

(12) 3.6.1944 – Towards 00.40 enemy contact with one Lancaster at about 4,000m over Paris. Attack broken off due flak fire.

(13) 3.6.1944 – Towards 00.45 enemy contact with Lancaster at 4,000m over Paris. Attack broken off due risk of ramming (excessive speed and blinded due to flash bombs exploding).

(14) 10.6.1944. Enemy contact towards 00.15 with four-engined aircraft at about 1,800m near Paris. Attack broken off due to blinding from flash bombs.

(15) 24.6.1944 – Towards 01.30 enemy contact with Marauder near Abbeville in searchlight.

(16) 1.8.1944 – Towards 00.30 enemy contact with four-engined aircraft near Dieppe–Abbeville. Attack with Ju 88 broken off due starboard engine damage.

(17) 7.6.1944 – Towards 02.00 enemy contact with Short Stirling at 800m between Rouen and Caen (invasion coast). Enemy aircraft disappeared into cloud.

(18) 2/3.8.1944 – Low level attacks in St Michel Bay near Avranches at disembarking troop movements with 4 MG 151/20. Own aircraft Ju 88 G1 3C+EP heavily damaged by American light flak near Avranches–Rennes (fuselage, wings, and tail unit).

(19) 3/4.8.1944 (take-off 22.59) – Towards midnight contact with enemy long-range night fighter Mosquito between Avranches–Rennes after being hit by heavy American flak. Baled out of burning aircraft near Combourg–Fougeres.

Wahrscheinliche/Nicht Anerkannte Abschüsse

(1) 13.8.1941 – Towards 02.30 south-east Hamburg. Short Stirling at about 4,000m height. One attack with 4 MG 17 and 2 MG FF in searchlight cone. No hits in own aircraft Me 110 D3. A Stirling was found near Bremen with aircraft gunfire damage (rear gunner killed by gunfire). But already confirmed to a flak unit.

(2) 13.8.1941 – Towards 02.50 south of Stade. Vickers Wellington at about 2,500m height. One attack with 4 MG 17 and 2 MG FF in searchlight cone. Defence by rear gunner but no hits on own machine Me 110 D3. Enemy aircraft showed fire and strong smoke on starboard wing and engine and was finally shot down at about 200m height by 2cm flak near Wesermünde and confirmed to them.

(3) 1.6.1942 – Towards 00.50 north of Maastricht. Vickers Wellington at about 4,000m height. One attack with 4 MG 17 and 2 MG FF. Fire returned by rear and front gunners. Number of hits in own machine Me 110 E2. Effect of hits clearly observed in fuselage of Wellington; enemy aircraft went steeply down through clouds with long smoke trail. Attacks broken off due to engine trouble caused by hits and several hits in cabin and instrument panel. Radio operator Adam wounded. Crash of Wellington not found. Bomb jettison observed.

(4) 11.3.1943 – 21.49, west of Verdun, Short Stirling at 2,200m height. One attack with 4 MG 17. Fire in starboard inner engine, smoke trail. Enemy aircraft lost in dive at 200m height after having jettisoned bombs. No hits in own machine Me 110 F4 with *Lichtenstein*.

(5) 4.7.1943 – 01.40, east of Liege. Short Stirling at about 3,500m height. One attack with 4 MG 17 and 2 MG 151/20. Hits in fuselage, starboard wing root and starboard wing observed. Fire out after a short time. About two minutes later crash fire in area Verviers–Eupen observed. Crash site in forest and swamp area not found after days of search and therefore not confirmed.

(6) 2.10.1943 – 22.35, near Strassburg. Halifax at about 3,800m height. One attack with 4 MG 17. All 4 MG FF failed to fire. After initial fire and violent evasive action the enemy aircraft was lost. Some hits in own machine Do 217 N1. Bomb jettison observed, Halifax probably crashed on way home.

(7) 2.5.1944 – 00.30, south-west of Paris. One attack with 4 MG 151/20, after a few hits in fuselage and starboard wing total failure of guns.

Nearly a nasty accident. Bombs falling from above and hitting aircraft flying at a lower level were always a hazard during concentrated bombing raids. In this instance, Lancaster LM190 'R' of 49 Squadron suffered damage to its starboard outer engine by a bomb dropped from an aircraft immediately above over Sequeville, 7–8 August 1944. Fg Off G. Poole brought LM 190 safely back to Fiskerton, where the damage was immortalized on film the next day. The outline of the offending bomb, from the nose back to the fin, can be clearly seen. Coll. Leslie Hay.

> Enemy aircraft recognized as Lancaster went ever lower on return course, speed dropped and only flew straight ahead. Attack had to be abandoned.

HIGH-TECH AIRWAR

During 1943 and early 1944, Bomber Command had been transformed into a mighty four-engined force equipped with a wide range of technical aids for navigating, target-marking, blind-bombing and electronic warfare. Combined with major tactical developments such as diversionary and 'spoof' raiding, the introduction of the Master Bomber, and the use of high-flying Oboe-equipped target-marking Mosquitoes, these enabled the bomber crews to deliver devastating blows to the Third Reich. The Command's transformation is illustrated by W/O Angus Robb, who joined 405 (RCAF) Squadron PFF as a second-tour air gunner in September 1944. He compares the operational conditions on bombing raids at this stage with his experiences during 1943, when he completed a tour in 431 and 432 Squadrons:

> Our crew were Blind Illuminators, and it was our job to get to the target a few minutes before the 'H' hour of the raid and, along with usually five other Blind Illuminator crews, drop a stick of ten illuminating flares over the target. These flares were 'hooded' from above which made it possible to look 'through' them and so allow the other crews involved in the early part of the raid, the Master Bomber and the Primary Visual Markers, to ensure that the RAF were in the right place before allowing the raid to proceed. The dropping of the flares required the aircraft to fly in a straight line for 100 seconds, they were dropped at ten-second intervals, and you can believe me when I tell you that 100 seconds is an eternity when you are flying over a heavily defended target and cannot take evasive action no matter what happens.
>
> When it was decided that the RAF were in the right place, the raid was allowed to go ahead, the rest of the marking was done and the Main Force dropped their bombs on the PFF markers, whose official name was Target Indicators, or TI's to us.
>
> The Master Bomber was a new arrangement as far as I was concerned. In 1943 the individual crews made their own arrangements and dropped their bomb load when they felt the moment was opportune. Now the Master Bomber could stop the bombing, tell the attacking aeroplanes to go higher or lower before bombing, instruct them to ignore certain markers if he felt they were in the wrong place and generally act as a real 'busybody'. That is unfair – they were brave men, the crews of the Master Bombers, doing a highly dangerous job. They all had to stay in the target area for all of the raid, twenty or so minutes, sometimes longer, whilst the rest of us got the hell out of it as soon as we possibly could.
>
> The other thing that was different was the numbers of aeroplanes involved. As an illustration: on 8 April 1943, 392 aircraft attacked Duisburg in the Ruhr. On 14 October 1944 the RAF attacked Duisburg with 1,013 planes, but were able to attack the same city on the following

One grey day in the second half of 1944, a 100 Squadron Lancaster is being serviced at Grimsby. 100 Squadron re-formed in 1 Group Bomber Command in December 1942 and flew Lancasters from Grimsby and Elsham Wolds on 280 raids. For 3,984 sorties flown, ninety-two aircraft were lost, plus twenty-one Lancasters destroyed in crashes. Coll. Maurice Paff.

evening with 1,005 bombers. The logistics of putting this number of planes in the air on successive nights is quite staggering, and illustrates the strides made in the planning aspects of aerial warfare in such a short time.

It should also be noted that the raids we were a part of were, in most cases, not the only large-scale operations that were taking place on the same night, or day, as on my second tour we did several daylight raids.

FEAR

Although the night airwar changed almost beyond recognition during 1943 and 1944, one thing did not alter. The fear that operational flying engendered still affected the crews flying in Bomber Command as it had their pioneering predecessors. Australian Flt Sgt Bill Pearce, WOp/AG in Flt Lt Andy Pelly's crew with 100 Squadron started flying on ops in late August 1944. He tells of a narrow escape on the night of 12–13 September 1944, when he learned the meaning of real fear:

> On the night of September 12, we flew a night op, of seven hours fifteen minutes, to bomb the railway yards at Frankfurt. This proved to be a pretty rugged trip, as we were attacked by night fighters four times. However, thanks to the gunners' alertness, and the skipper's skills, we fought our way out of the four combats without any significant damage. This was one of the times when I hung on in the cabin, my stomach in a very tight knot, listening to it on the intercom, and expecting something to happen at any moment. After each engagement, the skipper would calm us down with a few quiet words, and we would settle down and get on with it.
>
> What happens during a night fighter attack is a violent manoeuvre called the 'corkscrew'. This is carried out by the pilot, on instructions from the gunners, firstly diving in the direction of the attack, and then continually changing direction whilst diving and climbing, to give the effect of a corkscrew track through the air. The idea is to alter the angle at which the fighter must aim to try and hit the bomber, a continual alteration of the angle of deflection.
>
> What I meant when I said I was hanging on in the cabin was that at the bottom of a dive my stomach would be forced down towards my boots, and at the top of a climb, then the start of a dive, I would float up off my seat. I would be held there by jamming my knees under my small desk. My parachute pack would float up off the floor, and then settle back again at the bottom of the dive. I would hear our guns being fired, this came over the intercom as a 'tick tick ticking' noise, and I could smell the burning cordite from the gasses caused by the exploding ammunition. All the while, I would wait for something to happen to our aircraft, like the awful explosive noise as bullets or cannon shells find a mark. (I was to experience this later.) To 'get away with it' was a good feeling, but not really felt until I climbed out of the aircraft at our dispersal area, and once again had my feet on the ground.
>
> When I flew on ops, I felt as if a hand had been pushed into my stomach, grabbed a handful of my insides, twisted them tight, and held them there. That hand would not let go, or the feeling relax, until I was back on the ground. I was no 'hero type', far from it, I was always afraid. We all were; any man who flew with Bomber Command will tell you this, if he doesn't he is being untruthful, or, rarely, a rather unique person. Fear rode on my shoulder, I knew that there was 'something out there' trying to get me, and stop me from doing what I was there to do. But it was not the kind of fear that had me 'hiding under the table'. I knew it was there, I ignored it, I didn't think about it, I just kept on doing what I was supposed to be doing.
>
> Something else that contributed to my 'fear thing' was this; as the wireless op I was mostly attending to my equipment in the cabin of the aircraft, which was blacked out for obvious reasons. Therefore, I didn't see a lot of what was going on outside. I would know about it, I would hear the talking on the intercom between the pilot and the engineer, or the gunners, or the bomb-aimer. I would also feel the movement of the aircraft. I have never been able to decide

> which was the worst, or the best: to see it all happening on the outside, or to be shut off in the cabin, waiting for the worst to happen, for instance, in a fighter attack, or the sudden sliding dive to avoid a searchlight beam, or to avoid another aircraft in the bomber stream. These were always pretty anxious moments, when I could see nothing, and waited for something to happen.

The worst did happen to Bill Pearce and his crew on 20–21 February 1945, whilst serving in 156 (PFF) Squadron. On the bombing run to the target on their forty-second op, the Rhenania Ossag oil refinery at Reisholz, they were surprised by a sudden attack from below from a *Schräge Musik*-fitted Ju 88. Three of the crew were killed, the five others bailing out safely.

VILLAGE INN

Perhaps surprisingly, the defensive firepower of the British heavy bomber aircraft was hardly improved in the course of the War. Despite the fact that the bombers' main type of armament, the Browning .303-inch machine gun of First World War vintage, had proved early in the offensive to be no match for the standard heavy calibre 13mm machine guns and 20mm cannon used in the German fighter aircraft, little effort was put into providing the bombers' gunners with a more suitable type of defensive gun and gun turret.

There were, however, one or two exceptions to the rule. (Unsuccessful) experiments were undertaken to fit a .50-inch belly-gun in the Halifax and Lancaster aircraft during 1943–44, and No. 1 Group had installed the .50-calibre machine guns in the new Rose rear turrets of 83, 101, 153, 170 and 460 Squadrons' Lancasters during mid-1944. Another improvement was tried out on operations between July 1944 and early 1945, when five Lancaster squadrons (Nos 49 (5 Group), 101 and 460 (1 Group), 156 and 635 (both 8 Group)) were equipped with the radar-assisted Airborne Gunlaying in Turrets (AGLT). Code-named Village Inn, this device consisted of a rear turret with a small parabolic radar scanner fitted to the bottom of it. The radar scanner sent out a beam that was reflected by any aircraft at the rear up to 1,500 yards. These reflections were in the form of blips which got faster as the aircraft got nearer, and were also shown on the Fishpond, a radar scanner operated by the crew's wireless operator and which could detect aircraft to the rear of the bomber at up to 2,000 yards. The rear gunner and the W/Op searched independently as the W/Op's range on Fishpond was much greater. When one of them located an aircraft he would immediately alert the crew.

The rear gunner operated his turret in the usual way, but he could also, on a glass screen, track an aircraft closing on his aircraft, and thus open fire without actually seeing the hostile fighter. The rear gunner had pedals with which to work an image of the attacking aircraft on his glass screen, with a circular type of graticule in the form of dashes, rather like a clock, which enabled him to lay off the deflections required according to the position of his own aircraft in relation to the fighter. Fg Off Leslie 'Uncle Will' Hay, a pilot serving with 49 Squadron during 1944 and 1945 recalls the introduction and the use at the sharp end of Village Inn:

> The plan was for the rear gunner to search continually with a view to picking up the night fighters, and for the wireless operator to watch his screen. When an aircraft was engaged, the problem of being friend or foe was overcome by all aircraft being fitted in the nose with a gadget that transmitted infra-red signals and dots and dashes working opposite to morse code. These could be picked up by the rear gunner who had an infra-red telescope attached to his guns. The code could be changed nightly.
>
> The drill was for the rear gunner to pick up an aircraft in conjunction with the wireless operator and, as it came in to attack, the gunner would give the order to 'GO' (port or starboard depending on the direction of attack). The pilot would then go into an avoiding system known as a corkscrew which is just what he did, but the manoeuvres had to be made so that the gunner knew just where he was in the sky and how much deflection

Sgt Harry Swift (mid-upper gunner, left) and Flt Lt John Smith (rear gunner) proudly posing with the newly fitted .5 Rose Gun Turret on their 101 Squadron Lancaster at Ludford Magna in September 1944. Two of the most exposed and vulnerable crew positions in Bomber Command heavies were the mid-upper and rear gunner's. Flt Sgt Harry 'Paddy' Kelso, an Irish air gunner with 101 Squadron gives a graphic account of his experiences over Ludwigshafen, manning the Frazer Nash Type 50 mid-upper turret of Lancaster ME419 on his crew's first operation on 1–2 February 1945:

> *At around 20.40, the navigator advised the Skipper 'Target ahead fifteen minutes' and gave the bomb-aimer a course on to the bombing run. Nerves were on edge and everyone was alert with no need for 'Wakey Wakey' tablets. Our Special Operator advised us of enemy fighters ahead as he had heard Ground Control issue the order to scramble. I must have checked my guns a dozen times during this period. We were now experiencing heavy flak as the Ludwigshafen defences knew where we were heading. Shells seemed to be exploding everywhere and searchlights were combing the sky all around the target. From my mid-upper turret I could get an all-round view and looking ahead I saw this massive concentration of bursting shells and weaving searchlights and thought 'God Almighty have we got to go through that.' There was also the frightening sight of exploding aircraft from direct hits.*
>
> *We managed somehow to get on to our bombing run and I heard Jack say 'Bomb doors open, steady, left, left, steady – right a bit, steady,' then after what appeared to be a long pause 'Bombs gone.' The aircraft seemed to heave a sigh of relief as 12,000lb of bombs dropped away to fall on hapless Ludwigshafen. We still had to fly straight and level for another ten seconds (which seemed an hour) in order to photograph the results of our bombing. During this time shells were exploding all around us and we could do nothing but fly a level course. Searchlights seemed everywhere and it seemed a miracle they didn't find us. At last the pictures were taken and we headed for home thinking the worst was over.*
>
> *We had only just cleared the target area and were feeling quite exhilarated at having completed our first op when suddenly a stream of tracer came up from port quarter down. Bill Green in the rear turret saw the gun flashes and immediately gave the order 'Fighter port quarter down – corkscrew port – go,' we both opened fire in the general direction of the fighter but I doubt if we hit anything as it was very difficult to aim accurately from a diving aircraft and we only had a few seconds to do so.*
>
> *On getting the command to corkscrew, Ted, our pilot, threw the Lancaster into the most violent downward turn I had experienced. We had practised corkscrews in training, but nothing like this, I think Ted must have thought he was flying the Tiger Moth on which he did his initial training. We jinked and weaved all the way down from 20,000 to 12,000 feet where Ted saw a large bank of cumulus cloud into which we dived and managed to escape the fighter's attention.*

Coll. Tony Neve.

to lay off. The pilot would call out what he was doing, for example 'down port rolling', 'up starboard rolling' – these calls and actions were made at precise pre-calculated speeds by which the gunner could assess his deflections which appeared on a glass plate showing a small aircraft. The protrusion of the scanner on the rear turret resulted in the aircraft swinging up to 5 degrees off course with every turn of the turret, a thing which I found rather tiresome.

Part of the squadron was stood down for training until 10 September 1944 during which time we practised, practised and practised with Village Inn. The others continued to operate and the roles were reversed as training was completed. At the start, we flew in daylight with Spitfires attacking from the rear. Cameras were fitted on the fighter and to our rear guns and we developed a co-ordination between the wireless operator, rear gunner and pilot. Needless to say the mid-upper gunner took the opportunity to practise, but he did this on his own. Later we flew in daylight with the rear turret blacked out. This simulated the conditions under which we would operate. Fighters came up at our request and, after each trip, we would go back and look at the films taken from both aircraft to assess our progress. It was a long and tedious business, very hot as it was mid-summer.

It was then decided that the squadron had the experience to make its first operation using Village Inn and our briefing was particularly careful because of the circumstances surrounding the trip. The target on 11 September 1944 was Darmstadt, it was our eighth operation. Each aircraft was briefed to lag behind the bomber stream and stacked in echelon upwards as if we were late and trying to catch up. These were usually the aircraft that the fighters were able to pick off. We were given individual heights to fly and I found that I was right at the back, the uppermost aircraft. I must say that I wasn't keen on being in that position. It seemed too much like being a staked-out goat waiting for the tiger, and would probably be the first to get picked up.

There was always a possibility that there would be some genuine late-comers – there generally were – and their infra-red identification or 'Z' equipment as it was called might not be working. To overcome this we were briefed not to open fire this side of 3 degrees east (the other side of Paris) unless we identified the aircraft visually as an enemy one. We had to be absolutely certain that we were not shooting down our own bombers. It was a bit hair-raising as it seemed to me that we had to leave so much to chance before we would get to grips with anything that might come up. We could only wait and see what happened.

We took off in PB354 'G' as usual but later than the other squadrons, trailing behind and working on a time basis, to Reading then to the coast, guns tested and bombs fused. Here we go. We had hardly crossed the French coast when our wireless operator Sgt J.H. 'Harry' Jenkinson reported that his Fishpond radar screen showed that two aircraft were at 2,000 yards and had been there a little while. The rear gunner Fg Off J.F. Hall was unable to pick them up at that range so we just waited. They then moved closer to about 1,500 yards and Fg Off Hall got them on his radar, their blips sounding on our intercom, but no 'Z' equipment was flashing. The night was dark, no moon, but visibility was quite good.

We had not expected two aircraft like this and were a bit apprehensive, so I climbed 1,000 feet. They followed. I altered course 30 degrees starboard, they followed. With a further alteration of 60 degrees to bring us back to track, they stayed with us. They must be enemy, but we had no visual identification as per briefing and it seemed to me that we must wait, take the first attack and try avoiding action. Our advantage was that we knew that they didn't know that we knew that they were there.

We hadn't long to wait, they drew apart – difficult, whichever side we took the avoiding action we were meat for the other one – but they didn't know that we knew! Sgt Jenkinson: 'Coming in from starboard quarter level, 1,200, 1,100, 1,000, 900, 800, (the blips were now very rapid) 700.' I turned into the oncoming aircraft and dived. A few moments later, the mid-upper Sgt A.E. 'Bill' French said in his best Cockney accent 'I've got him. He's a 188, just gone over the top of us.' We breathed again – now we were ready and straightened out.

There was no time lost. Sgt Jenkinson reported that the other was coming in astern, 1,000, 900, 800, 700, I dived to port and Fg Off Hall opened fire and, almost immediately, the enemy dropped back to 1,500 yards – it seemed to me like the proverbial scalded cat. He never got near us, certainly not within 600 yards and was obviously hit. The two aircraft then flew behind us, close together. (Interesting to think how they were able to locate each other – presumably using us as a reference point.) We assumed that their RT was red hot and wished that we could hear their conversation.

In a short time they were joined by a third and flew in a triangle (all this being reported by Sgt Jenkinson working on Fishpond). This was real trouble. They then spread out and proceeded to make a series of attacks on us, Sgt Jenkinson reported their movements, I was working a continuous corkscrew and Fg Off Hall beat off every attack. It was just as we had practised so many times over the friendly fields of Lincolnshire.

They attacked again and again; the rear guns were almost out of ammunition with only two guns left firing. I told the bomb-aimer Sgt A.J. 'Mac' Mackay to take the ammunition from the front guns to the rear which he endeavoured to do, but as he was moving about and therefore not on intercom, could not hear my commentary, and had no knowledge which way I was going to throw the aircraft. Also he was not on oxygen and the floor was strewn with spent shells, but he got the ammunition to the rear just as the fighters, after making an attack from 450 yards, broke off at 400 yards and abandoned the engagement.

We assessed the situation. No damage – as far as we knew – and the guns were reloaded. However, we were disappointed. Why had we not shot any down? We didn't know it then, but next day when we tested the aircraft we estimated that the probable cause was the ranges sticking due to humidity which meant that the cone of fire did not centre on the enemy. The navigator Plt Off P.W. 'Charlie' Smith reported that there had been ten attacks in twenty minutes, and immediately gave us a new course for the target.

After the exciting start, the rest of the 11–12 September 1944 trip to Darmstadt proved uneventful for Fg Off Hay and his crew. Extracts from the 49 Squadron AGLT/Village Inn combat reports reveal that between 11–12 September 1944 and 7–8 February 1945, its Lancasters became engaged in combat with German night fighters on five occasions using AGLT, without either side scoring a confirmed kill. Although it was intended to use Village Inn at general Bomber Command squadron level, it proved to be difficult to use, prone to mechanical failure and, consequently, no general service use was forthcoming.

LIGHT NIGHT-STRIKING FORCE

The Light Night-Striking Force (LNSF) had been established in 8 (PFF) Group during the summer of 1943 after 'nuisance' raiding by Mosquitoes had proved very successful earlier in the year. Eventually, the LNSF totalled eleven squadrons with an establishment of some 200 Mosquitoes, which tormented Germany throughout 1944–45. The aircraft's high speed made it almost immune to fighter interception, and the Germans never really found a suitable answer to combat the high-flying Mossies. Flt Lt Chas Lockyer DFC was a veteran of Bomber Command's pioneering days in 1941, when he completed a tour of ops flying Hampdens with 106 Squadron from Coningsby. After a spell of instructing at No. 14 OTU he converted on to the Mosquito, teaming up with Scots navigator Fg Off Bart 'Jock' Sherry DFC & Bar and starting his second tour in August 1944 flying Mossies with 608 Squadron from Downham Market. Flt Lt Lockyer recalls his time spent with the force:

With a Lancaster (635) and a Mosquito squadron sharing the same airfield there was, naturally enough, a lot of good-humoured rivalry and banter between the respective aircrews. Our cause wasn't helped by some idiot naming the Mosquito squadrons of 8 Group 'The Light Night-Striking Force', leading us wide open to sarcastic suggestions that the qualification for service on a Mosquito squadron was presumably an inability to see in the dark! It was later changed, I believe, to 'The Fast Night-Striking Force', equally clumsy but less ambiguous.

Always with the aid of 'window', the Mossies were given a wide variety of different tasks in attempts to fool the enemy and tempt the fighters away from the main force of heavies, including such niceties as dropping route markers and target indicators over a false target while the main force pressed on elsewhere. With the introduction of the 'pregnant' Mosquito version, adapted to carry 'cookies' (4,000lb bombs, or 'blockbusters') we became a reasonably lethal bombing force in our own right, particularly as we could operate in weather conditions which grounded the heavies. The inhabitants of Berlin would be the first to acknowledge that 100 Mosquitoes each carrying a cookie weren't the most welcome visitors night after night.

RAF Oakington, 29 November 1944. 571 Squadron 'A' Flight crews in front of one of the unit's Mosquito XVIs, ready to set out on 8 Group's first Mosquito formation daylight raid of the War, against the tar and benzol plant in the Meiderich district of Duisburg. Formed in April 1944, 571 Squadron flew 2,681 Mosquito sorties in the Light Night-Striking Force during the last twelve months of the War, for the loss of just eight aircraft, or 0.8 per cent. Coll. Norman Mackie.

Additionally, when bad weather grounded the main force, small groups of Mosquitoes could be sent to a wide variety of targets in the Reich with the objective of getting a large part of Germany out of bed and into the shelter so there were very few nights when the sirens were silent over there.

We were fortunate at Downham in having a FIDO installation – the fog dispersal system consisting of a double line of burners running parallel to either side of the runway which burned large quantities of petrol on the primus stove principle. The intense heat so generated burned off the fog and thereby enabled the airfield to remain operational when the rest of the area was blanketed in fog. Coming in to land when FIDO was operating was rather like descending into the jaws of hell and proved a very useful incentive to keeping straight after touch-down!

Our first op was to Berlin, my first visit to the Big City (on 15–16 September 1944, when twenty-seven Mosquitoes of the LNSF were despatched to raid Berlin, nine others going to Lübeck and eight to Rheine airfield. One aircraft, KB239 6T-G of 608 Squadron, failed to return. At 02.30, it crashed into the railway station at Rangsdorf, Flt Lt B.H. Smith RCAF and Sgt L.F. Pegg both perishing. Both men were buried in a joint grave at the Berlin 1939–1945 War Cemetery). We'd just released the bombs and had completed the required straight and level run for the benefit of the camera when a master searchlight switched straight on to us and we were immediately coned as its satellites joined in the fun. At the same moment Jock, who had scrambled back from the bomb-aiming position in the nose, spotted an FW 190 closing in on us but slightly high. The pilot obviously hadn't seen us yet or his cannon shells would have blown us out of the sky by now and we were apparently in the blind spot created by the 190's large radial engine.

This situation posed a bit of a problem as any sort of diving turn on our part would undoubtedly bring us into his line of vision and a highly probable early end of our tour. The only alternative seemed to be to try to stay in his blind spot so I throttled back slightly until he was immediately above us and for the next three weeks (well it seemed like three weeks but it was probably about ten minutes) we performed a graceful *pas de deux* over the city, watching him like a hawk and responding as soon as we saw his wing dip as he searched left and right for his prey.

Finally, and to our profound relief, he gave up and turned steeply to starboard while we turned equally steeply to port and high-tailed it for home. We had a few chuckles on the way back trying to guess the gist of the conversation (for want of a better word) which must have gone on between the 190 pilot and his ground controller, with the latter asking what sort of short-sighted *dumkopfs* the *Luftwaffe* were recruiting these days and the pilot responding by asking the controller to kindly clean his screen as he didn't want to spend the rest of the night being vectored on to fly dirt.

After this initiation our second trip to Bremen (on 17–18 September 1944, when forty-two Mosquitoes of the LNSF raided Bremen, and six others Dortmund, all without loss) promised to be a bit of an anticlimax, particularly as we were assured by the Intelligence Officer at briefing that his information was that the anti-aircraft guns at Bremen were now being manned by women and old men owing to the demand for man power to stem the Allied and Russian advance.

Once again we'd just completed our bombing and camera run over Bremen when all hell broke out around us as we were introduced to one of the problems of ops in Mossies. We were often used on diversionary raids, involving extensive use of 'window', the semi-silverised strips of paper which produced a blip on radar screens similar to that produced by an aircraft. This could be used in a variety of permutations to confuse the enemy and give the controllers problems as to where to send up their fighters, and one popular ploy was for the Mosquitoes to overfly the main force of heavies and heave out masses of these strips as the Main Force either continued or diverted to its target while the Mossies carried on to an alternative target, leaving the Germans to decide which was the Main Force. Sometimes they got it right and sometimes they didn't, but the net result as far as we were concerned was that only a limited number of us would finally bomb our particular target and Jerry was able to dispense with his usual box barrage and concentrate on one aircraft at a time. What was happening at Bremen left us in no doubt that we'd drawn the short straw that night.

Climb and dive, twist and turn as we might, the flak was deadly accurate and it was only a matter of time before the flying shrapnel found a vulnerable spot. That spot turned out to be the cooling jacket around the starboard engine and a violent juddering, accompanied by belching smoke, signified the imminent loss of interest of the engine in any further proceedings. Jock feathered the propellor whilst I throttled back and trimmed the aircraft for single-engine flight and his finger hovered anxiously over the fire extinguisher button as we watched the trailing smoke, but there was no fire, the smoke ceased and we breathed again.

We were now faced with a further problem, however, as the returning Mossies would be tracked by German radar so they would soon know our course for home, we would be spotted as a straggler at our reduced speed and fighters would be sent up to intercept. Some more accurate flak near Groningen convinced us it would be somewhat unwise to continue on this course and a hasty cockpit consultation resulted in our turning due north to get out to sea as quickly as possible. This wasn't going to get us any nearer home, but would help to throw off the tracking radar and also deter the German night fighters, who were always reluctant to venture too far out to sea. The bright red 'Boozer' light (receiver tuned to the transmissions of the different types of German radar) in the cockpit soon turned to dull red and finally went out and we thankfully turned westward for home.

On learning that we only had one engine, Downham control promptly diverted us to Coltishall on the well-worn principle 'We're alright, Jack, but if you're going to make a cobblers of your landing we'd rather you cluttered up someone else's flarepath rather than ours'. Welcome home!

After two operations like this, Jock and I were somewhat thoughtful about our chances of doing another fifty-three to complete the tour, but the good old law of averages prevailed and the next half-a-dozen ops were comparatively uneventful. (On 3–4 November, whilst taking off in Mosquito XXV KB426 for another Berlin raid, their aircraft swung to the left due to the port engine suddenly losing power. Flt Lt Lockyer closed the throttles but he was unable to prevent the Mosquito from crashing into the Radar Hut at the other side of the perimeter track. Both men's top front teeth were knocked out, but they were fit to fly again three weeks later. KB426 was a complete write-off.)

At the end of November there was a somewhat more unwelcome diversion in our flying programme when somebody at Command decided to try a daylight raid, employing the American pattern of flying in tight formation, led by two Oboe Mosquitoes, and bombing in salvo. With no defensive armament we were inclined to think that this was carrying cockiness a bit too far, even though we were promised a fighter escort. (This operation took place on 30 November, with thirty-nine Mosquitoes of 8 (PFF) Group attacking the oil plant at Meiderich, Duisburg without loss.)

At the appointed time and place the Mossies rendezvoused, but with no sign of the fighter escort, and since our time schedule didn't allow us to hang about waiting for them we pressed on. The target was Duisburg, in the Ruhr, and we were halfway along the straight and level run up to the target when I spotted high above us a cluster of fighters – single engines and square wing tips, so probably Me 109s. If they were, then that famous 'corner of a foreign field' was going to accomodate twenty-four new permanent guests and it was with a tremendous sense of relief that we identified them as Mustangs as they dived towards us. Just at that moment the flak started to burst among us and they retreated as quickly as they'd arrived and stood off nicely out of range, eyeing us, as Jock put it so succintly, with morbid interest. They rejoined us when we were safely away from the target and we saw no sign of enemy fighters.

We flew two more daylights after that but luckily never encountered any enemy fighter opposition, but on one of the raids I saw a Fortress going down over Rotterdam, and watching that great aircraft helplessly spiralling earthwards was one of my saddest moments of the War. After that we were thankful for the cover of darkness again, although Berlin appeared on the board at briefing more and more often until Jock knew its street geography better than he knew his native Glasgow's.

We got belted once more on a low-level attack on Erfurt and flak pierced our hydraulics, resulting in a flight home with the bomb doors open. Without flaps we opted for the emergency landing strip at Woodbridge in Suffolk and landed without any further problems, although Jock had to use the emergency system to pump down the undercarriage. And so our tour drew towards its end, but we completed it in style with nine of our last eleven trips to Berlin and we finally finished about three weeks before the German surrender.

Statistics reveal that Mosquitoes of the Light Night-Striking Force carried out 27,239 operational sorties between May 1943 and 2–3 May 1945 for a loss of only 108 of their number. Additionally, eighty-eight Mosquitoes were written off as a result of battle damage. During these sorties, about ten thousand 4,000lb 'cookies' were dropped on Germany. Operating in the LNSF between August 1944 and May 1945, 608 Squadron (Flt Lt Lockyer's unit) contributed 1,726 sorties to this impressive record, losing just nine aircraft or 0.5 per cent in the process.

RAF SINK ISLAND

One of the striking facts of the devastating Bomber Command offensive during the final year of the War is that over a third of its sorties were flown in daylight during this period. Loss rates on these daylight raids were even lower than on the current night-time attacks, averaging below 1 per cent, a clear indication of the almost total Allied air superiority by this time.

Although it has never received much publicity, October 1944 witnessed one of the Command's major daylight bombing campaigns of the War. It was directed towards the Dutch peninsula of Walcheren with the aim to flood and destroy the German coastal gun batteries at Walcheren which dominated the approaches to the vitally important supply port of Antwerp. On 17 and 23 September 1944, two major bombing attacks had already been carried out on gun emplacements at Flushing, Westkapelle and Biggekerke, but with little success. The Allies had only scant information on the exact locations of the guns, which led to many dummy positions being bombed on these two raids.

During September, the Allies contemplated an airborne attack on Walcheren, but not enough troops were available and German opposition was considered still to be too strong. Consequently, at the beginning of October, it was decided to flood Walcheren through air attack, as this was believed to be the only solution to eliminate the threat of the German gun positions on the island. On 2 October, two B-17s of 406 Bomb Squadron with an escort of fifteen Mustangs of the 20th Fighter Group, dropped leaflets informing the population of the impending bombing attacks, and advising the Zeelanders to seek a good place to hide. Next day, the sea wall at Westkapelle was subjected to a heavy bombing raid by 247 Lancasters and seven Mosquitoes attacking in eight waves between 11.56 and 15.05, causing a forty-metre wide breach in the sea wall. The successful raid earned the bomber crews big newspaper headlines, the *Daily Mirror* using the headline 'RAF Sink Island' in letters two inches high across the front page.

Between 13.22 and 14.26 on 7 October, a further force of 120 Lancasters and two Mosquitoes dropped 730 tons of high explosives on the sea walls near Flushing, because aerial reconnaissance had revealed that the water only slowly took possession of the peninsula as a result of the 3 October attack. Again, the attacking force suffered no losses, and the dyke was successfully breached. Still, the raid was not a 'piece of cake' for all crews involved, as Fg Off Roy Hill, WOp with 207 Squadron remembers all too well of his eleventh trip:

> We felt quite confident about this one, which promised to be short and sweet, just about the nearest to a hit-and-run raid that Bomber Command were ever likely to devise, and in sharp contrast to the much longer night-time marathons that Lancaster crews were normally called upon to endure.
>
> In what seemed no time at all, we were homing in on our objective, with not a fighter in sight, and only sporadic flak. We were in the first wave, and from my birds-eye view in the astrodome, I could clearly see the sticks of bombs straddling the sea-walls, with little apparent effect – this most certainly wasn't going to be a repeat of the DamBusters epic!
>
> Then just as we dropped our bombs, Jerry opened up with the heavy stuff, ruffling our composure. It was far too close for comfort, you could hear the explosions above the din created by our four labouring Merlins, and our Lanc started to buck in a most alarming fashion. Suddenly, over the intercom came a cry of anguish, which ended abruptly. Looking astern from my vantage point, nothing seemed amiss, then I noticed a neat hole drilled into the perspex dome of the mid-upper turret, and Jock Sweeney, the unfortunate incumbent, slumped forward over his guns. Having relayed this information to George Wall, our Aussie pilot, I scrambled back down the fuselage, and with the help of Artie, the navigator, managed to unbuckle the mercifully unconscious Jock, and laid him out on the rest bed. There was lots of blood about, and from a cursory examination it appeared that quite a sizeable chunk of shrapnel had entered his right shoulder, leaving a jagged wound. We did what we could, injecting morphia and applying dressings. It was vital to get

him home as soon as possible; despite all our efforts he was still losing blood.

Leaving Artie to tend the hapless gunner, I, for the first and last time on ops, strapped myself into the mid-upper turret. Although a fully trained gunner, the occasion had never arisen for me to put my expertise to the test, and the circumstances were, to say the least, daunting. There was a fearful gale blowing through the damaged perspex, and never in my life have I felt so utterly isolated and exposed, with my head and shoulders high above the fuselage, so different from the comparative snug security of my radio compartment.

We had by this time cleared the target area, but were still being dogged by flak, and the plummeting silhouettes, which I recognized with a tightening of the throat as FW 190s, came hurtling down upon our gaggle of plodding Lancasters. Winky, our veteran rear gunner, alert as ever yelled out 'Dive starboard – Go!', simultaneously opening up with a long burst from his 'four-of-a-kind'. As the fighter, his attack frustrated by our manoeuvre, did a climbing turn past us, I swung my guns and opened fire. The feeling was one of intoxication, at long last I was able to vent my spleen on the Third Reich with something more tangible than a Morse key, and I watched hypnotically as the tracer curled towards and into the fighter. To my chagrin, the FW, showing no apparent signs of damage, wheeled away, promptly disappeared into cloud, and we lost touch. I still like to think we drove him away; maybe that's wishful thinking, but it was something to have survived a full-blooded onslaught by so lethal a foe, equipped as he was with immensely superior firepower and speed.

With the injured Jock aboard, George pulled out all the stops on the return journey. I vacated the turret and contacted base, alerting them of our situation. The ambulance ran alongside us as we touched down, and whisked Jock away, still unconscious and ashen faced. We heard subsequently that, following a large blood transfusion, the removal of the shrapnel and a comprehensive stitching job, there was every hope of a full recovery, but it meant the breaking up of our team, and introducing a replacement gunner.

At debriefing we described our combat, and Artie reckoned he had seen smoke belching from the Focke-Wulf as it entered the cloud, but no one else could confirm this, so we hadn't the temerity to claim a 'possible'.

After Walcheren, our tour progressed rather erratically until, on trip number eighteen, to Heilbronn in the Ruhr on 4–5 December, we 'bought it', being shot down in Alsace on our way home by an Me 109, piloted by Major Friedrich-Karl Müller of I./NJG11 (we were the twenty-seventh of his eventual formidable total of thirty victims). Three of our crew perished that night, both gunners, including Ted Sharpe, who had replaced the perhaps not so unfortunate Jock, and Artie, the navigator. We four survivors spent the dying months of the War as guests of the German Government in Stalag Luft I up on the Baltic Coast.

Eventually, on 30 April 1945, Russian forces liberated our camp, and after long delays we were flown back to England by Flying Fortresses of the USAAF, a fortnight after VE Day. The trip home was made at low altitude, as we had no oxygen. So we had a Cooks' Tour of northern Germany, with its spectral towns, and also Holland and Belgium. We passed near Walcheren, and I was one of several crowding into the port gun-blister position, straining to catch a glimpse of the landscape below, and I was awed at what I saw. The scene was one of watery devastation, our visit had been only too successful, and one's heart went out to the thousands of poor innocents whose homes and lands had been despoiled. Doubtless the powers-that-be had been justified in ordering the dykes to be breached, and probably many Allied lives had been saved, but it was an awful price to pay, and left the Dutch with a daunting task of reclamation.

During the second half of the afternoon on 11 October, 160 Lancasters and twenty Mosquitoes of Nos 1 and 8 Group attacked the Fort Frederik Hendrik battery at Breskens and another 115 Lancasters of 5 Group pounded gun positions near Flushing with 612 tons of high explosives. Both attacks went well in the face of heavy flak opposition, although more than half of the Breskens force had to abandon the raid because their target was obscured by smoke and dust. 101 Squadron Lancaster LL771 was shot down by flak and crashed at Heille with the loss of its eight-man crew; it was actually the first aircraft going in to attack the Breskens' gun batteries. A further sixty Lancasters and two Mosquitoes of 5 Group successfully breached the sea walls at Veere without loss. Next day, eighty-six Lancasters and ten Mosquitoes of 1 and 8 Group dropped 531 tons of high explosive plus eighty-eight marker bombs on four gun positions near Breskens, destroying two, without loss. 17 October witnessed forty-seven Lancasters and two Mosquitoes of 5 Group attacking the breach in the sea wall at Westkapelle, after reconnaissance again had shown that the sea water had not advanced far enough between 7 and 17 October. All aircraft returned safely, but the gap in the dyke was not widened. On the 21st of the month, seventy-five Lancasters of 3 Group carried out accurate visual bombing of a coastal battery at Flushing, for the cost of Lancaster HK596 of 75 (RNZAF) Squadron falling victim to flak over the target, all of its crew perishing. The 23 October saw ninety-two Lancasters of 5 Group attacking the Flushing gun battery positions, but visibility was poor and consequently the bombing was scattered. Four aircraft (LM645 of 44 Squadron, NF989 of 467 Squadron, NF977 and PD620 of 463 Squadron with the loss of nineteen airmen plus eight taken prisoner) were shot down by moderate but accurate flak in the target area, with another twenty returning with severe battle damage. Fg Off Les 'Jim' Ovens, pilot with 630 Squadron, vividly recounts the 23 October raid, which was his crew's fifth operational sortie in LM287 LE-O:

> I do remember that the day of the gun emplacements raid was quite a nice one as far as the weather was concerned. Normally, we would learn of operations by about 11am, or soon after. When this time came and went I assumed we were going to be stood down. This suited us because we were going on a few days leave the next day. However, I assumed wrongly, because a little later myself, and I believe it was five other Captains, were called and told we were listed for a daylight operation.
>
> The briefing was absolutely clear that we were most unlikely to encounter much flak. We were told that the Canadian troops in the area would keep the German gunners occupied by launching an attack on them at the time we would be bombing. It did not work out that way and certainly my Lancaster came under heavy fire. True, we were down to only 4,000 feet because above that height we could not see the target properly. We had been briefed to bomb from 8,000 feet, and actually, we had been warned not to go below 6,000 feet as there might be barrage balloons up to that level.
>
> On the bombing run at 4,000 feet, the bomb-aimer was not too happy and was muttering something to the effect that it was a 'bloody suicide run'! Of course, each time we had changed altitude to try to get a better view of the target he had had to adjust the settings of his bombsight to compensate for the lower height. He took a dim view of it. We encountered no fighters, but as we got close, all hell broke loose as we were bracketed by anti-aircraft fire. Our Lanc was rocked by the explosions and bounced around the sky. Flak was whistling through the fuselage and cockpit, and at one point I thought I had been hit in the neck by it. I put my hand up to the spot expecting to see blood on my glove, but when I looked it was covered in a whitish powder. It seemed that a plug of the perspex of the cockpit was the cause, so no harm was done.
>
> The noise of the shells exploding was terrific, and we also had the acrid smell of burnt cordite. We had a saying in those days to the effect that when you could see, hear, and smell the flak, you were in real trouble. But we lived to tell the tale, I am very glad to say. The time of bombing was 16.36.
>
> A fellow squadron crew were surprised to see us back at base as they had seen us vanish in a cloud of black smoke and thought we had been shot down. We found many gashes and holes in our plane on arrival back at base, but nothing vital had been hit or damaged.

Before the month of October was out, three more major raids were mounted by Bomber Command against Walcheren. On the 28th, 155 Halifaxes, eighty-six Lancasters and thirty-six Mosquitoes of 4 and 8 Groups carried out raids on gun positions at five places on the rim of the flooded island. Halifax MZ599 of 76 Squadron and Lancaster HK602 of 90 Squadron crashed in the target area with the loss of all on board, but the bombing appeared to be successful. Next day, 358 aircraft (194 Lancasters, 128 Halifaxes and thirty-six Mosquitoes) of 1, 3, 4 and 8 Groups disgorged some 1,600 tons of bombs on eleven gun positions. Visibility was good and it was believed that all the targets were hit, and only one aircraft (Lancaster III PB630 60-A of 582 Squadron, Fg Off L.F. Croft RNZAF and crew all missing) was lost. Fg Off Lyle F. James, a Canadian pilot with 101 Squadron at Ludford Magna, Lincolnshire, recorded of his fifteenth op:

> On 29 October 1944 our squadron was detailed to attack a coastal gun position situated near the village of Domburg, on the North Sea coast of Walcheren island. I believe the gun was a 155mm calibre. There were several of these guns placed at strategic points along the coast, and were to provide a strong defence against Allied invasion forces. These guns were to be attacked simultaneously, with each gun being allotted to a different squadron. For this attack 101 Squadron sent twenty-four aircraft to attack the Domburg gun.
>
> This was my fifteenth operation (out of a total of thirty-two trips), time on target was 13.30, duration of flight was two hours and thirty minutes and it was the shortest trip of my tour. It was a beautiful Sunday, and when we found that we were to have a short trip to the Dutch coast, and then be home in time for tea, we were quite ecstatic! Little did I realize that this was going to be one of the scariest trips that I would make in my entire tour of operations! We were briefed to bomb at 4,000 feet. However, as we approached the Dutch coast, cloud built up to 10/10ths, and we descended to 1,800 ft, which was extremely low for a heavy bomber, and the lowest altitude from which I ever bombed. As we approached Walcheren, we could see that practically the whole island was under water due to the fact that the Germans had blown the dykes. However Domburg itself was high and dry by a few feet, and we could see cattle, sheep and goats tied up in the main street, where the farmers had brought them for safety. We could see no sign of human beings, doubtless they were in the shelters.
>
> We were the last aircraft to bomb. Approaching the target, my bomb-aimer, Fg Off Gordon Bulloch DFC, reported that the target was completely covered with smoke and debris, so that he could not identify the aiming point. He therefore requested that I 'go around' again. Accordingly, I did a 360-degree turn and flew out to sea for about five minutes. When we came back on our heading the target was completely clear, enabling Gordon to score a direct hit on the gun emplacement, and our camera to record such a clear record of the raid. I am proud to say that this picture became the official picture sent to No. 1 Group Headquarters RAF for this particular operation. I am also very happy to say that not one of the bombs dropped by our squadron did any damage to Domburg, which was about a quarter of a mile from the target.
>
> As soon as we unloaded our bombs, a very keen German gun crew rushed out to an 88mm flak gun, and proceeded to train their gun on us, with the intention of shooting us down! However, due to our low altitude, our mid-upper gunner, Flt Sgt Bill Dean had a perfect view of their actions. Dean immediately asked for permission to open up on this crew. I distinctly recall answering 'Hell yes.' Bill promptly opened up with his twin Browning .303s, stitching two lines of tracer right through the gun site, blasting the breach of the gun, and scattering the gun crew all over the place. At the same time, our rear gunner Flt Sgt Ian Walker spotted a German Jeep racing around the compound. Ian also opened up with the two .5 Brownings that our Lancs carried in the rear turret. His very accurate fire blasted the Jeep on to its side, whence it burst into flame.
>
> By now, with the target successfully bombed, my navigator, Fg Off Bob Irvine DFC, gave me

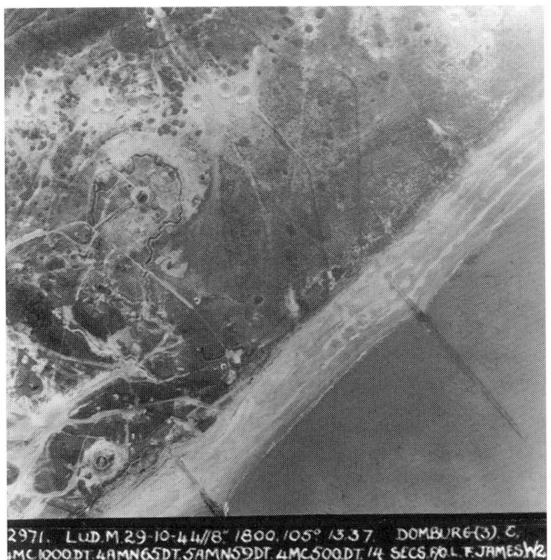

The Domburg target photograph which Fg Off Lyle F. James RCAF of 101 Squadron brought back from the 29 October 1944 Walcheren raid, and which became the official picture sent to No. 1 Group Bomber Command H.Q. for this raid. The coding on the photograph reads as follows: Ludford Magna 29-10-44, 8in (camera lens size), (altitude) 1,800 feet, (course) 105 degrees, (time) 13.37, (target) Domburg, (bomb-load) 4MC1000DT (1,000 pounders) 4AMN65DT, 5AMN59DT, 4MC500DT (500 pounders), 14 seconds (delay on camera), Flying Officer L.F. James, (flying aircraft) W2, 101 (Squadron). Coll. Lyle F. James DFC.

a course for home, and just as I was turning on to it, the rear gunner reported twelve Focke-Wulf 190s coming up on our stern! I distinctly remember thinking that this was the end of my career, and that we were all going to die within a few seconds! However, Flt Sgt Dean came through the intercom with 'Hell, those aren't 190s, they are Typhoons!' That was the most welcome news that I can ever remember hearing! It was a squadron of Canadian Typhoon fighter-bombers returning from a sweep over Germany. They waggled their wings, made some rude gestures towards us, then flew on towards England.

By now we were well out over the North Sea, completely relaxed, when all hell broke loose! Huge cumulo-nimbus clouds had been building up during the afternoon, and we became trapped in one of them. Almost immediately, we began to 'ice up', and I never before or after ever experienced such icing conditions. Immediately, the aircraft was enveloped in what all pilots feared more than anything else, the dreaded clear ice. Our aerials within seconds grew from one half an inch in diameter to over three inches. The wings and all horizontal surfaces built up such a load of ice that our big Lancaster lost all lift. Then to complicate matters further, all four engines cut out, due to the carburettors being choked with ice! I could not hold altitude at all, and we were being forced down towards the sea, losing height at about 1,000 feet per minute. Our wireless operator, Flt Sgt Lionel Wright began frantically sending out an 'SOS', hoping that Air–Sea Rescue in England would receive it. At the same time, my engineer, Flt Sgt Johnny Norrington, was working desperately to get the engines going again, by getting heat to the carburettors, and trying to get engines backfiring in order to blow the ice out.

Fortunately, we literally fell out of the bottom of this killer cu-nim, and we found out that it was raining hard beneath the cloud. This, and

The sea-wall breached on Walcheren in October 1944. Coll. Maurice S. Paff.

the warmer temperature at lower height, started to melt the ice which came off in huge chunks, rattling off the fuselage with a most welcome sound. Best of all, Flt Sgt Norrington's efforts began to pay off and as the ice melted out of the carburettor's intakes, all four Rolls-Royce Merlins picked up, and they began to sing their sweet song of power, our airspeed picked up to 165mph, and pretty soon the coast of England came into sight, and the rest of our trip back to base was uneventful.

30 October 1944 saw 102 Lancasters and eight Mosquitoes successfully attacking gun batteries at Walcheren Island, for the cost of Mosquito IV DZ640 of 627 Squadron and its crew who were lost over the sea due to a Target Indicator prematurely exploding in the bomb bay. It turned out to be the final Bomber Command raid in support of the Walcheren campaign and the opening of the River Scheldt to Allied shipping. Next day, the ground attack on Walcheren commenced, supported by hundreds of Typhoon fighter-bombers attacking various strong points near Flushing and Westkapelle. The island garrison surrendered after a week's heavy battle with Canadian and Scottish troops, including Commandos who sailed their landing craft through the breaches in the sea walls created earlier by Bomber Command. It took another three weeks to clear the Scheldt of mines and the first Allied convoy did not arrive in the port of Antwerp until 28 November.

THE BATTLE OF WITS: ELECTRONIC WARFARE

By early 1944, the night airwar over the Third Reich had increasingly become one of radio and radar measure and countermeasure, with each opponent seeking a technological loophole through which to gain an advantage over the other. In November 1943, virtually all the British electronic countermeasures had been concentrated in 100 (Special Duties, later Bomber Support) Group, and tasked to disrupt the German nightfighting organization.

This 'battle of wits' is clearly illustrated by Sgt Gerhard Heilig's story. Born on 19 April 1925 in Budapest, Hungary, of an Austrian journalist and a Hungarian mother, both members of Jewish families, thirteen-year-old Gerhard had been shipped to Great Britain in December 1938 on a special childrens' transport, thus escaping the threatening doom. During the early war years, after a spell at a Quaker school in Yorkshire, Gerhard learned the trade of electrician at a school for refugees in Leeds, and got a job as a telephone engineer in London. Meanwhile, he had become very interested in aviation, which led to him deciding to volunteer for aircrew duties in the spring of 1943. On reaching the minimum age in the summer of that year, he was trained as a radio operator, to become involved in the highly secret airborne jamming war, the predecessor of today's electronic warfare.

In early October 1943, shortly after I had arrived at No. 4 Radio School at Madley in Herefordshire, there was a call for all German speakers to put their names down. My part in radio countermeasures, the airborne jamming of the German fighter control frequencies, started when in mid-March 1944 another German-speaker from my course (Sgt Johnny Herzog, changed to Hereford prior to commencing operations) and myself were passed out ahead of our fellow students and posted to 214 Squadron at Sculthorpe for operations, soon to be followed by others with this qualification.

We were informed that the sole object of the squadron was to carry special operators like ourselves along in the main bomber stream and it would be our duty to find, identify and jam enemy fighter control transmissions, causing havoc and confusion to their defences. The whole thing was so secret that not even the Commanding Officer knew what it was all about.

No time was wasted in getting us trained on our equipment. It consisted of a control unit with a cathode ray tube scanning the German fighter frequency band. Any transmissions would show up as blips on the screen. We would then tune our receiver to the transmission by moving a strobe spot on to it, and select 'listen'

Bomber Ace Crew (II). Sqn Ldr Dave Leicester RAAF (second from right, back row) and his 35 Squadron Pathfinder crew posing with their Lancaster PB305 TL-F and faithful groundcrew at Graveley on 6 November 1944. They had just returned from the final trip of their second tour, a daylight raid on Gelsenkirchen in the Ruhr, which twenty-one-year-old Sqn Ldr Leicester led as Master Bomber. Kneeling second from the right is Sqn Ldr 'Pat' Patrick, navigator, who completed an amazing 110 operational sorties in Bomber Command during the War, being awarded a DSO plus DFC & Bar. In all, this crew was decorated with eight DFCs, two DFMs and one DSO, amassing 542 bombing sorties between them. Coll. David Leicester.

by throwing a switch for identification. This was where our knowledge of the language came in as the Germans were expected to come up with phoney instructions in order to divert our jammers. If the intercepted call proved positive, we would then switch on our own transmitters and, again using the cathode ray tube, tune our jammers on to that frequency, blasting off the ground controller's voice with a cacaphony of sound which in retrospect would put today's pop music to utter shame. Identifying a call as being positive was very cursory, time did not permit more. Just a quick listen in to hear whether it sounded genuine or just nonsense – otherwise it would have been too late to be effective. This equipment was named ABC (Air Borne Cigar). The transmitters were standard T1154 MF/HF transmitters converted to cover the *Luftwaffe*'s fighter control frequency band of 38–42.5MHz. Later on, specially designed equipment was to be used.

214 Squadron was not yet operational, having recently been converted from Stirlings. The B-17 Fortress had been chosen for the job, later to be followed by B-24 Liberators for 223 Squadron, as the American-type bomb-bay was better suited for the installation of the equipment than the British underfloor bays. New and more sophisticated equipment was being designed and, as far as I knew, installation and maintenance of this would be problematical on British bombers by reason of their general layout, this being for the carriage of large bombs and bomb-loads in a long underfloor bomb-bay. American bombers had their bomb-bay amidships, at wing level, the bombs being stacked vertically up either side with a catwalk between connecting the front and rear fuselage. This would be ideal for the installation of equipment and its access and maintenance from within the aircraft.

As there were not enough special operators to go round, we were allocated to whoever happened to be flying until our establishment would be complete and allow permanent crewing up. We soon made friends and found our favourite crews. The old hands, a number on their second tour, made us welcome and we soon lost the feeling of being intruding greenhorns. Training went on apace and we all felt it could not be long now before we became fully operational.

Johnny and I had been on the squadron a month when someone had the kind thought

Sgt Gerhard Heilig, German-speaking special operator (far right) did his first operational flight with 214 Squadron on Hitler's birthday, 20 April 1944, in Fortress SR386 BU-N (depicted here at Oulton in July 1944). His crew on that occasion was, from left to right: Plt Off Ken Hovers (nav.); Sgt Alf Read (RG); Sgt Jimmy Hollingsworth (WOp); Sgt Jack Hewitt RCAF (waist gunner); Flt Sgt Paddy Gilpin (mid-upper gunner); Fg Off Tommy Thomas (BA); Plt Off Jake Walters RCAF (Captain); Sgt Bill Howard (Flt Eng); Sgt Gerhard Heilig. Coll. Gerhard Heilig.

that, being now fully trained, a spot of overdue leave would not come amiss. It was the afternoon of 20 April and we were getting our things together when we were told to report to our section immediately. There we were told that we had been selected along with two others to take part in the squadron's first operational flight in its new role before proceeding on leave the next day as planned. Some of my special chums were flying that night and I had the pleasure of getting teamed up with Canadian Plt Off Jake Walters and his crew. Target was the railway marshalling yard of La Chapelle in Paris. We did not know it at the time but strikes against focal points of transport were part of the prelude to the Normandy landings. I had celebrated my nineteenth birthday on the day before and today was another birthday, Hitler's. I thought it rather appropriate that I should have the opportunity to start settling a personal account by helping to deliver a small present to That Man. We had an uneventful trip and after a few hours' sleep Johnny and I caught the train to London for a week's leave.

The squadron moved to Oulton on 16 May. One of our specialities were spoof raids, small groups of aircraft shoveling out great quantities of 'window' (aluminium foil strips) to simulate a bomber stream. Following the pattern of attacks on French railway marshalling yards, several of these had been flown over France, giving the real raids to Germany a clear run while the German night fighters were chasing 'window'. Then one night [17 July 1944?] we flew a spoof to the Dutch coast while the real attack consisted of a force of Mosquito night fighters over France. The Germans fell for it and flew straight into the waiting guns of our Mossies.

I have a deep and lasting impression of 214 Squadron as a happy unit with a high morale and a great sense of professionalism. Survival in war is largely a matter of luck, but it has always seemed to me that the high standard of airmanship in 214 must have had something to do with the fact that of the twenty-odd crews I knew, only four were lost.

On one of my leaves with 214 I had lunch with my father at a Czech emigré's club in Bayswater. Amongst the group of his friends there was a WAAF sergeant and I made polite conversation with her. To my opening questions she replied

> that her work was so secret that she could not even tell me where she was stationed. However, before many minutes had passed, I knew that her job was my own counterpart on the ground with 100 Group. When I started to grin, she told me indignantly that it was nothing to laugh about, it was all terribly important, but she was mollified when I told her that I was in the same racket. She then told me the following story.
>
> Receiver operators passed *Luftwaffe* radio traffic to a controller who then issued co-ordinated false instructions to transmitter operators designed to cause confusion to the enemy. One night there was nothing happening whatsoever. Then the controller was roused from his torpor by repeated calls for a homing which evidently remained unanswered. Mainly in order to relieve the utter boredom of a routine watch, he decided to give the lost sheep a course to steer to Woodbridge airfield in Sussex. The German pilot had been faced with the prospect of having to abandon his aircraft and was going to buy everyone concerned a beer on his return to base. He came down safely – to find himself a prisoner and could hardly be expected to keep his promise to stand drinks all round. The aircraft was a Ju 88, stuffed with the latest German equipment, quite a catch for Intelligence. The capture of this aircraft was made public at the time, but not how it had come about.

Indeed, in the early hours of 13 July 1944, Ogfr Mäckle of 7./NJG2 (a relatively inexperienced pilot credited with one *Abschuss*) had taken off from Volkel airfield in the Netherlands for a North Sea patrol to try and intercept one of the 100 Group flying jamming stations, in this case a Stirling, which had been heavily jamming the German early warning long-range radars of late. Inadvertently, Mäckle steered his Ju 88 G-1 on a reciprocal compass course over the North Sea and arrived over eastern England without realizing it. By that time, he was very low on fuel, and after being given a course to steer, it was a very relieved crew that touched down at RAF Woodbridge at 04.30 on their last drops of fuel. To their utter surprise (they had expected to be in the vicinity of Berlin!), the three men were immediately taken prisoner, and it only took the British 'boffins' a few days to unravel the secrets of the Ju 88's SN-2, *Naxos* and *Flensburg*, and to take effective countermeasures. This signed the beginning of the end for *Nachtjagd* as an effective fighting force. With its SN-2 now jammed by 'long window', and *Flensburg* and *Naxos* rendered virtually useless, it had nothing left to hit Bomber Command hard any more. Sgt Gerhard Heilig continues:

> We did our tenth op on July 17 and two days later I was told that I had been posted to 101 Squadron of 1 Group stationed at Ludford Magna near Louth in Lincolnshire along with Johnny and an Australian whose name I believe was Bluey Glick. 101 had pioneered airborne jamming and had continued the job as a sideline, they were short of specials and for some reason

Sgt Gerhard Heilig, German-speaking special operator with 214 and 101 Squadrons during 1944, depicted here in front of the rear entrance hatch of a 101 Squadron Lancaster in the autumn of 1944.
Coll. Gerhard Heilig.

had priority over 214. The three of us had to go and the powers that be had decided on us. 101 was a standard bomber squadron but was additionally fitted with special equipment and a special operator. In the Lancaster, ABC had been installed on the port side aft of the radio operator.

During my time with 101, I flew to a wide variety of targets in Germany and the occupied territories. My operations were not marked by any significant event and I finished my tour unscathed in October 1944. However, I did find my work most fascinating and, as far as I was able to judge, of considerable success. One night with 101 I decided to remain passive – just once – and just watch what went on. A blip duly came up, and almost immediately others appeared left and right, converged on to the original transmission and duly drowned it. My colleagues were evidently busy at it and most effective at their work. Having witnessed it once I went back to my active routine.

ABC was first used operationally by Bomber Command on the night of 7–8 October 1943, when 101 Squadron contributed its aircraft from Ludford Magna to a 342-Lancaster-strong force raiding Stuttgart. In fact, 101 Squadron was the only unit in the command which combined bombing and radar and radio countermeasures in its duties. All other RCM duties were carried out by the top-secret 100 Group. What Gerhard Heilig didn't mention in his story is that the special operators, when operating their set, had to switch themselves out of the crew's intercom circuit. This meant that, for most of the time that they were flying over enemy territory, the special operators were totally isolated from the rest of the crew. From their working position in the aircraft, all they could see of the crew was the mid-upper gunner's legs. As a result, they knew nothing of what was happening until they were well on their way home; they could see or hear nothing of what was happening around and below them.

The special operators were in a little world of their own, searching their cathode ray tube for German conversations between Ground Control

These two photographs were taken in quick succession of 101 Squadron Lancaster SR-B disgorging a standard area bombing load of a 'Cookie and Cans' (cans containing 4lb incendiaries) from its 33-feet-long bomb bay over Duisburg on 14 October 1944. Pilot of this aircraft, with its ABC transmission masts for jamming the German fighter broadcasts clearly in evidence, was Fg Off Grant RCAF. In all, 957 bombers showered 3,574 tons of high explosives and 820 tons of incendiaries on this important Ruhr communications centre within twenty-five minutes, in the heaviest single attack to that date made by Bomber Command. Within a few hours, Operation Hurricane *was continued with a night assault by 941 bombers dropping 4,540 tons of bombs on Duisburg. Bomber Command losses on these two devastating raids, which, as the directive stated, were intended 'to demonstrate to the enemy in Germany generally the overwhelming superiority of the Allied Air Forces in this theatre', only amounted to twenty-one aircraft.* Coll. Gerhard Heilig.

and *Luftwaffe* night fighters, which they then logged before jamming them with one or more of the three transmitters available. Those of the special operators who were sufficiently fluent in German would also transmit false instructions to the *Nachtjagd* crews on R/T, diverting them from the bomber stream. The jamming and transmitting of false instructions was very effective; in an effort to break through the jamming, German controllers tried to use slow morse, which was then countered by installing false slow morse transmitters in the 101 Squadron Lancasters. German conversations and callsigns were logged and passed to RAF Intelligence, before being countered. The frustration among the *Nachtjagd* controllers at times came to the surface when ABC operators suddenly heard 'Get off the air you English Swine!'

SECRET AIRWAR: NIGHT-FIGHTING MOSSIES

Apart from the very efficient Bomber Support RCM and ELINT (Electronic Intelligence) campaign, 100 Group's second major task was to hunt down the *Nachtjagd* crews over the Third Reich. From January 1944 onwards, Mosquito night fighter squadrons from 100 Group, later backed up by their colleagues from the 2nd TAF and the ADGB, launched a campaign to screen the bomber streams, and to intrude on *Nachtjagd* over the German night fighter aerodromes and at its radio beacons. Over the year, they gradually reversed the roles, the German night hunters now becoming the hunted. The ranks of *Nachtjagd* were seriously depleted with at least 487 German aircraft (the majority being *Nachtjagd* aircraft) claimed destroyed by the dreaded 'Wooden Wonder' during 1944–45. Flt Sgt Denis MacKinnon, nav/radar op with 85 Squadron recalls his tour of ops flying in Mosquito XII and XVII night fighters from Swannington during the final eleven months of the War:

> The usual rota was two nights on duty and two nights off. When on duty, the usual morning procedure was, in my case, to have a word with the radar technicians responsible for my 'Gubbins' (radar equipment) to make sure there were no problems. The afternoon was spent in doing an NFT, when we would more often than not practise interceptions with a colleague. Then it would be back to have some tea and a rest before the briefing.
>
> This would consist of the Duty Intelligence Officer giving us details of the night's operations, with the routes the bombers were taking in and out marked on a large map of Europe with red tape. Each crew would be given their task for the night: it could be Bomber Support, simple intruding on a random basis, patrolling beacons round which it was thought enemy fighters might congregate, or patrolling known enemy night fighter bases. Then after an 'any questions' session, the Meteorological Officer would take over and give us details of wind speed, direction and so on, at different heights, and then we navigators would be left to prepare our flight plan.
>
> On the flight I would have my head stuck in the box for most of the time in case I got a 'contact'. I think that German night fighter crews were always on edge. It was never an easy operation to home in on the enemy because there was constant weaving and height changing. On landing we'd be picked up at the dispersal point and taken back to the debriefing room where we were questioned on any activity we saw or on any unusual incidents. And then to bed.
>
> As regards life on the station, it was much the same as on most new airfields I think. No organized entertainment on the camp, except for an occasional game of rugby or soccer, and snooker and a game of cards in the Sergeants' mess. There was also transport into Norwich each night, which was the nearest town of any size. Transport round the camp for us meant picking up a bicycle where you could, then leaving it when you had finished for someone else to use. As aircrew we were allowed an occasional ration of chewing-gum, chocolate, eggs, and there was always a pitcher of milk in the mess to which we could help ourselves. So most of the nights when we were not on duty, it was a case of going to one of the country pubs around for a few beers, then

back to the mess before retiring to our Nissen Huts; freezing cold in the winter and hot as an oven in the summer.

As regards any memories of the operations, a few stand out. Our first operation over Europe was the night prior to the D-Day landings, when with my pilot Flt Lt Bill House we were assigned the task of intruding over the Cherbourg Peninsula while hundreds of gliders were being towed across the Channel. From early July to the end of August 1944 we were transferred to West Malling for Anti-Diver patrols. This operation was an attempt to intercept and shoot down V-1's which were raining down on London at that time.

My first encounter with the enemy was when I was flying on Bomber Support near Koblenz with Flt Lt Bill House on 13 September 1944. I'd never been to Night-Flying Training School; 85 Squadron were short of navigators at the time and I was posted straight from training as a navigator/radio to the squadron. So as you realize I'd never been in an aircraft that had occasion to fire any guns. Anyway I guided Bill on to an Me 110 near Koblenz, and managed it without the crew being aware of us. Bill opened fire and I thought it was us who were being attacked! The noise, to me, was terrifying. But to the enemy it must have been terrible. I think we must have hit its oxygen bottles, because the whole plane just blew up in front of our eyes.

'Achtung Mosquito' *was one of the most dreaded exclamations among* Nachtjagd *crews during 1944–45. Depicted here is a Mosquito XII of 29 Squadron in the summer of 1943, whilst the squadron was converting from the Beaufighter VIF to the Mosquito. After a spell of intruder training, 29 Squadron went on the offensive in May 1944, and was fully engaged on intruder operations until the end of the War in Europe. The German night fighter force was run ragged by Mosquitoes of the ADGB, 100 Group and 2nd TAF, at least 487 German aircraft being claimed destroyed during 1944–45.* Coll. Allan R. Wright.

Other memories stand out: the dreadful fires at Hamburg, the V for Victory flashes we saw occasionally flying over Holland, and the tracers climbing towards us, especially over the 'Happy Valley', the Ruhr. Then there was the time when I was with Ken Vaughan on Bomber Support in the Frankfurt area on 14 January 1945, when we followed a Ju 188 down to something like 1,000 feet before identifying and attacking it. We actually saw the aircraft hit the ground.

Another incident that stays in my mind concerns an American. His name was Peter Taylor and, because for some reason Ken was unavailable, I was detailed to fly with him on this particular night. He was completely new to the business of intruding, but nevertheless a very competent flyer. I picked up a contact near Heligoland and guided Peter on to it. It didn't take me long to identify it as a Lancaster, and advised Peter to get out of it as fast as he could. However, he said he wanted some experience and stayed behind it far longer than was healthy. Of course the inevitable happened, and we were rather badly raked by machine gun fire. Fortunately, neither of us was hit, but one engine was knocked out and other damage done, but we managed to get back on one engine. However, when we did try to land we crashed rather badly and ended up in a field next to the aerodrome. Neither of us were hurt.

There is one other incident. We were coming back from one operation and as we were crossing the Norfolk coast we were warned there were German intruders in the area and were diverted to another base. After landing there and getting a few hours' sleep, we were recalled back to our own base as we had to be back on duty that night. On taking off a booster coil went on one of our engines. Ken very wisely decided to leave the undercarriage down, but we smashed into a

Night hunters. Fg Offs J.E. Barry and his navigator/radar operator G. Hopkins ready to take off in their 29 Squadron Mosquito XIII on a night-flying test prior to an intruder operation over the Third Reich in 1944. Coll. Frank Pringle.

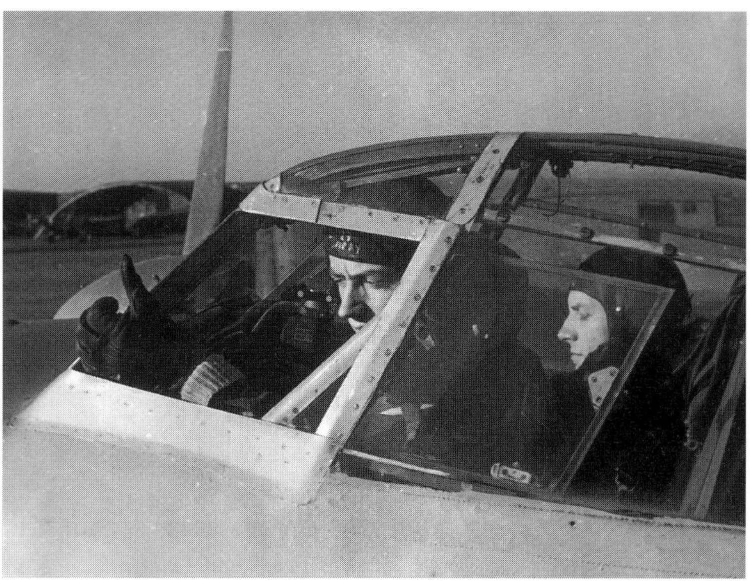

> bank of earth at the end of the runway. The undercart was completely ripped away, but we managed to escape unhurt. If Ken had left the undercart up we'd have probably gone straight into the bank and that would have been the end of us.

Apart from the two combat victories that Denis already described, he and his regular pilot Flt Lt Ken Vaughan claimed an He 219 destroyed in the Ruhr area on 16–17 January 1945. Whilst engaged on another Bomber Support operation the crew destroyed a second 'Owl' over Kiel on 13–14 April 1945.

MOUNTING ODDS: *NACHTJAGD* IN 1944

The German neglect of sufficient night fighter training must be considered as a major factor in the rapid dwindling of *Nachtjagd*'s striking power from mid-1944 onwards. With the establishment of *Nachtjagdschule* 1 (later NJG101) in the summer of 1941, training of future night-fighting crews seemed secured. However, the standard of instructing was lacking, and even after the Hamburg catastrophe in the summer of 1943, emphasis remained on *Himmelbett* operations, whilst long-distance flying, bad-weather landings and navigation were almost completely neglected. This left the rookie crews virtually unprepared for operating in the freelancing tactics adopted during mid-1943, and training often had to be completed at the operational units.

Between 15 September and 31 October 1943, operational losses in the First *Jagdkorps* (*Nachtjagd*'s main command), amounted to fifty-eight aircraft, with the majority of the crews killed or missing. However, due to lack of training facilities, the number of replacement crews lagged behind, which led to a drop in the command's number of combat crews over this period from 339 to 241. This, in turn, seriously affected the battle strength of *Nachtjagd* during the first half of the Battle of Berlin. Although the effects of this vicious circle were recognized and attempts were made to improve training conditions by late 1943, the serious fuel position and the necessity for employing every available pilot for operations made it impossible to remedy this grave situation.

This was at a time when the swift Allied advances in radar warfare, highly developed bomber tactics, long-range intruder activity and the necessity of countering the LNSF Mosquito raids, called for the *Nachtjagd* crews' highest performance in night flying and navigation and comprehensive tactical understanding. The serious situation for *Nachtjagd* is graphically summed up by Bordfunker Uffz Albert Spelthahn. On completion of their night-fighting training in NJG101, the NCO crew Uffz's Spelthahn, Franz Schulte (pilot) and Sigi Hinz (FE) were posted to 5./NJG2, which was equipped with the Ju 88, in May 1944.

> During our final training at München-Riem the *Himmelbett* area night-fighting was still being taught and practised. With such practice sorties, at first in daylight and later on by night, we had had enormous successes; we would have earned the Knight's Cross for Training. But in fact all we had learned there had long been overtaken by reality and worth nothing in later operational flights. It was all rubbish!
>
> At first sight it all looked very convincing and certain of success. But it had originated at a time when the British operated with but five or ten machines or even singly. These would then drop a few bombs, and even these would often land in fields or meadows. This was also the time when the Reichsmarschall Hermann Göring had said one could call him '*Meier*' if but one enemy aircraft would ever get through to Berlin. When Hermann had said that, he might even have believed it himself. But soon there came not ten, not even a hundred, but up to a thousand British bombers in a single night. Added to which, the 'comrades from the other side' had succeeded in disrupting our entire radar system with a simple but effective trick.
>
> That had been achieved by the dropping of millions of small strips of metal foil, the so-called *Düppel* ('window'), of which each one had the effect of appearing as a target on the radar screen thus making the identification of aircraft impossible. That made the ground control radars and our own airborne radar sets virtually worthless. And soon more British aircraft came to Berlin to drop their bombs by the ton than ever the name of '*Meier*' had appeared in its telephone directory. From then on area night-fighting could be consigned to the past. Without directions from the ground, left entirely to one's own resources and eyesight, the night fighters had to range freely and find their objectives as best they could.
>
> 'Objective' was the belittling expression for burning towns visible from afar. Finding these hardly ever required much in the way of direction. Taking off for instance from Cologne when it was Düsseldorf's or some other city's turn in the Ruhr, one would see the 'Christmas trees', the fires and the searchlights from at least 1,000 metres height. Ground Control – and also broadcasting stations – merely gave a running commentary of the direction of the bomber stream using grid references such as: 'Strong enemy formation from Otto-Paula-two to Otto-Konrad-four, *Kirchturm* (height) three-two to three-five.' This method, forced on us by circumstance, which depended entirely on the hunting instincts and luck of our crews, was officially named the *Wilde Sau Nachtjagd*, the 'Wild Boar' night-fighting. But this amusing-sounding expression had a less amusing aftertaste for the crews.
>
> A few days after our arrival we flew our first night-fighting sorties. Not so much in the invasion area however, as over the Ruhr, where almost daily the devil was loose. Like most of us, we achieved nothing; in fact, I believe, we never saw anything at all. And that in spite of the fact that most of the time some hundreds of British aircraft must have been in the air. After all, airspace is very large and three-dimensional. If one is not at nearly the same height as the enemy machines and close to their course, it is unlikely to see even one of them, to say nothing of shooting them down. Should one meet one on an opposite course or even across one's own, one cannot, like a cyclist, back-pedal and flip about. By the time one has turned a 13-ton machine like a Ju 88 flying at 400–450km/h, the enemy machine has long been swallowed up by the dark. Added to which is the difficulty of adjusting one's speed to that of the enemy. While we were hurtling along, the heavily laden bombers, such as the Lancasters, were flying at perhaps 250km/h towards their target. And when the

pilot was a clever old hand and noticed that one of us wanted to 'pee on his wheels', he lowered his flaps and perhaps his undercarriage as well. Then he hung there like a ripe plum and the night fighter flashed hopelessly past him. With luck he might get him into his sights at the last moment and give him a quick spurt. To turn around and get behind him again was hopeless. If all had gone as well with our SN-2 as during training it might have been very different.

But the nasty British not only placed with their millions of tin foil strips, the *Düppel*, veritable clouds of metal in the air; each formation also included a few machines which were brimfull of jamming transmitters and other electronic practical jokes from their box of tricks. With these they were able to prevent any useful radar measures on our part. One had to spot these fellows with one's own eyes before one was able to get at them.

After these frustrating sorties we usually landed back at the well laid-out airfield of Coulommiers. But already in the early dawn, before the ever-present fighter-bombers became active, we took off again for the short flight to the nearby 'shadow' airfield. This was a large, level meadow beside a wood, where our machines were hidden under trees and branches during the day. But it was inevitabe that in time our wheel tracks in the grass would be discovered. At dusk we flew our aircraft back to the main field to be ready for operations. That continued for quite a while, day after day, until the Yanks discovered our satellite field. They then destroyed a number of machines on the ground.

One day we witnessed an attack by several fighter-bombers on our main airfield from the safety of our barracks. We also saw a man from flying control shoot down an American Thunderbolt with his quadruple machine gun.

On another day with particularly good visibility we were able to observe from Bensberg an American attack with four-engined bombers on the centre of Cologne. Little distracted by our flak, they mercilessly dropped their bombs on the houses. A pure terror attack, as so often. The returning aircraft passed over Bensberg at a great height. We were in no danger ourselves and had to watch inactive and embittered as the buildings in Cologne collapsed or went up in flames under the deluge of bombs. With our binoculars we were able to observe every aspect of the attack and the immaculate formations of the B-17 bombers. The aircraft passing over Bensberg had already unloaded their deadly cargo over Cologne. Then suddenly we perceived a sinister rushing sound which escalated to a hellish scream. That must be a particularly heavy one which the Yanks had saved up for our especial delectation. It was as if a piano was hurtling down. 'Take cover!' In no time we all lay flat. Now the explosion must come! – but it only flopped down. One could hardly hear it. Evidently a super-heavy dud which had come down quite close to our childrens' home. We remained in cover for a little while just to make sure and then we went in search of the thing. And what did we find? A grey, sharp-edged cube of pressed metal foil held together by two steel bands. This rough cube had edges of only about 40cm. On closer inspection we realized that it was a package of the notorious 'window'. It had not broken up and scattered because the tiny charges at the steel bands had not gone off. The maker's name could be clearly made out and the present had come from Chicago. The infernal noise of this strange package had been caused by its sharp edges.

As I have already remarked, our airfields became more unsafe from day to day. It was therefore hardly surprising that one day the airbase of Cologne-Ostheim was bombed by the Yanks. The Allies had apportioned their tasks amongst themselves: the British came by night and the Americans by day. These had done a thorough job of their attack and the entire field, including the concrete runway, had been ploughed up. Bomb crater beside bomb crater. It was a real puzzle to mark out something like a provisional runway amongst all these holes. Anyone wishing to take off from there had to lift off very early because of the shortness of the strip, nor deviate even a little to the right or left. That would have been lethal. The distance to some of the craters was hardly more than five

During the final phase of Zerstörer *(Heavy Fighter) training, formation-flying practice featured on the flying programme regularly. This shot of Bf 110 CC+11 of the* Zerstörerschule *at Schleissheim was taken in early 1941.*
Coll. Anneliese Autenrieth.

metres from the wheel tracks. It was therefore left to the pilots whether they would risk a take-off under these difficult circumstances. Franz dared it and took off. Perfectly and without any difficulties! It says something for the abilities of our pilots that the entire *Staffel* got away without a single accident.

One had to be constantly on the alert, however, for the British long-range night fighters, the Mosquitoes, were increasingly active around our landing grounds. When they caught one of us in the particularly critical phase of approach and landing, then he'd had it. The special attractions of Bonn-Hangelar must have reached the ears of the British. During approach we heard ever frequently the warning over the radio: 'Attention, coin fakers at the station!' Then it would be as well if the radio operators kept their eyes open and made the machine guns ready. We were lucky and for the time being were spared the malicious Mosquito attacks. During this time two other aircraft were shot down during landing. We were able to observe the crashes from a greater height. After several crews had been lost in this way, one began to position 2cm quadruple light flak guns and searchlights along the approach lights. These had the task of illuminating the approach sector behind the landing night fighter. This improved our chances of survival if a Mosquito should position itself behind us. We very much welcomed this, for they gave us a degree of security during landing.

But otherwise we did not have a particularly good opinion of our flak units – especially the 88s. Not that we blamed our comrades for shooting down so few British bombers – in spite of an unbelievable consumption of ammunition. (After all, our own successes were also limited.) But the comrades from the flak fired not only at the British, but also at us. Had they once located one of us, they fired pretty accurately too.

During night operations, whether over the Ruhr or Darmstadt, the picture was very much the same. First came the so-called Pathfinders who marked the target with their 'Christmas trees'. That made the operational area visible from afar for us as well. Minutes later followed the inferno for the chosen city. For us from above, this picture presented a frightening fascination time and again. Thousands of explosive and incendiary bombs would flash below us, continually, wave upon wave. Such an attack would frequently last half an hour or more and soon the fires would spread and cover ever larger areas. We knew from our own experience what was happening to the people below. Compared to that, our night-fighting was a mere harmless pleasure flight.

Some thousands of metres above the town there was a similar picture. A ceaseless flashing of countless flak shells exploding in mid-air in between the searchlights, like groping fingers in empty space. The bulk of the bomber stream ought to be where the flak was at its most intense. Raging mad, and the firm will to get at last one of these four-engined bombers, we would fly to the centre of the flak fire time and again – frequently right into it; or place ourselves into the supposed approach or departure tracks of the bombers, straining our eyes. Although generally hundreds of aircraft would be involved in these terror attacks, it was very seldom that one of them would be seen. What made it even more difficult was the fact that the British would be flying at varying levels, which made it even more difficult to spot them.

In order to understand our irritation with the flak, it must be understood that they used not so much the searchlights as their radar for the direction of their fire. And that radar, as also our own SN-2, was made increasingly useless by the dropping of 'window' and other electronic tricks. We ourselves were, at least theoretically, made electronically immune against recognition and our own flak fire. Our machines carried special IFF equipment (FuG 25, with a range of 100km). Each evening the radio mechanic would insert into it a key carrying the recognition code of the day. This key carried a number of teeth, of which the appropriate ones would be broken out. The code itself consisted of two letters, such as Anton-Marta (dida-dada) which the equipment would transmit. There was also the daily changing 'ES' (*Eigen Schutz*), the recognition signal. These were signal rockets showing the colours of the day which could be fired off into the night with a large-calibre signal pistol. These would show for about ten seconds, such as one green and two red lights.

If we were caught by our own flak, that is their *Würzburg* radar, then our FuG 25 would automatically respond with its code. Slowly but clearly this would show up on the ground and the operator would know that he had caught a German machine. Be it that our comrades of the flak would not believe this, for the nasty British used all kind of tricks and even used our own codes or fired off the valid colours of the day; be it that our flak was pleased to have a clear picture at last (for we did not interfere) – they gave us all they got. The very first 'group' – the four shells always fired simultaneously by a battery – was often uncomfortably close. If it was to port, Franz would turn to port. If starboard, then to starboard. Always into the fire. For the good comrades always corrected after a group; if they were to the left, then they were pretty certainly far to the right after our flying into it. We called that the flak waltz. Franz was always very sour when the flak fired at us and refused to stop even after we had fired off the colours of the day. 'I'll stand the machine on its head and let them have

Bf 110s of NJG101 at Stuttgart, Spring 1943. Although NJG101 (formerly Nachtjagdschule *1) was primarily a night-fighting training wing, by the end of the War instructor crews of this unit had notched up some 200 confirmed aerial victories.* Coll. Peter Spoden.

it,' he said time and again, but he never did. We frequently saw the shells explode beside, behind or in front of us. And sometimes, when the 'group' went off below us, our machine was bounced upward to a greater or lesser degree. A queer feeling, that.

Anyone reading this must think that we would have our pants full on these night sorties. But that wasn't so in fact. Not because we were such fine fellows, or even 'heroes'. We were none of that. But compared to our comrades of the infantry whose nerves were torn by every shot and striking bullet, we experienced all these terrible events somehow at some distance. Apart from the soothing droning of our engines and the squeaks and voice on the radio we had no audible contact with the outside world. We were largely screened off from without and experienced the entire inferno below us and the firing of the flak almost as in a silent film. That was probably the reason that we were generally able to react relatively calmly and without fear.

Had the entire war and all we experienced not been such an inhuman and hardly imaginable madness, one could have laughed at times. One day someone with an obviously English accent came up on the German night fighter frequency and said, in an otherwise correct form: 'Make *Reise-Reise* to Dora-Paula-two!' (Or something like that.) To which the angry reply in an unmistakable Frankfurt dialect: 'Shut your gob, you arsehole, or I'll shut it for you!'

However unpleasant and sometimes hazardous our frequent misunderstandings with the flak might have been, the fast Mosquitoes continued to be the greatest danger to us all. The flak could be fooled if necessary, the Mosquitoes hardly. The aerial superiority of the British by night and the Yanks by day was altogether crushing. It was hardly conceivable that the *Luftwaffe* had once enjoyed total supremacy. For that one had to think far back: Poland, the campaign in France and other early theatres of the War – until about the autumn of 1941. But it was not only the countless aircraft at the Allies' disposal or the unlimited supply of fuel which had led to their supremacy. Added to this we were behind in electronics and partly also in our aircraft design. The Mosquito, for instance, was so fast because of its light and largely wooden construction.

It had become hardly worthwhile to switch on our own airborne radar, the SN-2. One could hardly make out a clear target amidst all the interference. It was better to keep one's eyes open and look outside rather than to keep staring into the flickering tube. But one night I was able to give Franz a clear target on my screen. Distance about 1,000 metres. I guided him at once to the correct height and directly behind the target. We were flying at full throttle, but the 1,000-metre range quickly grew to 1,500, then 2,000, and shortly afterwards it was gone altogether. No doubt it had been a Mosquito who, with its superior speed, had had no need to use 'window' or interfere in any other way. Our own Ju 88 G-6 with its two Jumo 213 engines (of some 1,500hp each) could hardly have been called slow, but here we simply could not compete.

After this first unreal contact with the fellows from the other side – if it could be called a contact at all – things soon began to be more realistic. We had known for a long time that we always had to reckon with Mosquitoes on landing; but now we had to be increasingly on the alert on our return flights at 3–4,000 metres height. One night we were returning peacefully on a straight course from a sortie in the Rhein-Main area. I had relaxed, was leaning back in my seat and had just acknowledged with a casual did-did-did-da-di-da a QDM (course to steer) I had obtained from a direction-finding station. But beside the squawks in my earphones, I also perceived a strange stuttering sound from outside. There was nothing to be seen, but then the sound was repeated. They were aircraft guns – quite close to us. 'Franz, we are being fired at!' I called to the pilot over the intercom who, like Sigi, had noticed nothing. Somewhat unbelieving and only as a precaution Franz swung the aircraft away a little. Then the Brit appeared a bare 100 metres away above our tailplane. At his first attack he had apparently raked us from below with his *Schräge Musik* [sic; the RAF never did use these upward pointing guns on

From left: Uffzs Sigi Hinz (Flt Eng), Franz Schulte (pilot), and Albert Spelthahn (Bordfunker) posing with a Ju 88 in Zerstörer *configuration, spring 1944.* Coll. Albert Spelthahn.

night fighters – author] and that was why he had remained hidden from our sight. Now was my chance. As Bordfunker I had an MG 131 mounted to the rear and was now able to give him something back. I had already turned on the electric mechanism and with sufficient light I had him fully in my sights. I calmly pressed the trigger. The breech snapped close but only made a click – nothing else. I cocked the gun again with that funny lever, the 'tin opener', reactivated the firing, pressed the trigger, and again nothing. Shit, shit! (I still say that today when the Brit appears in my dreams.) My great chance had gone, the thing would not work. Franz was meanwhile wide awake and did a fair display of aerobatics with our Ju 88.

Somehow we must get rid of these fellows who were so much faster than ourselves. Into the clouds, five minutes or longer, then out again. Franz had descended a couple of hundred metres, but as we emerged from the cloud at high speed, who was sitting close behind us? Those fellows! It went like that for about a quarter of an hour. We rejoiced at the tiniest cloud in which we could hide. It seemed like an eternity until we had finally got rid of the Mosquito. He must have had a good radar on board. The unplanned aerobatics had taken us somewhat off our direct course for home and we landed at the nearest airfield, at Mainz-Finthen. There we discovered that the Tommy had hit us with one of his bursts. The tailwheel tyre was flat and one part of our dipole aerial had been shot away. We had a few small, harmless-looking holes in the fuselage, mainly from splinters.

In these days we were not only hunters, but sometimes the hunted. It might well have turned out very different, especially the attack from below, where we were entirely unprotected. We were not so vulnerable to attacks from behind. Not only was there a 10mm-thick bulkhead directly behind my radio gear, the window around my machine gun was also thick and secure against gunfire. It was similar up front, where Franz and Sigi sat. They were also protected by a steel bulkhead. Then there was the windscreen of armoured glass which, with its numerous layers, was about 40mm thick. That was all very reassuring. Especially when on attacking a British bomber from behind one were to get defensive fire from his rear turret.

There was nothing we could do against being discovered by a Mosquito's radar. Apart from that, we made ourselves invisible as far as possible. When night-fighting first started our aircraft were camouflaged a dead black; this had now changed to a very light colour, almost white. Only the top parts of our Ju 88 had an

5./NJG2 crews at readiness in the crew room of Köln-Ostheim airfield, May 1944. From left: Uffz Fritz Laue (Flt Eng), his pilot Fw Erich Kubetz (survived the War with three Abschüsse*), and Uffz Gerhard Hug, their Bordfunker; Uffz Franz Schulte (pilot), and his Flt Eng Uffz Siegfried Hinz. Uffz Albert Spelthahn, Schulte's Funker, took this snapshot. Uffz Hug was most probably the only Bordfunker in* Nachtjagd *who is credited with shooting down a Mosquito night fighter, as he recalls:*

> *I cannot recall the exact date in the autumn of 1944, it was October or November. We took off in our Ju 88 from Cologne-Ostheim heading for the Ruhr. My SN-2 radar suffered such interference from 'window' that I was only able to give rough directions to my pilot for getting into the bomber stream. When, at 4,500 metres height, individual blips on the screen became clearer, the Flight Engineer had already sighted a four-engined enemy bomber. My own task was now to keep watch for attackers from behind. and I sat with my back to the pilot and heard over the intercom the other two getting ready for the attack, when suddenly a blip appeared on my SN-2 about 200 metres behind. That is an aircraft overtaking from behind. To the left of my head my MG 131 hung in a leather strap. During training I had learned that one should commence firing before taking aim in order to irritate the enemy with the tracer. I therefore opened fire before releasing the machine gun and at the same time called over the intercom – 'Indianer, Indianer!' ('Red Indians, Red Indians'). But at the same moment our aircraft went down into the attack and all four MG 151 2cm cannons went off. Our dive had caused the attacker to fly right into my burst and flames spurted from the starboard wing or engine, without my having taken aim. We broke off from the burning Lancaster in a turn to port and I observed my burning opponent disappearing into a layer of cloud. After landing, both victories were confirmed by the flak who had observed both these attacks.*

There were several nights during October and November 1944 when both Lancaster and Bomber Support Mosquitoes were lost on operations over the Ruhr and southern Germany: 6–7 and 19–20 October, 6–7 and 26–27 November, and 30 November–1 December 1944. Coll. Gerhard Hug.

irregular pattern on a light base, something like a dapple-grey horse. Thus we were not so easily recognizable when flying over low cloud or the smoke of a burning city. Supposedly. The blueish exhaust flames, which could be seen from afar, had been obscured by thick semi-stovepipe-like screens. Navigation lights, landing lights and the little lighting inside the cockpit were no longer allowed to be used. For internal lighting we had but a few tiny ultra-violet lamps. In order to see anything at all we had had our maps impregnated by some fluorescent material. These gave off a veritably magical glow under the ultra-violet lights.

One night, in spite of all these precautionary measures, we nevertheless had one more encounter with a British long-range night fighter. Whether it had been a pursuit or a chance encounter, we did not know. During the homeward flight from a sortie I suddenly spotted him on our starboard quarter. Distance a bare hundred metres. He was at our own level, a twin-engined aircraft, following us at our own speed. With no markings that could be discerned. Only the silhouette. Franz was startled and sour because I opened fire at once. He thought we had bought it this time. It was pretty noisy too, as I was firing from inside the cabin. Apart from that, it had been the first time that Franz and Sigi had experienced my gun in action. For at our first encounter with a Mosquito it had failed ignominiously. This time I wanted to see it work and lose no time about it. (On the principle of: He who shoots first, lives longer.) I was not accustomed to firing tracer, it dazzled somewhat in the dark. Then I was amazed, for I saw it for the very first time, that my tracer went away in a curve to the right while I was firing at an angle to the rear. That bothered me no end. The Brit took no evasive action and neither did he fire. So there were no wild manoeuvres as the first time. Perhaps he was perplexed. Anyway, I failed to hit him, to say nothing of shooting him down. Could be that he received a hit or two, but there was nothing to show that. After some time we somehow drew apart without any further incident.

Area night-fighting, with which they had driven us mad at München-Riem and which we had had to practise to perfection, had not been used for a long time. The SN-2, of which we had had such high expectations after the first practice flights, could now be forgotten. At best one might get a Mosquito within its range which then promptly flew off. Otherwise there was hardly a target to be found with it. And for the type of night-fighting which was now of necessity taking place we had not been trained. No one had been trained for it, because there was no such training and none could be set up. In order to have any success at all, one needed a good portion of luck, a great deal of experience and a hunting instinct which could only be developed in the course of time. We were therefore by no means the only ones amongst the more junior crews who had had no success after some ten or fifteen sorties. Even the old stagers on our *Staffel* had a hard time of it and hardly brought the British down by the score.

As we had done some nineteen or twenty sorties altogether, I reckon that the one on 2 November 1944 must have been our fourteenth or fifteenth. It had looked like a sortie like any other: trouble with the flak, nothing to be seen except Christmas trees, bomb explosions, fires and flak. This time it was Düsseldorf's turn. We had taken off from Cologne–Ostheim and only had a short distance to fly to the target. Only a few minutes after take-off one could see on the northern horizon where hell had broken loose. Towards 2 o'clock we arrived over the target. The radio droned its monotone commentary: 'Fat pantechnicons in Anton-Dora-two; church steeple three-four to three-seven.' Meaning: 'Enemy formation in grid position Anton-Dora-two at 3,400–3,700 metres height. The 'fat pantechnicons' over the 'church steeple' were not funny expressions or code words. Such and other similar expressions were used because they were particularly well understood accoustically. At that time, radio telephony was frequently little better than a barely distinguishable croak.

This time we orbited around the area of the presumed departure route of the bombers to the north-west of the town, hoping for luck. But there, by comparison to the air space over the city, it was pretty dark. Franz and Sigi strained their eyes at the darkness ahead. I looked out to the rear. I had not even turned on my SN-2. Judging by the heavy flak it must have been another major attack and not a diversionary spoof as sometimes still happened. We had already patrolled up and down at varying heights without having seen a thing.

Suddenly I heard Sigi's voice, breathless and almost whispering: 'Franz, there's one, up ahead!' I turned around and I could see him too, large and clear. A four-engined aircraft with twin rudders, a Lancaster. Our Ju 88 was caught in the slipstream. No time now for adjusting speed and careful aiming. Franz had to fire now, before we rushed hopelessly past him. Franz fired. But instead of the expected thunderclap of our four cannon, all that happened was a tired tack, tack, tack. Shit! Of our 2cm cannon only one had fired. But it had sufficed. Franz had hit the Brit in the port wing between the inboard engine and the fuselage. Flames burst from the wings. Not many hits were needed with our ammunition, it was very effective. It all happened so quickly that the Brit did not even have time to fire back. I can remember that in passing by I had fired into the huge fuselage of a bomber. Immediately after our attack Franz had turned off to port and down. He was able to observe the Lancaster disintegrating in the air and finally crashing. We made a note of the exact time and the approximate location. We needed that for the official confirmation of our success. For sometimes there were doubts whether it had been due to a night fighter or the flak. After landing we discovered a few dents in the leading edge of the wings, evidently caused by flying debris from the Lancaster.

I clearly remember that the Lancaster at which I had fired in passing had not been the same as the one which Franz had set on fire. It must have been a second machine, for 'my' Lancaster had not been on fire. I had spotted it about forty metres above me to the right when I, to Franz's alarm, had fired at its fuselage. I had not shot it down, but if Franz had not had those stoppages with his guns, a second or perhaps even a third *Abschuss* would have been possible that night.

That had been the second time we had had problems with our guns. The first time my machine gun had failed whilst having a Mosquito up our tail. This time we were really fed up; for once we had got on to an enemy formation, and then this. Sigi in particular swore and uttered expletives about the armourer. The very next day Sigi followed this up and had a go at the armourer. It turned out that only fifty-five rounds had been fired by our four cannon. Two had failed completely, one had fired five rounds and the rest had been fired by the fourth.

After a few days we heard that our *Abschuss* had been confirmed. We all received the EK2 (Iron Cross second class) and I was promoted to Unteroffizier. One might laugh about it; but we three – Sigi all of nineteen, Franz twenty-one and I twenty-one years old – were quite proud of this, however modest, decoration for valour. Our Staffel Kapitän, Hauptmann Hissbach, had pinned the Iron Cross complete with ribbon on to our chests in the presence of the entire unit. That was usually so. But only the black-white-red ribbon was worn. According to old military usage it was fastened to the third buttonhole from the top with only a modest part of it showing. It was not of course to be compared to the EK1, the 'fried egg', to say nothing of the *Dödel*, the *Ritterkreuz* or Knight's Cross; but this attribute did distinguish one from the mere beginners.

Indeed, Düsseldorf was the target for 992 aircraft (561 Lancasters, 400 Halifaxes, and thirty-one Mosquitoes) on 2–3 November 1944. This major raid was supported by thirty-seven RCM sorties, and fifty-one Mosquito patrols. More than 5,000 houses were destroyed or badly damaged in the northern half of the city, plus seven industrial premises destroyed and eighteen seriously damaged. In the hail of bombs, at least 678 people died and over 1,000 were injured. This was Bomber Command's last major raid on Düsseldorf. A total of eleven Halifaxes and eight Lancasters failed to return, four of these aircraft crashing behind Allied lines in Belgium and France. Ninety-two crew members perished, twenty-eight becoming PoWs. Five men succeeded in evading capture, and six ended up in Allied hospitals with (severe) injuries, one later succumbing to his wounds. *Nachtjagd* lost one aircraft and crew on 2–3 November 1944: Bf 110 G-4 G9+PZ of 12./NJG1 crashed to the north of Düsseldorf due to *Feindbeschuss* (enemy fire), with the loss of Uffz Johannes Kischke and his crew.

THE Bf 110 G-4 AND THE Ju 88 G-1/G-6 – AN OPERATIONAL COMPARISON

Throughout the War, the Messerschmitt Bf 110 and Junkers Ju 88 formed the backbone of *Nachtjagd*. Although both twin-engined types were facing obsolescence by 1944, they were constantly further developed to keep up with the rapid changes in the night airwar, and remained in front-line service until the end of the Third Reich in May 1945. One of *Nachtjagd*'s pilots who flew both aircraft on operations was Lt Helmut Bunje, who served with 4./NJG6 during 1944 and 1945. He scored his first two *Abschüsse* in the Bf 110 G-4: first a Halifax from a force raiding Stuttgart at 23.19, east of Wurmlingen on 15–16 March 1944, and secondly a Wellington attacking railway tracks to the west of Rome, crashing at 01.00 south-west of Rome on 3–4 June 1944. After his Gruppe had converted to the Ju 88 G-1 in the summer months of 1944, Lt Bunje went on to claim another ten victories (one Halifax and nine Lancasters) between 25–26 August 1944 and 16–17 March 1945 in the Junkers. He is therefore well-qualified to give an insight into the two aircraft:

> A comparison of the night fighters Bf 110 G-4 and Ju 88 G-1/G-6 during 1944–45 by a pilot of that period cannot be expected to have general validity. Much of this must be a matter of personal opinion. Night fighter pilots who had come from the former *Zerstörer* units generally preferred the Bf 110, also many pilots who had had a regular training at the *Nachtjagd* School No.1. Heinz Wolfgang Schnaufer, the most successful of all night fighter pilots with 121 claims, had preferred the Bf 110 to the end. Prinz zu Sayn-Wittgenstein had flown the Ju 88. A large proportion of the night fighters, who had later been transferred from tactical units, had difficulty in getting used to the highly sensitive control column of the Bf 110 and were glad to get their hands on the controls of the Ju 88 again.
>
> I myself – after several years' experience on many types – did not get into night-fighting until February 1944, flying with II./NJG6 and beginning with the Bf 110 G-4 without any problems. Looking back on these operational experiences and comparing these with the later experiences with the Ju 88 G-1 (from June 1944) and the Ju 88 G-6 (from November 1944), I arrive at the following comparison:
>
> The endurance of the Bf 110 G-4 was, in spite of drop tanks, only 3 to 3½ hours, which was frequently below the operational requirements and subsequent mostly lengthy search for a place to land. Lack of fuel caused many crews to abandon their aircraft. The drop tanks restricted the aircraft's speed and increased the risk of fire during combat, for which reasons they were to be jettisoned before entering a fight. But we did not consider the jettisoning process as sufficiently safe and were reluctant to risk it.
>
> The Ju 88 G-1 and also the Ju 88 G-6 had, even without external tanks, an endurance of about 4½ to 5 hours. That was a considerable advantage. I found that this allowed one to embark on the frequently extended chases of the *Zahme Sau* tactics with an easy mind.
>
> The speed of the Bf 110 G-4 was sufficient generally, but for extended approaches for infiltration into the bomber stream the type was often too slow. Frequently we simply arrived too late. The Ju 88 G-1 was appreciably faster, the speed of the G-6 exceeded that of the Bf 110 by about 60km/h. That was a clear advantage.
>
> The manoeuverability of the Bf 110 G-4 was perhaps better than the Ju 88 G-1/G-6, which, in a *Wilde Sau* dogfight with a well-flown Lancaster, was clearly not so superior.
>
> The armament of the Bf 110 G-4 with its four 7.9mm MG 17 in the upper part of the nose and two 20mm MG 151 in the lower gave it considerable firepower, but I had the

A fine air-to-air shot of Bf 110 G4 2Z+BF of 10./NJG6, probably in early 1944. Note the old Lichtenstein *BC radar, and underwing long-range fuel tanks for Tame Boar operations.* Coll. Hans Meyer.

impression that accuracy, as with the two twin 20mm MG 151 of the Ju 88, was not possible. We had the ambition to set on fire only one of the wing tanks, then the poor fellows there at least had a chance of baling out. The effectiveness of the excellent 20mm ammunition was assured. In the Bf 110 a further two 30mm MK 108 could be mounted in a belly-gun pack. But the noise and the vibration of their firing frightened me into thinking of having been hit myself. At the same time the enemy before me exploded into its component parts – a result which went against the fighter pilot's inner grain. I hated the MK 108. A particular advantage of the Ju 88 G-6 was the *Schräge Musik* of two 20mm MG 151 which we first had with this type. But it would not be right to show this as an advantage of the Ju 88, because at the same time the Bf 110 was also modified with this system, but regrettably often with MK 108.

The radar equipment of the Ju 88, for the operation of which a specialist operator was added as fourth member of the crew, was more modern, better and with more extensive capability than that of the Bf 110 G-4. Beside the active target-seeking FuG *Lichtenstein* SN-2, which both types carried (but which were very frequently jammed), the Ju 88 G-1 and G-6 mostly also carried the passive warning devices FuG 350 *Naxos* Z or even ZR and the FuG 227 *Flensburg*. With correct usage these devices could be decisive not only in the hunt, but also for shaking off enemy night fighters, the much-feared Mosquitoes.

The decisive advantage of the Ju 88 in the then increasingly complicated radio and high frequency struggle was the distribution of the various tasks to two crew members, whilst in the Bf 110 a single radio operator had to do it all.

(Above) '*The new Ju 88 G-6*'. *A fine impression of* Nachtjagd*'s standard night fighter of the final year of World War II, painted in watercolours by Lt Helmut Bunje of 4./NJG6 in 1944.* Coll. Helmut Bunje.

On the snow-covered Parndorf airfield in February 1945, Hptm Hans Krause's (Gr Kdr I./NJG4) Ju 88 G 3C+FK is being serviced. Coll. Hans Krause.

A further distinct advantage of the Ju 88 G-1/G-6 as against the Bf 110 G-4 was in my opinion the fact that, thanks to this fourth man on board, two pairs of eyes could be looking ahead. In a situation when the (not yet spotted) enemy must be close, the radar operator took his eyes off his equipment and searched the sky ahead and above together with his pilot. In the end, eye contact was the essential key to success! The two pairs of eyes to the rear in the Ju 88 were also an advantage.

In all important aspects the Ju 88, and especially the Ju 88 G-6, was superior to the Bf 110 G-4. From my own point of view, it was the best night fighter available to us during the last six months of the War. Nevertheless, most of us would have given a big cheer if we had had an enviably good aircraft which came off the British production lines: the Mosquito!

ALONE INTO GERMANY

One of the transportation targets selected for destruction by Bomber Command in the final year of the War was the Dortmund-Ems canal system. Several bombing raids were carried out on this target during the second half of 1944, which had the result of preventing smelting coke from the Ruhr mines reaching three important steelworks at Brunswick and Osnabrück, and which in turn proved a devastating setback to the German war industry. One of these raids took place on the night of 6–7 November 1944, when 235 Lancasters and seven Mosquitoes of 5 Group were detailed to cut the Mittelland Canal at its junction with the Dortmund-Ems Canal at Gravenhorst on the Dutch-German border. Lt Ted Howes SAAF, flying Lancaster LL948 ZN-V of 106 Squadron, recounts the raid.

The canals were vital to Germany in the transport of their materials and equipment of war. At briefing we were told of the importance of the target and of its proximity to Dutch civilians. The weather report was that we would be flying in bad conditions most of the way but that it would be clear in the target area for accurate bombing. Each Lancaster carried a bomb load of 14,000 pounds.

In the event, all the way to the target the weather was atrocious; we flew almost entirely in thick cloud, rain and ice through occasional flak-defended areas and other bright flashes and I sometimes could not distinguish between flak, lightning, or static discharges around my aircraft. Sometimes there was a gap in the cloud providing a glimpse of the stars up in the black sky. I do not remember the altitude at which we flew to the target and our planned bombing height, but I guess about 12,000 feet.

When I was about twenty minutes from my appointed time over the target, my tail gunner's voice warning me to take evasive action from an Me 109 night fighter attacking from our port quarter coincided with a stream of tracer cannon fire ripping through the aircraft between myself and the port inner engine. As the engine started flaming, in the light of those flames I could see petrol gushing out of the tank adjacent to it, between me and the flaming engine. I thought it could only be a matter of seconds before the flames and the leaking petrol came together.

With these events taking place in perhaps no more than a minute or so, the engineer, whose position was alongside me on my right, and I, had thrown the switches to stop the engine, feathered its propellor, activated the 'Gravenor' system to extinguish the flames in the engine, switched off the pump of port number one, and retrimmed the rudders. At the same time I put the aircraft into a dive to port as the first part of our standard manoeuvre against fighter attack, and the 109 disappeared into the darkness for the time being. I remember realizing that I could not win because if I slipped the aircraft to port the flames would spread towards the leaking petrol, and if I slipped it to starboard the petrol would wash towards the flames – both having the same explosive result with about a thousand gallons of petrol in the tanks.

At some stage in all of this discomfort – I cannot remember exactly when – an Me 109 came at us again. Perhaps he thought we were going down out of control because he did not fire at us, but our tail gunner got in a burst with his four Brownings and we then lost contact. Mercifully, the engine fire extinguishing system worked and the fire died out.

The second part of our standard manoeuvre, at each phase of which the gunners were trained in the deflections to allow in firing at an attacking fighter, was to bank the aircraft over at the bottom of the first dive and continue the dive to starboard, then pull the aircraft up and climb on the same course, then bank it over again and continue the climb to port. Theoretically, after completing this diamond configuration one would end the manoeuvre in the same vertical plane in which one had started and would be back on track. It worked well in daylight practice exercises over England with a friendly Spitfire or Hurricane for a playmate, but not quite the same in a damaged aircraft, with one engine out, loaded with 14,000 pounds of bombs, at night, and with an unfriendly Me 109.

The 106 Squadron crew that ventured alone into Germany in Lancaster LL948 on 6–7 November 1944. Back, left to right: Fg Off Bill Butterfield (nav.); Sgt Jock Robertson (rear gunner); Sgt Ron Grieve (WOp). Front, left to right: Lt Ted Howes SAAF (pilot); Sgt Brian Johnson (BA); Sgt Vic Smith (mid-upper gunner). Not in the picture is Sgt Les Barnett (Flt Eng), who probably took the photograph. Coll. Ted Howes DFC.

At the bottom of the manoeuvre, at the point to climb the other two legs of the diamond back to our original altitude, my Lancaster could not respond, in fact I could not even maintain height in straight and level flight. We reckoned we were about fifteen minutes from the target and could get there in spite of losing height all the time, and once we had released the bombs on the target our remaining three engines would get us home. The crucial consideration was to get rid of that huge load of bombs, but not to indiscriminately jettison them over friendly Holland.

As we approached the target I heard with alarm the Master Bomber transmit his code word for the attack to be abandoned. The weather was so bad that the target could not be clearly identified, so there was a risk that stray bombs might be inaccurately dropped on to Dutch people, houses, or farms. The Lancasters (minus casualties) would now return on the three-hour flight to their bases in England. But I could not do that – my damaged aircraft with one engine knocked out was steadily losing height, and with all the bombs on board I could not keep it flying long enough to reach England.

First priority was to offload the bombs, and as we were on our honour not to do so over Holland, I decided we must fly on alone into Germany. I am sure my crew were tempted to warn me that we would be tracked by German radar and become easy prey to a night fighter. But my crew silently accepted the decision and carried on with their jobs, although they all knew, as I did, that the German defence system would ensure that we had no chance of returning to England.

From the time that the Master Bomber abandoned the attack we flew on eastward for about thirty minutes until we were absolutely certain that we were well into Germany and able to jettison our bombs. We had been losing height steadily and I think my altimeter registered about 3,000 feet but I could not be certain of our height above the ground. I dearly wanted our bombs, finally, to do some damage in Germany, but if we were closer to the ground than we estimated, the explosion of 14,000 pounds of high-explosive bombs beneath us might give our own aircraft the final *coup de grace*. I opened the bomb doors, and with much reluctance and disappointment, ordered the bomb-aimer to release the bombs unarmed.

What sweet relief it was that my Lancaster came back to life after ridding itself of that burden. We now turned about and the navigator gave me a course to steer, almost directly westward, in the direction of England. On taking stock of our situation – one engine was dead, we had lost all the fuel out of the port number one tank, the main undercarriage wheel on the port side was hanging down, the bomb doors would not close after we had jettisoned the bombs, sundry holes and damage on the port side of the aircraft, and the foul weather had not cleared. All of these conditions affected the aerodynamics and airworthiness of the aircraft.

We climbed laboriously to about 5,000 feet which I hoped would provide enough time for all of us to abandon the aircraft if we were forced to do so, and I bombarded the navigator and engineer with questions about fuel remaining in the tanks, range, endurance, distance, and time. I felt that with careful nursing of the engines for optimum fuel economy we had a chance of reaching base in Lincolnshire, but if, en route, we ran out of fuel over the North Sea, that would be the end of us. I decided to continue in the direction of England and to consider our chances as we approached the Dutch coast before finally committing us to the flight across the sea. We flew on, resigned to the certainty of a night fighter, sooner or later, being alerted to our presence and finishing us off. At the coast, information from the navigator and engineer was encouraging and I took the decision to continue homeward over the sea to England.

And we made it! About ten minutes before estimated time of arrival we broke radio silence and signalled base that we were coming, and at the same time the engineer announced that all fuel gauges were on zero. I hoped they were slightly inaccurate, and as the navigator told me we were directly over base, I felt annoyed at having to do a couple of extra circuits waiting for the lights to mark the runway and the rest of the landing system. With the undercarriage lowered for landing we wondered if the troublesome port wheel was properly locked down or whether it would collapse when it touched the ground, but by this time I was almost beyond caring. To our surprise and relief the three-engine landing was not too bad, and the damaged undercarriage held firm.

We had arrived home at midnight, about one and a half hours late, after the rest of the returning crews had completed debriefing formalities and gone to bed. The next day, the officer in charge of the ground installations including the runway and circuit lights systems, irreverently known as the 'gas, light, and coke officer' was

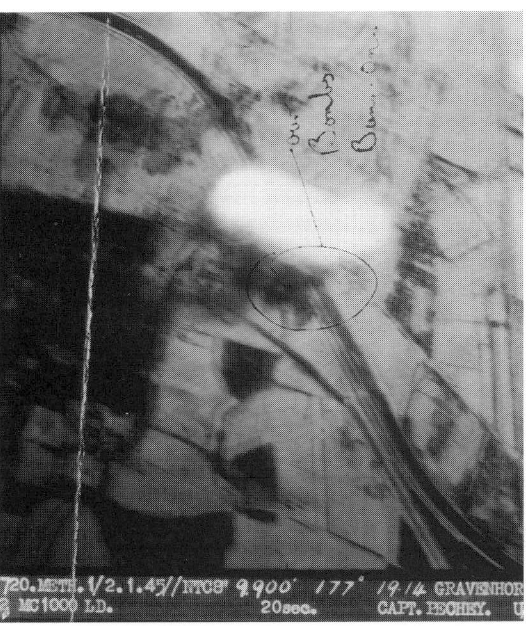

Target photo brought back by Capt Pechey (SAAF)'s Lancaster ZN-U of 106 Squadron from the 1–2 January 1945 attack on the Gravenhorst section of the Mittelland Canal. As a result of this 5 Group attack (by 152 Lancasters and five Mosquitoes), the bank of the canal was pitted with bomb craters for half a mile. Coll. C.P.C. Pechey DFC.

SAAF pilots in Monte Video, Uruguay, October 1943 en route to serve in Bomber Command in England. Far side of table, left to right: Peter Franklin; Jimmy Begbie; Charles McGregor. Near side of table, left to right: Ronnie Ackerman; Ted Howes; Edwin Swales. Ackerman and Howes were the only survivors at the end of the War, the other four being killed in air operations over the Third Reich. For his coolness under fire, Captain Edwin 'Ted' Swales was awarded the DFC for Pathfinder target-marking on his thirty-third op, with 582 (PFF) Squadron over Cologne on 23 December 1944. For outstanding gallantry whilst leading a 374-aircraft attack on Pforzheim as Master Bomber on 23–24 February 1945, in which he selflessly sacrificed his life in order to give his crew a chance to bale out of their stricken Lancaster, he was awarded the Victoria Cross, Britain's highest military award, on 24 April 1945. Coll. Ted Howes DFC.

> heard complaining of having to get out of bed to activate the system to bring us down!

Although by November 1944 hardly any single-seater aircraft were still operational in *Nachtjagd*, it is quite possible that Lt Howes' Lancaster was intercepted by a Bf 109 of I./NJG11, a specialist anti-Oboe single-seater *Gruppe* which operated from Bonn-Hangelar. Only thirty-one aircraft bombed the junction of the Dortmund-Ems canal before the Master Bomber ordered to abandon the raid due to unsuccessful marking of the target on 6–7 November. Ten Lancasters were lost, plus one crash-landing in England due to poor visibility. After this failed raid, it was successfully repeated on 21–22 November, when 138 Lancasters and six Mosquitoes of 5 Group managed to breach the canal banks near Gravenhorst. Next day, photographs brought back by a recce Mosquito revealed fifty-nine coke barges stranded on a thirty-mile section completely drained of water as a result of this raid.

After the end of single-engined Wild Boar night-fighting in March 1944, small-scale night-time employment of the Bf 109 and FW 190 continued throughout the last year of the War. It is quite possible that Lancaster LL948 flown by Lt Howes of 106 Squadron was intercepted on 6–7 November 1944 by a Bf 109 G-6 of I./NJG11, a specialist anti-Oboe single-seater Gruppe *which operated from Bonn-Hangelar. Depicted here is a Bf 109 G-4 'Yellow 42' at Schwäbisch Hall aerodrome in January 1945. On the right is the Ju 88 G-6 flown by Oblt Peter Spoden (Staffel Kapitän 6./NJG6) at that time.* Coll. Peter Spoden.

FIFTH *ABSCHUSS* OVER HEILBRONN

Between August 1944 and early May 1945, Bomber Command transformed most of the German industrial cities and transportation centres into heaps of rubble in a crushing resumption of the area bombing campaign, as ACM Harris still believed this to be the best way to hasten the collapse of Nazi Germany. This view was strongly supported after the War by *Nachtjagd*'s last C-in-C, General Schmid, who declared during interrogation that the British night attacks had had a decisive influence on the German downfall. He literally stated that '... in view of the astounding success in target-finding by night and in bad weather, and of the increased accuracy in aiming of the British bomber formations, the goal of paralysing the German war economy decisively could only have been a matter of time.'

The overwhelming power of the Command after the invasion in France is illustrated by the fact that almost half of the tonnage of bombs dropped on the Reich during the six-year conflict was dropped during the final nine months of the War. *Nachtjagd*, on the other hand, had become almost impotent to counter this devastating offensive, as the train of events for NJG6 on 4–5 December 1944 clearly illustrates.

At 19.05 on the evening of 4 December 1944, a force of 400 Bomber Command heavies, protected by a strong spearhead of Mosquitoes, was reported by the German ground control organization to be heading in the direction of Heilbronn and Karlsruhe (in fact, the figure was more than double the German estimates). Only minutes later, both these cities came under attack: Heilbronn between 19.18 and 19.30, and Karlsruhe between 19.25 and 19.50. Eighty-two per cent of the built-up area in Heilbronn were destroyed in a rain of 1,254 tons of bombs unloaded in only twelve minutes, and an estimated 7,000 people died in a firestorm. Karlsruhe also suffered heavily in a concentrated attack by 535 aircraft. To counter these raids, three Ju 88s and twenty-three Bf 110s were scrambled between 19.12 and 21.45 from Kitzingen and Gerolzhofen in the direction of Karlsruhe, whereas another nineteen Ju 88s of II./NJG6 headed for Heilbronn after taking off from Schwäbisch Hall and Echterdingen between 19.15 and 21.20. Among the first crews of his *Gruppe* to be scrambled, at 19.15 Lt Helmut Bunje lifted off from Schwäbisch Hall in his Ju 88G-6 of 4./NJG6 with his crew of Uffz Weimann (Funker), Fw Bergmann (FE), and gunner Ogefr. Ambs. Lt Bunje recalls events as follows:

> The order for take-off came very late. We were still taxiing, when suddenly, in the direction of take-off, the British markers lit up the sky. It was not far away, only forty kilometres as it turned out. So we took off and headed for the target with everything our Ju 88 had in it. The navigation was easy: we only needed to keep the fireworks a little to our left, then we should be able to join the approaching Tommies who were coming from the north. A bare ten minutes later we were on a course of 290 degrees at 2,300 metres height abeam of their objective. It was Heilbronn.
>
> The airspace was unusually lit up. Around the clearly visible town in which the first fires blazed with light-grey trails of smoke, flares had been set in a circular pattern. They appeared to hang motionless on white lines of smoke; like a huge chandelier. The visibility was excellent thanks to this newfangled illumination. As expected, a gaggle of five bombers suddenly crossed our course from starboard. They flew about 400 metres higher, slightly downward to their target, brightly lit from ahead and below. Their precise formation, keeping about 100 metres distance abreast, surprised us, also the zebra-striped camauflage. With a steep turn to port I tucked myself behind the last Lancaster on the right. First this one – then the one to its left – then the one in the centre – and so on ... that was my simple, though ambitious plan.
>
> But alas: to begin with we were a good thousand metres behind them, and they were as fast as we were ourselves! The distance to these bombers descending at maximum speed remained, excruciatingly, almost constant. Only when the clearly discernible bomb doors opened did we get a little closer. We were now also speeding along in a

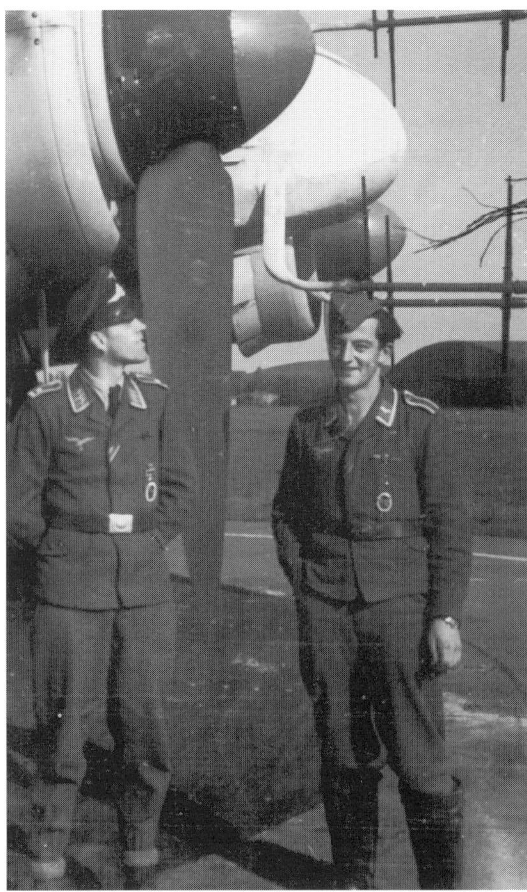

Fw Helmut Bunje (left) and his Bordfunker, Uffz Alfred Weimann of 4./NJG6 posing with their Ju 88 G-6 2Z+BM in November 1944. Coll. Helmut Bunje.

slight descent, ahead the city under a hail of bombs and the flicker of explosions, a little higher the brightly illuminated Lancaster. The distance was really still far too great, estimated some 600 metres – but it had to be now: at least one of these bombers should not get its load to the target! On its run-in our Lancaster flew a steady course – so I could take precise aim. First burst! It went low. A corrected second burst appeared to show hits. Now, after the longer third burst – most carefully aimed at the wing tank – its contents burst into flames! It burned! At this moment the first bombs dropped, in pairs. The Lancaster now turned to port, evidently not in panic – perhaps the Captain wanted to enable his crew to get out? – but then it continued to turn like in a slow roll, almost inverted for the plunge.

I now swung to port in order to get the next one. But he had left his place in the formation! Some bombers were flying some way off to port and lower; way above to our surprise an old Stirling wended its way . . . Whilst concentrating on the one on the right flank, I had subconsciously dreamt of a fiver-series, now that dream was over. Somewhat confused I watched our burning Lancaster going steeply down on an opposite course. It crashed close to the north-west of the city in open country. Fred noted the time: 19.34.The lost seconds could easily have had evil consequences.

'Two Lancasters behind! They're firing at us!' shouted Willy, the rear gunner. Hard turn to port! The tracers from the turrets of the bombers went wide. Turning back, I saw them disappear westwards into the night. We now had the fires on our beam, when several bombers crossed our course from port to starboard. After them! They were heading into the dark, only dimly lit from behind. But we, from their point of view, were coming from the light part of the sky! I was left with only their exhausts, weaving about in their evasive action, to aim at. I fired without effect. Now and then there was firing from the rear turret of the bomber, then he disappeared ... We tried a pursuit with our interfered-with radar.

Suddenly there were flashes close beside us – it rattled in the aircraft, crackled above my head – Karl-Otto, in front and to the right of me screamed – head wound – I heard him directly, not in the earphones, which had suddenly gone dead. Petrol fumes! Steep turn! The controls still responded, the engines too sounded unchanged, but all the electrics had gone and one tank was evidently leaking – well, at least it wasn't burning! We flew homewards to Schwäbisch Hall on reduced power, through the great smoke cloud hanging over Heilbronn, the smell of which penetrated into our oxygen masks. On landing I noticed that we had a flat tyre. Fortunately the undercarriage did not collapse. But our Junkers was completely riddled. She never flew again.

Lt Bunje's fifth *Abschuss*, a Lancaster on its bomb run towards Heilbronn, crashed at 19.34 some 10–20km to the north-west of the target from a height of 2,500 metres. In all, II./NJG6 crews claimed a mere five Lancasters destroyed in the target area, three of which fell to the guns of Lt Peter Spoden. In all, Bomber Command lost thirteen Lancasters and one Mosquito from exactly 1,000 sorties despatched on 4–5 December 1944. On the debit side, seven out of the forty-five Bf 110s and Ju 88s of II. and IV./NJG6 sent off were missing, at least four of which fell foul to Mosquitoes.

NACHTJÄGER OVER THE BULGE

During mid-December 1944, 140 Ju 88s and Bf 110s were withdrawn from *Nachtjagd Reichsverteidigung* duties and their crews ordered to carry out ground-attack missions in the Ardennes, in support of the advancing German troops in the last *Wehrmacht* ground offensive in the west, better known as the Battle of the Bulge. The aircraft were manned mainly by inexperienced and expendable crews, the '*Experten*' being held back in reserve to combat Bomber Command. Twenty-two-year-old Bordfunker Uffz Albert Spelthahn has told on pages 189–98 of his crew's night-fighting experiences with 5./NJG2 during 1944. By the final month of the year, Uffz Sigi Hinz, the crew's Flight Engineer, had been replaced by another third crew member, Uffz Hans Müllner, who acted as an extra Bordfunker. Flying the Ju 88 G-6, they were stationed at Eelde, a small field aerodrome to the south of Groningen in northern Holland, and where the 5./NJG2 crews were unpleasantly surprised when they received orders to attack Allied forward positions in Belgium in support of the German ground troops fighting in the Battle of the Bulge. Uffz Spelthahn vividly recounts the episode:

> We had recently started flying with two radio operators. The SN-2, with which we had not been very successful so far because of the 'dirty tricks' of the British, was now being installed in a different part of our machines. That should relieve the radio operator who, with his FuG 10 – together with his various receivers and transmitters – the D/F equipment, the FuG 16 for VHF voice communication and finally the MG 131, had already more than enough to cope with. From now on the SN-2 was mounted in front of the Flight Engineer, on the Pilot's right. That meant that the Flight Engineers – much to their sorrow – would no longer be part of the crew because their place would be taken by the second Bordfunker. In our case that was Hans Müllner, who for his part was only too happy to be able to fly with us. Some months before he and his pilot, Lt Ballier, had had a terrible crash at night. All three of the crew had survived miraculously with only light injuries. All that remained of their machine, a Ju 88, was an unrecognizable heap of metal scattered around the countryside.
>
> Our erstwhile and despondent Flight Engineer, Siegfried Hinz ('Sigi'), had flown with Franz and myself for a year and we had had some

Uffz Albert Spelthahn, Bordfunker with 5./NJG2 in full war colours, 1944. Coll. Albert Spelthahn.

hectic times together. We would now have to do without his delightful Saxon expressions, but we would be compensated by the lovely Viennese lilt of Hans Müllner. Apart from our own personal well-being, the situation at this time was more than grim. The Ardennes offensive, which had begun with great dash and success on 16 December under the command of Field Marshal Rundstedt, had petered out by Christmas and finally failed. The bad weather had cleared up and the Allies had re-established full air superiority. And that was the end of it. Only an utterly irrational confidence and a belief in one man, which had been hammered into us from childhood, and a vague hope for the promised miracle weapons kept our spirits up. That we should lose the War became more obvious with every day, one could almost grasp it with one's hands, only none of us could finally accept this fact.

In this situation we night fighters were, much to our surprise, from Christmas onward, ordered to carry out low-level night attacks on the Allied supply lines in Belgium. With only our fixed armament – we could not carry bombs – we were to improvise something. But at best these would be pinpricks and they could not hasten the 'final victory'. Anyway, on the second day of Christmas we took off – for the first time with our third man, Hans Müllner – for one of these crazy, nightly, low-level attacks. I cannot now recall our operational area or how we had approached it. We took off from Eelde, and we were very soon over Belgium. For some time now our *Staffel* had had the latest version of the Ju 88, the G6. The markings of our machine were 4R+KN. The visibility in these nights with clear, star-spangled skies and light snow on the ground was fantastic. Only of enemy traffic we saw next to nothing. Lacking better targets, Franz fired at a large gas holder with little significant effect. Then there was a railway engine which let off steam as a result. Meanwhile light flak fired tracer at us but did not hit us. That was something new, it looked pretty and appeared harmless.

For a while we flew around in our alotted area at 100 metres, looking for worthwhile targets. Suddenly, as if Franz had wanted to show our new crew member something interesting, we found ourselves over Liege and got heavily fired at from all sides. That looked very pretty too, but was, by comparison to the last lot, pretty dangerous. After landing we found a hole in the port wing. Overflying Liege was of course unintentional and pure chance. The city was covered by thick haze – a frequent winter occurrence. During our approach we had not been able to make out the town at first; it could just as well have been a patch of fog in a valley. It had turned out alright in the end, as so often before. What Hans Müllner thought about his 'initiation' I do not know; he might easily have got out of the fire into the frying pan. Now we knew what it was like when the Yanks were giving us all they had. As we were soon to discover, they had a machine gun mounted on every lorry, and with these they were able to put up a massive defensive fire.

By New Year's Eve the slight damage to our machine had been repaired and it was serviceable again. But who would, especially on New Year's Eve and New Year's Day …? so we thought, and looked forward to a jolly celebration at our pretty hotel 'Twee Provincies'. If I remember correctly, Hans Müllner had intended to play something on the piano in the evening and had started to practise soon after lunch. He could have spared himself the trouble.

In the afternoon we were told at a hastily convened briefing that we were to fly low-level attacks in the area of Huy, Namur and Brussels in the evening. In the same manner as on the second day of Christmas. Soon after dusk we drove out to the airfield to await orders. We passed the time as usual with card games or dozing in one of the deckchairs. Now and again we went outside, smoked a cigarette and admired the clear and starry sky. It was not cold. The moon shone and there was light snow on the ground. There were no lights and the airfield lighting had not been switched on. One could see for miles, it was so bright that one could have read a newspaper.

Shortly after 23.00 we were ordered cockpit readiness. It took a while before take-off and during this time I was able to set my frequencies at leisure. There would not be much to transmit;

or had we been ordered radio silence? I cannot remember now. As always, I then secured our talisman, a small yellow teddy bear, in his place in front of me. First we were to fly at 1,000 metres south to radio beacon Ida. On our map it was marked somewhere in the Eifel, south-west of Bonn. After the beacon we were to go on a westerly course to our operational area.

A quarter of an hour before midnight the green signal light went up. The order for take-off. Four other aircraft took off this night. I can remember only two of the pilots' names: Ofw Lubenka and Fw Kurz. As with the usual night fighter operations, each crew acted independently; none saw or knew anything about the other machines. Before the midnight hour of the New Year we were at our operational height of 1,000 metres as ordered. The machine was steady as a rock in the air. Below us in the moonlight every detail of the countryside and the blacked-out villages and towns could clearly be made out. Smoke rose almost vertically from the chimneys of the houses. Streams and railway tracks were silvery lines. There was a dreamlike beauty in the night, this last night of 1944. On the stroke of midnight – I heard part of Dr Goebbels' speech on the medium-wave frequency of the D/F set – Franz passed round a bottle of sparkling wine and we toasted each other high up in the sky.

Dr Goebbels adressed himself to 'our brave soldiers on all the fronts', but also to 'the comrades on the home front'. He believed – at least he said so – so utterly in the Führer and in the victory which we would achieve in the coming year as he had never believed in anything before. We were still flying over German territory. Here and there light flak fired a burst of tracer vertically into the air – but this time as a salute – no one wanted to do us any harm. The time came to silence Dr Goebbels and to tune our equipment to the radio beacon Ida.

There it was, the call sign was clear as a bell in my earphones as it came with its slow 'did, did dah did did, did dah' through the silence of the night. I had switched the indicator with its pointer over to Franz for him to follow. After some time the pointer sprang as expected to reciprocal and the signal in my earphones changed. We had just passed over the beacon and Franz went in a fairly steep turn on to a westerly course. We had meanwhile gone down to 100 to 150 metres height and followed the contours of the hilly Eifel countryside. Where exactly the front line lay we neither knew nor at first cared. The Rundstedt offensive had taken it somewhere between Monschau and Echternach in the direction of the Maas bend. The area around Aachen had been lost to the Americans during the second half of October and had remained in their possession. After some eight or ten minutes we were able to make out where the front line ran.

It started with a burst of tracer which approached us seemingly so slowly and which had its origin so far away that Franz was able to slide quite leisurely below it. We were fairly relaxed and hardly nervous; we'd seen it all before. Perhaps they too were celebrating the New Year. Anyway, it took quite a while before those fellows had woken up properly and started to fire at us accurately and from all directions in a most unfriendly manner. Perhaps it was an advantage that as radio operator I was sitting with my back to our direction of flight. The view of the fireworks from the 'better seats' in front must have been both more impressive and less pleasant. As radio operator one had to be somewhat of a fatalist; it was all part of flying backwards. They were certainly not short of ammunition, for now tracer was coming up at us from all directions and getting closer all the time. It was almost like being under a shower. Franz was now getting annoyed, he pushed the machine down and returned the fire. We also let go with tracer from our four guns. After this unfriendly reception and some evasive action and changes of course we seemed to have escaped from the worst. We took a deep breath.

Only a few persistent ones continued with fairly random fire. I was just thinking: thank God, that's over, when Franz shouted 'Jump'. I thought I had not heard right. Why? Is he joking? We were at perhaps 100 metres and flying quite normally; we were not on fire and I had not noticed any hits. Something might have

The Ju 88 G-1, which became the standard Luftwaffe *night fighter during the final year of the War, was powered by two air-cooled 14-cylinder 1,700hp BMW 801 D radial engines, giving it a maximum speed of 520km/h at 20,000ft. This 2./NJG4 aircraft was photographed at Mainz-Finthen aerodrome in the winter of 1944–45.* Coll. Charles F. Kern.

happened up front, but nothing noticeable. I wanted to ask why, when Franz again shouted 'Out!' Ah well, he was in command. (All this happened much more quickly than in reading it.) I don't know whether I had time to think 'shit'; Hans Müllner was already standing over the floor hatch and fiddled – apparently without success – with the well-known but never yet used red lever. The hatch, the only reliable exit, would not open. Well, there was another – also well-known but never yet used red handle in the cockpit roof above my head. I was left with no choice – whatever the tail structure – I pulled it down.

The entire roof, including the machine gun and Hans, disappeared as if by magic; for at the same moment Hans went through the floor hatch. Now there was a fresh breeze in our aircraft with nothing below and above. We must have had something like 400–450 on the clock. Well, it was more like a storm than a breeze. Now that Hans had got out of the hatch I wanted to do so too. But I had barely risen from my seat with my parachute than I found myself pushed up against the radio by the air pressure. Careful now! Don't get the rip-cord handle caught up in anything. Guard it with one hand; legs out through the hatch; away like an old rag and pull were like one single action. No time for fear. A slight jerk – and I'm hanging in the 'chute. Crazy situation. We had never practised it, but one knew by hearsay: feet together and take the shock on landing. The ground came up surprisingly quickly, watch out! Then a terrible shock; I think I am dead. But I could not be. (I think, therefore I am.)

Kiss my arse! It cannot be true. Would I ever find out why I had to get out? Where am I now? I hope I don't get caught by Belgian partisans with shotguns or so. Discard harness, roll up the 'chute and hide it in the bushes. And then? It was a singularly crazy situation. There was some pretty wild firing in the area, they were at it all the time and not very far away. Are the Yanks – or whoever – hunting for us already? I saw no one, neither Hans nor Franz. Had he even got out? He had to, and could only be, the last to leave. Like the captain of a sinking ship.

In fact no one had fired at us or at anyone else. Our aircraft had crashed nearby and had caught fire and our ammunition kept exploding. That had been this sound of 'combat fire'.

Although he had injured his left foot and right arm on baling out, Albert set out walking eastwards, hoping to make it to friendly forces on the other side of the front. Alas, after only a few hours on the loose, he stumbled across an American Ack-Ack battery, and was taken prisoner. He was taken to the nearby hamlet of Palenberg, north of Aachen, where his wounds were attended to in a house and:

After my cosmetic-medical treatment I was taken to another room. On the way there – what joy – I found, apparently hale and well, Franz and Hans.

A rare, if somewhat blurred, shot of the cockpit interior of a Ju 88 G-1 night fighter of 2./NJG4, taken from the entrance hatch below the aircraft. On the left, facing aft, is Oblt Kretschmer, Funker. His pilot, Lt Kern, is sitting lower down on the right. Mainz-Finthen, probably early 1945. Coll. Charles F. Kern.

Posing with the tail unit of Ju 88 G-1 Wrk.Nr. 714255 of 2./NJG4 at Mainz-Finthen in February 1945 are, from left to right: Lt Kern (pilot) and Oblt Kretschmer (Bordfunker). Note a second Ju 88 G-1 in the background. Coll. Charles F. Kern.

> The Yanks would not permit any exuberant display of our pleasure at finding each other again and so we had to content ourselves with brief greetings. But the question of why we had had to abandon our aircraft remained – at least for myself – still unanswered. That same night the three of us were taken by Jeep for a first interrogation and during this journey Franz was able to tell me what had happened. Our elevator control lines had apparently been shot through and Franz had been left with no control pressure on his stick. He had tried using the trim tabs but to no avail. In no time at all we would have bored ourselves into the ground had we not – really much too low – baled out at the very last moment. That explained everything. Franz had given the best order of his life.

As Uffz Spelthahn experienced, the night ground-attack missions proved to be a particularly hazardous business. From the *Nachtjagd* sorties directed to the Ardennes between mid-December 1944 and 1–2 January 1945, at least thirty-one aircraft failed to return, with ninety-four crew members being posted killed or missing. After a week of initial success, the German ground offensive was contained, without the *Nachtjagd* crews being able to even slightly delay the Allied advance.

CHAPTER 5

1945

FERNNACHTJAGD PLANS

Fernnachtjagd, or long-range night intruding over Great Britain, must be considered as the Cinderella of *Nachtjagd*. When the arm was created in 1940, General Kammhuber intended to establish both an offensive long-range night-fighting arm in parallel with a short-range defensive arm over the Continent. Kammhuber at that time appreciated the value and effectiveness of long-range night fighter operations, leading him to set about developing the strength of his intruder force to the maximum extent.

However, for various reasons his superiors resisted all his efforts to raise the intruder strength beyond just one *Gruppe*, I./NJG2. Although this unit made a very promising start during 1940–41, with claims submitted for 143 *Abschüsse* (the RAF admitted ninety-three aircraft lost), Hitler gave the far-reaching order on 12 October 1941 to cease all *Fernnachtjagd* activity. From then on, the Allied day and night bomber forces and training organizations were able to expand and develop in the UK in comfort and virtually without enemy interference. Without a doubt, this contributed materially to the later destruction of the German homeland and thereby to the loss of the War.

During 1943–44, many efforts were being made to rehabilitate *Fernnachtjagd*, mainly in the form of plans to launch a very heavy intruder attack with 600–700 aircraft from time to time, taking full advantage of surprise. Both Göring and Hitler

Nachtjagd*'s old workhorse. This Bf 110 G-4 of 7./NJG6 was photographed at Wiener Neustadt in late 1944, with, from left, Ofhr Manfred Tangelst (pilot) and his Funker Uffz Herbert Rockel. This crew completed a total of twenty-five operational sorties with 7./NJG6 between June 1944 and April 1945, during which time they had encounters with RAF aircraft on eight occasions, but could not claim any victories. This was typical for the young, green and inexperienced crews joining* Nachtjagd *during the final phase of the War.* Coll. Manfred Tangelst.

remained opposed to this sound form of offensive night-fighting though, until late 1944, by which time it was far too late to stem the tide. Uffz Albert Spelthahn, Bordfunker with 5./NJG2 between May and December 1944, expands on the plans:

> The *Himmelbett* night-fighting method had long become redundant, but the free-ranging one too, the *Wilde Sau* tactics, had been insufficiently successful to avert the British terror attacks on German cities. Long-range night-fighting offered therefore greater promise and our *Staffel* had lately been selected for this method. *'Adelheid'* was the code name for this operation. As we all knew, the British bomber units took off and landed at dozens of newly built airfields along the English south-east coast. The airfield lighting was arranged like a funnel and it was known that the bombers made their approach with full illumination, that is with navigation and landing lights. Night fighters which managed to inveigle themselves into these landings would cause the greatest confusion and were bound to have no end of success.
>
> Each crew was assigned one or two airfields as their hunting ground and I still remember very well how eagerly we studied the available air photos of the approaches and topographical situation of our target areas. The name of our assigned airfield was Graveley [a few miles WNW of Cambridge and SSE of Huntingdon, right in the heart of 'Bomber Country' – author]. Operation *Adelheid* announced itself by the receipt of additional clothing and equipment which we were to wear on all future operations. These were to prevent our drowning in case we were to come down in the drink. Not only was there a lifejacket, but also a rubber dinghy to be worn below it. In order not to die of hypothermia we received Angora underclothes, over which a so-called foam suit was to be worn. Then the uniform and on top the leather overalls. The foam suit was made of several layers and stitched together in a rhomboid pattern. These contained a material which, when soaked with water, expanded the entire suit as a protection against the cold. But that was not all with which we were to fly against England. In our pockets we had a bag of colouring with which we could produce a huge yellow patch in the water, and as emergency rations we had a couple of round tins of the popular Schoka-Cola. Around our right calves we strapped a belt of signal cartridges, then a signal pistol, pistol and a knife. This 'astronaut suit' was then completed with the parachute, which was part of our equipment anyway. With the flying helmet on our heads and a smart yellow scarf around our necks we made quite an impression.
>
> By the time I had heaved myself in all this gear up the narrow ladder to the cockpit, had sat down on the parachute dangling on my behind and had set up my frequencies, I was usually already covered in sweat. During the take-off I then had to bend down to the FuG 16 (ultra-short frequency radio receiver and transmitter on 38.5–42.3MHz bands) mounted near the floor before we were finally able to send and receive.
>
> Since *'Adelheid'* had appeared on the programme, it had become clear to us that apart from the usual kinds of landings such as by parachute, there were now other possibilities of getting down to earth. According to the old aviators' saying: 'No one yet has ever remained aloft for ever!' Now one could end up in the drink or even make an emergency landing in England. Even for this however unlikely eventuality, provision had been made. On the floor between my seat and that of the pilot there was a neat little black box about the size of a cigar box. Beside it, in an open, thick-walled steel tube, there was a small metal capsule with a handle. This gadget, which we treated with considerable respect, was an explosive device, with which we were to blow up the machine in the case of an emergency landing on British territory. On no account were secret technical devices to fall into enemy hands.
>
> The short remaining time left to us no longer offered much in the way for effective long-range night-fighting. Only once did we follow a bomber stream returning from an attack on the Ruhr, without catching sight of it, as far as the English coast. The picket boats were already seeking us with their searchlights. We had to break off due to lack of fuel.

An impressive watercolour of a Ju 88 G-6 shooting down a Lancaster during a Bomber Command raid in the final months of the War, illuminated against a background of the burning city under attack. Coll. Helmut Bunje.

OPERATION *GISELA*

Only in October 1944 did General Schmid finally get the green light to go ahead with his plans to carry out one or two massed intruder attacks over England. The actual operation, under the codename Operation *Gisela* was, however, repeatedly delayed by the High Command. With the inevitable defeat of Nazi Germany already in sight, on 3–4 March 1945 the long-fostered *Fernnachtjagd* plans finally came to fruition, when 142 Ju 88Gs of NJG2, 3, 4 and 5 were employed to intercept two forces of 234 and 222 Bomber Command heavies returning respectively from raids on Kamen and Ladbergen. During the course of the night, they claimed twenty-four Allied aircraft destroyed for the loss of twenty-five Junkers written off, forty-seven of the German crews perishing. Oblt Walter Briegleb, St Kpt of 7./NJG2 who ended the War with twenty-five night *Abschüsse*, recounts his experiences:

> Under the date of 3–4 March 1945 in my diary I read: ninetieth sortie. Long-range night-fighting in the area Lincoln/south-east England. The order for take-off for this sortie burst into a mess party with ladies in evening dress at Marx airfield (East Friesland). Preparations for Operation *Gisela* had been going on since October 1944 at our NJG2, with the crews being allocated their task during intensive training: infiltration of the night fighter units into the returning British bomber stream, free chase over the British airfields and low-level attacks on ground targets there. Between November 1944 and March 1945 the codeword *Gisela* had been given out to our *Gruppe* (III./NJG2), and each time the crews had been at cockpit readiness at the bases Marx, Varel, Jever and Wittmundhafen (all in East Friesland). But the order for take-off had never come.
>
> So my commander, Hptm Ferger, and I did not take the preliminary warning *Gisela* very seriously and enjoyed the merry company in the mess. But gradually the reports from operations became more insistent; as we hurried by bus to the dispersals three white signal lights rose into the air: orders for take-off! Fw Fischer, my first mechanic, assisted me into overalls and lifejacket and the engines of my Ju 88 G-6 were already running. The crew (Funkers Uffz Brant and Fw Weilbaucher, and Flight Engineer Uffz Bräunlich) were already in the machine. I rushed up the boarding ladder, strapped in – and we were off.
>
> The first turning point was the radio beacon Texel and from there at low level with backbearings in direction Lincoln/Waddington. Headings

and time had been pre-calculated countless times. Precisely as expected, the vertical searchlight beams marking the approach lane for the returning bombers appeared at the English coast, which we passed at a height of 1,500 metres. We felt exposed, like being presented on a salver, so bright was the sky. Our nerves were stretched to the limit, when the familiar darkness swallowed us up again after a short time and we could hardly believe our eyes: there they were, flying in front and above us, four-engined aircraft with full illumination. The dream of my night fighter's life come true!

I almost felt sorry for those boys as they flew about above me, presumably preparing for their landing: the pilot circled, for there was a great deal of activity, the radio operator was probably talking with the tower, the navigator packed his maps, the rear gunner could at last get out of his tight turret and stretch his limbs. And all of them would be glad to be back home.

These thoughts were interrupted by my Flight Engineer with the report of an *Abschuss* on our port quarter. Later on, after landing, time and place confirmed the report of my *Staffel* comrade, Fw Heinz Koppe, for whom it had been his ninth victory. Meanwhile I manoeuvred my Ju 88 under the nearest bomber into attacking position with my upward-firing guns. I quickly had the Lancaster 150m above me in my reflector sight, pressed the trigger, and nothing happened! Damn! 'Switch on guns!' I shouted. 'Are switched on' came the reply. Press firing button again, but again no shot fired. So, attack from behind! I pulled up the machine behind the Tommy, aimed briefly and hit him with the full power of my four MG151/20 right in the fuselage. The Lancaster burst at once into bright flames and went down like a comet.

Now there was no time to be lost, for our attack would no doubt have been observed from the ground. So at the next one whilst he was still showing his navigation lights. He flew relatively high, and I approached him with some difficulty. Suddenly he doused his lights and below us at the airfields it also got darker. We had been recognized. I was just able to keep sight of my dark target and observe as he commenced evasive action: continuous acrobatic changes of course, to port and upward, and starboard and down, and conversely. There was even a proper peel-off, amazing what such a huge kite could stand! With difficulty I was able to keep him in sight and follow his manoeuvres at a respectful distance.

He must have lost sight of us and thinking himself safe again, when after some ten minutes

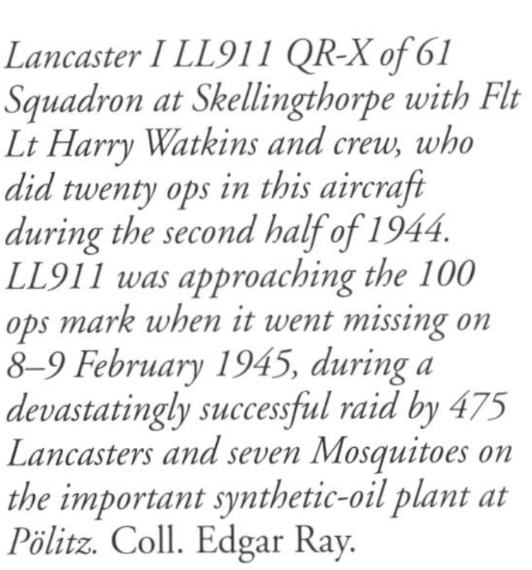
Lancaster I LL911 QR-X of 61 Squadron at Skellingthorpe with Flt Lt Harry Watkins and crew, who did twenty ops in this aircraft during the second half of 1944. LL911 was approaching the 100 ops mark when it went missing on 8–9 February 1945, during a devastatingly successful raid by 475 Lancasters and seven Mosquitoes on the important synthetic-oil plant at Pölitz. Coll. Edgar Ray.

he resumed level flight. I was at his level and some 400 metres to his starboard and now went slowly 200 metres below him, pulled my 'Berta' up behind him and let him have it with my guns. This was my twenty-fifth night *Abschuss* in fourteen months. Meanwhile, all the lights both in the air and on the ground had gone out.

Numerous fires showed the success of other shot-down aircraft and ground attacks. The British defences were presumably running in top gear and the Mosquitoes would be looking for us feverishly. We were intent to make this as difficult as possible for them, using every bank of cloud as cover and suddenly altering course and height during our return flight. Our tension only eased over the Dutch coast as we recognized that the wind and the weather had unexpectedly become much worse. Then we again had to keep our senses fully alert until we were safely home after four hours since take-off.

We were the first crew back and greeted the other returning and partly successful comrades with pleasure and pride. Only our commander, Hptm Ferger, was discontented; he had found a completely blacked-out England and had not been able to make out a single target either in the air or on the ground. The reason was soon discovered: some desk strategist had had the glorious idea to run Operation *Gisela* in two waves, at an interval of twenty minutes. My Commander had been in the second wave; it was logical that by then all lights had been doused. I felt sorry for him, his score in the past months had been twenty-nine, the thirtieth was not to be. On 10 April 1945 he and his gallant crew were shot down by a Mosquito during their approach to Lübeck; there were no survivors.

After the capitulation I had an opportunity to talk with three Mosquito long-range night fighters at the airbase of Leck in Schleswig-Holstein, who during the last year of the War had been engaged in 'looking after' the north-west German night fighter airfields of Wittmundhafen, Marx, Varel, Nordholz, Stade, Westerland, Leck, Lübeck and Schleswig. Amongst other things they wanted to know where under the 'controlled night-fighting' we had assembled after take-off, which radio or light beacons we had used, at what height and whether orbiting to port or to starboard.

The conversation showed how many puzzles our tactics had posed, even though our navigation aids had been well known and also used by themselves. The British Mosquito pilots commented on *Gisela* very positively. The planning of it had been known since November 1944, there must have been some careless talk, and they had been amazed that this idea had not been put into practice much sooner, for it would have caused Bomber Command considerable headaches and the means of defence for British night-fighting was very limited. With hindsight it must be said that Operation *Gisela* had been exceptional for all concerned – the night fighter's dream come true.

RONNIE'S DEATH

On 7–8 March 1945, Bomber Command mounted three major raids on Dessau, Hemmingstedt and Harburg. Among the 526 Lancasters and five Mosquitoes of 1, 3, 6 and 8 Groups that were detailed to attack Dessau in eastern Germany, were sixteen Lancaster IIIs from 405 (RCAF) Pathfinder Squadron. The bomb-load of the Blind Illuminator Pathfinder aircraft consisted of a Wanganui Flare, to achieve accurate target-marking in cloud-cover conditions, along with four 1,000lb and one 500lb bombs. W/O Angus Robb, veteran mid-upper gunner in Fg Off 'Bud' Larson's crew took off from Gransden Lodge in Lancaster PA965 'D', for his forty-eighth operational sortie.

The trip to Dessau was a disaster, as far as we were concerned, as it was on this trip that we lost W/O Ronnie Hainsworth, our rear gunner. We had been detailed to get to the target about two to three minutes after the raid had officially finished, to mark for any stragglers who had been delayed, and were therefore over the town virtually on our own. We bombed at 22.00, using an airfield as our aiming-point. The bombs had just left the aircraft when we were attacked by the

(Above) *Captain Ronny Martin (SAAF, third from left, back row), 'C' Flight 115 Squadron Commander and his crew, plus groundcrew, pose in front of their Lancaster I NG205 IL-D at Witchford in early 1945. By this time, 115 Squadron 'A' and 'B' Flights wore the squadron code KO, whereas 'C' Flight had the IL code. NG205 completed a total of fifty-one ops with 115 Squadron, plus four 'Manna' (food-dropping) and five 'Exodus' (repatriation of ex-PoWs) sorties.* Coll. Raymond F. Base.

Brothers in Arms. 405 (RCAF) Squadron PFF, Gransden Lodge, New Year's Day 1945. W/O Angus Robb, mid-upper gunner (left) tried in vain to save his mate W/O Ronnie Hainsworth, rear gunner (right), from burning to his death in the rear turret of Lancaster PA965 'D' for Dog on a trip to Dessau on 7–8 March 1945. Coll. Angus Robb.

first of three Ju 88s. The first one was shot down by Ronnie in the rear turret as it came into attack, but the second set the rear turret alight before I managed to get a short burst of gunfire into it, setting it on fire. It was then we heard Ronnie say 'For Christ's sake get me out of here.' The last words I suppose he ever said.

The third Junkers also hit us, putting my turret out of action, a cannon-shell moving the whole turret, with me in it, about a foot sideways, severing all the vital links: electricity, oxygen, oil and the intercom, and generally causing damage to the rest of our Lancaster. The fire in the rear turret had been caused by the severing of the hydraulic pipes and the ignition of the fluid. The fluid was being pumped into the turret by the engine-driven generator, fuelling the blaze, and the cut oxygen lines were making it burn with a terrifying intensity. The bottom of the turret appeared as a white-hot ball of fire, and the slipstream through the aircraft was blowing the flames behind us like a blow-torch.

Due to the attention of the remaining Ju 88, holes kept appearing in various parts of the airframe, and at frequent intervals the supply of ammunition for the rear turret kept exploding as they were hit by the gunfire. At one time I thought I had had my leg shot off as it suddenly gave way under me, but to my relief I had merely put my leg through a hole which had suddenly been blown in the floor of the Lancaster. Eventually, however, the wireless operator Plt Off Van Metre and I managed to get the fire in the rear turret under control, but by that time it was obvious to us there was little we could do for Ronnie. He was hanging half-in and half-out of the turret, and the metal had melted due to the heat of the flames. We took the decision, unspoken, and got him out of the aircraft, pulling his parachute rip-cord as he went. It seemed that the sooner he got medical attention the better, and we were a long way from home.

The remaining enemy fighter had, whilst all this was going on, continued his attacks, scoring hits on us at will, but it says much for the construction of the Lancaster that, despite it all, no fatal damage was done. We could only assume that he ran out of ammunition, as after about ten to fifteen minutes he drew alongside, waggled his wings and peeled off.

During our running battle with the remaining night fighter, Sgt B.A. Potter, our engineer, had been having his own hair-raising moments. In the nose of the Lancaster, aft of the bomb-aimer's position, a hole had been cut in the floor which allowed one of the crew to put his head out of the plane, looking underneath to spot any fighters coming up; a blind spot on all bombers, with the exception of those equipped with ball-turrets. This was the task generally assigned to the Flight Engineer during fighter attacks. The hole was protected by a bubble of perspex to disperse the slipstream. Our engineer was doing his duty, and had his head out of the hole when some of the fire from the attacker took the perspex bubble cleanly away from the nose, leaving him to the mercy of the night air. Naturally, he got up rather quickly, and in the process managed to open his parachute, which he had put on earlier in the attack, leaving himself with an armful of parachute silk. He apparently asked the pilot, with just a hint of pleading in his voice, that we were not going to evacuate the aircraft.

We had sustained a tremendous amount of damage. One engine was out of action, another had no cowling left and was running very roughly (this was due, we discovered on landing back at base, to the propeller blades being bent at right angles about a foot from each tip). The intercom was out of action, so it was a case of passing notes to each other or shouting in one another's ear. One rudder was waving freely in the breeze, and as we did not know how much damage had been done to the other, violent movement of the aeroplane was out of the question. The mid-upper and rear turrets were both out of action and there were large holes in the side and floor of the plane. Generally speaking, we were in a mess.

We had a discussion as to the merits of trying for the nearest emergency 'drome in England, but decided that 'Home is where the heart is' so we set our course back to Gransden Lodge. I can honestly say that at no time during the nine hours we spent airborne was there any real panic amongst the crew. At no time can I recall thinking that we were not going to come out of the situation other than in one piece. When we had taken the decision, by writing notes to each other, that we would try to make it back to Gransden Lodge, it seemed as if we all accepted the fact that we would make it.

Whilst engaged on an RCM sortie to Harburg on 7–8 March 1945, this 214 Squadron crew in Fortress KJ106 BU-G was mistakenly shot down by a Lancaster. From left: Fg Off N. Peters (RCAF, Spec. Op.) KIA; W/O J. Henderson (mid-upper gunner) PoW; Sgt K. Phelan (Starboard Waist AG) PoW; Sgt W.P. Mulham (FE) PoW; Fg Off G. Stewart (RNZAF, pilot) KIA; Sgt A.S. Goldson (Port Waist AG) PoW; Flt Sgt J. Matthews (RAAF, W/Op) PoW; Flt Sgt H.L. Henderson (RCAF RG) KIA; Flt Sgt J.W. Winstone (RNZAF, BA) KIA. Photograph taken at Oulton by Sgt H.M. McCylmont (nav.) KIA. Sgt Ken Phelan recalls:

As a crew we did twenty-seven operational flights, most of them very similar. We did our last operation on 7–8 March 1945. I suddenly heard over the intercom: 'Mid-upper gunner to Skipper. Enemy fighter on the starboard beam. I'm losing him. Can you see him, starboard waist gunner?' I replied: 'Starboard waist here. I've got him Skipper – starboard quarter down, flying on a parallel course, about 4,000 feet away. He's turning in, Skipper. Prepare for evasive action. He's at 3,000 feet. Corkscrew starboard GO.' I gave him a long burst of machine gun fire. The tracer bullets seemed to be going right through him. Then he lost interest and dived away. 'Attack broken, Skipper, resume course.' No smoke or debris, so we could not claim him.

Harry, the rear gunner, came on the intercom, 'Lancaster dead astern. My God, he's firing at us.' There was a noise like the sound of pebbles on a tin roof as the .303 bullets tore through the fuselage. One grazed my ankle. The port wing burst into flames. We veered to starboard and started to dive out of control. The G forced me to the roof, but somehow I got to the rear escape hatch. Jacky, the wireless operator, and Jimmy, the port waist gunner, were already there, trying to release the door. Pilot Officer Peters, our Special Operator, struggled up. He saw the position and went on to try the rear gunner's escape hatch. We never saw him again.

The three of us pushed again. Suddenly we were floating in space. I was pulled in and smashed against the tailplane. My left leg and jaw were broken and my shoulder dislocated. I am sure my guardian angel pulled my rip-cord. There was a blank – nothing more until I came to in a field surrounded by jackboots and uniforms. Harry, the rear gunner, was quite near me. He was calling for help. He screamed out 'No! No!' Then there was silence. I will say no more.

Eventually we were taken away for interrogation. We only had to give our name, number and rank. I was badly wounded so they left me alone, but the four crew members who remained had a very tough time. The Germans told them who they were, what they were doing and where they came from. They knew everything about 100 Group. Out of a crew of ten, only five of us remained. We were sure the skipper, navigator and bomb-aimer survived the crash. They were never seen again. I assume that the crew of the Lancaster which shot us down mistook us for an intruder. They may have claimed us but when we were reported missing, the action was conveniently forgotten. I am sure that somewhere there is someone who could answer that question.

Coll. Ken Phelan.

Our troubles though, were not yet over. We were steadily losing height due to the damage we had received and decided to lighten the aircraft where we could. We had got rid of most of the loose stuff lying around when the bomb-aimer remembered that we had some of our bomb-load still aboard. He opened the bomb doors and pressed the 'tit' to release the remainder. Unfortunately, it slipped his mind that our markers were barometric pressure-fused to go off at 3,000 feet. By this time we were quite a bit lower than that, so as soon as he let them go they exploded, filling the floor above the bomb bay full of pyrotechnics! It took the wireless operator and I a lot of kicking and stamping to eventually get rid of them.

So the long night wore on and we continued our way across Europe, slowly but surely and you can imagine how much of a relief it was to arrive back over our base at Gransden Lodge and take up our crash-landing positions – just in case – but we landed safely after just over nine hours in the air. It was then a case of being debriefed and spending the night in the sickbay, at the insistence of the MO, before being sent on survivors' leave for seven days.

As far as I can recall, our Lancaster 'D' for Dog never flew again, but we must have had a replacement, as after one trip in 'K' for King, my log book shows I did my remaining eight in 'D' for Dog.

Ronnie, sad to say, was dead when he reached the ground, being buried near the town of Dessau, but since the end of the War his body has been removed to the War Cemetery in Berlin where over 3,000 British servicemen lie, the majority of them aircrew.

I have often asked myself the question 'Did we do the right thing? Should we have done it any differently?', and to be honest I don't know. At the time it certainly seemed the right thing, in fact the only thing to do, and I suppose one has to live with that. I only know I lost a man who was the closest thing to a brother I ever had. To add further irony to the affair, the 7th of March 1945 was his twenty-third birthday, and the day previously he had become engaged to be married.

For their valiant efforts that night, Plt Off Van Metre was awarded the DFC, while W/O Angus Robb received the CGM (Flying) on 16 December 1946. In fact, their Lancaster PA965 was repaired and relegated to 1660 CU, and later to 1656 CU, 12 and 9 Squadrons before being struck off charge on 15 November 1946. From the 531 aircraft attacking Dessau on 7–8 March 1945, eighteen Lancasters were lost, but the raid was devastatingly successful, with the town centre, residential, industrial and railway areas all being hit.

Small forces of Ju 88 G-6s and Bf 110 G-4s of I., II. and IV./NJG6 were directed to the Dessau force, but the majority of the *Nachtjagd* crews didn't get at the bomber stream due to conflicting ground control instructions, and due to heavy jamming by 100 Group rendering the SN-2 radar all but useless in the target area. Still, at least two experienced crews of II./NJG6 managed to infiltrate the bomber stream, Oblt Spoden and Hptm Schulte claiming three Lancasters shot down over or in the vicinity of Dessau between 22.00 and 22.29. After claiming two Lancasters, one of the engines of Oblt Peter Spoden's Ju 88 G-6 2Z+DP was put out of action by return fire from a vigilant Lancaster gunner, and the crew was forced to bale out. Oblt Spoden came down safely and survived the War as Gruppen Kommandeur of I./NJG6, credited with twenty-four confirmed night victories, plus one probable B-17 kill in daylight on 6 January 1944.

The 4,000lb 'blockbuster' or 'cookie' bomb, typically dropped in combination with a load of incendiaries, was used to devastating effect in the RAF strategic bombing offensive. Sitting on a 'cookie', Fg Off Maurice Paff, navigator with 100 Squadron, is flanked on either side by groundcrew, before it is loaded into a squadron Lancaster at Grimsby in the autumn of 1944. Coll. Maurice Paff.

NACHTJAGD'S FINAL MONTHS

Lt Wolfhard Galinski served as an operational night fighter pilot in 8./NJG6 during the final nine months of the War. Mainly due to the acute shortage of fuel that plagued the *Luftwaffe* at this stage, he only flew six night-fighting and nine night-time ground attacking sorties before the end came. Lt Galinski gives a graphic personal account of life in III./NJG6 during these final months of hostilities.

Lt Wolfhard Galinsky, pilot with 8./NJG6, who shot down Mosquito NF.30 NT490 of 141 Squadron intruding on Neubiberg airfield with a double MG 181 in the early hours of 19 April 1945. Lt Galinsky rose to Generalmajor in the post-war Bundesluftwaffe. Coll. Wolfhard Galinsky.

One day at Schleissheim, our *Staffel* commander, Oblt Wilhelm Johnen (who survived the War as Hauptmann and Ritterkreuzträger with thirty-four night victories to his credit), called us together in the mess and asked us whether we were prepared to volunteer for an operation with little chance of survival (evidently piggyback flights in an Me 109 on a Ju 88, fully laden with explosives for shipping targets on the Atlantic coast). Apart from myself, only one other pilot volunteered. But for weeks we heard nothing more about training for this task ... and we doubted whether our solicitous Staffelkapitän had passed on our names at this stage of the War. (In fact, he had not.)

One fine day we were suddenly transferred to join the rest of our *Gruppe* at Leipheim, together with two *Staffeln* of Me 110s and a Staff Flight and one other *Staffel* equipped with the Ju 88. The airfield of Leipheim had a wonderfully long runway. For many months we had not had a concrete runway and had been used to the smallest of grass strips. We were delighted with our new airfield.

Another surprise was the test unit for the fantastic Me 262 stationed there which, from an assembly line in a forest clearing (with netting camouflage) on the other side of the Autobahn, daily received five of these unbelievable new aircraft for testing. I soon met two instructors of blind-flying from Alt-Lönnewitz who were in this fabulous testing business. They thundered down the runway with their kites and waved to us joyfully at the end of their run with a brief pulling of the stick, for this machine had to be pulled into the air. It did not lift off at flying speed by itself like other aircraft. This was news to us, and otherwise there was just pure joy at the completely new flying sensation of this ultra-modern type. The tested aircraft were then flown mainly to the airfields of Lechfeld and Schwäbisch Hall. Major Knauth, the Commander, offered our Staffelkapitän a flight under his instructions from the ground, and so we saw our brave and exemplary leader flying an Me 262. The landing and especially the speed was something pretty new for an experienced Me 110 pilot, and it was no simple matter for him to get safely back on the ground.

Centurion. Lancaster III EE139 BQ-B for Baker of 550 Squadron, better known as the 'Phantom of the Ruhr', at North Killingholme in the autumn of 1944. Fg Off Joe C. Hutcheson took the Phantom on a bombing raid against German troop concentrations in Le Havre on 5 September 1944 for its 100th sortie. During its operational life with 100 and 550 Squadrons between July 1943 and November 1944, the Phantom logged 121 trips, surviving four night fighter attacks plus a strafing run by an intruder, being hit by incendiary bombs from above, returning with severe flak damage five times, and landing on three engines six times. After being transferred to 1656 CU and later 1660 CU, it soldiered on post-war before finally being SOC unceremonially on 19 February 1946. Coll. Len Browning.

As a result, none of us got permission to undertake such a trial flight. Quite rightly, concern for the troops had precedence, for the *Luftwaffe* had had more than enough losses through such larks.

The days passed, one noticed that there was a war on, but on the whole we were spared from damage, for our aircraft were dispersed along the airfield by the Autobahn and well camouflaged among the bushes. The link to the Autobahn had been given a solid surface in order to be able to use this road as an auxiliary runway, particularly for the Me 262. When we had five days of bad weather, twenty-five finished machines stood waiting for their test flight. One was impressed by this fleet and the achievements of our war industry. One day, when I had to drive to Munich on a duty trip, I was amazed at the sight of all these Me 262s parked in bays along this Autobahn awaiting collection – flight was evidently very limited due to lack of fuel. Also at the air base of Schleissheim, where I had to go, I found some 60–80 Me 110s parked in a wood, which however had been heavily damaged by Allied splinter bombs, leaving hardly any serviceable aircraft to be found. But even that worked out and in the end I was able to fly one back to Leipheim.

There was still plenty of good food in the mess. We were stationed out in the country. But we now had to share the rooms with the uniformed girls who had the upper part of the building and also a block of officers' accommodation beside the mess. Sometimes after dinner in the evening, one could hear a pin drop when Magda, one of these girls, sang in her beautiful voice accompanied by a piano – to great applause.

Our days at Leipheim were suddenly over, for in mid-February 1945 we were about to be transferred to Neubiberg near Munich – with considerable changes, for the unit was to be reduced in size, without the Ju 88, and Hptm Wilhelm Johnen would be our new Commander, because 'Poldi' Fellerer (Hptm Leopold Fellerer, who survived the War as *Ritterkreuzträger* and credited with forty-one kills) had been under treatment for a stomach ailment for some considerable time. All of us were affected and some of us were not very happy about it, although our *Nachtjagdgruppe* remained fully operational to the very end of the War thanks to good leadership and maximum effort. I now had my old Staffelkapitän as my new *Gruppen* Kommandeur and was more than satisfied, for one could hold nothing against 'Wim' Johnen. He was always a good example in all situations, though one might have liked a more personal contact at times, but this was not possible in Munich because the crews were accommodated in private quarters, and because, especially by day, air-raids had now become permanent. But he must have liked me, for everyone who had so far failed to score a kill had by now to be transferred to the paratroopers – and I got the privilege as so-called 'still promising crew' to remain with the old, nice and model comrades. Perhaps I had done something accidentally for him by saving his life one night during a Mosquito attack, because during a car ride to one of our flak sites I gave the 'order' to get out of the car at one of our dispersals, where later on we discovered that a bullet of the attacker would have hit the driver. Together with Lt Kögler we finally shot down this Mosquito, which earned me the award of the EK II on 20 April 1945! (Lt Galinski was credited with shooting down Mosquito NF.30 NT490 TW-R of 141 Squadron, which was on an intruder sortie of München-Neubiberg aerodrome, with a twin MG 181 machine gun of the Neubiberg airfield defences, in the early hours of 19 April 1945. The New Zealand crew of W/O R.G. Dawson and Fg Off C.P.D. Childs both perished and were buried in Dürnbach War Cemetery.)

At our new airfield of Neubiberg, we further found that several hangars had been destroyed and that fragments of the huge transport machine 'Gigant' lay about, which hinted at the stationing of this other impressive new construction of the Messerschmitt works. The workshops and other facilities were unharmed and the airfield remained usable without significant limitations. We officers were accommodated beside the nice mess and were more comfortable than for a long time now.

We soon flew our first night fighter operations from here, against enemy aircraft flying to the Main area, Neuremberg or Munich. Here we had the best-equipped, already legendary British night fighters with their Mosquitoes to contend with, who now hung around our airfields or followed our own returning aircraft in order shoot them down on landing. This implied for us the closest co-operation with our controllers in order to land with a minimum of airfield lighting. In spite of taking the greatest care, the enemy succeeded to get our Staffelkapitän after a night operation. Only their immediate abandoning of their aircraft as soon as it had come to rest on the runway enabled the pilot and crew to survive. Having had a thorough fright, we were able to welcome these comrades in the mess while the aircraft burnt outside. Time and again one needed luck as well as skill.

Together with other not yet successful pilots I now flew on night operations against American truck convoys in the Elsass and Rhein-Main areas, using high explosive and splinter bombs and our guns (two 3cm and two 2cm cannon as forward-firing guns in the Me 110).

One day seventeen bomber formations attacked Ulm/Neu-Ulm and interrupted the last major north–south railway line, as well as causing

Bomber Veteran. Sqn Ldr Peter Sarll DFC, sporting a typical bomber aircrew handlebar moustache, is photographed here with NG243 BQ-M2 and his 550 Squadron crew in the winter of 1944–45. Peter was in the thick of the action, flying Blenheims with 21 Squadron on daylight ops during 1939–1940, being one of only a handful of pre-war regulars to survive the murderous daylight battles of the Low Countries and France during May–June 1940. After a spell of instructing in the mid-war years, he became operational again in 1944 as 'C' Flight Commander 550 Squadron on Lancasters, finishing his second tour in style by bombing Hitler's mountain retreat 'Eagle Nest' and SS guard barracks at Berchtesgaden in daylight on 25 April 1945. Coll. Frank Pritchard.

other major damage in the city. The following day our night fighter *Gruppe*, 170 men under my command, had to travel by rail to Neu-Ulm, the last part on foot, in order to repair the main line under the instructions of railway engineers. The result was that by evening the main lines were usable and the locomotives could travel again. We were quite proud of ourselves.

One day we had another surprise when the night fighter *Gruppe* had to transfer fifty men to other military units. As compensation fifty young girls were on their way from the Vienna area in order to take over clerical, stores, armoury and other tasks. So in the evenings our cockpit windows were cleaned by nice uniformed beings, no bad thing – besides the improved pleasantries for all ranks. During air-raids we made for the Danube meadows with this female enrichment. This soon became very necessary as the airfield was attacked and our lovely runway badly cratered. A considerable proportion of the bombs failed to explode and these were cleared during the following days by personnel of the SS camp at Dachau. These men stood in deeply dug holes and burrowed down to the bombs. Any questioning of these people was immediately stopped by harsh words from the guards. Thank God none of these unfortunates was injured.

Almost daily during April 1945, NJG6's operational airfields of Ingolstadt, Schleissheim and Neubiberg were subjected to bombing and strafing attacks by roaming Mustangs, Thunderbolts and Lightnings by day, and Mosquitoes at night. On 9–10 April, nine Bf 110s and eight Ju 88s of 1./NJG6, Stabs *Staffel*, and the *Geschwader* reserves were destroyed at Schleissheim, and a heavy raid by 210 B-17s of the 3rd Air Division, 8th USAAF dropping 606.3 tons of bombs on Ingolstadt on 11 April left only four aircraft of Stab, 4. and 10./NJG6 intact at this 'drome.

Still, over this period, NJG6 despatched an estimated 162 sorties, resulting in one *Abschuss* (a Halifax, possibly MZ467 of 462 Squadron, by Ofw Heinrich Schmidt of 2./NJG6 for his fifteenth victory at 03.44 on 17 April, observed to crash 12km north of Gablingen), and dozens of Allied vehicles left blazing in ground strafing attacks. Losses however mounted to fourteen aircraft failing to return or being heavily damaged in crash-landings, with the majority of the aircrews killed or missing. The curtain for NJG6 finally fell in the last week of April, when its airfields were overrun by advancing American ground forces.

STIRLING MASSACRE

Although the Short Stirling had been phased out as a Main Force bomber at the end of 1943, the aircraft remained in service in a wide variety of operational roles such as gardening, radio and radar jamming in 100 Group, and in G-H (blind-bombing) experiments. From December 1943, in 38 (Airborne Forces) Group the aircraft was even given a whole new existence, in glider towing, paratroop dropping and SOE/SAS duties. By early 1945, its squadrons became involved in tactical bombing to assist the advancing Allied Forces. One of these bombing operations took place on 21–22 February 1945, when 299 (SD) Squadron dispatched six Stirling IVs on a supply dropping operation to Norway, with all aircraft returning safely. Another force of six 299 Squadron Stirlings were sent on a low level bombing raid of Rees in the Ruhr Valley. Flt Sgt Tom Toll had served as a Flight Engineer in 295 and 570 Squadrons from September 1944, before being posted to RAF Shepherd's Grove, Suffolk and 299 Squadron in Sqn Ldr Spear's DFC, DFM, AFC crew in November of that year.

SOE ops followed, mostly low level, carried out individually on moonlit nights, as navigation was all DR and map-reading, to southern France, the Alps, Holland and Norway. The latter were code-named DOOMSDAY.

By mid-January 1945, the requirement for SOE operations on the Continent was beginning to ease off and operations to Norway were hampered by severe weather conditions. The airborne assault on the Rhine was some way off. We were kicking our heels and Group then had the bright idea that with our experience on

299 Squadron Stirling IV LK124 X9-'Q' for Queenie at Shepherd's Grove dispersals, April 1945. Flt Sgt Tom Toll (Flt Eng), is peering out of the cockpit window with his regular groundcrew looking on. On 21–22 February 1945, five out of six 299 Squadron Stirlings were shot down by flak whilst engaged on a low-level tactical bombing raid against Rees in the Ruhr. The sixth participating Stirling was destroyed by a German Intruder when coming in to land back at base, with the loss of the crew's rear gunner. Coll. Tom Toll.

accurate low-level work and the fact that the Stirling was by far the most highly manoeuvrable of the heavy bombers, we could be usefully employed on close support and special low-level bombing operations.

21 February – my twenty-seventh op. Briefing at 14.00, the target was Rees in the Ruhr Valley – a busy river crossing point, with three bridges, barge traffic and major railway marshalling yards. Take-off time was 18.30. Six aircraft were detailed, each carrying twenty-four 500lb G/P bombs to be released at half second intervals, and the aircraft to be over target at five-minute intervals at 7,000 feet. This wasn't low level? It would be a piece of cake – a picnic – we were told. We were to be the first away with 5G-C Charlie, a converted MkIII which we had never flown before. Our own aircraft 5G-G George went u/s on air test the previous day. It was squadron procedure to conduct an air test prior to an operation and as C-Charlie had not been air tested, the skipper suggested that we should all go out to the aircraft earlier than we would normally do to give her a very thorough going-over. He also insisted that we should all exchange our parachutes, despite our protests that we had done so only two weeks earlier and we didn't have all that much time to spare. The procedure was to pull the rip-cord on handing it over to the WAAF packer in the parachute section. The navigator's didn't work!

We took off on time – visibility was near perfect. Climbing steadily we crossed the coast at Orford Ness and droned our way across the North Sea to Schouwen Island and the Dutch coast. We were dead on course, engines were running sweetly, the familiar patchwork of Holland sliding below in the moonlight as we made our way to Eindhoven. Here we altered course to the north to bring us towards our target area with forty-five miles to run and sixteen minutes to target. At this point the skipper asked for 2400rpm +2 boost, pitch levers fully up fine, mixture normal, this gave more control response. I also at this stage selected main fuel tanks to all four engines in case we should have to take evasive action. Our IAS was 155mph. On intercom: 'Navigator to skipper. Five minutes to enemy lines.' 'Skipper to crew. Keep a good look out, seems unusually quiet, could be fighters about.' 'Navigator to skipper. Alter course 070 degrees. Fifteen miles to run.' At this time the Rhine was clearly visible in the moonlight like a big silver ribbon. Some light anti-aircraft fire and the odd searchlight was also visible, but well to the north of us. Gabby Allen, our bomb-aimer who had been down in his position for quite some time map-reading and readying his equipment, requested bomb doors open. I flicked the switch and the green light came on.

Almost immediately, light and medium anti-aircraft shells were bursting around us. The skipper took evasive action, however evasive action doesn't stop you flying into a shell burst, which we did. The port outer first poured black smoke, then flames. I shut off the fuel cock and closed the throttle whilst the skipper pressed the fire extinguisher button. I then feathered the prop. The fire went out, but by this time, half the cowling had gone.

We managed to escape the immediate area and the skipper asked for a damage report. Apart from a few shrapnel holes everything seemed to check out. The controls were OK and no one seemed to be injured. I took this opportunity to clip on my parachute. We came round again, quite tight this time with the intention of dropping our bombs and then diving down to come out on the deck. As we approached the target for the second time, a blue radar-controlled master searchlight beam latched on to us. Geordie, our rear gunner, opened fire and the blue beam slowly faded away, but not before we were coned by four or five white searchlights; we were very vulnerable at this height. The target was dead ahead and we had to keep straight and level. A shell burst immediately under us. The aircraft reared like a bucking bronco. The skipper immediately pulled the bomb jettison toggle – I turned to look over my shoulder and could see just a flicker of flame in the centre section, but before I had even time to get out of my seat I could see the extent of the damage. We must have taken a direct hit. A couple of bombs still in the racks had punched a hole clean through the floor. The starboard inner engine was on fire and the fuel balance pipes in the centre section were pouring burning 100-octane fuel. The whole cockpit was bathed in an eerie glow, reflected back from the windscreens.

I was still on the intercom and the skipper, who was desperately trying to maintain control, gave the order to abandon aircraft. It was obvious it was becoming impossible. He shouted at me to 'get out'. I wasted no time descending the two steps into the nose section where the front escape hatch was located. The wireless operator and navigator were already down there, both miraculously unscathed. The bomb-aimer was very badly wounded and whilst he was getting attention I kicked open the hatch catch bar to release the hatch. The noise and debris took us all by surprise. All three of us then eased the bomb-aimer through the escape hatch and out into the night. My turn next, someone gave me a push, when I hit the slipstream it was like being hit by an express train. I felt like my whole body was being torn apart. Then oblivion.

Tom Toll came to gently swinging under the open canopy, the rip-cord still in his hand. Soon after, he hit the snow-covered ground at speed, badly spraining his ankle. Undaunted, he set off walking westwards towards the Rhine, which he reached after a hellish trek through mud, woods and country roads two days and two nights later. In a small boat, he barely managed to cross the wildly pounding current of the river. Having safely reached the western river bank, Tom proceeded through the vast area of pine trees called the Reichswald Forest, before he finally encountered advancing Allied vehicles some forty-eight hours after crossing the Rhine.

After recovering in hospital, Tom was sent back to Shepherd's Grove and 299 Squadron, where he was informed that of the six Stirlings participating in the Rees raid, five had been shot down over or near the target area. The sixth was destroyed by an intruder when coming in to land back at base with the loss of the crew's rear gunner. Of Sgt Tom Toll's own crew, the skipper Sqn Ldr Spear DFC, DFM, AFC and rear gunner Flt Sgt Geordie Wilson were killed in the crash and buried in the Reichswald War Cemetery at Kleve. Fg Off Gabbie Allen, bomb-aimer, and Flt Lt Jock Henderson, the WOp, were taken prisoner, with Fg Off Dave Saunders, the crew's navigator, managing to escape to Allied lines.

SCHNAUFER'S FINEST HOUR

Lt Fritz Rumpelhardt was the most successful Bordfunker in *Nachtjagd* during World War II, being credited with 100 *Abschussbeteiligungen*, or 'contributions to claims'. This incredible record was achieved in the course of just 130 sorties flown with his regular pilot, Major Heinz-Wolfgang

St Trond, October 1944. Hptm Heinz-Wolfgang Schnaufer, Kommandeur of IV./NJG1, reached the historic mark of 100 night victories on 9–10 October 1944, when he destroyed two Viermots *for his 99th and 100th kills. The first was shot down at a height of 5,200 metres to the south of Bochum at 20.32, his 100th going down thirty-three minutes later from a height of 5,000 metres in grid square JO. Next day, Schnaufer's comrades presented him with a 'lucky pig' named Fridolin, which we see here about to receive its baptism from Hptm Drewes. From left: Ofw Wilhelm Gänsler (the most successful air gunner in the German night-fighting arm, who participated in seventeen victories whilst flying with Oblt Ludwig Becker in 6./NJG2 during 1942, and in ninety-eight of Schnaufer's final 121 night victories during 1943–45. Ofw Gänsler was awarded the* Ritterkreuz *in July 1944 and nominated for the award of the Oak Leaves in March 1945); unknown Fw; Oblt Georg Fengler (who ended the War with sixteen confirmed kills in NJG1 and 4); Hptm Martin Drewes (*Ritterkreuz *with Oak Leaves, forty-nine* Abschüsse *by the end of the War); Hptm Schnaufer; Hptm Hermann Greiner (*Ritterkreuz *with Oak Leaves, fifty-one victories in IV./NJG1).* Coll. Martin Drewes, via Rob de Visser.

Schnaufer, who ended the War as *Nachtjagd*'s top-scoring ace with 121 confirmed kills. Rumpelhardt had teamed up with Lt Schnaufer during night-fighting training in 1941, and together they were posted to 5./NJG1 in November of that year. It took six months before they succeeded in bringing down their first adversary, a Halifax which was shot down at a height of 3,500 metres on 2 June 1942. According to Schnaufer's *Leistungsbuch* or 'Log of Achievements', the aircraft crashed at 01.55 near Grenz-Donau, some 15km south of Louvain, Belgium. Before the year was out, the two men had become aces with seven confirmed kills. In the meantime, they had been joined by Fw Wilhelm Gänsler, an experienced air gunner with formidable night vision, who had previously flown with Oblt Ludwig Becker and who had shared seventeen kills with him.

Over the next one-and-a-half years, Rumpelhardt guided his pilot to a further sixty-one victories, which earned him the award of the *Ritterkreuz* in August 1944. Schnaufer gained a further twenty-one victories over this period with other Bordfunkers (amongst them Fw Handke, who shared in the destruction of five bombers; Lt Baro (twelve kills), and Oblt Freymann (two victories)). In the previous month, Ofw Gänsler had reached the eighty-kills mark, for which he also received the *Ritterkreuz.* By that time, Schnaufer commanded IV./NJG1, his personal tally having risen to eighty-nine confirmed victories by night, for which he had been awarded the *Ritterkreuz* with Oak Leaves and Swords. In spite of the ever worsening operational conditions in which *Nachtjagd* had to combat Bomber Command after the Allied invasion of the Continent, the team kept accumulating their score. At 20.09 on 3 February 1945, Major Schnaufer, now Kommodore of NJG4, claimed his 107th *Abschuss*, a *Viermot* which was shot down from a height of 4,500 metres in 'grid square LO'.

The next success came on 21 February 1945, with the crew claiming two Lancasters destroyed at 01.53 and 01.58 in 'grid squares MM-MN'

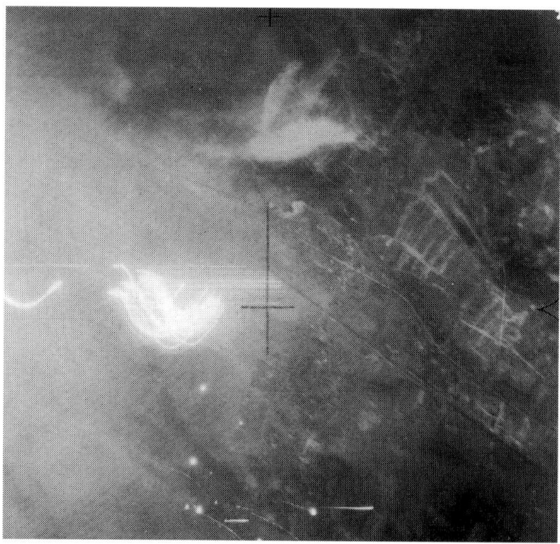

This photograph shows a typical view of the ground over a German city under bombing attack. The ground is illuminated by flares, and the streaks and stars are the German gun flashes and shells exploding. 'It was nerve-wracking to keep the aircraft absolutely steady for about 15–20 seconds on the bomb-run in a situation in which the world seemed to have gone mad, and I used to lower my seat to its lowest position to concentrate only on my instruments and avoid being blinded or distracted by the madness.' (Capt Ted Howes DFC, flying Lancaster 'N' of 97 (PFF) Squadron, who brought back this target photograph of Hamburg on 21–22 March 1945, when the Deutsche Erdölwerke were put out of action by 151 Lancasters and eight Mosquitoes of 5 Group, for the loss of four Lancasters.) Coll. Ted Howes DFC.

and 'MM' respectively during a sortie lasting two hours and nine minutes. After landing back at Gütersloh airfield, the three men rested until late afternoon, when they air tested their regular mount, Bf 110 G9+EF, for the coming night's operations. Lt Rumpelhardt vividly recalls the following events, of what would become their most successful night-fighting sortie of the War.

> For Schnaufer, it was a matter of honour to be the first in the air when operations were ordered in order to give his unit early information on the situation. Now, during this second sortie on 21 February 1945, fate played an unexpected card. I was all alone in the standby room in order to fortify myself for possible operations by consuming an ample evening meal. The order for 'increased readiness' had not reached me. When 'cockpit readiness' was immediately followed by the order for take-off and the Kommodore discovered that he had an utterly unprepared and surprised Bordfunker, his comments were anything but pleasant.
>
> It all went head over heels – but to no avail. The others were in the air and on their way to the area of Düsseldorf before our trusty 'EF' was ready and at last had taken off at 20.08. But the supposed mishap was to turn out to be of considerable significance later on. We were far behind, flying on the course ordered by ground control, while the *Geschwader* was already approaching the area where the attacking British bombers were supposed to be. We could not understand why there were no signs of enemy or flak activity to be seen. Schnaufer could not make up his mind whether to keep on his set course, when abeam to the north – it must have been in the area of Münster – intense light flak activity

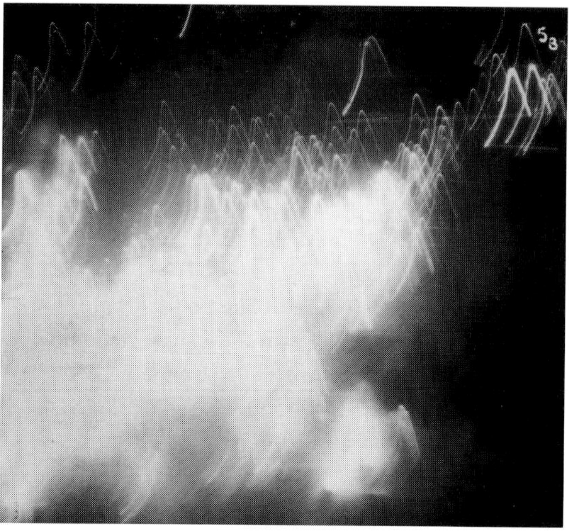

When a bomber aircraft weaved during the short period in which the camera flash exploded to take a target photograph, this is the picture that was brought back. A 550 Squadron Lancaster took this target photograph over Stettin in late 1944 or early 1945; the white areas are fires on the ground and tracer shells being hosed up by the ground defences. Coll. Len Browning.

Between August 1944 and April 1945, one third of all Bomber Command sorties were flown in daylight, which underlined both the overwhelming Allied air power and the almost complete impotence of the Luftwaffe *by this time. Depicted from a height of 17,500 feet is the airfield at Heligoland smothered in bomb bursts on 18 April 1945. Nine-hundred-and-sixty-nine aircraft released 11,776 bombs on the Island between 12.24 and 13.25, with only three Halifaxes being lost to the island's flak defences. Ninety-five per cent of all the houses on Heligoland were destroyed in this devastating attack, leaving 2,000 civilians homeless. Some fifty German soldiers were killed, another 150 injured, and the island's defences, airfield and U-boat base were knocked out.* Coll. Bill Harvey.

could be observed. As it turned out later on, the target had been the Dortmund-Ems Canal. Now then – light flak which reached only up to 2,000 metres against British bombers, which generally flew at 3,500 to 6,000 metres – there must be something wrong there. But there was no need for long reflection. Schnaufer went into a descent and went on a north-westerly course in order to intercept the returning bombers, passing through a thin layer of cloud at about 2,500 metres on the way. Several targets appeared on the SN-2 radar and we found ourselves under a thin layer of cloud. Beyond that was the moon which made the clouds appear like a white sheet, or 'death shroud' as we called it, beneath which we were able to make out the returning bombers like dark shadows at relatively long range.

Schnaufer selected a Lancaster, somewhat off-set to the right and at about 1,700 metres, seemingly flying unconcerned on a steady course. We had been in the air just over half an hour when the Kommodore went into position for an attack from below. As always, whenever possible, he aimed the vertical guns, the *Schräge Musik*, between the two starboard engines. This is where the fuel tanks were placed, making this method the quickest and most effective one. But this also gave the enemy the best chances of survival, generally allowing them to escape unscathed by parachute.

Well, this attack was crowned by success at 20.44. The Lancaster's starboard wing was heavily damaged by an explosion. A bright flame lit up the night sky far around. After a brief level flight, which gave the crew ample time to leave the stricken bomber by parachute, it nosed down and crashed, as was later ascertained, in grid square 'HQ-HP'. Now one event followed hard upon the other. Schnaufer was able to pick and choose his targets and displayed his exceptional skill in night-fighting. The bomber pilots had been warned and tried to escape the attacking fighter by 'corkscrewing'. In order not to get into their defensive fire, Schnaufer was forced to follow their manoeuvres. Only that way was it possible to get into the blind spot under the wing and to stay there. It was Schnaufer's particular talent to judge just the right moment for an attack. There was no time to be wasted. In one case he had no option but to fire his almost vertically mounted guns whilst in a seemingly impossible position standing vertically on his wing tip. That some of the projectiles might strike the fuselage could not be avoided. I will come back to that. What made it more difficult for us was that on overflying the front line the American flak gave us considerable trouble. Within precisely nineteen minutes Schnaufer had succeeded to set seven bombers afire without our Me 110 receiving a single hit from the defending guns of the enemy. This proves that the Major had unbelievably steady

Fg Off Arthur 'Whitty' Whitmarsh DFC and his 460 Squadron 'B' Flight crew posing on Lancaster III ND968 AR-O for Oboe II at Binbrook prior to taking off for a record 1,079 aircraft daylight assault against Essen on Sunday 11 March 1945. Although the city of Essen was completely cloud-covered, 4,661 tons of bombs were accurately dropped on Oboe-directed sky-markers, for the loss of only three Lancasters in the target area. Coll. David Fellowes.

nerves, made each attack with considered precision and succeeded with a relatively short burst at minimum range. With daredevil flying skills and split-second timing he was able to keep out of the danger zone each time.

No. of Abschuss	*Type*	*Time*	*Grid Square*	*Height*
110	Lancaster	20.44	HQ - HP	1,700m
111	Lancaster	20.48	HP - HO	1,600m
112	Lancaster	20.51	HP - HO	1,600m
113	Lancaster	20.55	HP - HO	1,600m
114	Lancaster	20.58	IO - JN	1,600m
115	Lancaster	21.00	JN - KM	1,700m
116	Lancaster	21.03	KM - KL	1,700m
(Probable claim)	Lancaster	21.10	KM - KL	1,700m

During these violent combats I hardly had time and opportunity to note down the details. On the other hand, however, the already mentioned 'Death Shroud' relieved me of the important task of guiding the pilot on to the bomber by radar in the dark of night. Once again Wilhelm Gänsler was the steadying influence in the crew. As so often already, he knew how to give Schnaufer good advice. But these did not help during two further attempts to attack. During the eighth attack the *Schräge Musik* failed at the critical moment – it fired not a single shot and Schnaufer had his work cut out to escape the concentrated defensive fire of the bomber's crew. Now there only remained the horizontally mounted guns in the nose of the Me 110 which also failed to fire during the ninth attack. With that our pursuit of the returning bomber stream was over.

On our return we overflew the active American flak on the front line. The psychological, but also the physiological powers, of the Kommodore had meanwhile been strained beyond measure. Via our previous base at Dortmund I requested all possible assistance for our final stage to the airfield of Gütersloh. Searchlights pointed and signal rockets showed us the way and so Schnaufer was able to land our faithful G9+EF with a final effort at 21.55 at the base of Gütersloh. When the machine had taxied to its dispersal and the engines had stopped, there was silence amongst the crew. Leaning forward, for some minutes each of us tried to order our thoughts. These thoughts also included the crews of the shot-down Lancasters, in particular the hopes that their parachutes might have proved a saving grace. Years later I received a letter from an Englishman, Stan Bridgman from Welwyn Garden City. He had been the Flight Engineer in Lancaster JO-Z of 463 Squadron which had been shot down over Holland on 21 February 1945 at 21.02. So the crews of a bomber and a night fighter got to know each other. An exchange of letters, presents and a meeting in summer 1980 resulted in a friendship between former opponents. Unfortunately Major Heinz-Wolfgang Schnaufer was unable to share in this friendship. In 1950 he was killed in a car accident in France.

Before the end of the War, Major Schnaufer and his crew flew two more successful sorties: on the evening of 3 March they claimed two Lancasters shot down at 21.55 and 22.04, and added three more Lancasters on the evening of 7 March (at 20.41, 20.47 and 21.56). This brought Schnaufer's final score to an all-time record of 121 victories, plus one probable, in 164 night-fighting sorties, after which he was grounded for the remaining two months of the War. His tally included 114 *Viermots* (six Stirlings, the others all Lancasters and Halifaxes), Lt Rumpelhardt having shared in 100, and Ofw Gänsler in ninety-eight of his victories.

THE JET AGE

One of the most spectacular German innovations in the night airwar during the closing stages of the conflict was the introduction of the twin-engined Me 262 jet fighter into *Nachtjagd*. However, when the first handful of these revolutionary aircraft were committed to battle in '*Kommando Welter*' during December 1944, it was already too late to have a significant impact on the night airwar. Lt Herbert Altner, who ended the War with twenty-six confirmed victories with 7./NJG3, 8./NJG5, and 10./NJG11, recalls how he was propelled into the jet age:

A few days after my last success with a Ju 88 on 8–9 February 1945, when I had shot down three aircraft over Stettin, Oblt Welter landed with his Me 262 A-1a in Lübeck-Blankensee. I got into conversation with him about the jet fighter, which of course interested me very much. Barely three weeks later, Oblt Welter had me posted to his unit which went under the name 10./NJG11 (or *Kommando Welter*). At this time Kommodore Welter only had the single-seater version of the Me 262. With these, the few pilots of the unit flew *Wilde Sau* sorties over Berlin, which means flying by the light of the searchlights especially against Mosquitoes which, due to their high speed, could not be caught by other fighters.

Oblt Welter told me that he was waiting for two-seaters of the type Me 262 B-1a/U1, which would be equipped with the FuG 220 *Lichtenstein* SN-2. As I already had a great deal of experience in night-fighting with the Bf 110 and had an excellent radar operator in the person of Reinhard Lommatzsch, Welter had selected me to fly these two-seaters.

My type training on the Me 262 took place on 7 March 1945 on the single-seater. After a brief theoretical introduction with Oblt Welter standing beside me on the wing, I did several take-offs and landings with this fantastic kite. I was impressed looking at my air-speed indicator needle which did not come to rest until 800km/h. I can only confirm General Adolf Galland's words: 'It was as if an angel were pushing.'

On 11 March 1945, having completed about fifteen circuits, my practical training was completed. I got permission from Oblt Welter to do a cross-country flight to my former unit, NJG5 at Lübeck-Blankensee. I did a low-level run over the airfield there and was greeted after landing by my former comrades with great joy and not a little respect.

On 15 March 1945 I did one last night fighter sortie with a Ju 88, which unfortunately ended with the total loss of the machine and the baling out of the entire crew. We had probably been made out by a British long-range night fighter and set on fire.

On 22 March I flew to Staaken with an Me 110 in order to take over the first two-seater Me 262 B-1a/U1, test it, and then fly it to my unit.

Although the flying of the Me 262 was generally without problems, the night fighter version, which the *Lichtenstein* SN-2 made considerably heavier than the single-seater, required more concentration. Especially at the airfield of Burg near Magdeburg it was difficult to get airborne from the short field when there was no wind.

On a transfer flight from Staaken, I landed at Lübeck. My Me 262 was pushed into a wooden hangar. During the night the airfield suffered a bombing attack and in the morning we found that the hangar roof had fallen on to my Me 262 through the force of an explosion. As far as I can recall today, I had flown four two-seaters from Staaken to Burg or Lübeck. These four were the only Me 262 B-1a/U1 to get into action.

On 27 March I flew my first night fighter sortie on the 262, during which my radio operator located a Mosquito on his radar. But my own speed was too high and I passed below it. On throttling the engines too quickly, both failed. As a restart of the engines of the Me 262, especially at night, was impossible, we were left with no choice but to bale out. We released our straps and, having jettisoned the roof, I briefly raised the nose of the aircraft and then pressed it forcefully down, causing us both to be thrown out. Unfortunately my radio operator struck the tail, lost consciousness and hit the ground without having opened his parachute. My successful radio operator Reinhard Lommatzsch died this night the airman's death. This happened in the vicinity of Havelberg.

At the beginning of April, while again fetching a two-seater from Staaken, the airfield of Burg was put out of action by a bombing raid and I took the machine to Lübeck. On 6 April, together with another radar operator, Hans Fryba, I succeeded to shoot down a Mosquito [of 305 Squadron, 2nd TAF, Sqn Ldr Hanbury and crew]. During this night I had contact with another Mosquito but, as all my guns failed to fire, we flew together in formation over Berlin.

In order to avoid bombing attacks, we transferred our machines during the day to the motorway Lübeck-Hamburg, near Reinfeld. But the night sorties were always flown from Lübeck, transferring our aircraft there at dusk, for the motorway had no airfield lighting.

On 6 May I flew with my mechanic Karl Braun in our good old 'Red 12' from the motorway near Reinfeld to Schleswig-Jagel, where the last two Me 262 B-1a/U1 of the *Luftwaffe* were surrendered to the RAF. That was the end of the War for me and I had done my duty. I remember with pride that I had flown the first operational jet aircraft of the world, and to have been the only pilot of the *Luftwaffe* to have flown the two-seater version on night-fighting operations.

Hptm Heinz Rökker, St Kpt of 2./NJG2, concentrating before taking off in his Ju 88 G-6 from Twente airfield in early 1945. Hptm Rökker survived the War as the eighth highest scoring Nachtjagd *ace of World War II with sixty-four* Abschüsse *(including fifty-five* Viermots*) amassed in 161 sorties, for which he was decorated with the* Ritterkreuz *with Oak Leaves.* Coll. Heinz Rökker.

NACHTJAGD'S FINAL KILL

Right up until the final caving-in of Germany's home frontiers, the suspense built up by the drama of the night airwar never slackened, and the experienced *Nachtjagd* crews remained a force to be reckoned with. As we have seen above, pilots like Major Schnaufer kept accumulating kills

German Airmen Land
at Gormanston
Three German airmen landed at Gormanston, Co. Meath, on Saturday morning.
They had flown from Aalborg, in Denmark.

This 1./NJG3 crew of Ju 88 G-7a D5+GH, consisting of Ogefr Kruschyna, Ofw Herbert Giesecke (an ace with at least seven night Abschüsse *in 1./NJG3) and Uffz Schmidt, are posing with their night fighter aircraft after landing at the Irish Air Corps base at Gormanstown near Dublin in the early hours of 5 May 1945. Wrk Nr 621642 was allotted RAF serial number VK888 and was on charge of the Enemy Aircraft Flight, Central Fighter Establishment, Tangmere, for over two years.* Coll. Theo Boiten, via Eric Bakker.

until the end of the conflict. Other '*Experten*' stand out: Hptm Heinz Rökker, St Kpt of 2./NJG2, scored twenty-four of his final sixty-four *Abschüsse* between October 1944 and 15–16 March 1945, whereas Hptm Martin 'Tino' Becker, Kommandeur of IV./NJG6, claimed seventeen of his total of fifty-eight *Viermot* kills between September 1944 and 16–17 March 1945.

Oblt Herbert Koch, who had scored his first victory on 20–21 April 1943, downing an 83 Squadron Lancaster (*see* pages 81–3), had become an ace, with twenty-two confirmed victories by late April 1945 and was now in command of 1./NJG3. He recounts his final *Abschuss* on the night of 24–25 April 1945:

> I had a special relationship with the *Himmelbett* box Schakal ('Jackal', on the northern tip of Jütland), as I did both my first and my last operational flights in this box. Shortly after midnight on 24 April 1945, at 00.19, I took off from Grove in Ju 88 G-6 D5+AH for a patrol in Schakal. The difficult thing about this sortie was having to fly at relatively low level and in bad visibility. I could not afford to take my eyes off the altimeter at any time.
>
> Apart from regularly giving me courses to steer, the JLO often urged me to '*Express, Express*' ('pour on the coals'). He obviously feared that the target aircraft would escape by getting out of the effective range of the ground radar. Shortly after receiving his message 'You should be in visual range', I caught sight of my adversary, it was a four-engined aircraft. We were at that time flying at a height of only seventy metres. A short burst of fire at long range and from directly behind, and an explosion of flames erupted from the bomber. I turned away for home even before I watched the doomed machine hitting the surface of the sea, trailing a sheet of flames. I called up the Ground Controller asking him if he could see the flaming aircraft, but he told me he could not, as it was too far out to sea. My flying log book records the place of the crash to the west of Skagen at 01.21. I landed back at Grove again at 02.32, after a sortie lasting for 133 minutes.

Oblt Herbert Koch's twenty-third victory has gone down in history as *Nachtjagd*'s 7,308th and final kill during World War Two. Actually, his victim was Halifax GR.II JP299 of 58 Squadron, which was flying an armed reconnaissance over the Skagerrak in the hands of twenty-one-year-old Flt Lt Arthur T.C. Wilmot-Dear DFC, in search of the German vessel *Tübingen*. There were no survivors from the Halifax crew. The 5,452 ton *Tübingen* was bombed and sunk by another Halifax crew, of 502 Squadron, at 00.39.

'FORGIVE, YES, BUT NEVER, EVER FORGET'

In the course of almost six years of war, Bomber Command lost 8,655 aircraft on ops, plus some 1,600 through accidents and write-offs. Of a total of approximately 125,000 aircrew serving in front-line units, casualties amounted to 73,741, of whom 55,500 were killed. W/O Angus Robb, who completed two tours of ops as air gunner in Wellingtons with 431 and 432 (RCAF) Squadrons, and 405 (RCAF) Squadron PFF in Lancasters between December 1942 and April 1945, reflects on the War:

> I often wondered, through the tears, if the sacrifice of so many young lives was worth it all. I made a visit a few years ago to the British War Cemetery in Berlin, where my friend Ronnie is now buried, along with about 3,000 others, the majority of them aircrew in their twenties. I wondered, again, was it worth this? On the same trip we were taken to Dachau, the site of the infamous concentration camp which is now a memorial to the millions who died in the camps. It was in that, still sorrowful place, I thought to myself; if it stops anything like this ever happening again, yes, their sacrifice was worthwhile. But I would make this plea to the ones this was really written for, my grandchildren: Try to ensure it never happens again. *Forgive, yes, but never, ever forget.*

'At the end of hostilities in Europe, a number of bomber crews were allowed the privilege of flying about over Germany in daylight to view the results of their efforts. I was appalled at the destruction of that country. We just cruised about at a couple of thousand feet for three or four hours, and every city and town seemed to be reduced to rubble and devastation.' (Capt Ted Howes DFC, SAAF, pilot, who completed twenty-eight ops with 106 and 97 (PFF) Squadron between October 1944 and April 1945.) This is a typical view of a completely gutted district of Cologne at the end of the War. Coll. Maurice S. Paff.

Glossary of German Terms

Abschuss: Confirmed victory in air combat.
Abschussbeteiligung: Contribution to a confirmed victory in air combat.
Bordfunker/Funker: German Radar/radio operator.
Dunkle Nachtjagd: Radar-directed night-fighting without the aid of searchlights.
Eisernes Kreuz (EK): The Iron Cross.
Emil-Emil: Radio Telephony (R/T) code for '*Lichtenstein* airborne radar'.
Express-Express: R/T code for 'hurry up'.
Feindberührung: Contact with an enemy aircraft.
Feldwebel (Fw): Sergeant (Sgt).
Fernnachtjagd: Long-range night-fighting or intruding.
Gefreiter (Gefr): Aircraftman 1 (AC1).
Geschwader: Operational unit comprising three *Gruppen*.
Gruppe: Operational unit comprising three *Staffeln*.
Hauptmann (Hptm): Flight Lieutenant (Flt Lt).
Helle Nachtjagd: Illuminated night-fighting.
Himmelbett: Close-range and radar-controlled night-fighting.
Kapelle: R/T code for 'height of target aircraft' (in hectometres).
Karussell: R/T code for 'orbit'.
Kirchturm: R/T code for 'altitude' (in hectometres).
Kleine or Grosse Laterne: R/T code for 'small' or 'large radio beacon'.
Kommandeur: CO of a *Gruppe*.
Kommodore: CO of a *Geschwader*.
Kurier: R/T code for 'Allied heavy bomber'.
Leutnant (Lt): Pilot Officer (Plt Off).
Lichtenstein: Airborne interception radar.
Lisa: R/T code for 'turn ten degrees to left'.
Major (Maj): Squadron Leader (Sqn Ldr).
Marie: R/T code for 'distance to target' (in kilometres).
Nachtjagd: Night-fighting arm.
Oberfeldwebel (Ofw): Flight Sergeant (Flt Sgt).
Oberleutnant (Oblt): Flying Officer (Fg Off).
Oberst: Group Captain (Gp Capt).
Oberstleutnant (Obstlt): Wing Commander (Wg Cdr).
Pauke-Pauke: R/T code for 'going in to attack'.
Reichsverteidigung: Air defence of the Third Reich.
Reise-Reise: R/T code for 'break off engagement, return to base'.
Ritterkreuz: Knight's Cross to the Iron Cross.
Rolf: R/T code for 'turn ten degrees to right'.
Schräge Musik: Upward firing guns in night fighter aircraft.
Seeburgtisch: Plotting table used in *Himmelbett*.
Staffel: Operational unit comprising of nine aircraft.
Staffel Kapitän: CO of a *Staffel*.
Tampen: R/T code for 'fly in direction …'
Viermot: Four-engined Allied bomber aircraft.
Viktor: R/T code for 'have received and understood message'.
Wilde Sau ('Wild Boar'): Freelance night-fighting tactic over Bomber Command's targets under attack.
Zahme Sau ('Tame Boar'): Night-fighting tactic of feeding night fighter aircraft into a Bomber Stream and then letting them 'swim' with the stream whilst shooting down as many bombers as possible.
Zerstörer: 'Destroyer', Bf 110 fighter aircraft.

Bibliography: Published and Unpublished Works

Aders, Gebhard, *Geschichte der deutschen Nachtjagd 1917–1945* (Stuttgart 1978)

Balss, Michael, *Deutsche Nachtjagd. Personalverluste in Ausbildung und Einsatz – fliegendes Personal* (Eich 1997)

Blepson, Wing Commander, *Luftflotten Kommando Reich*. AP/WIU (2nd TAF) *Report No. 70/1945* (Unpublished, National Archives, Washington DC)

Boiten, Theo, *Nachtjagd. The Night Fighter versus Bomber War over the Third Reich 1939–1945* (Marlborough 1997)

Bosomworth, Jack, *I'm lucky – I believe* (Market Rasen 1998)

Bowman, Martin W. & Boiten, Theo, *Raiders of the Reich. Air Battle Western Europe: 1942–45* (Shrewsbury 1996)

Bowman, Martin W. & Cushing, Tom, *Confounding the Reich* (Sparkford 1996)

Bowyer, Chaz, *For Valour. The Air VCs* (London 1992)

Brookes, Andrew, *Bomber Squadron At War* (London 1983)

Bruce, D., Chorley, W.R., & de Haan, J.G.J., *Roll of Honour 115 Squadron Royal Air Force 1939–1945* (1996)

Chorley, W.R., *In Brave Company. 158 Squadron operations* (Salisbury 1990)

Chorley, W.R., *Royal Air Force Bomber Command losses of the Second World War, 1939–1945* (six volumes, Earl Shilton 1992–1998)

Davis, Jim, *Winged Victory. The Story of a Bomber Command Air Gunner* (London 1995)

Decker, Cynrik de & Roba, Jean-Louis, België in Oorlog 5. *Luchtgevechten boven België 1941–1942* (Charleroi-Erembodegem 1994)

Derix, Jan, *Vliegveld Venlo* (Vols I & II) (Horst 1990)

Dierich, Wolfgang, *Die Verbände der Luftwaffe 1935–1945* (Stuttgart 1976)

Felkin, Group Captain S.D., *The History Of German Night-fighting. ADI (K) Report No. 416/1945* (unpublished, National Archives, Washington DC)

Franks, Norman, *Forever Strong. The story of 75 Squadron RNZAF 1916–1990* (Auckland 1991)

Gomersall, Bryan B., *The Stirling File* (Revised Edition) (Tonbridge 1987)

Goulding, James & Moyes, Philip, *RAF Bomber Command and its aircraft 1936–1940* (London 1975)

Greenhous, Brereton, Harris, Stephen J., Johnston, William C., and Rawling, William G.P., *The Crucible of War 1939–1945, Vol. III* (Ministry of Supply and Services Canada 1994)

Griehl, Manfred, *Deutsche Nachtjäger im 2. Weltkrieg* (Friedberg 1986)

Gunston, Bill, *Night Fighters. A development & combat history* (Bar Hill 1976)

Halley, J.J., *The Lancaster File* (Tonbridge 1985)

Handke, Erich, *Private diary on night-fighting as Bordfunker in NJG1, 1942–1945* (unpublished)

Harris, Sir Arthur, *Bomber Offensive* (London 1947)

Held, Werner and Nauroth, Holger, *Die deutsche Nachtjagd. Bildchronik der deutschen Nachtjäger bis 1945* (Stuttgart 1982)

Hinchliffe, Peter, *The Other Battle. Luftwaffe night aces versus Bomber Command* (Shrewsbury 1996)

Huhn, Heinz, *Private diary on night-fighting as Bordfunker in II./NJG2 and IV./NJG1* (unpublished)

Various issues of *Jägerblatt: Offizielles Organ der Gemeinschaft der Jagdflieger e.V.* (1954–1998)

James, Ron, *... I was one of the Brylcreen boys* (unpublished manuscript 1992)

Jansen, Ab A., *Wespennest Leeuwarden* (Vols I–III) (Baarn 1976–78)

Jürgens, Hans-Jürgen, *Zeugnisse aus unheilvoller Zeit* (Jever 1991)

Kock, Werner, *Das Kriegstagebuch des Nachtjagdgeschwaders 6* (Wittmund 1996)

Kümmritz, Dr Ing. Herbert, *Geschichte und Technik der deutschen Nachtjagd* (unpublished article)

Leeuwen, Peter van, *Terschelling en zijn rol in de luchtoorlog 'Tigerstelling'* (Barchem 1997)

Lutgert, Drs W.H. & de Winter, Drs R., *Nederland en de Duitse Nachtjacht* (in: *Militaire Spectator*, 1994/12 & 1995/1, Rijswijk)

Lyall, Gavin (Ed.), *The War In The Air 1939–1945* (London 1994)

McQuiston, John. H., *Tannoy Calling. A story of Canadian airmen flying against Nazi Germany* (New York 1990)

Messenger, Charles, *Cologne. The first 1,000 Bomber Raid* (London 1982)

Middlebrook, Martin, *The Nuremberg Raid 30–31 March 1944* (London 1973)

Middlebrook, Martin, and Everitt, Chris, *The Bomber Command War Diaries* (Harmondsworth 1985)

Mitcham, Samuel W., *Eagles of the Third Reich. Hitler's Luftwaffe* (Shrewsbury 1988)

Mourton, Douglas, *Lucky Doug. Memoirs of the RAF 1937–1946* (unpublished manuscript, Ham Street 1997)

Moyle, Harry, *The Hampden File* (Tonbridge 1989)

Murray, Williamson, *Luftwaffe, strategy for defeat 1933–45* (London 1985)

Nowarra, Heinz J., *Die Ju 88 und ihre Folgemuster* (Stuttgart 1978)

Obermaier, Ernst, *Die Ritterkreuzträger der Luftwaffe 1939–1945. Band I Jagdflieger* (Mainz 1989)

Pearce, William G., *The Wing Is Clipped* (unpublished manuscript, Camp Hill 1994)

Price, Alfred, *Messerschmitt Bf 110 Night Fighters* (Windsor 1967)

Ries, Karl & Obermaier, Ernst, *Bilanz am Seitenleitwerk* (Mainz 1970)

Ring, Hans, *Nachtjagd pilots victory list* (unpublished, via Gebhard Aders)

Robb, Angus, *RAF Days* (unpublished manuscript, Blackpool)

Robinson, Albert E., *Ontmoeting met de Grijze Monnik* (Hallum 1979)

Rökker, Heinz, *Chronik I. Gruppe Nachtjagdgeschwader 2* (Zweibrücken 1997)

Schnaufer, Major Heinz-Wolfgang, *Leistungsbuch* (unpublished)

Scutts, Jerry, *Luftwaffe night fighter units 1939–1945* (London 1978)

Sharp, C. Martin & Bowyer, Michael J.F., *Mosquito* (London 1971)

Sherring DFC, Charles C., *For Your Own Eye* (privately published autobiography 1945)

Spelthahn, Albert, *Erinnerungen eines Bordfunkers* (unpublished manuscript, Mainz 1986)

Streetly, Martin, *Confound & Destroy. 100 Group and the bomber support campaign* (London 1985)

Webb, Alan B., *At First Sight* (Romford 1991)

West, Kenneth S., *The Captive Luftwaffe* (London 1978)

Zijl, Annejet van der, *Missing*. In: *HP De Tijd*, 3 May 1991.

Index

USAAF PERSONNEL

PLACES AND AIRFIELDS